EBI Studies in Banking and Capital Markets Law

The European Banking Institute

The European Banking Institute based in Frankfurt is an international centre for banking studies resulting from the joint venture of Europe's preeminent academic institutions which have decided to share and coordinate their commitments and structure their research activities in order to provide the highest quality legal, economic and accounting studies in the field of banking regulation, banking supervision and banking resolution in Europe. The European Banking Institute is structured to promote the dialogue between scholars, regulators, supervisors, industry representatives and advisors in relation to issues concerning the regulation and supervision of financial institutions and financial markets from a legal, economic and any other related viewpoint.

As of May 2021, the Academic Members of the European Banking Institute are the following: Universiteit van Amsterdam, University of Antwerp, University of Piraeus, Alma Mater Studiorum–Università di Bologna, Universität Bonn, Academia de Studii Economice din Bucureşti (ASE), Trinity College Dublin, University of Edinburgh, Goethe-Universität, Universiteit Gent, University of Helsinki, Universiteit Leiden, KU Leuven University, Universidade Católica Portuguesa, Universidade de Lisboa, University of Ljubljana, Queen Mary University of London, Université du Luxembourg, Universidad Autónoma Madrid, Universidad Carlos III de Madrid, Universidad Complutense, Madrid, Johannes Gutenberg University Mainz, University of Malta, Università Cattolica del Sacro Cuore, University of Cyprus, Radboud Universiteit, BI Norwegian Business School, Université Panthéon - Sorbonne (Paris 1), Université Panthéon-Assas (Paris 2), University of Stockholm, University of Tartu, University of Vienna, University of Wrocław, Universität Zürich.

Supervisory Board of the European Banking Institute:

European Banking Institute e.V.
TechQuartier (POLLUX), Platz der Einheit 2
60327 Frankfurt am Main, Germany
Website: www.ebi-europa.eu

Edoardo D. Martino

EU Bank Governance and Bail-In

A Legal and Financial Analysis on the Role of Long-Term Creditors

palgrave
macmillan

Edoardo D. Martino
Amsterdam Center for Law
and Economics
University of Amsterdam
Amsterdam, The Netherlands

ISSN 2730-9088 ISSN 2730-9096 (electronic)
EBI Studies in Banking and Capital Markets Law
ISBN 978-3-032-20698-5 ISBN 978-3-032-20699-2 (eBook)
https://doi.org/10.1007/978-3-032-20699-2

Cover illustration: Teekid/gettyimages

This Palgrave Macmillan imprint is published by the registered company Springer Nature Switzerland AG
The registered company address is: Gewerbestrasse 11, 6330 Cham, Switzerland

Financial levers, economic levers, information levers: the three fundamental levers of every genuine social, political, and cultural construction. When these levers are missing, all that remains is the meagre solace of resorting to rhetorical speaches about the value of the human person.

From a letter by G. La Pira to A. Fanfani
13 February 1955

To my mother, whose resilience knows no limits
To Giorgio, who sparked my curiosity

Competing Interests The author has no competing interests to declare that are relevant to the content of this manuscript.

CONTENTS

About the Author

Edoardo D. Martino is Associate Professor of Law & Finance at the University of Amsterdam (UvA), Programme Director of the Master's in Law & Finance, and a Research Associate at the European Banking Institute (EBI).

Edoardo earned his PhD in Law and Economics at Erasmus University Rotterdam (EUR), an LLM degree from the European Master's in Law and Economics—EMLE (with distinction) and a Law Degree from the University of Florence (summa cum laude). He held visiting positions in several Universities, including the European University Institute, Goethe University Frankfurt, LUISS University, and Oxford University.

Edoardo's research spans in the broad field of Law & Finance, focusing on (sustainable) banking regulation, private money regulation and bank recovery. On these topics, he published book (chapters) and edited volumes in houses such as Elgar, Palgrave Macmillan, OUP and Routledge; as well as articles in journals such as the *Computer Law & Security Review, European Business Organization Law Review, Journal of Corporate Law Studies, Journal of Financial Crises, and Yale Journal on Regulation*. He is a guest contributor to, among others, the Columbia Law School Blue Sky Blog, Oxford Business Law Blog, ProMarket and VoxEU Columns.

About the Author

Abbreviations

AIFMD	Alternative Investment Fund Manager Directive
AT1	Additional Tier 1 Instruments
BCBS	Basel Committee for Banking Supervision
BIS	Bank of International Settlements
BRRD	Bank Recovery and Resolution Directive
CBR	Combined Buffer Requirement
CCB	Capital Conservation Buffer
CDS	Credit Default Swap
CEBS	Committee of European Banking Supervisor
CEO	Chief Executive Officer
CET1	Common Equity Tier 1 Instruments
CMDI	Crisis Management and Deposit Insurance
CoCos	Contingent Convertible Instruments
CRA	Credit Rating Agency
CRD	Capital Requirement Directive
CRR	Capital Requirement Regulation
DCCP	Deferred Contingent Capital Plan
DGS	Deposit Guarantee Scheme
EA	Euro Area
EBA	European Banking Authority
EBU	European banking Union
ECB	European Central Bank
EDIS	European Deposit Insurance Scheme
EMU	Economic and Monetary Union
EU	European Union
FDIC	Federal Deposit Insurance Corporation

FSB	Financial Stability Board
GDP	Gross Domestic Product
G-SIB	Globally Systemically important banks
IF&PF	Insurance Firms and Pension Funds
MDA	Maximum Distributable Amount
MiFID	Markets in Financial Instruments Directive
MiFIR	Markets in Financial Instruments Regulation
MMF	Money Market Fund
MPOE	Multiple Point of Entry
MREL	Minimum Requirement for Own Funds and Eligible Liabilities
NCA	National Competent Authority
NCWO	No Creditors Worse Off
NPV	Net Present Value
OECD	Organisation for Economic Cooperation and Development
OFIs	Other Financial Institutions
PAF	Partner Asset Facility
RWAs	Risk Weighted Assets
SHS	Security Holding Statistics
SPOE	Single Point of Entry
SRD	Shareholders Right Directive
SREP	Supervisory Review and Evaluation Process
SRM	Single Resolution Mechanism
SRMR	Single Resolution Mechanism Regulation
SSM	Single Supervisory Mechanism
SSMR	Single Supervisory Mechanism Regulation
SVB	Silicon Valley Bank
T2	Tier 2 Instruments
TBTF	Too Big to Fail
TLAC	Total Loss Absorbency Capacity
UCITS	Undertakings for Collective Investment in Transferable Securities

List of Figures

Chapter 6

Chapter 7

List of Tables

CHAPTER 1

Introduction

The Global Financial Crisis of 2007–2008 had a sensational impact in many different areas of the society.[1] Almost 20 years later, the cultural effects of this impact is this vivid. Its effects were not confined to the financial and economic domain. On the contrary, the spillovers of the crisis spanned from strong political reactions, media commotion, to a deeper and long-lasting cultural impact, especially for the generation that experienced the crisis while approaching adulthood.

The famous sociologist Zygmunt Bauman claimed that the latest financial crisis represented a disruptive generational event, defining the end of the previous generation and introducing a "new normal" according to which people's hopes, fears, and expectations were re-calibrated.

> Every generation has its measure of outcasts. There are people in each generation assigned to outcast status because a 'generation change' must mean some significant change in life conditions and life demands likely to force realities to depart from expectations implanted by the conditions-quo-ante. […] When looking back from the second decade of the 21st century, we can hardly fail to notice that when confronted with the profound changes brought about by the latest economic collapse, each

[1] Zygmunt Bauman and Carlo Bordoni, *State of Crisis* (John Wiley & Sons 2014).

E. D. Martino, *EU Bank Governance and Bail-In*, EBI Studies in Banking and Capital Markets Law,
https://doi.org/10.1007/978-3-032-20699-2_1

> one of those previous passages between generations may well seem to be an epitome of inter-generational continuity. Indeed, after several decades of rising expectations, the present-day newcomers to adult life confront expectations falling – and much too steeply and abruptly for any hope of a gentle and safe descent.[2]

In recent decades, such an impact in the Western world can only be matched by 9/11 and the Covid Pandemic. This generational event provoked an impressive and almost unprecedented regulatory response by several national and supranational institutions, shaping a new regulatory architecture both at global and regional level.[3] This holds true especially for the European Union, where the regulatory framework proved completely inapt to face a systemic crisis, especially because of fragmentation of national laws.[4]

Looking back at the financial crisis, two striking features capture the attention of each and every layman in Main Street[5]: the gigantic amount of bailout money given out by states[6] and the absurd level of compensation to bankers whose bank went underwater because of the disproportionate risks they undertook.[7] The first aspect relates to how

[2] Zygmunt Bauman and Neal Lawson, *A Chronicle of Crisis: 2011–2016* (Social Europe Edition 2017) 1.

[3] Chris Brummer, *Soft Law and the Global Financial System: Rule Making in the 21st Century* (Cambridge University Press 2015).

[4] Charles Enoch and others, *From Fragmentation to Financial Integration in Europe* (International Monetary Fund 2013).

[5] Used in opposition to Wall Street, referring to people that are not part of the financial world.

[6] For instance, in the U.S. the Emergency Economic Stabilization Act of 2008 established the Troubled Asset Relief Program (TARP), the more relevant source of bailout money for US financial institutions. The TARP had the authorisation to spend up to 700 billion $. In the EU, the European Commission approved State Aid measures for 4.5 trillion euro, equivalent to the 37% of the EU GDP of 2008. See, European Commission, New crisis management measures to avoid future bank bailouts, MEMO/12/416. Available at https://ec.europa.eu/commission/presscorner/detail/en/IP_12_570 (accessed 30/09/2025).

[7] Lucian A Bebchuk, Alma Cohen and Holger Spamann, 'The Wages of Failure: Executive Compensation at Bear Stearns and Lehman 2000–2008' (2010) 27 Yale J. on Reg. 257. It has been estimated that between 1993 and 2007, while serving as CEO, Mr. Fuld received almost half a billion dollars.

banks fail, whereas the second pertains to the domain of bank governance and the incentives faced by bankers when making risky decisions.

Unsurprisingly, these areas attracted the attention of the post-crisis legislators. Politicians on both sides of the Atlantic committed to do everything within their power to prevent a similar meltdown to happen again in the future. The key motto was: "Never again".

For instance, in presenting the Dodd-Franck Act, former President Obama stated:

> This economic crisis began as a financial crisis, when banks and financial institutions took huge, reckless risks in pursuit of quick profits and massive bonuses. When the dust settled, and this binge of irresponsibility was over, several of the world's oldest and largest financial institutions had collapsed, or were on the verge of doing so. [...] Never again will the American taxpayer be held hostage by a bank that is 'too big to fail'.[8]

In the EU, one of the major cornerstone of the post-crisis financial reforms consisted in establishing a European Recovery and Resolution Framework for ailing banks, whose declared main goals are to preserve the stability of the European financial market and to avoid "to the largest extent possible" resorting to the use of public money in handling banks' crises.[9]

This book investigates the post-crisis regulatory framework, assessing to what extent those political commitments have been implemented in practice. More specifically, it investigates whether and to what extent those are actually contributing to avoid (i.e., minimise the probability of) future financial meltdowns. In more technical words: this research assesses the impact of the resolution framework on the governance of banks, i.e., on the quality of their decision-making.

[8] Remarks by the President on Financial Reform, 21 January 2010. Available at https://obamawhitehouse.archives.gov/the-press-office/remarks-president-financial-reform (accessed 30/09/2025).

[9] See Recital n 1 BRRD: "The financial crisis has shown that there is a significant lack of adequate tools at Union level to deal effectively with unsound or failing credit institutions and investment firms ('institutions'). Such tools are needed, in particular, to prevent insolvency or, when insolvency occurs, to minimise negative repercussions by preserving the systemically important functions of the institution concerned. During the crisis, those challenges were a major factor that forced Member States to save institutions using taxpayers' money. The objective of a credible recovery and resolution framework is to obviate the need for such action to the greatest extent possible".

1 The Problem of Bank Governance and the Role of Long-Term Debt

The main problem this book endeavours to address is the impact of the recovery and resolution framework for ailing banks on the governance of European banks. The ultimate aim is to understand how and to what extent a clear and credible institutional framework regulating banks' failures enhances the decision-making process of banking institutions and, in turn, their resilience.

This query involves many different aspects of banks' behaviour and their inter-relations. It is, thence, important to disentangle the main elements to be addressed: bank governance and the recovery and resolution framework for ailing banks. Bank governance represents the central aspect of this book. Poor decision-making and excessive risk incentives in the period leading up to the crisis proved to boost, if not to cause, the financial meltdown. In this regard, the final report of the "High-Level Group on Financial Supervision in the EU", chaired by Jacques de Larosière, stated:

> [Corporate Governance] is one of the most important failures of the present crisis. [...] Looking back at the causes of the crisis, it is clear that the financial system at large did not carry out its tasks with enough consideration for the long-term interest of its stakeholders.[10]

In a similar vein, a growing body of empirical research demonstrates how banks with "better" corporate governance performed worse during the crisis. For instance, Beltratti and Stultz concluded that

> Our results show that no evidence exists that banks with a better alignment of the CEO's interests with those of the shareholders had higher stock returns during the crisis. Some evidence shows that banks led by CEOs whose interests were better aligned with those of their shareholders had worse stock returns and a worse return on equity.[11]

[10] Jacques De Larosière and others, 'Report of the High-Level Group on Financial Supervision in the EU' [2009] European Commission. Brussels.

[11] Andrea Beltratti and René M Stulz, 'The Credit Crisis around the Globe: Why Did Some Banks Perform Better?' (2012) 105 Journal of Financial Economics 1.

Nowadays, there is ample evidence showing that the shareholder-centric governance paradigm incentivises excessive risk-taking, especially in good time, and that such excessive risk-taking contributes to build-up systemic risk. These special features of bank governance result in the impossibility to foster social welfare by maximising shareholders' value.

Those few remarks suffice to understand a certain tension between the governance of non-financial corporations and bank governance. And even more, on the concept of "good corporate governance" for bank. In fact, in the aftermath of the financial crisis, the idea that "bank governance is special" attracted a certain degree of consensus.[12] Such specialty would open the door to substantial departures from the plain "shareholder value" maximisation paradigm, widely employed in non-financial firms.[13] Nevertheless, both the academic and the regulatory debates over bank governance fell short in operationalising the fact that bank governance is special.[14]

For instance, professors Armour and Gordon, discussing the desirable regulatory reforms in the area of bank governance, stated:

> We should emphasize that we are far surer of the significance of the problem we document than we are of the efficacy of our proposed solutions, which we present primarily as a heuristic framework for debate.[15]

Thus, when it comes to bank governance and the incentives stemming therein, proposing a theoretical framework to operationalise those specialties represents a quintessential goal. For such framework to be suitable, it must be grounded on the inter-linkages between bank governance and regulation, and on the role of debt. This latter observation directly leads to the second central component of this research. In fact, the European

[12] Marco Becht, Patrick Bolton and Ailsa Röell, 'Why Bank Governance Is Different' (2011) 27 Oxford Review of Economic Policy 437.

[13] The book does not enter in the debate over the "shareholder value maximisation" paradigm in non-financial firms, but simply takes it for granted and evaluates whether the argument grounding this approach for non-financial firms hold in banking.

[14] Christoph van der Elst, 'Corporate Governance and Banks: How Justified Is the Match?' (2015) 284/2015.

[15] John Armour and Jeffrey N Gordon, 'Systemic Harms and Shareholder Value' (2014) 6 Journal of Legal Analysis 35, 40.

Legislator established a new and unprecedented framework on recovery and resolution of banks.[16]

The framework harmonises the tools and procedures to deal with bank distress through the whole European Union. The Bank Recovery and Resolution Directive (BRRD) regulates the procedures, the tools and the powers to handle bank distress, from the phase of preparation to resolution. It mandates Member States the task to designate an administrative authority, the Resolution Authority, to exercise the powers provided by the Directive.[17] Moreover, in the process leading to the "European Banking Union", a central Resolution Authority was established for the Eurozone countries.[18]

For the time being, it suffices to say that the overarching idea behind the recovery and resolution framework is that banks failures must be paid by the investors in the bank and not by the generality of taxpayers through bailout money. Such overarching policy goal largely shapes the tools provided by the BRRD, especially in the phase of resolution. In particular, the bail-in, as opposed to bailout, represents not only the most innovative tool provided by the Directive, but the quintessential concept behind the whole framework.[19]

In performing a bank bail-in, the Resolution Authority exercises the power to write down or convert into ordinary shares eligible liabilities issued by the bank under resolution. Among the instruments eligible for bail-in, the Directive includes equity, other instruments that are part of regulatory capital as well as long-term debt instruments. Therefore, the Directive creates a category of creditors, the bail-inable creditors, that are prone to suffer losses upon the decision of an administrative authority should the bank enter in distress.

[16] Bank Recovery and Resolution Directive (BBRD) - Directive 2014/59/EU of the European Parliament and of the Council of 15 May 2014 establishing a framework for the recovery and resolution of credit institutions and investment firms [2014] *OJ L 173*.

[17] Article 3 BRRD.

[18] Single Resolution Mechanism Regulation (SRMR) - REGULATION (EU) No 806/2014 OF THE EUROPEAN PARLIAMENT AND OF THE COUNCIL of 15 July 2014 establishing uniform rules and a uniform procedure for the resolution of credit institutions and certain investment firms in the framework of a Single Resolution Mechanism and a Single Resolution Fund and amending Regulation (EU) No 1093/2010.

[19] Paul Calello and Wilson Ervin, 'From Bail-out to Bail-In' 30 *The Economist* (2010).

It is pivotal to stress from the very beginning that bail-inable investors do not enjoy the gains from excessive risk-taking in good times nor they have a say in corporate decisions according to statutory corporate law. Yet, in resolution, they face losses in the same way shareholders do, according to the seniority of their claim. Accordingly, the link between governance incentives, regulation, and the role of (bail-inable) creditors represents the core problem to address throughout this book. Indeed, debt governance represents the area of corporate governance where the departure from corporate governance in non-financial firms is more pronounced. Moreover, the situation of bank creditors is highly dependent on the existing regulation, being it the resolution framework for bail-inable creditors or the deposit insurance scheme for depositors.

Nevertheless, the potential role of bail-inable creditors in the governance of financial institutions did not represent the goal of the resolution framework. On the contrary it has been widely neglected.[20] In fact, from an ex-ante perspective, the fact that banks cannot rely any longer on the implicit guarantee of the State on their solvency is widely considered the main channel through which the resolution framework should influence bank decisions and markedly decrease the moral hazard of bankers in undertaking excessive risk.[21]

Therefore, discussing the ex-ante expectations stemming from the recovery and resolution framework necessarily means to engage in a set of problems that relates to the role of bail-inable creditors.[22] Among these, a central feature is "resolvability". In the context of the book, resolvability is defined as the combination of two linked but separate aspects: the practical feasibility of a resolution (e.g., issuing enough bail-inable securities)[23] and the political appetite for resolution. In fact, the first anecdotal attempts to use resolution powers clashed with considerable resistance by

[20] Iris HY Chiu, 'Corporate Governance: The Missing Paradigm in the Mandatory Bail-in Regime for Creditors of Banks and Financial Institutions' [2014] Journal of business law 611.

[21] Jianping Zhou and others, 'From Bail-out to Bail-in: Mandatory Debt Restructuring of Systemic Financial Institutions' [2012] Journal Issue 3.

[22] Emilios Avgouleas and Charles Goodhart, 'Critical Reflections on Bank Bail-Ins' (2015) 1 Journal of Financial Regulation 3.

[23] Minimum Requirement for Own Funds and Eligible Liabilities (MREL).

politicians, striving to avoid imposing losses on the investors of bank in resolution.[24]

Having defined the subject matter, three kinds of problems arise. The first of these problems relates to how bank governance and financial regulation and supervision weave together. In this respect, two competing approaches exist. On the one hand, the first approach postulates the assimilation of bank corporate governance with the governance of any other corporation. According to the assimilation theory of bank governance, the peculiarities of banking impacting on the incentives of decision-makers should be tackled by substantive regulation, such as capital, liquidity requirements, and supervisory oversight.[25] Thus, regulation and supervision should mimic market forces, substituting for the governance features that the peculiarity of banking disable, such as the ability of creditors to impose discipline on their borrowers.[26]

On the other hand, the second approach proposes the complementarity of governance with regulation and supervision.[27] In this view, providing appropriate incentives to corporate actors complements the possible flaws and deficiencies of substantive regulation and of supervisory oversight. The complementarity approach clearly hints at the possibility of shaping the incentives of bank decision-makers not only through substantive regulation, but also through governance regulation.

So far, both the literature and the policy maker focused mainly on how governance regulation can complement substantive regulation and supervision.[28] In this regard, the regulation of remuneration packages and the regulation of board committees represent paradigmatic examples.[29]

[24] Tobias H Tröger, 'Too Complex to Work: A Critical Assessment of the Bail-in Tool under the European Bank Recovery and Resolution Regime' (2018) 4 Journal of Financial Regulation 35.

[25] Dewatripont Mathias and Jean Tirole, *The Prudential Regulation of Banks*, vol 1 (MIT Press 1994).

[26] Lane defined market discipline as the ability of financial markets to provide signals leading borrowers to engage in projects consistent with their solvency. Timothy D Lane, 'Market Discipline' (1993) 40 IMF Staff Papers 53, 55.

[27] John Armour and others, 'Bank Governance' (2016) ECGI Law Working Paper 316/2016.

[28] David A Becher and Melissa B Frye, 'Does Regulation Substitute or Complement Governance?' (2011) 35 Journal of Banking & Finance 736.

[29] See Articles 91–95 of the Capital Requirements Directive, Directive 2013/36/EU of the European Parliament and of the Council of 26 June 2013 on access to the

Yet so long as governance regulation does not consider the specificities of bank governance, this represents a narrow-minded approach and could cause unintended consequences.[30]

This research builds on this second stream of literature and aims to address the abovementioned shortcomings of the literature and policy-making. In particular, this book adds to the scientific debate on bank governance and regulation the necessity to fine-tune substantive and governance regulation. This could provide bankers with a coherent and compelling incentive structure oriented towards the long-term resilience of the institution.

The second problem deals with the impact of the current resolution framework on bank governance. This implies a positive analysis of the recovery and resolution framework and of the expectations it ingenerates on bank decision-makers ex-ante.

This represents a specific aspect of the relationship between bank governance and substantive regulation that the book will focus on. For the time being, it suffices to say that the impact of the resolution framework on bank governance represents a heavily understudied issue.[31] Moreover, the interception between governance and resolution mainly comprises debt governance, i.e., the incentives and channels through which creditors can influence the decision-making of their borrower in a way consistent with their solvency.[32]

In addressing this gap in the literature, the book will show how the new resolution framework for ailing bank has the potential to enhance the quality of bank governance as well as the bank resilience. Last but not least, the third main problem related to the subject matter is to identify room for further regulatory interventions fine-tuning debt governance

activity of credit institutions and the prudential supervision of credit institutions and investment firms, amending Directive 2002/87/EC and repealing Directives 2006/48/EC and 2006/49/EC. OJ L 176/2013.

[30] As noted by Luca Enriques and Dirk Zetzsche, 'Quack Corporate Governance, Round III? Bank Board Regulation Under the New European Capital Requirement Directive' (2015) 16 Theoretical Inquiries in Law 211; Kevin J Murphy, 'Regulating Banking Bonuses in the European Union: A Case Study in Unintended Consequences' (2013) 19 European Financial Management 631.

[31] With some notable exceptions, see for instance Chiu (n 21).

[32] Lane (n 27) 55.

with the substantive resolution regulation and, consequently, enhancing the quality of bank governance.

2 Debt Governance and the Resolution Framework: A Perfect Match?

Based on the presentation of the problem, the book aims to answer a fundamental question: *Can the resolution framework for distressed banks enhance the quality of banks' decision-making?*

The answer to this overarching question cannot be given all at once. On the contrary, this question must be disentangled in sub questions that will form different building blocks of the analysis. In fact, assessing the impact and the potential of a regulatory framework requires answers to smaller, intermediate questions.

First, the book investigates the relation between bank governance and the substantive financial regulation. And, in particular, the relation between debt governance in banking and the resolution framework.

This first sub-question involves the fundamental and somehow philosophical question of what good governance for banks is. To answer this question the main economic theories on both corporate governance and banking regulation are critically discussed, highlighting the inter-relations between the two spheres and discussing how these influence one another. In particular, the traditional paradigm of "shareholder value maximisation" as the benchmark of "good corporate governance" fostering social welfare is questioned. In fact, due to the specific capital structure of banks and the institutional design of financial regulation, there are compelling reasons to argue that some deviations from that traditional paradigm are warranted.

This allows to take the analysis a step further as compared to the well-documented fact that "bank governance is special" and attempt to operationalise such specialty. In so doing, bank governance and the rules shaping it are conceptualised as a medium between the peculiar incentives of bank's decision-makers and the goals of the substantive regulations.

The main take away point is that regulators cannot take for granted the fact that the incentives of bankers can be aligned to their desiderata simply through regulation. On the contrary, bankers' incentives may need to be fine-tuned with regulatory goals through corporate governance rules. The discussion on bank corporate governance and its relationship with substantive regulation highlights the crucial role of debt governance and of a sound resolution framework as a missing piece in the academic and regulatory debate.

This opens the way to narrow down the focus of the analysis to the specific impact of the European Resolution Framework on the governance of European banks, wondering whether it actually, or potentially, enables debt governance.

Compared with the previous literature, the book brings a step forward the debate on the relationship between governance and regulation. The analysis embraces the complementarity approach to bank governance and enriches the existing literature by analysing the role of governance regulation.[33]

Establishing the link between the resolution framework and bank governance also adds to the existing state of the literature on bank resolution, where governance considerations are largely neglected. From the perspective of bank governance, linking it to the resolution framework provides a fresh view on the long-lasting debate on "good bank governance",[34] advancing the understanding of how to operationalise the special features of bank governance in regulation.

Second, the book analyses the impact of the current resolution framework on bank governance.

The second sub-question is to understand the impact of the resolution framework as it is on the corporate governance of banks. Predominantly, this work will look at debt governance. More specifically, this question addresses whether the resolution framework alters the incentives of debtholders in a way consistent with the long-term stability and resilience of the bank. This general query boils down to many specific questions related to the specific channels through which debt governance operates in non-financial firms. Does the resolution framework enhance the level market discipline imposed on banks? Does the resolution framework allow contractual solution with which the investors can efficiently allocate control powers? Does the composition of the investors in bail-inable securities matter for corporate governance?

[33] The role of governance regulation, with a sharply different approach and result, was also the focus in Steven L Schwarcz, 'Rethinking Corporate Governance for a Bondholder Financed, Systemically Risky World' (2017) 58 Wm. & Mary L. Rev. 1335.

[34] Renée B Adams and Hamid Mehran, 'Is Corporate Governance Different for Bank Holding Companies?' (2003) 9 Economic Policy Review 123.

These smaller, more specific, questions are answered through the scrutiny of the regulatory design of the resolution framework. The analysis discusses whether and how it impacts on the incentives of debtholders and their relationship vis-à-vis other corporate constituencies. In other words, these aim at understanding whether corporate governance incentives of bankers are fine-tuned with the goals set down by the resolution framework.

Answering this sub-question widens the understanding of the current literature on the ex-ante impact of the EU resolution framework. Up until now, the debate focuses on whether and to what extent the resolution framework increases the ability and willingness of investors to correctly price bank subordinated debt, internalising the costs of a future failure.[35] The book shows how such a debate is only a small fraction of the entire picture. In so doing, the book considers the price adjustment channel but is not limited to that. It also takes into consideration other channels of creditors' influence, such as contracts and closed-door pressure. In this latter regard, the composition of debtholders proves to be quintessential, tough almost completely neglected by the existing literature.[36]

Third, the book moves to normative considerations, investigating how to improve the fine-tuning of governance incentives with the resolution framework.

Finally, this third question moves to a more normative approach to the subject matter, wondering whether additional statutory intervention on bank governance can help fine-tuning bankers' incentives with the regulation. In so doing, the proposals do not aim at completeness and exhaustiveness. Rather, those address two salient aspects of corporate governance such as remuneration and voting rights, relating those to a broader view of bank governance in which debt governance plays a central role in fostering the long-term solvency and resilience of the bank.

The specific contribution of each policy proposal to the existing scientific and policy debate is discussed more at length in Sect. 5 and in the proceeding of the book. Nonetheless, at this point, it is important to point out that the book will consider both cash flow rights of bank

[35] See Tröger (n 25). From an empirical perspective see Fabrizio Crespi, Emanuela Giacomini and Danilo V Mascia, 'Bail-in Rules and the Pricing of Italian Bank Bonds' (2018) 25 European Financial Management 1321.

[36] Wolf-Georg Ringe and Jatine Patel, 'The Dark Side of Bank Resolution: Counterparty Risk through Bail-In' (2019) 31.

management and voting rights of constituencies other than shareholders. The two aspects necessarily complement each other. This already represents an aspect of originality compared to the existing literature that often approaches separately to cash flow and voting right, as if they were watertight containers.

3 Methodological Approach(es)

Generally speaking, the methodological approach is shaped by the need to identify and understanding the relation between two traditionally distinct spheres: governance and substantive financial regulation, and in particular resolution regulation.

The theoretical framework builds on the traditional theoretical approaches to both corporate governance and financial regulation. In particular, bank corporate governance is approached through the agency theory of the firm.[37] The agency approach to governance is enriched by insights from the incomplete contract theory and contingent allocation of control,[38] that is particularly suitable for the analysis of the ex-ante creditors' role in corporate governance. On the other hand, the traditional theory on banking and banking regulation helps explaining how incentives in the financial sector are different from the ones assumed in the governance of non-financial firms. The discussion builds on the standard model of bank fragility and run risk.[39] Another crucial contribution shaping the methodological approach is the moral hazard resulting from the implicit guarantee on banks' solvency.[40]

Finally, a further important element is the concept of "systemic externalities" stemming from banking activities, i.e., the idea that the risks

[37] Michael C Jensen and William H Meckling, 'Theory of the Firm: Managerial Behavior, Agency Costs and Ownership Structure' (1976) 3 Journal of financial economics 305. Following agency theory, Andrei Shleifer and Robert Vishny defined corporate governance as: "the ways in which suppliers of finance to corporations assure themselves of getting a return on their investment". Andrei Shleifer and Robert W Vishny, 'A Survey of Corporate Governance' (1997) 52 The journal of finance 737, 737.

[38] Philippe Aghion and Patrick Bolton, 'An Incomplete Contracts Approach to Financial Contracting' (1992) 59 The review of economic Studies 473.

[39] Douglas W Diamond and Philip H Dybvig, 'Bank Runs, Deposit Insurance, and Liquidity' (1983) 91 Journal of political economy 401.

[40] A crucial aspect of the analysis is, indeed, to assess whether moral hazard concerns have been addressed by the new regulatory framework.

undertaken by individual institutions spill over the entire financial system and the real economy.[41] This feature reveals to be crucial for the incentive analysis. Indeed, banks in making decisions about their risk profile do not internalise the (systemic) social costs of their activities.[42] This implies that traditional wisdom in corporate governance, according to which maximising shareholders value fosters social welfare, is not likely to hold true in banking.

Within the framework built on these methodological specifications, the question of the impact of regulation on the decision-making of banks is, ultimately, an empirical matter. Yet, the book does not engage itself in statistical and econometric exercises for a number of reasons. First, granular data on transactions, prices, supervisory decisions, etc., are not publicly available.[43] Second, the resolution framework was established in the EU relatively recently. Its implementation has been accompanied by political and media commotion and its enforcement is to this date uncertain. Therefore, any statistical exercise would be weakened by the high degree of noise surrounding bank resolution. Third, no bulletproof design for causal identification of the impact of governance on the stability of individual banks and the financial system as a whole is currently employed in the literature.

Hence, qualitative methods investigating the incentives structure of relevant actors in bank resolution appear to be more promising in fostering the understanding on bank corporate governance and the ex-ante effects of the resolution framework.

Nevertheless, it is important to bear in mind that available empirical evidence should, to the largest extent possible, drive the research. Consequently, empirical studies carried out by financial economists on the role of governance in the latest financial crisis will be largely relied upon.

As mentioned, the causal identification of the role of governance in causing and/or fostering the crisis has not been established. Yet, all the available studies point at one clear-cut evidence: the banks that, according

[41] Steven L Schwarcz, 'Systemic Risk' (2008) 97 Geo. LJ 193.

[42] Armour and Gordon (n 16).

[43] For instance, Chapter 6 attempts to assess the composition of the holders of bailinable securities. Yet, only data aggregated at country level are available; whereas granular data at transaction level are collected by the competent and resolution authorities but kept confidential.

to traditional metrics, were thought to have a better corporate governance performed worse during the financial crisis.[44] Therefore, when proposing departures from the standard paradigms of corporate governance, available empirical studies will play the role of "validity check" of the arguments proposed in the analysis.

Assumptions represent an inevitable part of any research. Through the book, assumptions are kept to a minimum, so not to lose a complex view of the reality. Nonetheless, few assumptions are necessary so to make sense of the convoluted relation of governance incentives and regulation. Specifically, the full credibility of the resolution framework will often be assumed. Full credibility of the resolution framework means that the powers granted to the competent and resolution authorities are always and consistently used so that market players can base their decisions also on the expectation of the future application of the resolution powers.

This is functional to identify the discrete impact of resolution in the governance mechanisms. Nonetheless, the assumption is subsequently relaxed to provide a more nuanced picture of the incentives in a world where bank resolution is not fully credible.

To satisfactorily answer the research question(s), the book employs positive and normative methodologies.[45] Specifically, positive analysis is employed in the formulation of a theoretical framework for examining the role of corporate governance of banks in their resilience and their relationship with the rules on resolution of distressed banks. Again, a positive approach is used for assessing the impact of the new European Resolution framework on bank corporate governance.

On the contrary, normative and prescriptive analysis drives the last part of the book, where specific policy proposals are advanced, with the aim of enhancing bank governance in relation with the resolution framework.

In fact, the aim of the book is not to stop to positive economics, answering the question "what is", but endeavours to take a step forward

[44] The load of literature on this specific issue is now considerable. Many studies will be reviewed and discussed throughout the book. For the time being, it suffices to refer to one of the first and most influential study by Andrea Beltratti and René Stultz, showing that banks whose governance was more aligned to shareholders' interests performed worse during the crisis. See Beltratti and Stulz (n 12).

[45] Jan M Smits, 'Law and Interdisciplinarity: On the Inevitable Normativity of Legal Studies' (2014) 1 Critical Analysis of Law 75.

and study "what ought to be". Yet, normative questions cannot be independent of positive questions.[46] Rather, answering positive questions represents a necessary precondition to approach normative questions in a sensible way. It follows that the book is of a consequentialist nature: the positive part builds on the theoretical framework. In turn, the normative part builds on the shortcomings of bank governance highlighted in the positive analysis.

4 The Scope of the Analysis

The ways in which the resolution framework for ailing banks shapes the incentives of bail-inable creditors in good times represent the focal point of the book. This, indeed, appears as the most suitable focal point to answer the research questions. In particular, the subject of investigation is threefold. First, how the shift in incentives affects the role of bail-inable creditors on the governance of banks. Second, the relationship of the bail-inable creditors with banks and vis-à-vis other corporate actors, such as the management or shareholders. Third, whether the changes in bank governance and the role of creditors have the potential to enhance the stability and resilience of banks.

This research clearly questions a multiplicity of dimensions, and it might appear difficult to clearly identify its specific scope. To this end, defining its borders by subtraction and highlighting its limitations seem to be the more sensible way to proceed. The proceeding of this section defines the limitations of this research across its relevant dimensions. Namely, its geographical, time-related, subjective and objective dimensions.

As for the geographical limitation, the research mainly focuses on the European Union and, in some instances, more specifically on the Eurozone. In fact, there is a dichotomy in the EU law on banking regulation between substantive rules and the rules pertaining to the institutional framework and the procedures of implementation and enforcement of the substantive regulations.

The substantive rules are set for each and every Member State, with the aim to build a level playing field in the internal market. On the

[46] Uskali Maki and Uskali Mäki, *The Methodology of Positive Economics: Reflections on the Milton Friedman Legacy* (Cambridge University Press 2009) 4.

other hand, in the aftermath of the global financial crisis and the European sovereign debt crisis, the European legislator undertook the task to create a European Banking Union for the countries belonging to the Eurozone.[47] In undertaking this gigantic effort, the European legislator created, for instance, a centralised authority in charge of the supervision and resolution of the banks located in the Eurozone.[48] It is not time to lose our way in the intricacies of the institutional architecture of the European Banking Union. Yet, this brief caveat proved necessary as this research mainly focuses on substantive rules that in principle apply to the whole European Union. Yet, in some instances, the specific way of proceeding within the Eurozone makes not only an institutional difference, but also a substantive one. In this case, the discussion will also focus specifically on the Eurozone.

Conversely, this research does not carry on a comparative analysis of different regulatory regimes. Thus, the references to US and UK regulations are limited and strictly functional to better focus the key concepts of the European regime.

The second dimension to consider is the time-related dimension. This aspect pertains to the fraction of the lifecycle of a bank considered. The focus of the research is on the expectations generated by the regulatory framework and the backward induction that decision-makers might do. Thus, no in-depth study on the immediate vicinity of insolvency neither the governance incentives in resolution procedures is conducted. Rather, the analysis zooms in the incentives of the relevant actors in good times: when the economy is booming and bankers have incentives to take disproportionate risks contributing to piling-up systemic risk.[49]

The third relevant dimension concerns the subjects on the spotlight. In this regard, bail-inable creditors have, indisputably, the leading role. Granting bail-inable creditors the leading role on the scene means that the book will develop those as round characters rather than flat once, highlighting all their relevant characteristics and the evolutions are experiencing. The scene also features a wide array of supporting casts, such

[47] Herman Van Rompuy and others, 'Towards a Genuine Economic and Monetary Union', vol 5 (2012).

[48] Jean Pisani-Ferry and others, 'What Kind of European Banking Union?' [2012] Brugel Policy Contribution.

[49] Claudio Borio, 'The Financial Cycle and Macroeconomics: What Have We Learnt?' (2014) 45 Journal of Banking & Finance 182.

as other corporate constituencies and regulatory agencies. Yet, those other actors are mainly part of the scene for their relationships vis-à-vis bail-inable creditors. Thus, their full characterisation is not always indispensable so that the reliance on existing literature is extensive.

Finally, the last relevant dimension to consider is the object of the analysis. In fact, several aspects of the resolution framework have the potential to ingenerate expectations on corporate actors. However, it is not possible to devote the same degree of attention to all these different aspects. Throughout this book, the decisive element prompting the inclusion of a specific aspect is the role the bail-inable creditors have in that regard. Therefore, the main objects of the investigation are the expectations ingenerated by the resolution tools, particularly the bail-in, and the potential those have to impact the decision-making of corporate constituencies ex-ante.

Following this line of reasoning, the preparation phase to resolution, and especially the rules on resolution planning and resolvability assessment, are not directly addressed. Few sporadic references are made so long as those are functional to better examine the position and the governance role of bail-inable creditors.

In the same way, a plethora of rules, standards, and guidelines on more traditional features of bank governance are not directly part of the research. This is the case for the rules on the risk management function, the composition of the board, the fit-and-proper requirements for bank directors and owners, the group structure, and the rules on group governance. Some degree of attention is instead devoted to the rules concerning remuneration of directors and risk-takers and on the board committee. In fact, those governance mechanisms are addressed in the final part of the book in relation with bail-inable debt and the potential role of bail-inable creditors in corporate governance.

5 Structure of the Book

It is now convenient to provide a synopsis of the arguments, key concepts, theories and ideas shaping the book. This roadmap will help the reader to keep sight of the overall flow of the book, without losing the way in the labyrinthic details of EU banking regulation.

The book is conceptually structured into three main parts: the first builds the theoretical framework (Chapters 2–3). The second performs a positive analysis of the impact of the BRRD on the governance of banking institutions (Chapters 4–6). The third proposes two distinct normative improvements to the current regulatory framework and assesses the recent banking crises against the framework (Chapters 7–9).

Chapter 2 introduces bank governance, highlighting why and how corporate governance of financial institutions is special as compared with non-financial corporations. It discusses the role of negative (systemic) externalities of banking activities, and the perverse incentive structure faced by shareholders, especially in good times.

The second part of the chapter moves the focus to the main regulations on bank governance and pinpoints how these pieces of regulation are often not tailored to the specificities of bank governance. Rather, these often represent a mere crystallisation of existing best practices or, even worse, an attempt to extract political benefit from a harsh attitude towards the banking industry in the aftermath of the financial crash.

Finally, the chapter discusses the role of debt governance in banking and how its usual channels are largely unavailable. It argues that, if appropriately enabled by specific regulatory intervention, debt governance has the potential to positively complement the effort of the regulator and the supervisor in achieving the resilience of the bank. In this respect, governance regulation should be conceptualised as a medium, necessary to fine-tune the special incentives of bank constituencies and goals of substantive regulation.

Compared to the rest of the literature, this chapter proposes a new approach to operationalise the specialty of bank governance, identifying two crucial features: the role of regulating governance in linking substantive regulation and governance incentives and the importance of debt governance.

Chapter 3 operationalises the theoretical construct proposed in the previous chapter. Indeed, it wonders whether the new European recovery and resolution framework for ailing bank might, almost inadvertently, represent an effective medium between substantive regulation and governance incentives.

To this end, the chapter discusses the institutional as well as substantive architecture of the new regulation. Subsequently, it zooms in the resolution tools provided by the BRRD and in particular the bail-in tool, discussing the expectations it is supposed to ingenerate. The chapter also links the ex-ante potential of the BRRD with debt governance. In so doing, it shows how and the conditions under which their intertwinement can enhance the quality of bank governance trough the role of bail-inable creditors.

This chapter mainly review and systematise the existing literature on bank resolution and its potential to have ex-ante effects. Nonetheless, building upon the framework of Chapter 2, this chapter marginally innovates the literature on bank resolution. In particular, the chapter discusses the conditions necessary for debt governance to be enabled. Moreover, the approach to debt governance is broader as compared with the rest of the literature on ex-ante effects of resolution, taking into consideration not only price adjustments, but also contracts and the role of different holders of bail-inable securities.

Chapter 4 addresses a traditional channel of debt governance, which is market discipline through price adjustment. This chapter shows that the BRRD provides inherently suboptimal incentives to bail-inable creditors to monitor bank's activities and accordingly adjust pricing because of competing policy objectives pursued by the Directive.

In dealing with market discipline through price adjustments, the existing literature had focused on the elements of uncertainty, over complexity and lack of credibility. The chapter adds to the existing literature, highlighting how disciplining incentives are inherently diluted, even assuming smooth functioning and full credibility of the resolution framework.

Chapter 5 investigates whether bail-inable creditors can discipline their borrower (i.e., the bank) through contractual arrangements attached to bail-inable securities. This chapter, building on the incomplete contract theory of debt, passes through the main contractual disciplining mechanism checking whether they are available to bail-inable creditors given the current financial regulation, highlighting once again a trade-off between financial stability and market discipline.

The chapter concludes that financial contracting over bail-inable securities lacks the potential for disciplining banks because of the existing regulation on qualitative requirements for capital and eligible liabilities, whereas Contingent Convertible instruments have the potential to positively impact on corporate governance.

The analysis of financial contracting fills a void in the literature. In fact, no specific studies focused on the available contractual mechanisms for long-term creditors in the banking context. In so doing, the chapter finds that the financial stability considerations prevail over market discipline ones. This finding also adds to the wider literature on the trade-off between financial stability and moral hazard.

Chapter 6 intends to address the composition of bail-inable debtholders and the relevance of counterparty risk in resolution. This chapter underlines a widespread inattention of both academics and policy makers on these issues, addressing the relevant trade-offs and providing informative data on bail-inable security holders. It highlights that the market is adjusting towards a desirable composition of holders even though a considerable room for improvement is still available and a mix of different investors might yield superior outcomes.

This exercise deepens the current understanding on the impact of the new framework on market preferences, providing evidence on both the credibility of the resolution framework and the perspectives of effective application of the new tools.

Finally, the chapter discusses some possible ways forward, underlining the importance of increasing the share of sophisticated investors that are specialised in dealing with bail-inable securities, especially for junior positions. It proposes a balanced mix of investors with different business models and time horizons so to minimise systemic risk while maximising governance benefits. The chapter concludes that to incentivise market players to shift towards more efficient composition, granting ex-ante governance rights is warranted.

Chapter 7 proposes a radical change in the current remuneration practices, including bail-inable debt within the variable component of remuneration packages. In fact, the current regulatory framework and resulting practices in the EU are to be considered heavily unsatisfactory since they decreased the link between pay and performance. Moreover, it does not consider the specificities of bank corporate governance; consequently, the negative externalities it generates are still not accounted for.

The chapter sets the economic rationale for remuneration, highlighting the special case of the banking industry and explaining why debt can be particularly useful in such framework. Against this theoretical framework, the EU regulation on the structure of remuneration packages is critically assessed. This highlights how the policy goal of optimising risk-taking incentives of bankers is far from being reached and, more importantly, that it cannot be reached without a radical change in the regulatory paradigm.

The chapter shows why such shift necessarily implies to include bail-inable debt in remuneration packages. It also shows how it would tighten the link between pay and performance and address the specificities of bank governance. Finally, as an additional positive spillover, remuneration through debt would also enhance the resolvability of the institution. The final part of the chapter develops a detailed policy proposal that focuses both on the content of the regulation and on the possible implementation strategies.

The chapter builds on the extensive literature on remuneration in banking and innovates in two main ways. First, it fine-tunes governance incentives and the resolution framework. This allows not only to have positive effects on the incentives of bankers, but also to have positive spillovers on the credibility of the resolution framework and the resolvability individual institutions. Moreover, the chapter demonstrates that cash flow rights should be adjusted to the specificities of bank governance through mandatory regulation.

Chapter 8 proposes a deep statutory reform in the area of bank governance, exploiting the potential positive synergies with the BRR framework and, in particular, the incentive structure of the so-called "bail-inable creditors". The overarching aim of such proposal is to fine-tune bank governance and substantive regulation and, subsequently, truly enhancing the quality of decision-making of banks in terms of risk-taking. At the same time, the proposed reform should increase the ex-ante credibility of resolution.

The second part of the chapter operationalises that theoretical construct, proposing to grant bail-inable creditors with a limited set of decision and appointment rights. This limited set of rights should be complemented by a general principle of sufficient accountability of banks governance arrangements towards bail-inable creditors, so to allow for differentiated and proportionate implementation.

The analysis demonstrates how granting bail-inable creditors with ex-ante governance rights can represent a tool to correct for shareholders' perverse incentives and make debt governance work in banking. The policy proposal advanced in the chapter would complement substantive regulation and the oversight activity of the competent authority. The governance role of creditors has the potential to be particularly helpful in preventing disproportionate risk-taking decisions in good times, when regulatory and supervisory standards are lax and systemic risk piles-up.

Chapter 9 examines the 2023 banking crisis, focusing specific on the case of Silicon Valley Bank (SVB) and Credit Suisse (CS). The analysis focuses on the features of these crises pertaining to debt governance, testing the theoretical contribution of this book.

In so doing, the chapter analyses how and why key mechanisms intended to foster market discipline and bank resolvability, including contingent convertible bonds (CoCos), underperformed under stress. The analysis reveals that while both banks faced idiosyncratic vulnerabilities, the system is still vulnerable to runs and resolution lacks credibility. The chapter highlights that the (lack of) effective debt governance deepens these vulnerabilities.

The chapter shows that the mere existent of ex-ante regulatory and contractual tools are not sufficient to discipline banks unless embedded within a credible institutional framework favouring timely enforcement. Specifically, in the SVB case, the *de facto* bailout of uninsured depositors disrupted expectations of loss-sharing, while in the CS case, the wipeout of AT1 bonds revealed critical flaws in their contractual design. Across both cases, supervisory reluctance to act timely, prompting bank recovery, contributed disorderly resolution.

CHAPTER 2

Bank Governance

1 Introduction

In the aftermath of the Global Financial Crisis, corporate governance failures were blamed as one of the chief causes of the meltdown in Europe and elsewhere. The OECD, for instance, published a condemnatory report on bank governance, claiming that "the financial crisis can be to an important extent attributed to failures and weaknesses in corporate governance arrangements".[1]

Such a negative and clear-cut judgement triggered a season of political attention and activism in regulating bank governance. The aim was to restrain excessive risk-taking and correct perverse incentives of financial regulation. However, many scholars immediately raised serious concerns about this regulatory wave and its potential to promote good governance of banking institutions.[2]

[1] Grant Kirkpatrick, 'The Corporate Governance Lessons from the Financial Crisis' (2009) 2009 OECD Journal: Financial Market Trends 61.

[2] See, for instance, Luca Enriques and Dirk Zetzsche, 'Quack Corporate Governance, Round III? Bank Board Regulation Under the New European Capital Requirement Directive' (2015) 16 Theoretical Inquiries in Law 211; Guido Ferrarini, 'CRD IV and the Mandatory Structure of Bankers' Pay' (2015) 289; Kern Alexander, 'Regulating Bank Governance and the EU Capital Requirements Directive' (2017) 28 European Business Law Review 809.

E. D. Martino, *EU Bank Governance and Bail-In*, EBI Studies in Banking and Capital Markets Law,
https://doi.org/10.1007/978-3-032-20699-2_2

Moreover, when it comes to corporate governance of financial institutions, there is a more profound and still under-explored question: what is good governance for banks? There is a widespread idea that bank governance is special and that what is good governance in banks and non-financial institutions may differ.[3] Nonetheless, a compelling theory on good bank governance and its defining tools is currently missing. Moreover, the load of theoretical and empirical studies on bank governance consistently produced evidence that banks with better governance according to traditional metrics performed worse during the Global Financial Crisis.[4]

Improving the decision-making of financial institutions through governance regulation represents an impossible task as long as what good bank governance is remains largely unknown. This chapter takes off from such a conundrum and discusses what is good bank governance.

In this chapter, I aim to show that good bank governance does not arise endogenously, simply allocating control to those who values it most. Therefore, both substantive and governance regulation need to stimulate the emergence of good governance. In so doing, governance regulation should closely mirror the special features differentiating bank governance from corporate governance in non-financial corporations. At the same time, governance regulation should fine-tune banks' decision-making to the policy goals set by substantive regulation.

[3] Among many others, see Marco Bodellini, 'Corporate Governance of Banks and Financial Stability: Critical Issues and Challenges Ahead' (2018) 39 Business Law Review 160.

[4] Andrea Beltratti and René M Stulz, 'The Credit Crisis around the Globe: Why Did Some Banks Perform Better?' (2012) 105 Journal of Financial Economics 1; Rüdiger Fahlenbrach and René M Stulz, 'Bank CEO Incentives and the Credit Crisis' (2011) 99 Journal of Financial Economics 11; David H Erkens, Mingyi Hung and Pedro Matos, 'Corporate Governance in the 2007–2008 Financial Crisis: Evidence from Financial Institutions Worldwide' (2012) 18 Journal of Corporate Finance 389; Luc Laeven and Ross Levine, 'Bank Governance, Regulation and Risk-taking' (2009) 93 Journal of Financial Economics 259; Luc Laeven, Lev Ratnovski and Hui Tong, 'Bank Size, Capital, and Systemic Risk: Some International Evidence' (2016) 69 Journal of Banking & Finance S25; Allen N Berger, Björn Imbierowicz and Christian Rauch, 'The Roles of Corporate Governance in Bank Failures during the Recent Financial Crisis' (2016) 48 Journal of Money, Credit and Banking 729.

Following this approach, the analysis confirms and systematises the dissatisfaction towards the current governance regulation, with a particular focus on the EU regulation of bank governance.[5]

Thereafter, the analysis spotlights debt governance: the distinctive features of bank governance consistently deal with the role of creditors. Thus, this chapter claims that any consideration of good bank governance ought to embed debt governance and this potentially calls for governance regulation. Finally, such regulation should be fine-tuned to the new recovery and resolution framework for ailing banks.[6] Indeed, regulatory innovation considers the incentives of bank creditors, conditionally on the maintenance of banks' solvency. Relatedly, it crucially claims to eliminate the bailout expectations.

2 Why Bank Governance Is Special?

2.1 Corporate Governance: Definitions and Basic Features

The governance of modern corporations represents one of the most widely studied topics in social sciences, from many different perspectives: company law, corporate finance, business management, industrial organisation, just to name the ones of utmost relevance.[7] Different approaches to social science tend to have different definitions of what corporate governance is and its constitutive mechanisms. It is informative to briefly go through those approaches that will prove insightful in the development of the analysis.

[5] The Capital Requirement Directive - Directive 2013/36/EU of the European Parliament and Of the Council of 26 June 2013 on access to the activity of credit institutions and the prudential supervision of credit institutions and investment firms, amending Directive 2002/87/EC and repealing Directives 2006/48/EC and 2006/49/EC.

[6] The Bank Recovery and Resolution Directive (BRRD) - Directive 2014/59/EU of the European Parliament and of the Council of 15 May 2014 establishing a framework for the recovery and resolution of credit institutions and investment firms. OJ L 173, 12.6.2014 and the Single Resolution Mechanism Regulation (SRMR) - REGULATION (EU) No 806/2014 OF THE EUROPEAN PARLIAMENT AND OF THE COUNCIL of 15 July 2014 establishing uniform rules and a uniform procedure for the resolution of credit institutions and certain investment firms in the framework of a Single Resolution Mechanism and a Single Resolution Fund and amending Regulation (EU) No 1093/2010.

[7] For an overview, see Jeffrey N Gordon and Wolf-Georg Ringe, *The Oxford Handbook of Corporate Law and Governance*, vol 1 (Oxford University Press 2015).

First, from a legal perspective, it is possible to rely on the definition provided by the Cadbury Code[8]: "*Corporate governance is the system by which companies are directed and controlled. Boards of directors are responsible for the governance of their companies. The shareholders' role in governance is to appoint the directors and the auditors and to satisfy themselves that an appropriate governance structure is in place*".[9] This approach focuses on the rights and duties of corporate constituencies and takes for granted the existence of a given financial structure of the corporation. Moreover, it mainly focuses on managerial rights directly stemming from ownership rights of shareholders while neglecting the underlying cash flow rights intrinsically linked to the ownership.

A different and complementary approach is proposed by Corporate Finance literature, which can be summarised with Shleifer and Vishny's words: *«Corporate Governance deals with the ways in which suppliers of finance to corporations assure themselves of getting a return on their investment. How do the suppliers of finance get managers to return some of the profits to them? How do they make sure that managers do not steal the capital they supply or invest it in bad projects? How do suppliers of finance control managers?»*[10] Therefore, governance mechanisms are linked to the financial structure of the corporation and consist of a bundle of income and control rights stemming therein,[11] defining the property rights related to firms.[12]

At any rate, corporate governance undoubtedly deals with corporate decision-making; its legal and economic implications have generated a

[8] The Cadbury Report was drafted in 1992 for the London Stock Exchange by a committee chaired by Sir. Adrian Cadbury. It represents the first example of Corporate Governance code of best practices and played a pivotal role in the development of this kind of instruments that are now well spread in most of the developed countries.

[9] Adrian Cadbury, *The Financial Aspects of Corporate Governance - Report with Code of Best [Cadbury Report]* (Gee Publishing 1992).

[10] Shleifer and Vishny (n 8).

[11] Johan Devriese and others, 'Corporate Governance, Regulation and Supervision of Banks' (2004) 2 Financial Stability Review 95.

[12] On the proprietary approach to corporations see John Armour and Michael J Whincop, 'The Proprietary Foundations of Corporate Law' (2007) 27 Oxford Journal of Legal Studies 429. Property as a bundle of rights is the standard representation for defining Property Rights in Law & Economics literature. See Harold Demsetz, 'Toward a Theory of Property Rights' (1974) 57 The American Economic Review 347.

gigantic load of academic models and debate.[13] In this regard, the seminal contribution on the agency theory of the firm by Jensen and Meckling represents a cornerstone of the discussion on corporate governance.[14] The agency theory highlights the costs stemming from the separation of ownership and control, its implications for governance decisions, and its impact on the cost of capital.[15] It remains to this day the leading model to approach corporate governance research. In a nutshell, given the existence of agency problems between different corporate constituencies, governance arrangements should design corporate relationships capable of solving or minimising the existing agency costs, yielding a second-best outcome.[16]

The corporate governance literature relying on agency theory in its different specifications focused on three main agency conflicts.

First, the conflict between shareholders and managers stemming from the separation of ownership and control. This has been acknowledged since the early 30 s thanks to the seminal work by Berle and Means.[17] Dispersed shareholders have little incentive to monitoring because of the little individual stake they have invested in the company. This results in a risk of expropriation of dispersed shareholders by managers, who become the real "owners" of the company.

[13] For excellent surveys, see Andrei Shleifer and Robert W Vishny, 'A Survey of Corporate Governance' (1997) 52 The journal of finance 737; Marco Becht, Patrick Bolton and Ailsa Röell, 'Corporate Law and Governance', *Handbook of law and economics*, vol 2 (Elsevier 2007).

[14] Michael C Jensen and William H Meckling, 'Theory of the Firm: Managerial Behavior, Agency Costs and Ownership Structure' (1976) 3 Journal of financial economics 305. For a legal operationalisation of the agency theory, see Frank H Easterbrook and Daniel R Fischel, *The Economic Structure of Corporate Law* (Harvard University Press 1996).

[15] An alternative theory based on proprietary rights has emerged in the last twenty years. See Henry Hansmann and Reinier Kraakman, 'The Essential Role of Organizational Law' (2000) 110 Yale Law Journal; John Armour and Michael J Whincop, 'The Proprietary Foundations of Corporate Law' (2007) 27 Oxford Journal of Legal Studies 429. For an attempt to systematise this approach, see Eva Micheler, *Company Law: A Real Entity Theory* (Oxford University Press 2021).

[16] Frank H Easterbrook, 'Derivative Securities and Corporate Governance' [2002] The University of Chicago Law Review 733, 740.

[17] Adolf Augustus Berle and Gardiner Coit Means, *Modern Corporation and Private Property* (Transaction Publishers 1932).

Second, the conflict between majority and minority shareholders. This second stream of literature insists on situations where a controlling blockholder may pursue his private interests while running the company. This conflict arises when there is a majority shareholder that might extract private benefits from their control, expropriating minority shareholders.[18] While the former flow of literature was born and developed in the Anglo-Saxon world of dispersed ownership, this latter one is more peculiar to the European world of concentrated ownership.[19]

Third, the conflict between insiders (shareholders, managers, etc.) and creditors: equity and debtholders have intrinsically different claims towards the corporation.[20] The equity holders earn the residual income and bear part of the losses due to limited liability. On the other hand, debtholders enjoy fixed contractual payments and do not enjoy upside when the venture succeeds. Therefore, interests of equity and debtholders might differ significantly, especially on the verge of distress.[21] This third agency conflict is in the banking industry and represents the focal point of this book.

The agency theory of the firm is not immune to criticism and gaps. Accounting for all the competing theories of the firm and all the refinements to agency theory is beyond the scope of this analysis.[22] However, it

[18] Henry Hansmann, 'Ownership of the Firm' (1988) 4 Journal of Law, Economics, & Organization 267; Rafael La Porta and others, 'Investor Protection and Corporate Governance' (2000) 58 Journal of financial economics 3.

[19] Fabrizio Barca and Marco Becht, *The Control of Corporate Europe* (Oxford University Press 2001). See also Alessio Pacces, *Rethinking Corporate Governance: The Law and Economics of Control Powers* (Routledge 2013).

[20] This specific agency problem has been analysed in particular by the corporate finance literature, see Jean Tirole, *The Theory of Corporate Finance* (Princeton University Press 2006) 213–220. Legal consequences of this conflict have been tackled, up to a certain extent, by the LLSV literature that sees the legal protection of creditors as a substitute for the lack of shareholder's protection in civil law countries. See La Porta and others (n 17).

[21] For an introduction to the agency costs of debt, see John Armour and others, *The Anatomy of Corporate Law: A Comparative and Functional Approach* (2017) ch 5.

[22] Among them, it is worth mentioning the transaction costs theory and the stakeholder's theory. See, respectively, Oliver E Williamson, 'Transaction-Cost Economics: The Governance of Contractual Relations' (1979) 22 The journal of Law and Economics 233; R Edward Freeman, 'A Stakeholder Theory of the Modern Corporation' (2001) 3 Perspectives in Business Ethics 144.

is important to discuss the proprietary theory of the firm based on incomplete contracts since it represents an essential complement and extension to the agency theory of the firm.[23] In a world of complete contracts, agency conflicts should not be a problem since every future course of action is contractible ex-ante and verifiable in courts ex-post. Yet, we live in a world of incomplete contracts that makes it impossible or, at the very least, excessively costly to contract over all the possible future courses of actions.

Thus, a crucial feature of corporate contracting is the allocation of residual control rights, i.e., the right to decide on the non-contracted contingencies. This goes to the core of what equity contracts are about: shareholders retain the residual control rights over corporate decisions even though such allocation is not absolute. In contrast, debt contracting, as modelled by Aghion and Bolton,[24] provides a mechanism for allocating control contingent on future and uncertain events.[25] The interplay between equity control rights and debt intrusions (contingent on default or other contracted contingencies)[26] goes to the core of corporate governance. Indeed, it portrays the available mechanisms through which the main suppliers of finance, equity, and debtholders assure themselves of getting a return on their investments.[27]

To sum up, the legal and corporate finance approaches to agency governance are complementary in describing corporate operations as well as the close link between governance rights and the financial position of the claim holder vis-à-vis the corporation. Moreover, the incomplete contract approach highlights the importance of the allocation of residual control rights in shaping the relation between corporate constituencies.

On top of that, the underlying "institutional matrix" is also crucial for understanding corporate governance, especially in financial institutions.

[23] For its original formulation see Sanford J Grossman and Oliver D Hart, 'The Costs and Benefits of Ownership: A Theory of Vertical and Lateral Integration' (1986) 94 Journal of political economy 691.

[24] Philippe Aghion and Patrick Bolton, 'An Incomplete Contracts Approach to Financial Contracting' (1992) 59 The review of economic Studies 473.

[25] For a review of the possible contractual devices available to creditors, see Patrick Bolton, 'Corporate Finance, Incomplete Contracts, and Corporate Control' (2013) 30 The Journal of Law, Economics, & Organization i64.

[26] Think for instance of covenants or security interests.

[27] Shleifer and Vishny (n 8).

Indeed, in defining governance, the Basel Committee on Banking Supervision (BCBS)[28] incorporates the regulatory environment, stating that: "*Effective implementation of sound Corporate Governance requires relevant legal, regulatory and institutional foundations. A variety of factors, including the system of business laws, stock exchange rules and accounting standards, can affect market integrity and systemic stability*".[29] The remainder of this chapter discusses the roots and consequences of the specialty of bank governance, highlighting its relations with the regulatory framework.

2.2 The Special Features of Bank Governance

The idea that the mechanisms underpinning bank governance are special is not new.[30] However, the roots of such specialty were more attentively scrutinised only in the aftermath of the Global Financial Crisis.[31] Banks possess specific features that differentiate them from any other non-financial firm. Crucially, any of these features entails a negative externality for other players of the financial system and, more broadly, to the financial system itself.[32]

First, banks are highly leveraged institutions,[33] i.e., the amount of equity held against banks' assets is particularly low. In terms of corporate governance, and the conflict between the bank and its creditors, this raises two main issues: risk-shifting and debt-overhang. On the one hand, in good times, equity holders are willing to take on much more risk than

[28] BCBS, 'Corporate Governance Principles for Banks - Guidelines' (2015).

[29] Ibid 21.

[30] See, for instance, Jonathan R Macey and Maureen O'Hara, 'The Corporate Governance of Banks' [2003] Economic Policy Review 91, where the authors acknowledge the specialty of bank governance and propose a different liability regime for directors to tackle such specialties. See at length Chapter 8.

[31] With some notable exceptions. See, for instance, Renée B Adams and Hamid Mehran, 'Is Corporate Governance Different for Bank Holding Companies?' (2003) 9 Economic Policy Review 123; Macey and O'Hara (n 29).

[32] Steven L Schwarcz, 'Systemic Risk' (2008) 97 Geo. LJ 193.

[33] Capital regulation is meant to limit excessive leverage. See Articles 72 and ff of the Capital Requirement Regulation (CRR). Professors Hellwig and Admati argued in favour of a sharp increase of regulatory capital to limit leverage-related distortions. See Anat Admati and Martin Hellwig, *The Bankers' New Clothes: What's Wrong with Banking and What to Do about It* (Princeton University Press 2014).

what is socially optimal. Thanks to limited liability, they shift most of the downside risk of their investment to debtholders.[34] On the other hand, in bad times, when the bank approaches insolvency, equity holders are still, and even more, willing to take on value-destroying bets, but they are also likely to pass up positive net present value projects since these would mainly benefit debtholders.[35]

Second, the core business of commercial banks is to perform transformation activities; namely, liquidity, maturity, and risk transformation.[36] Banks transform short-term and liquid (deposits and wholesale funds) into long-term and illiquid assets, by way of granting credit (retail, corporate, mortgages, etc.). This provides an essential service to the economy but, at the same time, it makes banks particularly prone to liquidity shocks.[37] Thus, the funding decisions of banks tend to generate liquidity externalities.[38] Indeed, banks massively rely on short-term financing and the defining characteristic of those short-term funds is that they are runnable, meaning that their holders can freely decide to withdraw or not roll-over their exposure towards the bank.[39]

[34] Marco Becht, Patrick Bolton and Ailsa Röell, 'Why Bank Governance Is Different' (2011) 27 Oxford Review of Economic Policy 437, 445.

[35] Linus Wilson, 'Debt Overhang and Bank Bailouts' (2012) 5 International Journal of Monetary Economics and Finance 395.

[36] John Armour and others, *Principles of Financial Regulation* (Oxford University Press 2016), 277.

[37] In the literature liquidity has been defined in a number of ways. Brunnermeier and Pedersen define liquidity negatively, focusing on the definition of market illiquidity as the "difference between the transaction price and the fundamental value". See Markus K Brunnermeier and Lasse Heje Pedersen, 'Market Liquidity and Funding Liquidity' (2009) 22 Review of Financial studies 2202. On the contrary, Pistor defines it positively and more generally as the "ability to sell any asset for the other assets or cash at will". See Katharina Pistor, 'A Legal Theory of Finance' (2013) 41 Journal of Comparative Economics 315, 316. The latter definition, although more general and somehow vague, has the advantage that there is no need to determine the fundamental value of the asset.

[38] Liquidity regulation aims at minimising the creation of such externalities requiring the bank to hold some stable funding against illiquid assets. See Article 415 and ff. of the Capital Requirement Regulation.

[39] Perhaps the most famous run of the history is the Northern Rock one, when not-fully-insured depositors physically formed gigantic queues to withdraw their money. Nowadays, the possibility of a physical run is rather small because of full protection of deposit insurance, and the focal point is now shifted to the risk of wholesale creditors stopping to roll over credits, even though theoretically more sophisticated investors, as wholesale investors are, should not panic. See Hyun Song Shin, 'Reflections on Northern

If liquidity dries up, either because of an idiosyncratic or systemic shock, those transformation activities (and the entailed mismatch in liquidity and maturity) jeopardises the cash flow solvency of the bank, which may be forced to fire-sale its illiquid assets, leading—in turn—to balance sheet insolvency and, thus, triggering the crisis.[40]

Third, bank assets are opaque, i.e., banks have a sizeable advantage in assessing the value of their asset. Therefore, the ability of outside investors and supervisors to monitor the quality of banks' assets is limited. The bank acts as an intermediary by performing a (costly) "delegated monitoring" activity over its assets. Thus, the bank has more information than the general public.[41] Again, such informational advantage incentivises the incumbent management to take excessive risk. The pervasiveness of these perverse incentives skyrocketed in the last two decades as financial assets became more and more complex.[42]

Tightly related to assets opacity, the fiduciary nature of banking activities needs attention. Banking services can be labelled as "experience goods" and perhaps even as "credence goods".[43] This is the standard argument for special consumer protection in banking, but it also has governance spillovers. Indeed, the difficulty of correctly pricing the assets and make consistent inter-temporal choices creates incentives for the bank

Rock: The Bank Run That Heralded the Global Financial Crisis' (2009) 23 Journal of economic perspectives 101.

[40] There is nowadays a wide consensus on the fact the even the big evil of the financial crisis, Lehman Brothers was not completely insolvent from a balance sheet point of view, but just from a liquidity When wholesale creditors panicked and stopped to roll out Lehman's liabilities, Lehman was forced to fire-sale its illiquid assets and, eventually, became balance sheet insolvent as well. For greater detail on Lehamn failure see Jeffrey N Gordon and Wolf-Georg Ringe, 'Bank Resolution in Europe: The Unfinished Agenda of Structural Reform' in Guido Ferrarini and Danny Busch (eds), *European Banking Union* (Oxford University Press Oxford, UK 2015) 16.

[41] Douglas W Diamond, 'Financial Intermediation and Delegated Monitoring' (1984) 51 The review of economic studies 393.

[42] For instance, think about the repo market, the structured assets, the swap instruments, etc. See Gary Gorton and Andrew Metrick, 'Securitized Banking and the Run on Repo' (2012) 104 Journal of Financial economics 425.

[43] This aspect grasps the very nature of banking activity, as the word "credit" itself derives from latin *credere*", meaning "trust", Alessio M Pacces and Dirk Heremans, 'Regulation of Banking and Financial Markets', *Encyclopedia of Law and Economics - Volume 9* (Edward Elgar 2012) 559.

management to behave opportunistically, take on too much risk, and extract a rent from unsophisticated investors.

Fourth, the social costs of failure are larger than private ones: shareholders bear only a fraction of the potential social costs of the bank failure, especially in systematically relevant institutions.[44] Banks do not internalise the costs of their failure and have suboptimal incentives to take socially efficient prudential measures to avoid bankruptcy. Moreover, there was—and there still is—a reasonable expectation of a state bailout in case of failure, increasing the risk of moral hazard by shareholders.[45]

Finally, each individual bank is part of a wider and interconnected financial system. This raises at least two issues: the correlation of risk portfolios and the interconnectedness of individual banks.[46] Risk correlation hints at the fact that all individual banks diversify their portfolio in a similar manner, so that a bank portfolio is likely to correlate with that of other banks. This can create systemic stability issues in bad times as the asset value of interconnected banks simultaneously decreases.[47] Interconnectedness is crucial to understand systemic risk and the perverse incentives arising therein since it entails contagion risk.[48] The contagion spreads through both "real" and "informational" channels.[49] The former refers to domino effects triggered by mutual exposure on financial instruments or through inter-bank deposits.[50] The latter relates to trust as the quintessential feature in the financial system: as trust declines because

[44] Matej Marinč and Razvan Vlahu, 'The Economic Perspective of Bank Bankruptcy Law' (Springer Science & Business Media 2011) 310.

[45] Chris Bates and Simon Gleeson, 'Legal Aspects of Bank Bail-Ins' (2011) 5 Law and Financial Markets Review 264; Charles Goodhart and Emilios Avgouleas, 'A Critical Evaluation of Bail-in as a Bank Recapitalisation Mechanism' in Franklin Allen, Elena Carletti and Joanna E Gray (eds), *Bearing the Losses from Bank and Sovereign Default in the Eurozone* (FIC Press 2014).

[46] Peter O Mülbert and Ryan D Citlau, 'The Uncertain Role of Banks? Corporate Governance in Systemic Risk Regulation' (2011) 179 16.

[47] Viral V Acharya, 'A Theory of Systemic Risk and Design of Prudential Bank Regulation' (2009) 5 Journal of financial stability 224.

[48] Anne-Caroline Hüser, 'Too Interconnected to Fail: A Survey of the Interbank Networks Literature' (SAFE 2016) 91.

[49] Olivier De Bandt and Philipp Hartmann, 'Systemic Risk: A Survey' (ECB working paper 2000) 35.

[50] For what mainly pertain cross-holding of bank debt see Wolf-Georg Ringe and Jatine Patel, 'The Dark Side of Bank Resolution: Counterparty Risk through Bail-In' (2019)

of the bad news coming from one or few financial institutions, mistrust spread quickly, harming the rest of the system.[51]

Undoubtedly, overlaps among these special features of banking exists and perhaps the list is not exhaustive. Nonetheless, this section makes clear how these impact the decision-making process of banks, i.e., their corporate governance.

2.3 *Bank Governance: Assimilation v. Specialty*

The fact that bank corporate governance is special was overlooked for decades. The acknowledgement that the mechanisms underpinning the decision-making in banking were different did not lead to acknowledge that bank governance should be treated specially. The dominant idea, building on the fundamental model of banking was that the rigorous regulation and supervision were enough to handle the limitation of decision-making mechanisms in banking.[52]

The policy and academic debate focused mainly on the inability of creditors, and especially depositors, to efficiently discipline their borrowers, the banks. The primary cause behind such an inability consists of the implicit or explicit state guarantee on bank solvency. In this setting, Dewatripont and Tirole[53] expressed their "representation hypothesis" according to which the banking supervisor acts as a substitute for standard corporate governance mechanisms. The supervisor should mimic what market players would do in the absence of the state guarantee.

The model behind the representation hypothesis postulates that the most efficient way to carry out banking activities is to empower managers, align their incentives with the shareholder maximisation benchmark, and make them accountable *vis-'a-vis* the supervisor. In the post-crisis

31; Benjamin Bernard, Agostino Capponi and Joseph E Stiglitz, 'Bail-Ins and Bailouts: Incentives, Connectivity, and Systemic Stability' (2017) wp23747.

[51] For the standard case of "bank run", see the seminal contribution by Douglas W Diamond and Philip H Dybvig, 'Bank Runs, Deposit Insurance, and Liquidity' (1983) 91 Journal of political economy 401.

[52] What professor Armour and co-authors calls "Assimilation Theory of Bank Governance". See John Armour and others, 'Bank Governance' (2016) ECGI Law Working Paper 316/2016.

[53] Dewatripont Mathias and Jean Tirole, *The Prudential Regulation of Banks*, vol 1 (MIT Press 1994).

literature, this approach took the label "assimilation theory" of bank governance.[54]

After the global financial crisis, the "assimilation theory" was heavily criticised. Poor decision-making, especially in terms of risk profile, was considered one of the boosters that led the financial system to blow up in 2007.[55] Hence, many proposed to consider the special features of bank governance and suggest governance as a complement to regulation and supervision.[56] The key difference is that the assimilation theory acts as a strict substitute for governance. In contrast, the specialty of bank governance postulates a complementary relation between governance and regulation.

The special nature of banks' governance does not represent just a theoretical speculation. To operationalise the argument proposed so far, it is useful to briefly review the empirical literature on the matter.

The study by Beltratti and Stulz is the most famous and widely cited.[57] The authors studied the determinants of bank performance during the crisis, measured by stock return, in a sample of 98 banks across the world. Even though they did not find governance to be the main determinant of the financial crisis, they detected a systematic negative effect of what is commonly labelled as "good governance" in banks' performance during the crisis. This result is consistent with the findings of many other empirical pieces of research on these issues. Erkens and co-authors found that financial institutions with more independent boards and higher institutional ownership experienced worse stock returns during the crisis.[58] Fahlenbrach and Stulz found that better alignment between shareholders' interests and CEO compensation yielded worse performance during the

[54] Armour and others, *Principles of Financial Regulation* (n 35).

[55] See, in particular, Luigi Zingales, 'The Future of Securities Regulation' (2009) 47 Journal of Accounting Research 391; Jean-Michel Sahut and Sandrine Boulerne, 'Flaws in Banking Governance' (2010) 15 International Journal of business 319.

[56] Just to name some prominent study, see Becht, Bolton and Röell (n 33); Guido Ferrarini, 'Understanding the Role of Corporate Governance in Financial Institutions: A Research Agenda' (2017) 347/2017; Armour and others, 'Bank Governance' (n 52).

[57] Beltratti and Stulz (n 5).

[58] Erkens, Hung and Matos (n 5).

crisis.[59] In a similar vein, Anginer and co-authors found that shareholder-friendly corporate governance is positively associated with bank risk of insolvency.[60]

The picture emerging from these findings has no straightforward explanations. The fact that what is commonly known to be "good governance" yields bad performance is, to say the very least, counterintuitive. A possible explanation is that factors other than governance better explain the performance during the financial crisis.[61] An alternative interpretation is that what is good governance for non-financial and financial firms may not coincide.[62] The two interpretations are not mutually exclusive, and it is reasonable to argue that both are, to an extent, true.

2.4 How to Deal with Bank Specialty?

Nowadays, there is a certain consensus about the mistakes that occurred in the past: above all, poor risk management and poor remuneration.[63] Financial regulation and supervision did not mitigate those problems. On the contrary, they provided perverse incentives to bankers, worsening their decision-making.[64]

Beyond such a consensus, there is the domain of a vast number of ideas proposed to address the determinants of the financial crisis, especially the systemic risk issue.[65] It appears clear that the standard approach to

[59] Fahlenbrach and Stulz (n 5).

[60] Deniz Anginer and others, 'Corporate Governance and Bank Insolvency Risk' (2014) 7017.

[61] Beltratti and Stulz (n 5) 16.

[62] Renée Birgit Adams, 'Governance and the Financial Crisis' (2012) 12 International Review of Finance 7.

[63] Lucian Bebchuk and Jesse Fried, *Pay without Performance*, vol 29 (Cambridge, MA: Harvard University Press 2004).

[64] Russ Roberts, *Gambling with Other People's Money: How Perverse Incentives Caused the Financial Crisis* (Hoover Press 2019). See also, Peter Laaper and Danny Busch, 'How to Behave Like a Good Banker?' (2022) 18 European Company and Financial Law Review 899.

[65] Nonetheless, some authors radically refused the idea that banks governance could play a decisive role in enhancing the overall financial stability, preferring a pure macro-founded supervision approach. See Markus Konrad Brunnermeier and others, *The Fundamental Principles of Financial Regulation*, vol 11 (ICMB, Internat Center for Monetary and Banking Studies 2009).

governance (i.e., maximising shareholder value) in banking fails to incentivise an efficient risk and crisis management.[66] This claim is linked to the shape of agency conflicts in banking as well as the systemic implications of bad decision-making. Hence, this should represent the starting point for framing corporate governance as a complement to financial regulation and supervision.

Some scholars emphasised the role of banks' governance for financial stability,[67] focusing in particular on risk management and remuneration policies as a complement to financial regulation and supervision.[68] These contributions mainly deal with the internal corporate governance mechanisms, with primary emphasis on executive remuneration, board committees, and risk management functions. These proposals aim to marginally improve the governance of financial institutions, but they are not suited to fully internalising the externalities stemming from the special nature of bank governance.[69]

More interestingly, some others have proposed a broader approach,[70] focusing on a wider range of agency problems stemming from banking activities[71] in particular: the conflicts between shareholders and creditors.[72] All the peculiar features of bank governance relate to three shortcomings: the inability of financial regulation and supervision to be effective; the inability of creditors to discipline the decision-making of

[66] On these mechanisms see, widely, John Armour and Jeffrey N Gordon, 'Systemic Harms and Shareholder Value' (2014) 6 Journal of Legal Analysis 35.

[67] Mülbert and Citlau (n 45).

[68] Ferrarini (n 56); Becht, Bolton and Röell (n 33).

[69] For an ex-post analysis on board composition and expertise during the banking crises of 2023, see Harald Hau, Tim-Ole Radach and Marcel Thum, 'Insufficient Supervisory Board Competence as a Risk Factor for Banks' *VoxEU Column* (10 June 2024) <https://cepr.org/voxeu/columns/insufficient-supervisory-board-competence-risk-factor-banks> (accessed 30/09/2025).

[70] Jens-Hinrich Binder, 'The Banking Union and the Governance of Credit Institutions: A Legal Perspective' (2015) 16 European Business Organization Law Review 467; Iris HY Chiu, 'Corporate Governance: The Missing Paradigm in the Mandatory Bail-in Regime for Creditors of Banks and Financial Institutions' [2014] Journal of business law 611.

[71] As categorised by Dirk Heremans and Katrien Bosquet, 'The Future of Law and Finance after the Financial Crisis: New Perspectives on Regulation and Corporate Governance for Banks' [2011] U. Ill. L. Rev. 1551.

[72] Those insights are going to be developed thoroughly in Sect. 5.1.

banks and their managers; and, crucially, the interaction between these two.

In non-financial firms, creditors are usually able to assure themselves a return on their investment through contractually agreed control rights and monitoring activities.[73] On the contrary, the special features of bank governance generally prevent them from efficiently doing so.[74] According to the representation hypothesis, regulation and supervision are in place to cope with such deficiency. Therefore, if one wants to move away from the representation hypothesis of bank governance, and embrace the complementarity between governance and regulation, the role of creditors is the place to look at.[75]

Coming to regulation, several doubts arise about its ability to single-handedly yield efficient outcomes. The dynamic and ever-evolving nature of financial markets makes the financial world inherently difficult to regulate.[76] Moreover, there is a well-documented tendency of supervisory forbearance to delay any intervention fearing the public reaction.[77] Additionally, there is a more subtle but relevant element of such inefficiency: regulation usually addresses individual institutions, whereas it fails to account for the systemic environment each institution is part of.[78]

[73] Clifford W Smith Jr and Jerold B Warner, 'On Financial Contracting: An Analysis of Bond Covenants' (1979) 7 Journal of financial economics 117.

[74] There is an everlasting debate on the market discipline ability of bank creditors. For a survey see Mark J Flannery and Robert R Bliss, 'Market Discipline in Regulation: Pre- and Post-Crisis' in Allen N Berger, Philip Molyneux and John OS Wilson (eds), *Oxford Handbook of Banking* (3rd edn, Oxford Handbook of Banking (3rd edition), Oxford University Press, 2018).

[75] This line of argumentation is developed in Sect. 5.2.

[76] Charles W Calomiris, 'Financial Innovation, Regulation, and Reform' in Michael Spence and Danny M Leipziger (eds), *Globalization and Growth: Implications for a Post-Crisis World* (World Bank Publications 2011).

[77] Charles M Kahn and Joao AC Santos, 'Allocating Bank Regulatory Powers: Lender of Last Resort, Deposit Insurance and Supervision' (2005) 49 European Economic Review 2107.

[78] Luca Enriques, Alessandro Romano and Thom Wetzer, 'Network-Sensitive Financial Regulation' (2019) 45 J. Corp. L. 351; Jeremy C Kress and Jeffery Y Zhang, 'The Macroprudential Myth' (2023) 112 Geo. LJ 569.

Therefore, a closer scrutiny of the relationship between governance and regulation is crucial. Stating that governance should complement regulation and supervision sounds appealing[79]; yet, understanding how such a complementary role should operate is all but straightforward.

3 Governance and Regulation

Banking regulation applies to all entities that are chartered as banks and aims to influence and constrain the decision-making of the regulated entities and their managers. For instance, regulating minimum capital requirements influences the decision on the structure of both the asset and liability side of the bank's balance sheet.[80] It mandates holding a minimum amount of capital against risk-weighted assets.[81] In absence of such piece of regulation, some or all banks would opt for a different level of equity or a different mix of risky assets.[82]

In terms of impact on decision-making, not all the pieces of regulation are equal. It is possible to draw a broad distinction between regulation of substance and regulation of governance.[83] Examples of substantive regulation are capital and liquidity requirements, the resolution framework, the mandatory deposit guarantee schemes, etc. Examples of governance regulation are mandatory board structure, the regulation of executive compensation, the special rules on managerial responsibility, etc.

Substantive regulation usually imposes restrictions on the possible courses of action available to the bank. As a result, the control powers of shareholders and managers over the corporation are limited not only by the undertaken contractual obligations but also by regulatory

[79] Katarzyna Sum, 'Bank Governance in the EU: A Substitute or Complement of Banking Regulation?', *Post-Crisis Banking Regulation in the European Union* (Springer 2016).

[80] Article 92 CRR.

[81] See, for instance, Patricia Jackson and others, 'Capital Requirements and Bank Behaviour: The Impact of the Basel Accord' (1999) 1.

[82] Following professors Pacces and Heremans: "all aspects of the behaviour of financial firms can be ultimately understood as corporate governance issues". See Pacces and Heremans (n 41) 597.

[83] Such distinction has already been drawn, with a slightly different approach, by professor Schwarcz. See, Steven L Schwarcz, 'Misalignment: Corporate Risk-Taking and Public Duty' (2016) 91 Notre Dame L. Rev. 1, 19. On the differences between the two approaches see note 90.

constraints. Governance regulation consists of restrictions on how to make decisions (e.g., mandatory nomination committee) or the tools for incentivising managerial decisions (e.g., regulation on remuneration). Therefore, governance regulation does not limit control power but limits the modes through which corporate constituencies exercise control. The goal of these regulatory restrictions is to preserve the safety and soundness of the regulated bank, pursuing—*latu sensu*—the public interest.

The relevance of such differentiation is limited in non-financial corporations, whereas it is pivotal in framing bank governance. First of all, financial institutions are by far more regulated than virtually any other industry. Moreover, outside financial institutions, it is hard to make a solid case for regulating governance. Substantive regulation is usually employed to address market failures, such as externalities and information asymmetries.[84] In this framework, regulation limits the control powers over future and uncertain courses of action, protecting the counterparties that are unable to contractually protect themselves.[85] Thereafter, the corporation will seek to maximise shareholder value given the regulatory constraints. According to the standard approach, this is supposed to yield socially optimal results.[86] Therefore, the room for regulating governance is rather limited in such framework,[87] as it is thought to yield suboptimal results limiting entrepreneurship.[88]

[84] Ian B Lee, 'The Role of the Public Interest in Corporate Law' in Claire A Hill and Brett H McDonnell (eds), *Research Handbook on the Economics of Corporate Law* (Edward Elgar Publishing 2012) 124.

[85] Think for instance of environmental regulation limiting emissions or prohibiting environmentally hazardous activities.

[86] Milton Friedman, 'The Social Responsibility of Business Is to Increase Its Profits' *N.Y. Times* (13 September 1970). See also Eugene F Fama, 'Efficient Capital Markets: A Review of Theory and Empirical Work' (1970) 25 The journal of Finance 383.

[87] Among several examples, one can think of the Italian case. To address the specific, highly concentrated, ownership structure of the vast majority of the Italian corporations and protect minority investors, the Italian policymaker decided to introduce the so-called "slate-voting" procedure for both the board of director and the board of auditor. See, respectively, Articles 147-ter and 148. Such provisions allow a qualified minority of shareholders to appoint at least on director and internal auditor. On the point, see Armour and others, *The Anatomy of Corporate Law: A Comparative and Functional Approach* (n 20) 80.

[88] See David F Larcker, Gaizka Ormazabal and Daniel J Taylor, 'The Market Reaction to Corporate Governance Regulation' (2011) 101 Journal of Financial Economics 431. The authors studied, following standard methodologies for event studies, the impact of

Banking regulation has proved to be flawed and unable to keep pace of financial innovation. Moreover, the ability of regulation to account for systemic externalities and to adjust for other special features of banking is limited.[89] In particular, the role of creditors in external governance is impaired as compared with non-financial firms. Their protection is, therefore, delegated to substantive regulation such as deposit guarantee. However, the positive impact of creditors' oversight and discipline is not entirely replaced by regulation.[90] Therefore, the argument according to which, given regulatory constraints, the decision-making of the corporation will yield efficient outcome seems not to hold at least in banking.

This last observation opens up the case for special governance regulation for banking institutions. Nonetheless, the case for regulating governance does not stem directly from the fact that bank governance is special.[91] On the contrary, restricting decision-making modes is only

the announcements of governance-related regulatory interventions in the U.S. on shareholder's value, measured through movements on stock prices. These reforms, from the classical agency-theory perspective, are supposed to be value-enhancing for shareholders as they reduce the possibility for managers to extract a rent out of their office. Nevertheless, the authors found an insignificant impact for *executive pay* announcements in general and even a negative impact for companies with higher compensation packages, conditioned on industry and size. A negative, though weak, relationship was found for reform announcements concerning *proxy access*. Finally, the authors found a significant negative impact of reforms announcing the *ban of staggered boards or CEO-Chairman duality*. Those results are striking, and their interpretation is nothing but clear-cut. Regardless the specific policy conclusions drew by the authors; those findings clearly indicate that governance-related reforms are a sensible issue that has to be handle carefully.

[89] Macro-prudential regulation so far has not been a success and, in general, suffers of the same problem of micro-based regulation and supervision: regulatory and supervisory forbearance and delay. See Luca Amorello, 'Europe Goes "Countercyclical": A Legal Assessment of the New Countercyclical Dimension of the CRR/CRD IV Package' (2016) 17 European Business Organization Law Review 137.

[90] There is nowadays ample evidence on the fact that creditor's governance is value increasing for the corporation itself at least in some states of the world. See, for instance, Greg Nini, David C Smith and Amir Sufi, 'Creditor Control Rights, Corporate Governance, and Firm Value' (2012) 25 The Review of Financial Studies 1713; Sudheer Chava and Michael R Roberts, 'How Does Financing Impact Investment? The Role of Debt Covenants' (2008) 63 The Journal of Finance 2085.

[91] The correspondence between bank governance specialty and bank governance regulation represents the approach taken by prof. Schwarcz, which makes his argument not compelling. His claim to introduce a "public duty" to bankers stems from the fact that regulation is not able to handle all externalities of bank governance. Yet, he fails to explain how governance regulation, i.e., the restriction of the available decision-making modules,

advisable as long as restricting courses of action is not sufficient to induce socially optimal decision-making. Hence, regulatory interventions in bank governance must be strictly functional to aligning banks' incentives with regulatory goals.

Governance regulation as a medium between bank governance and substantive regulation moves away and beyond the representation hypothesis. It acknowledges that normal governance mechanisms cannot work smoothly in banking, but also account for the fact that regulation and supervision cannot, themselves, mimic efficient outcomes.

Thus, governance regulation should aim to reduce, and hopefully fill, the wedge between regulatory goals and banks' incentives. Accordingly, regulating substance and regulating governance are not alternatives to achieve the same result. Rather, these are in a circular relation: substantive regulation sets the goal and the scope of the regulatory intervention, whereas governance regulation provides incentives to the banks and bankers to achieve such a goal.

This line of argumentation leads to a crucial consequence: good bank governance does not arise endogenously, simply allocating control to those who value it the most,[92] rather it needs to be stimulated and shaped by a coherent mix of substantive and governance regulation. Remuneration can serve as a paradigmatic example and make this theoretical construct more tangible. Regulating remuneration packages of bankers means limiting the ways of incentivising senior management.[93] This limitation is desirable so long as it is functional to achieving regulatory goals that, despite substantive regulation, would not be achieved otherwise.[94]

This leads to the conclusion that governance regulation should fine-tune substantive regulation and bank governance.[95] Governance and

would incentivise the banks and their managers to engage in efficient decision-making given the current regulatory constraints. See Schwarcz (n 83) 20.

[92] Ronald H Coase, 'The Problem of Social Cost' (1960) 3 ournal of Law and Economics 1.

[93] Anna Zalewska, 'A New Look at Regulating Bankers' Remuneration' (2016) 24 Corporate Governance: An International Review 322.

[94] See at length Chapter 7.

[95] In this regard, the EU regulation on remuneration can be and has been harshly criticised. See, for instance, Kevin J Murphy, 'Regulating Banking Bonuses in the European Union: A Case Study in Unintended Consequences' (2013) 19 European Financial Management 631; Ferrarini (n 3).

substantive regulation should not merely co-exist in watertight compartments but need to be adaptive to one another. In this adaptive dynamic, governance regulation should be calibrated to the specific features of bank governance[96] that impede the market from working in the first place,[97] i.e., the reasons incentivising banks to take poor decisions.

The position of bank creditors represents one of the major sources of specialty so that the natural way to proceed is to scrutinise debt governance and the related substantive regulation. Before moving to debt governance, it is informative to briefly review the "special" governance rules for European banks.[98]

4 A Critical Assessment of the Current Governance Regulation

During and in the immediate aftermath of the Global Financial Crisis, corporate governance of banking institutions was blamed as one of its main drivers[99] in the policy debate.[100] For instance, analysing the causes of the financial crisis, the OECD stated that: "the financial crisis can be to an important extent attributed to failures and weaknesses in corporate governance arrangements".[101]

[96] Rather than on generic claims about bank risk-taking that are mainly meant to gain political consensus than to actually solve problems. In this regard, see Enriques and Zetzsche (n 3); Ferrarini (n 3).

[97] In this regard see again Pacces and Heremans (n 33) 597, where the authors state: "Hence, within the present corporate governance debate, more attention should be given to specific agency problems for financial institutions. In particular, the corporate governance of banks should also be viewed from a financial stability perspective. This approach implies corporate governance recommendations for financial firms which may differ from corporate governance for non-financial firms".

[98] The analysis will mainly refer to the provisions embedded in the Capital Requirement Directive, Articles 88–94.

[99] No scientific evidence of bad governance causing the crisis has been established so far; yet, as discussed in Sect. 2 there are several evidences that bad governance boosted the crisis.

[100] See Jacques De Larosière and others, 'Report of the High-Level Group on Financial Supervision in the EU' [2009] European Commission. Brussels para 23 and 24; Kirkpatrick (n 2).

[101] Kirkpatrick (n 2) 61.

Such a harsh stance led to considerable political activism in regulating bank governance in the area of remuneration, risk management, and board composition. The European Legislator granted a great deal of attention to governance-related issues also before the financial crisis broke out. The Directives 2000/12/EC[102] and the 2006/49/EC[103] regulated board composition, requiring sufficient expertise,[104] and governance arrangements requiring the definition of the organisational structure, a transparent line of responsibility and accountability for risk-taking, and a system of internal controls.[105]

In the aftermath of the financial crisis, the regulatory effort of the European Legislator increased significantly. In 2010, the CRD III[106] additionally mandated to include in the governance arrangements both remuneration policies and practices consistent with effective risk management.[107] Member States were required to issue guidelines for implementing those arrangements.

The fourth iteration of the Capital Requirement Directive massively tackles corporate governance arrangements.[108] In particular, the CRD IV dedicates several and intrusive provisions to the governance of banking institutions, making a long list of compulsory requirements on the composition of the board of directors and remuneration policies. This non-exhaustive list summarises the salient provisions[109]:

[102] Directive 2000/12/EC of the European Parliament and of the Council of 20 March 2000 relating to the taking up and pursuit of the business of credit institutions.

[103] Directive 2006/49/EC of the European Parliament and of the Council of 14 June 2006 on the capital adequacy of investment firms and credit institutions.

[104] See, Article 6 of Directive 2000/12/EC.

[105] See Article 22 of Directive 2006/49/EC.

[106] Implementing Basel II accords, Directive 2010/76/EU of the European Parliament and of the Council of 24 November 2010 amending Directives 2006/48/EC and 2006/49/EC as regards capital requirements for the trading book and for re-securitisations, and the supervisory review of remuneration policies.

[107] See Article 1 3 a of Directive 2010/76/EU.

[108] Directive 2013/36/EU of the European Parliament and of the Council of 26 June 2013 on access to the activity of credit institutions and the prudential supervision of credit institutions and investment firms, amending Directive 2002/87/EC and repealing Directives 2006/48/EC and 2006/49/EC.

[109] For and excellent and detailed review of the governance regulation in CRDIV, see Klaus J Hopt, 'Corporate Governance of Banks and Other Financial Institutions after the Financial Crisis' (2013) 13 Journal of Corporate Law Studies 219. For an

(1) the chairman of the management body in its supervisory function of an institution must not, in principle, exercise simultaneously the functions of a chief executive officer[110];
(2) systemically relevant institutions must establish a nomination committee composed only of non-executive directors[111];
(3) the management must possess sufficient knowledge, skills, and experience; it must be adequately differentiated in order to possess a broad range of experiences and must be of sufficiently good reputation[112];
(4) the board members must devote to their office a sufficient amount of time[113];
(5) the remuneration policy should incentivise an optimal level of risk-taking, the resulting remuneration package must consist of both a fixed and variable part. The variable component shall not exceed 100 per cent of the fixed remuneration, sufficiently deferred, and provide for malus and clawback arrangements[114];
(6) systemic institutions must establish both a remuneration and risk committee.[115]

On top of the regulatory requirements set down by the European legislator, Bank Governance Codes issued around the world provide guidelines and instruction for the governance of financial institutions. Van der Elst carried out a thorough analysis of the provisions embedded in such codes.[116] He did not find any bank-specific governance tools in the 11 Bank Governance Codes analysed, including the guidelines issued by the

updated analysis, see Klaus J Hopt, 'Corporate Governance of Banks and Financial Institutions: Economic Theory, Supervisory Practice, Evidence and Policy' (2021) 22 European Business Organization Law Review 13.

110 Article 88(1)(e) CRDIV.

111 Article 88(2) CRDIV.

112 Article 91 (1) CRDIV.

113 Article 91 (2) and (3) CRDIV.

114 Article 94 CRDIV.

115 Articles 95 and 76(3) CRDIV.

116 Christoph van der Elst, 'Corporate Governance and Banks: How Justified Is the Match?' (2015) 284/2015.

Basel Committee in 1999.[117] The author did not find any specific tool or guidelines to tackle bank specialty, apart from some rare and rather vague references to the importance of taking into account financial stability in determining the risk profile and the executive remuneration package.[118]

After this brief review, one may wonder: is the current governance regulation for European banks consistent with the framework depicted in Sects. 2 and 3? In other words, is the EU bank governance regulation tailored to the specific features of bank governance, acting as a medium between substantive regulation and banks incentives?

The answer is, unsurprisingly, markedly negative. Existing governance provisions are an end in themselves and not a medium between bank governance and substantive regulation. Most importantly, these provisions largely ignore the features of bank governance, especially when it comes to debt governance.

Some of the rules, such as the ones related to board composition, represent a crystallisation of best practices inside and outside the financial industry.[119] Others, as in the case of remuneration regulation, consist of little more than a political stance against bankers.[120] In a nutshell, the existing bank governance regulation fails to fine-tune governance and substantive regulation.

As Van der Elst noted: "The 'stakeholders' gap, left by bank governance codes, provides legislative room for improvements".[121] This will, therefore, represent the next step of the analysis, arguing that regulating debt governance has the potential to improve bank governance.

[117] And then updated in 2006, 2010 and 2015.

[118] Those references appear, for instance, in the Italian and in the Dutch governance codes.

[119] Enriques and Zetzsche (n 3).

[120] Murphy (n 95).

[121] Van der Elst (n 116).

5 A Quest for Good Governance

5.1 Bank Governance and Debt

In banking, the standard channels for debt governance are, to a considerable extent, impaired. Monitoring banks' activities is inherently difficult because of the opaqueness of their balance sheet.[122] Additionally, for a sizeable part of banks' creditors, i.e., depositors, the willingness to monitor is undermined by the deposit insurance, making them insensitive to the financial developments of their borrower.[123]

A similar argument goes for the contractual protection of creditors. Designing state-contingent contracts granting creditors control rights over future contingencies turns out to be more complicated and costly in banking than in non-financial firms.[124] This is both due to the opacity of banks activities and the dispersed composition of bank creditors. Moreover, granting creditors the right to speed up repayments contingently on a contracted situation would endanger the stability of the bank. Those would face funding difficulties precisely in the moment of distress. For this reason, covenants on junior unsecured debt are statutorily restricted.[125]

The impossibility of efficiently designing state-contingent contracts to protect creditors' entitlements represents one of the foundations of the representation hypothesis, with regulation and supervision substituting for creditors' contractual rights.

[122] Macey and O'Hara (n 29) 93.

[123] In Europe deposits are insured up to 100.000 euro, see the Deposit Guarantee Schemes Directive - Directive 2014/49/EU of the European Parliament and of the Council of 16 April 2014 on deposit guarantee schemes. A long-lasting theoretical debate focuses on the desirability of leaving some skin in the game to depositors to increase their willingness to monitor and discipline their bank. Such debate is now closed once and for all after the depositors run during the Northern Rock crisis. U.K. bank deposits were fully insured only up to 2,000 pounds, and then only 90% of their deposits up to an upper limit of 35,000 pounds. Hyun Song Shin, 'Reflections on Northern Rock: The Bank Run That Heralded the Global Financial Crisis' (2009) 23 Journal of economic perspectives 101.

[124] As discussed by prof. Flannery: "Because bank assets do not have contractible, easily described risk properties, covenants governing firm risk changes are unusually ineffective for banking firm". See Mark J Flannery, 'Debt Maturity and the Deadweight Cost of Leverage: Optimally Financing Banking Firms' (1994) 84 The American Economic Review 320, 321.

[125] A throughout analysis of the relationship between contractual mechanisms and regulatory foreclosures is developed in Chapter 5, Sect. 3.2.

Banks' funding models markedly adjusted accordingly and moved towards short-term and securitised funding. Both assure bank creditors a return. Through a quick and cheap exit for overnight debt or through property entitlements for secured debt. However, both models entail considerable systemic risks[126] and their disciplining mechanisms yield value-decreasing outcomes during the latest financial crisis. Those were unable to signal the build-up of risk in good times, with artificially low haircuts on repos.[127] On the contrary, once the crisis broke out such mechanisms worked excessively, pushing out of the market weaker banks.[128] According to the framework depicted above, neither short-term nor secured creditors have the potential to improve the decision-making process of banks.

On the contrary, junior long-term, unsecured, and uninsured debt has the potential to improve debt governance and, thence, bank governance. So far, they have exerted no noteworthy governance role as they could quietly rely on the implicit government guarantee to bailout failing banks.[129]

In the aftermath of the financial crisis, the policymakers worldwide rebelled against bailouts and set down resolution frameworks that, allegedly, ruled them out.[130] So long as such policy stance is credible,[131]

[126] Short-term funding has been described as an inefficient equilibrium in Douglas W Diamond and Raghuram G Rajan, 'A Theory of Bank Capital' (2000) 55 The Journal of Finance 2431. As for secured debt and its implication for financial stability, see Reimo Juks, 'Asset Encumbrance and Its Relevance for Financial Stability' (2012) 3 Sveriges Riksbank Economic Review 67.

[127] Gary Gorton and Andrew Metrick, 'Securitized Banking and the Run on Repo' (2012) 104 Journal of Financial economics 425.

[128] Constantinos Stephanou, 'Rethinking Market Discipline in Banking: Lessons from the Financial Crisis' (2010) 5227 3.

[129] Decreasing the cost of finance and the willingness to engage in monitoring accordingly. See Kenichi Ueda and B Weder Di Mauro, 'Quantifying Structural Subsidy Values for Systemically Important Financial Institutions' (2013) 37 Journal of Banking & Finance 3830.

[130] Todd A Gormley, Simon Johnson and Changyong Rhee, 'Ending "Too Big to Fail": Government Promises versus Investor Perceptions' (2014) 19 Review of Finance 491.

[131] John Armour, 'Making Bank Resolution Credible', *The Oxford Handbook of Financial Regulation* (Oxford University Press Oxford, UK 2015). Crucially, the bank resolution triggers the possibility for junior creditors to be positive actors in bank governance as long as the no-bailout commitment is credible. Conversely, the ability of bank creditors to play a positive governance role, i.e., taking concrete actions to secure the

junior unsecured debtholders are in a position to improve bank governance as they are prone to bear losses should the bank fall into distress. At the same time, junior creditors are not subject to perverse incentives generating systemic externalities and, if any, they are prone to be victim of those through, for instance, debt-overhang and asset substitution.

Therefore, debt governance should focus on the role of junior unsecured and uninsured creditors, as these represent a category of creditors having the potential to actually improve the decision-making of the bank and coping with its specialty.

In so doing, debt governance needs to be fine-tuned to the relevant substantive regulation. Specifically, the framework for recovery and resolution of failing banks represents the natural point of reference. This framework allocates losses on bank creditors in case of distress in the form of principal write-down or conversion into equity. A major issue is the credibility of the resolution framework and, in particular, of the credibility of the no-bailout commitment. In this view, governance regulation ought to handle the wedge between investors' expectations and the regulatory goal set down by the resolution regulation.

5.2 EU Regulation of Bank Failure and Debt Governance

The Bank Recovery and Resolution Directive harmonised the framework for handling bank distressed throughout the EU. For the Euro Area Countries, the Single Resolution Mechanism Regulation supplements the Directive.[132] The recovery and resolution framework provides rules and procedures for smooth management of a banking crisis, with provisions ranging from preparing for a future crisis,[133] to the resolution of the crisis

return on their investment, is crucial for the credibility of the resolution framework. On this point, see more at length Chapter 6 and Chiu (n 68).

[132] The BRRD applies to all the Member States, whereas the Single Resolution Mechanisms is in charge of enforcing it in cooperation with national authorities within the Euro Area.

[133] Jens-Hinrich Binder, 'Resolution Planning and Structural Bank Reform within the Banking Union' in Juan Castaneda and others (eds), *European Banking Union. Prospects and challenges* (Routledge 2015).

once it materialises.[134] The pivotal tool set down by the BRRD is the so-called "bail-in" tool,[135] the power of the Resolution Authority to impose losses on the "bail-inable creditors", i.e., unsecured and insured creditors whose claim fulfils specific qualitative requirements.[136] The Resolution authority can reduce the principal amount of the debt claim to set off losses and/or convert debt into equity to restore regulatory capital.[137]

Such rules not only govern the resolution of failing banks but also provide incentives to market players in good times. By backwards induction, bail-inable creditors should anticipate future losses and be willing to take every action to maximise the expected value of their claim. This is true only as long as the regulatory goals set down by the BRRD and bank (debt) governance are fine-tuned.

Building on the previous analysis, two hurdles are noteworthy.

(1) First, investors might not apply backwards induction in the first place since they do not deem the no-bailout commitment credible;
(2) Second, due to the special features of bank governance, bail-inable creditors might be short of suitable tools to influence or improve the decision-making of the borrowing bank. Should this be the case, direct regulation of debt governance might provide a valuable option to the European legislator.

6 Conclusion

Bank governance is different from the corporate governance of non-financial firms. Among its many special features, debt governance is of crucial relevance. Based on the distinctive features of bank governance, this chapter developed a framework for the analysis of the relationship between financial regulation and bank governance, where governance regulation acts as a medium between the regulatory goals and the special features of bank governance.

[134] Bates and Gleeson (n 44).

[135] Karl-Philipp Wojcik, 'Bail-in in the Banking Union' (2016) 53 Common Market Law Review 91.

[136] See Article 44 and 45 of the BRRD.

[137] Article 46 BRRD.

Following that framework, the analysis re-considers the regulation on bank governance, arguing that it does not capture the essence of bank governance, nor does it promote better decision-making. Against the unsatisfactory state of the art, this chapter proposes to focus on debt governance and to fine-tune it with the newly established resolution framework for ailing banks as a way to improve banks' decision-making in good time and, hence, promote good governance.

Fine-tuning bank governance and regulation is a complex task. This framework represents the backbone of the entire book. From now onwards, the analysis focuses on the role of long-term creditors. Therefore, the natural next step is to analyse the main piece of legislation related to such creditors. Chapter 3 focuses on the analysis of the legal design of the Bank Recovery and Resolution Directive, focusing on the aspects (aiming at) impacting on the ex-ante behaviour of banking institutions. Thereafter, one needs to assess if the current legal design of the BRRD is already apt to fine-tune governance and regulation. Therefore, the book proposes a thorough positive analysis of the impact of the BRRD on the incentives of bail-inable creditors, assessing whether and to what extent resolution is credible and the tools available to creditors are sufficient (Chapters 4–6). Finally, the third part of the book will draw policy implications and discuss two specific proposals on how to regulate bank governance under the present framework (Chapters 7and 8). The final part of the book discusses the latest development in the banking industry, looking at the governance components of the 2023 crisis and the proposals to reform the resolution framework (Chapters 9 and 10).

CHAPTER 3

The EU Bank Resolution Framework and Its Ex-ante Potential

1 Introduction

The 2007–2008 Global Financial Crisis spectacularly demonstrated that the social cost of bank failures outweighs the private cost.[1] The failure of one significant bank carries several negative systemic spillovers: it imposes losses on interconnected counterparties possibly triggering contagion and endangers the trust of the rest of the market in the solvency of other banks. What is more, it usually entails complex cross-border issues that are particularly difficult to handle given the short time window available for resolving banking crises and, therefore, usually leads to further value destruction.[2]

During the global financial meltdown, European countries experienced both of these downsides, due to several failures of cross-border banks.[3]

[1] Ex pluribus, see Matej Marinč and Razvan Vlahu, *The Economics of Bank Bankruptcy Law* (Springer Science & Business Media 2011).

[2] Dirk Schoenmaker and Sander Oosterloo, 'Financial Supervision in an Integrating Europe: Measuring Cross-Border Externalities' (2005) 8 International Finance 1.

[3] In this respect, there are several paradigmatic cases happened during the latest financial crisis. Think for instance of Fortis that entered in distress in 2008 after the acquisition of part of ABN AMRO together with Royal Bank of Scotland and Banco Santander. In that situation, the necessity to resolving the crisis in a cross-border context worsened the crisis, delaying the necessary interventions. On this point, see Rosalind Wiggins,

E. D. Martino, *EU Bank Governance and Bail-In*, EBI Studies in Banking and Capital Markets Law,
https://doi.org/10.1007/978-3-032-20699-2_3

This led to an overall lack of trust in the entire EU banking system, perceived as on the verge of collapse. To prevent such collapse from happening, the European Commission approved €4.5 trillion of state aid measures for banks between 2008 and 2011, amounting to 37% of EU GDP.[4]

In the aftermath of the crisis, the need for a deep reform of banking regulation appeared clear. In particular, the need for a common framework to resolve troubled entities arose as one of the main gaps in the regulatory framework. The European Legislator tried to fill the gap with the approval of the Bank Recovery and Resolution Directive (BRRD).[5] The main aim of the new framework is effectively summarised in its first recital: "to prevent insolvency or, when insolvency occurs, to minimise negative repercussions by preserving the systemically important functions of the institution concerned. During the crisis, those challenges were a major factor that forced Member States to save institutions using taxpayers' money. The objective of a credible recovery and resolution framework is to obviate the need for such action to the greatest extent possible".[6]

Natalia Tente and Andrew Metrick, 'European Banking Union D: Cross-Border Resolution—Dexia Group' [2014] Yale Program on Financial Stability Case Study. Landsbanki, the biggest Icelandic Bank, provides another clear example: the bank operated in the UK through a branch and refused to repay depositors after a run. In response the UK government froze the assets of Landsbanki in the UK making use of an anti-terrorism piece of legislation. On this case, see Arwin G Zeissler, Thomas Piontek and Andrew Metrick, 'Ireland and Iceland in Crisis C: Iceland's Landsbanki Icesave' [2015] Yale Program on Financial Stability Case Study.

[4] European Commission, New crisis management measures to avoid future bank bailouts, MEMO/12/416. Available at https://ec.europa.eu/commission/presscorner/detail/en/IP_12_570 (accessed 04-04-2020).

[5] The Bank Recovery and Resolution Directive (BRRD) - Directive 2014/59/EU of the European Parliament and of the Council of 15 May 2014 establishing a framework for the recovery and resolution of credit institutions and investment firms. OJ L 173, 12.6.2014.

[6] Recital n. 1 BRRD.

The BRRD harmonises at the European Union level several substantive rules for bank insolvency,[7] from preparation to resolution.[8] The quintessential idea behind the harmonised resolution framework is, as highlighted by the recital, to minimise bailouts in the future and therefore protect taxpayer money. However, saving taxpayers' money ex-post is not the only advantage of eliminating bailouts, and, arguably, is not the most important either. Banks and their financiers ex-ante expect to be rescued should anything go wrong, providing them with perverse incentives.[9]

The Directive aims to operate a shift from the bailout paradigm, to a new "bail-in" paradigm, in which shareholders and junior and senior bondholders bear the costs of the crises to the largest extent possible. To this end, a public agency specifically designated by national and EU provisions, the "Resolution Authority", can write down the claim of eligible creditors or convert these into ordinary shares.[10]

This approach to bank insolvency should, in theory, enhance the decision-making process of banks ex-ante; since creditors are at actual risk of bearing losses in resolution should impose higher and better discipline

[7] National insolvency laws remain of crucial relevance and, potentially, represent an obstacle to resolution. On the relation between insolvency law and resolution, see Lynette Janssen, 'Bail-In from an Insolvency Law Perspective' (2017) 26 Norton Journal of Bankruptcy Law and Practice.

[8] In the Eurozone, the SRMR establish a central agency, the Single Resolution Board, to handle the resolution of banking institutions. The SRMR establish mainly procedural rules, the power of the SRB and the relation between the SRB and the national resolution authorities. Regulation (EU) No 806/2014 of the European Parliament and of the Council of 15 July 2014 establishing uniform rules and a uniform procedure for the resolution of credit institutions and certain investment firms in the framework of a Single Resolution Mechanism and a Single Resolution Fund and amending Regulation (EU) No 1093/2010. OJ L 225, 30.7.2014, p. 1.

[9] Reint Gropp, Christian Gruendl and Andre Guettler, 'The Impact of Public Guarantees on Bank Risk-Taking: Evidence from a Natural Experiment' (2014) 18 Review of Finance 457.

[10] On the determination of the National Resolution Authority, see Article 3 BRRD. For the Euro Area Countries, the Single Resolution Board is tasked with resolution planning and resolution decisions, while the implementation remains with the National Resolution Authority. On the importance of agency cooperation for an effective resolution regime, see Jens-Hinrich Binder, 'Inter-Agency Cooperation Within the SRM: Legal and Operational Challenges for the Cooperation Between Banking Supervision and Resolution Authorities in the EU and With Third-Country Authorities' (2023) 19 European Company and Financial Law Review 900.

on the risk-taking appetite of the borrowing bank.[11] The alleged elimination of any bailout expectation increases the skin in the game of junior creditors that, threatened by a future bail-in, should be incentivised to preserve the solvency of the bank.[12]

These theoretical expectations are reasonable so long as the commitment of governments not to bail out banks is fully credible. Yet, the first years of application of the new regime cast severe doubts on the credibility of the resolution framework.[13]

The existing studies mainly focus on how this lack of credibility and the excessive complexity of the resolution framework prevent creditors from disciplining banks. This represents a sensible approach; yet it falls short in positioning the problem in the broader context of bank corporate governance: can better debt governance enhance the resilience of financial institutions? And of the financial system as a whole? To incorporate these questions in the analysis of the EU resolution framework, this chapter widens the scope of the analysis and links debt governance to the resolution framework, discussing the incentives matrix stemming from the combination of the two.

This remainder of this chapter assesses whether the resolution framework designed by the BRRD can enhance ex-ante the resilience of individual institutions and/or system stability. The analysis focuses on the role of long-term unsecured (bail-inable) debtholders in corporate governance. In particular, this chapter discusses the problematic relation between the ex-ante potential of the resolution framework and its lack of credibility.

[11] Decision-making and risk-taking incentives have been blamed to be a major driver and booster of the financial crisis. In the European context, see Jacques De Larosière and others, 'Report of the High-Level Group on Financial Supervision in the EU' [2009] European Commission. Brussels 29.

[12] For fist attempts to empirically investigate the credibility of such threat, see Edoardo Martino, 'Subordinated Debt under Bail-in Threat' (2017) 2 University of Bologna Law Review 252; Fabrizio Crespi, Emanuela Giacomini and Danilo V Mascia, 'Bail-in Rules and the Pricing of Italian Bank Bonds' (2018) 25 European Financial Management 1321.

[13] Various doubts have been cast about the credibility of the bail-in. See Tobias H Tröger, 'Too Complex to Work: A Critical Assessment of the Bail-in Tool under the European Bank Recovery and Resolution Regime' (2018) 4 Journal of Financial Regulation 35; John Armour, 'Making Bank Resolution Credible', *The Oxford Handbook of Financial Regulation* (Oxford University Press Oxford, UK 2015).

2 A Very Brief Introduction to the European Banking Union

In the aftermath of the financial crisis, the need for substantial and procedural harmonisation of several areas of financial regulation became clear. The crisis hit harshly across the whole European Union and in particular the Eurozone. The reasons behind the financial and Eurozone crises are complex and entangled.[14] Nonetheless, it is safe to argue that two of the key elements at play were the lack of cross-border coordination[15] and the vicious circle between Member States and their national banking systems, where the former guarantees the solvency of national champions and the latter heavily engages in the market for sovereign bonds issued by the home country.[16]

The reforms were numerous and profound, ranging from market infrastructures to a completely new institutional design for supervision and resolution. A comprehensive analysis and assessment of these reforms falls outside the scope of this book.[17] However, a brief introduction to the salient elements of the European Banking Union is necessary to correctly frame the ex-ante potential of the resolution framework.[18]

[14] For an excellent and comprehensive review, see Andreas Nölke, 'Economic Causes of the Eurozone Crisis: The Analytical Contribution of Comparative Capitalism' (2016) 14 Socio-Economic Review 141.

[15] Jens-Hinrich Binder, 'Cross-Border Coordination of Bank Resolution in the EU: All Problems Resolved?', *Research Handbook on Cross-Border Bank Resolution* (Edward Elgar Publishing 2019). In the EU this was revealed for instance in the Dexia case. See Wiggins, Tente and Metrick (n 3).

[16] Valerie De Bruyckere and others, 'Bank/Sovereign Risk Spillovers in the European Debt Crisis' (2013) 37 Journal of Banking & Finance 4793. See also Anastasia Kotovskaia and Tobias H. Tröger, 'National Interests and Supranational Resolution in the European Banking Union' (2023) 34 European Business Law Review 781.

[17] For a comprehensive survey of the economic and functional significance of these reforms, see Darrell Duffie and others, 'Financial Regulatory Reform after the Crisis: An Assessment' (2018) 64 Management Science 4835. For a more recent account of the impact of the resolution reforms, see Ioannis Asimakopoulos and David Howarth, 'Stillborn Banking Union: Explaining Ineffective European Union Bank Resolution Rules' (2022) 60 JCMS: Journal of Common Market Studies 264.

[18] For a deeper legal scrutiny of the Institutional setting and substantive aspects of the Banking Union, see D Busch and G Ferrarini, *The European Banking Union* (Oxford: Oxford University Press 2020).

The Banking Union has been the major innovation in the European financial system after the crisis. Commissioner Barnier, responsible for the internal market and financial services in the period that led to the approval of Banking Union's pieces of regulation, described it as a revolution and the "most ambitious project since the creation of the Euro".[19] It has, primarily, the goal of supplementing the Monetary Union. Indeed, many argued that the incompleteness of economic and monetary integration was another key vulnerability of the Eurozone, especially during the Sovereign Debt Crisis of 2011–2012.[20]

The Banking Union consists of three main pillars.[21] First, the establishment of common European rules and authority on banking supervision[22]; second, the establishment of harmonised crisis management and a central resolution authority[23]; third, further harmonisation of deposit guarantee

[19] Commissioner Barnier Speech at the Peterson Institute for international Economics, Washington DC, June 13, 2014. Available at http://europa.eu/rapid/press-release_SPEECH-14-465_en.htm.

[20] Jean Pisani-Ferry and others, 'What Kind of European Banking Union?' [2012] Brugel Policy Contribution. For the policymaker perspective, see Herman Van Rompuy and others, 'Towards a Genuine Economic and Monetary Union' (2012) 5 European Council. Brussel.

[21] On the contrary, many studies that focused mainly on the institutional arrangement governing the Banking Union defined it narrowly, including only the procedural rules that specifically apply to Eurozone countries and define the powers and mandate of the relevant central agency and institution. See, for instance, Stefan Grundmann, 'The Banking Union Translated into (Private Law) Duties: Infrastructure and Rulebook' (2015) 16 European Business Organization Law Review 357.

[22] Council Regulation (EU) No 1024/2013 of 15 October 2013 conferring specific tasks on the European Central Bank concerning policies relating to the prudential supervision of credit institutions.

[23] Directive 2014/59/EU of the European Parliament and of the Council of 15 May 2014 establishing a framework for the recovery and resolution of credit institutions and in- vestment firms; the BRRD had been supplemented, for the Eurozone, by a regulation establishing a centralised Single Resolution Mechanism, Regulation (EU) No 806/2014 of the European Parliament and of the Council of 15 July 2014 establishing uniform rules and a uniform procedure for the resolution of credit institutions and certain investment firms in the framework of a Single Resolution Mechanism and a Single Resolution Fund and amending Regulation (EU) No 1093/2010. For an analysis of evolution of the recovery and resolution legislation within the banking union, see Christos V. Gortsos, 'The Bank Recovery and Resolution Directive (BRRD): Evolution Within the System of EU Banking Law over the Period 2014–2024' (2025) 26 European Business Organization Law Review 5.

schemes.[24] The Banking Union is here defined in a broad sense, including both substantive and procedural rules.

On top of these three fundamental pillars, the European Banking Union is complemented by the Single Rulebook,[25] developed by the European Banking Authority. It aims at harmonising the interpretation of substantive norms as well as the supervisory practices across Europe.[26] This represents the core of the Single Rulebook; however, the EBA mandate in terms of regulatory and implementing standards, guidelines, and recommendations is particularly wide.[27] Therefore, many technical rules set down by the EBA belong to the "penumbra" of the Single Rulebook,[28] dealing with the quality of banks' relationships with client and counterparties and on banking activities.[29] The remainder of this section briefly introduces the first and third pillars of the European Banking Union, whereas the second pillar is discussed more at length in Sect. 3.

[24] Directive 2014/49/EU of the European Parliament and of the Council of 16 April 2014 on deposit guarantee schemes.

[25] Regulation (Eu) 1093/2010 Of The European Parliament And Of The Council of 24 November 2010 establishing a European Supervisory Authority (European Banking Authority), amending Decision No 716/2009/EC and repealing Commission Decision 2009/78/EC. Article 8 of the regulation Article 8(1)(a) provides the EBA with the mandate to develop the Single Rulebook: "The Authority shall have the following tasks: (a) to contribute to the establishment of high-quality common regulatory and supervisory standards and practices [...]".

[26] The importance of the Single Rulebook for the completion of a genuine and effective European Banking Union let commentators to label it as the fourth centrepiece of the Banking Union. See Grundmann (n 24).

[27] See, respectively, Articles 10, 15, and 16 of the Regulation (Eu) 1093/2010. On the role of EBA within the Banking Union, see Christos V Gortsos, 'The Role of the European Banking Authority (EBA) after the Establishment of the Single Supervisory Mechanism (SSM)', *Regulating and Supervising European Financial Markets* (Springer 2016).

[28] Following the terminology used in Christos Hadjiemmanuil, 'The Banking Union and Its Implications for Private Law: A Comment' (2015) 16 European Business Organization Law Review 383.

[29] Such the Payment Services Directive (Directive 2015/236/EU, OJ 2015 L 337/35); the Consumer Credit Directive (Directive 2008/48/EC, OJ 2008 L 133/66.), the Mortgage Credit Directive the Distance Marketing of Consumer Financial Services Directive (Directive 2014/17/EU, OJ 2014 L 60/34), the Anti Money Laundering Directive (Directive 2015/849/EU, OJ 2015 L 141/73), or the provisions in MiFID II (Directive 2014/65/EU, OJ 2014 L 173/349).

The first pillar of the Banking Union chiefly consists of the new Regulation establishing the Single Supervisory Mechanism (SSMR).[30] The new Single Supervisory Mechanism represents a decisive innovation towards a "genuine economic and monetary union".[31] The Single Supervisory Board (SSB), composed of a dedicated unit of the ECB and the National Competent Authorities (NCAs), is in charge of the supervision over Eurozone banks. The SSM directly supervises all "systemically relevant" institutions as defined by Article 6 of the SSMR, representing around 80% of the market. Whereas, for the less significant institutions, the NCAs retain primary responsibility for direct supervision, in close cooperation with the SSM.[32]

The main goal of this new institutional design is to break the vicious circle between domestic banks and their sovereign since it is considered one of the main determinants of the Sovereign Debt crisis of 2010–2011.[33]

The supervisory powers are assigned, within the SSM, to the ECB and the NCAs.[34] Of crucial importance is the Supervisory Review and Evaluation Process (SREP),[35] complemented by the Supervisory Examination Program[36] and yearly Stress Tests.[37] To carry out, implement

[30] Council Regulation (EU) No 1024/2013 of 15 October 2013 conferring specific tasks on the European Central Bank concerning policies relating to the prudential supervision of credit institutions. OJ L 287/2013.

[31] Van Rompuy and others (n 20). For an initial assessment on those issues see, widely Guido Ferrarini, 'Single Supervision and the Governance of Banking Markets: Will the SSM Deliver the Expected Benefits?' (2015) 16 European Business Organization Law Review 513.

[32] Article 6 SSMR.

[33] As explicitly stated in the recital n. 6 of the Single Supervisory Regulation: "The stability of credit institutions is in many instances still closely linked to the Member State in which they are established. Doubts about the sustainability of public debt, economic growth prospects, and the viability of credit institutions have been creating negative, mutually reinforcing market trends. This may lead to risks to the viability of some credit institutions and to the stability of the financial system in the euro area and the Union as a whole and may impose a heavy burden for already strained public finances of the Member States concerned".

[34] See Article 6 SRMR.

[35] Article 97 CRD.

[36] Article 99 CRD, where the results of stress tests and evaluation process are condensed in an action program to handle all possible risks and flaws detected.

[37] Article 100 CRD.

and enforce the Supervisory activities, Article 104 of the CRD grants the competent authority with intrusive powers, such as requiring banks to hold own funds above the minimum requirements, imposing specific liquidity requirements, requiring additional disclosure, etc.

The third pillar of the Banking Union is the harmonisation of the Deposit Guarantee Schemes. It does not represent a revolution, as the first European Directive in the field dates back to 1994[38] and the consensus around the importance of a full guarantee on retail deposits has consolidated since the Northern Rock run.[39] Accordingly, deposits are guaranteed up to 100.000 euro and protection remains at the national level.

A political agreement on a single deposit insurance scheme is not currently achievable nor for the European Union at large, neither Euro-zone countries. Therefore, the 2014 Directive represents an attempt to make the deposit insurance mechanism more efficient and trustworthy, speeding up the procedure for the reimbursement and the settlement mechanisms between national deposit insurances. Such marginal improvements enhance the protection of depositors, especially if cross-border issues are at play.

Many highlighted that the lack of a single deposit insurer makes the European Banking Union inherently incomplete.[40] Therefore, in November 2015, the Commission put forward a proposal to set up a European Deposit Guarantee Scheme (EDIS) in the Euro Area.[41] To this day, no political convergence on EDIS has formed, and this is unlikely to happen in the coming years. Setting up a single deposit insurer would

[38] Directive 94/19/EC of the European Parliament and of the Council of 30 May 1994 on deposit-guarantee schemes. OJ L 135/1994.

[39] Hyun Song Shin, 'Reflections on Northern Rock: The Bank Run That Heralded the Global Financial Crisis' (2009) 23 Journal of economic perspectives 101. The authors points out that the physical run on retail deposits was only the consequence of the previous run on wholesale ones; yet, the limited insurance (up to 90%) of such deposits contributed to worsening the situation of Norther Rock.

[40] Jacopo Carmassi and others, 'Completing the Banking Union with a European Deposit Insurance Scheme: Who Is Afraid of Cross-Subsidisation?' (2018) 208; Daniel Gros, 'Completing the Banking Union: Deposit Insurance' (2015) 335.

[41] Proposal for a Regulation of the Parliament and of the amending Regulation (EU) 806/2014 in order to establish a European Deposit Insurance Scheme. COM/2015/0586 final - 2015/0270 (COD).

require Member States to accept a mutualisation of risk within the Eurozone.[42] This quest for risk-sharing lost political traction, so that an agreement on EDIS seems, nowadays, far from being reached.[43]

In the new regulatory landscape, DGSs are tightly related to the resolution framework for ailing banks. Indeed, DGSs provide protection to depositors when a financial institution loses its banking licence without qualifying for resolution, the so-called "paybox function".[44] Furthermore, DGSs can come into play to safeguard insured depositors within a resolution procedure.[45]

3 The EU Resolution Framework

3.1 From Bailout to Bail-In: The Rationale

The Bank Recovery and Resolution Directive (BRRD), and, for the Eurozone, the Single Resolution Mechanism Regulation (SRM) were approved in 2014. This reform package represents the second Pillar of the European Banking Union and deals with the crisis management of distressed banks. It changes the institutional design for Eurozone resolution procedure, allocating many of the responsibilities to the Single Resolution Board. Moreover, and most importantly for the purpose of this analysis, it

[42] On the road towards EDIS, see Christos V Gortsos, 'The European Deposit Insurance Scheme', *Research Handbook on EU Economic Law* (Edward Elgar Publishing 2019).

[43] See, nonetheless, Agnès Bénassy-Quéré and others, 'Reconciling Risk Sharing with Market Discipline: A Constructive Approach to Euro Area Reform' 8, where EDIS is one of the key points of a proposal put forward by French and German economist to reconcile market discipline and risk-sharing in the Euro Area.

[44] See Recital n. 14 of Directive 2014/49/EU of the European Parliament and of the Council of 16 April 2014 on deposit guarantee schemes. OJ L 173, 12.6.2014, p. 149.

[45] Article 109 BRRD. On the use of deposit guarantee schemes to finance resolution and its configurability as a State Aid, see Cases T-98/16 *Italian Republic and Others v European Commission*. For a comment of the decision, see Mariateresa Maggiolino, 'The Tercas Case, State Aid, and Antitrust: Are There Holes in the Warp?' (2022) 8 Italian LJ 745. For a specific analysis on the role of deposit guarantee schemes in resolution, see Irene Mecatti, 'The Role of Deposit Guarantee Schemes in Preventing and Managing Banking Crises: Governance and Least Cost Principle' (2020) 17 European Company and Financial Law Review 657. For an analysis of the reforms for the State Aid regime under the proposal for a Crisis Management and Deposit Insurance (CMDI) framework, see Michael Anderson Schillig, 'CMDI Resolution Funding and State Aid Control' (2025) 26 European Business Organization Law Review 221.

harmonises and innovates the substantive rules for dealing with banking crises, widening the set of available tools to resolution authorities. As the key aspect of this analysis is on substantive rules, the analysis focuses on the BRRD rather than on the SRM.

The failure of banking institutions displays many peculiarities and complexities, making insolvency proceeding unfit.[46] In banking, the goal itself of bankruptcy seems to differ sharply from standard corporate insolvency law. On the one hand, for corporate insolvencies, the legal framework provides bankruptcy and reorganisation procedures to cope with creditors' collective action problems[47] and reduce agency costs in distressed corporations.[48] This should lead to the maximisation of returns for creditors[49] and, from an ex-ante perspective, should minimise the cost of debt finance.[50] In a nutshell, the private interests of creditors and companies outweigh public interest considerations, at least in the mainstream literature.[51]

On the other hand, in banking, the primary objective is to preserve the continuity of their essential functions and avoid systemic contagion,[52] i.e.,

[46] For a comprehensive explanation of the economic underpinnings of the specialty of bank failure, see Matej Marinč and Razvan Vlahu, *The Economics of Bank Bankruptcy Law* (Springer Science & Business Media 2011).

[47] Robert Gertner and David Scharfstein, 'A Theory of Workouts and the Effects of Reorganization Law' (1991) 46 The Journal of Finance 1189.

[48] David D Li and Shan Li, 'An Agency Theory of the Bankruptcy Law' (1999) 8 International Review of Economics & Finance 1.

[49] Douglas G Baird and Thomas H Jackson, 'Corporate Reorganizations and the Treatment of Diverse Ownership Interests: A Comment on Adequate Protection of Secured Creditors in Bankruptcy' (1984) 51 The University of Chicago Law Review 97.

[50] See Alan Schwartz, 'A Contract Theory Approach to Business Bankruptcy' (1998) 107 The Yale Law Journal 1807. For a comprehensive even though outdated survey of the Law & Economics literature on insolvency see John Armour, 'The Law and Economics of Corporate Insolvency: A Review' (2001) wp197.for a more up to date review see also Nadine Levratto, 'From Failure to Corporate Bankruptcy: A Review' (2013) 2 Journal of Innovation and Entrepreneurship 20.

[51] Armour (n 52).

[52] Article 31(2)(b) BRRD: "When applying the resolution tools and exercising the resolution powers, resolution authorities shall have regard to the resolution objectives [...]. The resolution objectives referred to in paragraph 1 are: [...] (b) to avoid a significant adverse effect on the financial system, in particular by preventing contagion, including to market infrastructures, and by maintaining market discipline".

public interest considerations are predominant. This should be a sufficient argument for implementing an *ad hoc* normative framework.[53]

The externalities generated by bank failures generate the need for a "special" bankruptcy regime.[54] These fall outside the scope of corporate insolvency rules. Specifically, four sets of externalities linked to bank distress are worth analysing. First, informational linkages[55] among banks and the role of trust. In non-financial industries, the failure of a firm represents an advantage for the other firms in the market that can try to capture the market share of the failing competitor. This is not the case in the banking industry, since the failure (or even severe distress) of one institution may have negative spillovers on all the relevant market, decreasing the level of trust among retail and wholesale customers.[56] Standard bankruptcy procedures, aimed at solving a collective action problem among creditors, are unable to make creditors and insiders internalise those negative spillovers in the whole banking market.

Second, the risk of contagion. The negative spillovers deriving from the failure of a bank do not end in increasing mistrust in investors. Financial institutions are more and more interconnected, and the banking

[53] Until BRRD entered into force, many European jurisdictions heavily relied on corporate bankruptcy procedures, supplemented by some specific rules. The level of specialty of bank bankruptcy in different European jurisdictions had huge variability and it is not possible neither useful now to report them. For a survey on the pre-crisis insolvency regimes in several European countries see Eva HG Hüpkes, 'Insolvency - Why a Special Regime for Banks?', *Current developments in monetary and financial law, Vol. 3* (International Monetary Fund 2002).

[54] In recital 4 of BRRD, the European Legislator acknowledges both the need for harmonisation at European level of bank insolvency regimes and the necessity for a special regime: "[…] the financial crisis has exposed the fact that general corporate insolvency procedures may not always be appropriate for institutions as they may not always ensure sufficient speed of intervention, the continuation of the critical functions of institutions and the preservation of financial stability".

[55] Peter O Mülbert and Ryan D Citlau, 'The Uncertain Role of Banks? Corporate Governance in Systemic Risk Regulation' (2011) 179 17.

[56] On the role of trust in financial market and regulation see, among many others, Carin van der Cruijsen, Jakob de Haan and David-Jan Jansen, 'Trust and Financial Crisis Experiences' (2016) 127 Social Indicators Research 577.

market is systemic.[57] Therefore, the insolvency of even a single systemically significant institution[58] might trigger a domino effect because of the counterparty exposures as well as the correlation of the risk profiles of financial institutions.[59]

Third, the social costs of failure are larger than private ones. Shareholders bear only a fraction of the risk of failure and management is, therefore, incentivised to take on excessive risk. In non-financial corporations, the *ex-ante* threat of future bankruptcy represents a disciplining mechanism for incumbent management, incentivising it to take on optimal risk.[60] However, this is not the case in banks, where the highly levered nature of the balance sheet impedes the internalisation of the adverse effects of excessive risk-taking. Most of the risk is shifted to creditors.

Fourth, the implicit State guarantee on banks solvency (i.e., bailout expectation). The debate over the desirability of saving banks with taxpayers' money is still nowadays open.[61] Two sets of costs of bailouts are unquestionable. On the one hand, there are raw costs borne by the State (i.e., taxpayers) for bailing banks out.[62] Moreover, and arguably more importantly, the *ex-ante* incentives have been perversely shaped due to

[57] On systemic risk, see the formal model by Viral V Acharya, 'A Theory of Systemic Risk and Design of Prudential Bank Regulation' (2009) 5 Journal of financial stability 224; and its empirical application in Viral V Acharya and others, 'Measuring Systemic Risk' (2017) 30 Review of Financial Studies 2.

[58] A list of Global Systemically Important Banks (G-SIBs) is produced by the Financial Stability Board and updated annually. An up to date list can be found in the FSB website at https://www.fsb.org/work-of-the-fsb/policy-development/addressing-sifis/global-systemically-important-financial-institutions-g-sifis/ (accessed 05-02-2020). For a critical evaluation of the designation procedure see Katarzyna Parchimowicz, 'Three Hidden Issues in the List of Global Systemically Important Banks' (2020) Oxford Business Law Blog <https://www.law.ox.ac.uk/business-law-blog/blog/2020/01/three-hidden-issues-list-global-systemically-important-banks> . (accessed 05-02-2020).

[59] Mülbert and Citlau (n 57) 20.

[60] Timothy D Lane, 'Market Discipline' (1993) 40 IMF Staff Papers 53.

[61] Especially in Europe, where this debate is linked to the State Aid regulation as a measure to preserve competition.

[62] During the 2007-08, crisis almost 37% of aggregate EU Member State GDP was spent to avoid banks failure. See ECB, EU Banking Structure, September 2010.

the expectation of a future bailout, inducing moral hazard in carrying out banking activities.[63]

Finally, the distress of financial institutions needs a quick solution to be effective, so that judicial-based bankruptcy procedures are inherently inappropriate to match this requirement.[64] Therefore, it appears reasonable and proportionate to design a quick administrative procedure that minimises the time necessary to enforce and implement the resolution.[65]

In the aftermath of the crisis, the general public and many politicians emphasised the raw and direct costs of bailing-out banks, strongly proposing a paradigm shift from bailout to bail-in to safeguard taxpayers' money.[66] Such proposals gained political momentum and led the Financial Stability Board to draft the "Key Attributes of Effective Resolution Regimes for Financial Institutions"[67] and subsequently in the EU to the BRRD.

3.2 The Bank Recovery and Resolution Directive (BRRD)

The first draft of BRRD was published in June 2012. Thereafter, in August 2013, the European Commission issued a Banking Communication establishing a mandatory burden-sharing of losses among shareholders and subordinated debtholders.[68] Accordingly, the Burden Sharing Communication stated that the contribution of inside investors (namely,

[63] Emmanuel Farhi and Jean Tirole, 'Collective Moral Hazard, Maturity Mismatch, and Systemic Bailouts' (2012) 102 American Economic Review 60.

[64] The resolution of distressed institutions needs to begin after the closing of Wall-Street on Friday and before the opening of Japan and China stock exchanges on Monday, in a time-window of about 38 hours. See Thomas Huertas, 'European Bank Resolution: Making It Work!' (2016) 9.

[65] See Recital 92 BRRD.

[66] Jianping Zhou and others, 'From Bailout to Bail-in: Mandatory Debt Restructuring of Systemic Financial Institutions' [2012] Journal Issue 3; Paul Calello and Wilson Ervin, 'From Bailout to Bail-In' 30 *The Economist* (2010). For a recent critical review of the tool, see Christos Hadjiemmanuil, 'Bail-in's Unfulfilled Promise' (2025) 26 European Business Organization Law Review 89.

[67] Financial Stability Board, 'Key Attributes of Effective Resolution Regimes for Financial Institutions' (2011).

[68] Communication from the Commission on the application, from 1 August 2013, of State aid rules to support measures in favour of banks in the context of the financial crisis ('Banking Communication'). 2013/C 216/01.

stockholders, hybrid capital holders, and subordinated debtholders) should represent the condition for any public intervention (State Aid) in banking crises.[69] That document informed the approach of the European Legislator in addressing bail-ins, seen at first as a mechanism to redistribute losses, in response to the widespread perceived unfairness of bailouts.[70]

In May 2014, the European Parliament approved the Bank Recovery and Resolution Directive.[71] The aim of allocating risks and responsibility differently appears crystal-clear already in the recital No.1: "During the crisis, those challenges [lack of tools for addressing banking crises] were a major factor that forced Member States to save institutions using taxpayers' money. The objective of a credible recovery and resolution framework is to obviate the need for such action to the greatest extent possible".[72]

The resolution framework consists of mainly three parts: Preparation (Title II), Early intervention (Title III),[73] and Resolution (Title IV). The Directive provides four main resolution tools: the sale of business tool, the bridge-bank tool,[74] the bridge institution tool,[75] the asset separation tool,[76] and the bail-in tool.[77] Among these tools, the bail-in represents the most innovative and intrusive one.[78]

[69] Banking Communication, para 3.1.2.

[70] Wolf-Georg Ringe, 'Bank Bail-In between Liquidity and Solvency' (2016) 92 Am. Bankr. LJ 299.

[71] As mentioned before in fn (n 8), the SRMR complements the BRRD for the Euro Area Counties. Given the general nature of the analysis, that can applies to all European Member States, the rest of this chapter as well as the proceeding of the book only refers to the BRRD provision, since the SRMR provision are almost always identical and the slight differences never impact on the general validity of the arguments proposed here.

[72] Emphases added.

[73] For an analysis of the (in)effectiveness of these tools, see David Ramos-Muñoz, '"Twilight Troubles". Early Intervention, Resolution Preparation and Triggers, and the Urgent Need to Reform Them' (2025) 26 European Business Organization Law Review 133.

[74] Article 38 BRRD.

[75] Article 40 BRRD.

[76] Article 42 BRRD.

[77] Article 43 BRRD.

[78] Therefore, it was deemed proportionate to let it enter into force one year after the rest of the Directive, the 1st January 2016 Articles 130 and 131 BRRD.

A bail-in of a distressed bank consists of the power of resolution authorities to write down[79] or convert into ordinary shares[80] eligible liabilities issued by the resolved bank.[81] This materialises as a balance sheet operation to recapitalise and restore the viability of the distressed bank.[82] As a first approximation, the bail-in is a mechanism that preserves a "likely to fail" institution as a going-concern without any government intervention.[83] To make this possible, shareholders and creditors mandatorily bear the losses, according to the seniority order of their claims. Therefore, bank failures no longer threaten taxpayer money.[84]

The idea of bailing-in insiders is particularly attractive since it promises to offer the regulator an alternative to State intervention for the resolution of too big, too complex, or too international to fail institutions.[85] Indeed, both the Financial Stability Board and the Basel Committee have stressed the importance of implementing the bail-in reform specifically for SIFIs.[86] In contrast, the EU adopted the one-size-fits-all approach to establish a level played field within European banking market.[87] In the policymaking desiderata, the bail-in should avoid resorting to taxpayers'

[79] Article 63(1)(e) BRRD.

[80] Article 63(1)(f) BRRD.

[81] See in particular Chris Bates and Simon Gleeson, 'Legal Aspects of Bank Bail-Ins' (2011) 5 Law and Financial Markets Review 264; Thomas Conlon and John Cotter, 'Anatomy of a Bail-In' (2014) 15 Journal of Financial Stability 257; Emilios Avgouleas and Charles Goodhart, 'Critical Reflections on Bank Bail-Ins' (2015) 1 Journal of Financial Regulation 3; Bart PM Joosen, 'Bail in Mechanisms in the Bank Recovery and Resolution Directive', *Annual Conference of the Netherlands Association for Comparative and International Law* (2014); Armour (n 12).

[82] John Armour and others, *Principles of Financial Regulation* (Oxford University Press 2016).

[83] Bates and Gleeson (n 79) 4.

[84] Zhou and others (n 68) 5.

[85] Bates and Gleeson (n 79) 2.

[86] Systemically Important Financial Institutions.

[87] Charles Goodhart and Emilios Avgouleas, 'A Critical Evaluation of Bail-in as a Bank Recapitalisation Mechanism' in Franklin Allen, Elena Carletti and Joanna E Gray (eds), *Bearing the Losses from Bank and Sovereign Default in the Eurozone* (FIC Press 2014) 30. For empirical validation, see oão AC Santos, 'Evidence from the Bond Market on Banks''Too-Big-To-Fail'Subsidy' [2014] Economic Policy Review 29.

money and wipe out, once and for all, the too-big-to-fail policy by eliminating the government implicit guarantee on domestic bank solvency.[88] Nonetheless, tremendous uncertainties and worries remain about bail-in effectiveness and efficiency. The first decade of application has made clear that an open-bank bail-in will never happen because of the reluctance of resolution authorities to affect non-shareholders investors.[89] That is the result of both the perceived unfairness of involving creditors in the resolution procedure[90] and the persistence of bailout expectations.[91]

Such persistence of bailout expectations and, conversely, the lack of credibility of bail-in is rooted in several ambiguities inherent to the resolution framework.[92] At first, important legacy issues prevented a full-fledged application of the new rules. For instance, a substantial fraction of eligible liabilities outstanding was issued before the FSB Key Attributes, the first draft of BRRD and the 2013 Banking Communication. Therefore, holders could not price in the bail-in possibility when purchasing those financial instruments and the application of the new rules may seem unfair and face legal challenges. Moreover, especially in some countries, such as Italy, unsophisticated investors (mostly households) hold a considerable amount of those instruments without having a sufficient understanding of the entailed risk (Fig. 1).[93] That is one of the reasons why the Italian

[88] See, among many others, John C Coffee Jr, 'Systemic Risk after Dodd-Frank: Contingent Capital and the Need for Regulatory Strategies beyond Oversight' (2011) 111 Colum. L. Rev. 795.

[89] Ringe (n 72) 29. See also Christos Gortsos, '10 Years of Banking Union Case-Law: How Did CJEU Judgments Shape Supervision and Resolution Practice in the Banking Union?' (European Banking Institute Working Paper Series 2024) <https://www.europarl.europa.eu/thinktank/en/document/IPOL_STU(2024)755730> accessed 3 February 2025.

[90] Iris HY Chiu, 'Corporate Governance: The Missing Paradigm in the Mandatory Bail-in Regime for Creditors of Banks and Financial Institutions' [2014] Journal of business law 611.

[91] Armour (n 12).

[92] Giulio Velliscig and others, 'The Bail-in Credibility: Barking Dogs Seldom Bite' (2024) 25 Journal of Banking Regulation 1.

[93] Martin R Götz and Tobias Tröger, 'Should the Marketing of Subordinated Debt Be Restricted/Different in One Way or the Other? What to Do in the Case of Mis-Selling?' (2016). For a deeper and wider analysis, see Chapter 6.

Resolution Authority (Resolution Unit of the Bank of Italy) is resistant to make use of bail-in powers.[94]

Second, there is no clear consensus about the needed calibration of bail-in eligible liabilities.[96] At first, the BRRD asked for bank-specific

Holders of banks subordinated debt (Data in billion €)

Holders	Amount	Share
- Italian Banks	3	5,11%
- Italian Households	31	52,81%
- Italian Institutions of which	8,1	13,80%
other financial intermediaries	3,1	5,28%
investment funds	2,2	3,75%
companies	2,2	3,75%
- Foreign investors	13,2	22,49%
- Not classified	3,4	5,79%
Total	**58,7**	**100,00%**

Fig. 1 Banks subordinated debt market in Italy[95]

[94] Ringe (n 72) 29. Onthe MontePaschi Siena case, see Christos Hadjiemmanuil, 'Monte Dei Paschi: A Test for the European Policy Against Bank Bailouts' (2017) Oxford Business Law Blog <https://www.law.ox.ac.uk/business-law-blog/blog/2017/05/monte-dei-paschi-test-european-policy-against-bank-bailouts> . (Accessed 05-02/2-2-) . For a more recent analysis of the implications related to the precautionary recapitalisation of Monte Paschi Siena, see Edoardo D Martino and Andrea Perini, 'Rescued Banks Back to the Market?' (European Banking Institute Working Paper Series 2023) 157 <https://papers.ssrn.com/sol3/papers.cfm?abstract_id=4646777> accessed 3 February 2025.

[95] Bank of Italy, 'Informazione Sui Detentori Di Obbligazioni Subordinate [Information about Subordinated Bond Holders]' (2015) <https://www.bancaditalia.it/media/approfondimenti/2016/obbligazioni-subordinate/index.html> .

[96] Christos Hadjiemmanuil, 'Bank Stakeholders' Mandatory Contribution to Resolution Financing: Principle and Ambiguities of Bail-In', *ECB Legal Conference 2015 - From Monetary Union to Banking Union, on the way to Capital Markets Union* (2015); Armour and others (n 82).

Minimum Requirements of Eligible Liabilities (MREL).[97] At the international level, the Financial Stability Board issued guidelines for SIFIs requiring, in a not yet wholly defined timespan, to comply with a "Total Loss Absorbency Capacity" (TLAC) requirement[98] that should amount to 18% of RWA by 2022.[99] The 2019 revision of the BRRD amended the rule for MREL calibration, aligning those to international standards for systemic institutions.[100] The future implementation strategy of the resolution authorities will reveal whether such attempt will suffice.[101]

Third, beyond the ambiguities due to the lengthy implementation and phase-in period, the very ability of bail-in to cope with systemic crises is doubtful. While there is a widespread consensus that bail-in is a superior mechanism to address idiosyncratic crises of non-systemic institutions, many scholars argued that bail-in might even increase systemic risk and facilitate contagion in case of a systemic crisis.[102]

Fourth, another problematic issue pertains to the moment and the condition in which the resolution has to be triggered. The normative framework sets two general and non-quantitative criteria for triggering a resolution procedure: the institution has to be failing or likely to fail,

[97] Article 45 BRRD.

[98] Financial Stability Board, 'Principles on Loss-Absorbing and Recapitalisation Capacity of G-SIBs in Resolution - Total Loss Absorbency Capacity' (2011).

[99] According to some authors setting capital requirements and TLAC requirement high enough represents a necessary and sufficient means to avoid any future banking crisis. See Jeffrey N Gordon and Wolf-Georg Ringe, 'Bank Resolution in the European Banking Union: A Transatlantic Perspective on What It Would Take' (2015) 115 Colum. L. Rev. 1297; Anat R Admati and others, 'Fallacies, Irrelevant Facts, and Myths in the Discussion of Capital Regulation: Why Bank Equity Is Not Socially Expensive' (2013) 23.

[100] Directive (EU) 2019/879 of the European Parliament and of the Council of 20 May 2019 amending Directive 2014/59/EU as regards the loss-absorbing and recapitalisation capacity of credit institutions and investment firms and Directive 98/26/EC. OJ L 150, 7.6.2019.

[101] Edoardo D Martino and Katarzyna M Parchimowicz, 'Go Preventive or Go Home–the Double Nature of MREL' (2021) 18 European Company and Financial Law Review 608.

[102] Neel Kashkari, 'Lessons from the Crisis: Ending Too Big to Fail', vol 16 (2016); Steven L Schwarcz, 'Misalignment: Corporate Risk-Taking and Public Duty' (2016) 91 Notre Dame L. Rev. 1, 26.

with no prospect that any other measure will solve the distress.[103] Moreover, the resolution has to be "necessary for the achievement of and is proportionate to one or more of the resolution objectives referred to in Article 31" (public interest test).[104] These criteria stated by the Directive leave considerable discretion to the resolution authority. Therefore, their concrete implementation will depend on a choice of resolution policy.[105] Ringe argued in favour of an early resolution trigger, treating the distressed institution in a going-concern.[106] That approach follows how the understanding of the bail-in nature has developed: from a "redistribution" towards a "stabilisation" focus.

The last noteworthy issue still closely relates to the development of bail-in towards a stabilisation mechanism. A bank bail-in consists of a mandatory recapitalisation of a distressed institution operated by an administrative authority. From a stability perspective, a mere recapitalisation of a bank is a necessary but not sufficient step to assure its viability. The bailed-in bank will need extensive liquidity assistance. The inability to credibly provide sufficient liquidity in resolution currently represents one of the most debated and fundamental shortcomings of the entire framework, sensibly decreasing the credibility of resolution.[107]

[103] Such determination is taken by the competent and not by the resolution authority. Hence, for significant Eurozone banks the SSM is entitled to determine whether a bank is failing or likely to fail.

[104] Article 32 (1) and (5) BRRD. See Ricardo Cabral, 'The Banking Union's Resolution or Liquidation Approach' [2024] Journal of Banking Regulation.

[105] The public interest test was crucial in the resolution decision of the so-called Veneto Banks in 2017. The SSM certified that the banks were "failing or likely to fail" but the SRB decided that a fully-fledged resolution was not in the "public interests" so that the banks were liquidated according to Italian Law on bank insolvency (Articles 80 and ff. of the Consolidated Banking Law). See Ioannis G Asimakopoulos, 'The Veneto Banks Resolution: It Shall Be Called "Liquidation"' (2018) 15 European Company Law 156. This case sparked new interest on the divergences among national liquidation procedures. See Jens-Hinrich Binder, 'Towards Harmonised Frameworks for the Liquidation of Non-Systemically Relevant Credit Institutions in the EU?' (2021) 18 European Company and Financial Law Review 555.

[106] Ringe (n 72). See also Goodhart and Avgouleas (n 87) 10.

[107] See Ringe (n 72). See also the policy report by the European Parliament. Willem Pieter de Groen, 'Financing Bank Resolution: An Alternative Solution for Arranging the Liquidity Required' (2018) PE 624.423.

4 Ex-ante Tools and the Credibility of Resolution

As discussed in the previous section, there are several theoretical and practical issues undermining the credibility of the EU resolution framework. The first attempts to resolve failing banks confirmed these hurdles. So far, there are only two full-fledged resolution cases: Banco Popular Español and Sberbank.[108]

In the case of Banco Popular, the bank entered in resolution on 7 June 2017, after the Single Resolution Board's decision.[109] The resolution happened through a "sale of business" tool, transferring all the shares to Banco Santander.[110] Aside from these two cases, other cases of distressed banks happened after the BRRD entered into force were handled out of resolution.[111]

The lack of credibility and the high level of uncertainty may cast doubts about the usefulness of having a resolution framework in place. An overall welfare assessment of the resolution framework is beyond the scope of this book. However, it is worth noting that the resolution framework embeds several features having the potential to improve ex-ante the resilience of the individual institutions and, to a more limited extent, of the financial system as a whole. To this end, two main channels are worth discussing.

First, regulating the "end game" changes the incentives of the bank and its risk-takers also ex-ante, through backwards induction. In more rigorous terms, financial institutions discount the ex-ante probability of

[108] For an overview of the judicial review on resolution decisions, with a specific focus on the Banco Popular case, see Marco Lamandini and David Ramos Muñoz, 'Bank Resolution and Judicial Review: Lessons of the Banco Popular Litigation' (2025) 26 European Business Organization Law Review 47.

[109] The ECB, in its supervisory capacity, declared the Banco Popular failing or likely to fail on 6 June.

[110] On the resolution of Banco Popular, see more generally Isabel Fernández Acín, 'Caso Banco Popular (Banco Popular Case)' (2018) <https://papers.ssrn.com/sol3/papers.cfm?abstract_id=3132293> .

[111] It is not here possible to provide a detailed description of all the case. For an excellent survey, see Karel Lannoo, 'Uneven Progress in Implementing Cross-Border Bank Resolution in the EU' (2017) No 2017–26.

incurring losses ex-post in resolution, adjusting their risk appetite accordingly.[112] For this kind of mechanism to work, the credibility of ex-post application is crucial: the bank is going to discount losses in resolution as long as it believes that losses will materialise in case of distress. However, the level of credibility that is needed is not the certainty about the full application of the resolution framework, but some degree of probability to bear at least a fraction of losses should the bank enter distress. In this respect, the post-crisis state of affairs sharply improved and burden-sharing exercises,[113] even without fully applied resolution, are now relatively common.[114]

Second, to make the resolution process feasible from both a theoretical and practical perspective, granting the resolution authority ample and discretionary powers once a resolution is triggered is not enough: both the resolution authority and the bank need to be ready for the resolution.[115] For this reason, the BRRD encompasses many tools that ease the task of the resolution authority in resolution and, at the same time, have the potential to change the behaviour and the incentives of financial institutions in good time. For the time being, it is sufficient to generally refer to resolution planning as the quintessential tool in this respect.[116]

[112] The argument is the same for bankruptcy law in non-financial corporation. See widely Robert K Rasmussen, 'The Ex Ante Effects of Bankruptcy Reform on Investment Incentives' (1994) 72 Wash. ULQ 1159; Douglas G Baird and Robert K Rasmussen, 'Private Debt and the Missing Lever of Corporate Governance' [2006] University of Pennsylvania Law Review 1209. For a formal model explaining why different "end game" rules affect behaviours in good time, see Francesca Cornelli and Leonardo Felli, 'Ex-Ante Efficiency of Bankruptcy Procedures' (1997) 41 European Economic Review 475.

[113] Banking Communication 2013.

[114] In this sense, the decision to allow the precautionary recapitalisation of the Monte dei Paschi Bank is paradigmatic. Commissioner Vestager declared: "Commissioner Margrethe Vestager, in charge of competition policy, said: "We have approved Italy's capital injection into MPS in line with EU rules, which will help MPS meet capital needs in case economic conditions were to worsen unexpectedly. [...]. This capital injection could only be approved after junior bondholders and shareholders have contributed to the costs of restructuring, in line with "burden-sharing" requirements under EU state aid rules". See EU Commission Press-release (4 July 2017), available at https://ec.europa.eu/commission/presscorner/detail/en/IP_17_1905 (accessed 05-02-2020).

[115] Armour (n 12) 14.

[116] Emilios Avgouleas, Charles Goodhart and Dirk Schoenmaker, 'Bank Resolution Plans as a Catalyst for Global Financial Reform' (2013) 9 Journal of Financial Stability 210.

The fact that the resolution framework has an impact on behaviours and incentives in good time raises the question of whether, how and to what extent, such an impact is desirable. The answer to this question crucially depends on the type of crisis one has in mind. The case of an idiosyncratic crisis, where a bank enters in distress for reasons specific to its business model and funding structure with little or no spillovers on the rest of the financial system, sharply differs from a systemic crisis.

In the case of idiosyncratic events, the credibility of the bail-in is going to be comparatively higher once, if ever, the legacy issues discussed in the previous section will be solved. Therefore, it is reasonable to argue that efficiently exploiting the ex-ante potential of the BRRD tools would reduce the probability of an idiosyncratic crisis, as bankers would have incentives to discount ex-ante the probability of a bail-in. Or, in other words, internalise at least some of the social costs of future bankruptcy. Moreover, the ex-ante effect of the resolution framework, especially for the part related to bail-inable creditors and debt governance, can in turn increase the credibility of the ex-post resolution, triggering a virtuous circle between ex-ante effect and ex-post credibility. Increasing the role of junior creditors in the decision-making of the bank makes, from a political perspective, the use of a bail-in more viable.[117]

On the contrary, in the case of a systemic event, the threat of a plain open-bank bail-in is likely never to become credible. In the financial system "trust" plays a quintessential role, and the existence of a public back-up reassuring the market players is of utmost importance: governments are likely to always back up systemic banks in a systemic crisis.[118] However, better risk incentives decrease the probability and the severity of systemic events. From this perspective, debt governance through bail-inable creditors can play a positive role in limiting the build-up of systemic risk in good times.

[117] Chiu (n 91) 617.

[118] On the role of trust in banking and the disruptive effects of mistrust during the Global Financial Crisis, see David-Jan Jansen, Robert HJ Mosch and Carin AB van der Cruijsen, 'When Does the General Public Lose Trust in Banks?' (2015) 48 Journal of Financial Services Research 127. For the role of the public backstop with specific reference to the European financial system, see Gros and Schoenmaker (n 43).

5 The Ex-ante Potential of the Resolution Regulation and Debt Governance

The legal and financial literature has discussed the limited ability of bank creditors to impose discipline on the borrowing banks over the last decades.[119] Such inability was mainly attributed to the implicit or explicit bailout expectations.[120] Therefore, the enactment of a comprehensive resolution framework aiming to end the bailout expectations also promised to bring about a functioning market-based discipline from long-term creditors, capable of complementing financial regulation and supervisory oversight.[121]

The positive spillovers of the resolution framework to this day have remained mostly undelivered. This is because of several reasons. First and foremost, the resolution framework and its no-bailout commitment are not fully credible. However, this cannot fully explain the failure of debt governance. As argued earlier in Sect. 4, even though plain open-bank bail-ins have not yet been used, burden-sharing exercises with sizeable losses allocated to junior bondholders have become somehow common.[122] In other words, even if the bail-in threat were fully credible, market discipline would remain suboptimal.[123]

There are, indeed, other elements preventing market discipline from properly functioning. Some tightly relate to the legal design of the resolution framework; others are more fundamentally grounded on the basic mechanisms underpinning the business models and operating practices of banks.

Among the elements related to the legal design of the resolution framework, the literature focused particularly on the excessive complication of the resolution framework, especially when it comes to the requirements

[119] For a comprehensive and up to date survey, see Mark J Flannery and Robert R Bliss, 'Market Discipline in Regulation: Pre-and Post-Crisis' in Allen N Berger, Philip Molyneux and John OS Wilson (eds), *Oxford Handbook of Banking* (3rd edn, Oxford Handbook of Banking (3rd edition), Oxford University Press, forthcoming 2018).

[120] Following the seminal model by Douglas W Diamond and Philip H Dybvig, 'Bank Runs, Deposit Insurance, and Liquidity' (1983) 91 Journal of political economy 401.

[121] Financial Stability Board (n 69); Zhou and others (n 68) 23.

[122] See, for instance, the discussion on the precautionary recapitalisation of Monte dei Paschi Bank, back in note 118.

[123] See at length Chapter 4.

and procedure to set MREL.[124] Moreover, the competing policy objectives set down in Article 31 of the BRRD, among which the "maintenance of market discipline" generated a legal framework not completely apt to correctly incentivise bail-inable creditors to exert adequate discipline.[125]

To understand the more fundamental aspects impairing market discipline, it is worth taking a step back and spelling out how debt governance functions in non-financial firms. Creditors can impose discipline on the borrowing firm by monitoring its activities and correctly pricing the issued debt as well as through contractual entitlements embedded in debt contracts, granting the creditor specific control rights.[126] These rights, such as a right to speed up principal amount repayments, can be activated if the situation of the borrowing firm deteriorates over a certain threshold defined in the contract.

Should bailout expectations disappear, debt governance would function as well as in non-financial firms, and creditors would discipline the borrowing banks. However appealing this may sound, it also implies an underlying and often unspoken assumption: the traditional channels for debt governance are going to function smoothly. Yet, this is unlikely to be the case. Bank governance is, nowadays, known to be special as compared with corporate governance of other non-financial firms.[127] Many elements make bank governance "special". Among these, two stand out for our analysis: the opaqueness of bank assets and the peculiar link between governance and regulation.[128]

The ability to monitor and price the debt issued by the banks crucially relies on the ability to convey and compute all the relevant information on the value of banks' assets. However, banks' assets are inherently opaque, making the task of effective and efficient monitoring particularly burdensome for bank creditors.

[124] Tobias Tröger, 'Why MREL Won't Help Much' (2019) 20 Journal of Banking Regulation.

[125] See at length Chapter 4. On the specific case of No Creditors Worse Off principle, see Chiu (n 91) 627.

[126] "Market discipline means that financial markets provide signals that lead borrowers to behave in a manner consistent with their solvency". See Lane (n 62) 55.

[127] Marco Becht, Patrick Bolton and Ailsa Röell, 'Why Bank Governance Is Different' (2011) 27 Oxford Review of Economic Policy 437.

[128] For an extensive analysis of these mechanisms, see *supra* Chapter 2, Sect. 3.

Second, the ability of creditors to contingently allocate some control rights through contracts, as they do in non-financial firms, is severely limited by regulation.[129] There is a tension between market discipline imposed by creditors ex-ante and financial stability considerations.[130] Coming back to the previous example of financial covenants, the right to ask for early repayment of the debt conferred upon creditors contingent on the deterioration of banks' performance represents a disciplining mechanism, as it provides the borrowing firm with incentives compatible to avoid such deterioration (i.e., avoid taking gambles that increase the risk of breaching the covenant). Yet, if that happened in banking, it is likely to create stability concerns. Indeed, a bank whose capitalisation is decreasing would need to repay part of its creditors in a moment when attracting fresh funds in the market is particularly challenging. Therefore, the rules on both capital instruments and the minimum requirement for eligible liabilities (MREL) disqualify instruments embedding this type of clauses in their contracts.[131]

From the discussion above, it became clear that having a resolution framework for failing banks in place is strictly necessary, though not sufficient, to improve debt governance and make it a valuable complement to current regulation and supervisory oversight. Possible policy strategies to make debt governance effective are discussed later on in the book.

6 Conclusion

This chapter discussed the rationale of the European Resolution framework and briefly discussed the context in which it is embedded, the European Banking Union, as well as its main features. Particular attention was devoted to the key shortcomings of the resolution framework,

[129] See at length Chapter 5.

[130] For an interpretation that absolutely prioritises financial stability, see Jonathan Bauerschmidt, 'Financial Stability as the Objective of the Banking Union' (2020) 17 European Company and Financial Law Review 155. For a broader perspective, see Vincenzo Bavoso, 'Rethinking Banks and Banking Regulation in the Age of Financial Instability' (2023) 17 Law and Financial Markets Review 306.

[131] This point is widely developed in Chapter 5. See also Fiona Mann and others, 'Market Discipline and UK Bank Bondholders' (2017) 57 Bank of England Quarterly Bulletin 26.

undermining the credibility of the application of the resolution framework.

The link between the ex-ante credibility of resolution and the ability of bail-inable debtholders to discipline the borrowing bank is crucial for understanding whether having the resolution framework in place helps to improve the resilience of banking institutions.

The analysis reveals that the existence of a resolution framework is a necessary yet not sufficient element to exploit the full potential of debt governance in financial firms. Moreover, this chapter argues that the credibility of the resolution framework is not the only element at play. On the one hand, the full and consistent credibility of resolution and predictability of its outcome are not strictly necessary. The expectation of suffering non-trivial losses, also in the form of burden-sharing, can provide bail-inable creditors with incentives to discipline the borrowing institution towards risk-taking appetite that is consistent with bank solvency. On the other hand, there are legal and material obstacles for bail-inable creditors to exert efficient discipline, and such obstacles go beyond the credibility of the resolution framework.

CHAPTER 4

The Legal Framework for Market Discipline and Debt Governance

1 Introduction

For decades, regulators and academics have discussed the ability of junior creditors to correctly and continuously assess the risk profile of their borrower, promptly react to that information and, thus, impact managers' behaviour.[1] Nevertheless, the creation of the Banking Union and, more specifically, the implementation of the Bank Recovery and Resolution Directive (BRRD)[2] bestowed a new fashion to the market discipline debate in the banking sector.

This chapter heavily draws from Edoardo D Martino, 'The Bail-in beyond Unpredictability: Creditors' Incentives and Market Discipline' (2020) 21 European Business Organization Law Review 789.

[1] BCBS, 'A New Capital Adequacy Framework' (1999); Timothy D Lane, 'Market Discipline' (1993) 40 IMF Staff Papers 53.

[2] DIRECTIVE 2014/59/EU OF THE EUROPEAN PARLIAMENT AND OF THE COUNCIL of 15 May 2014, establishing a framework for the recovery and resolution of credit institutions and investment firms. Hereinafter, "BRRD" or "the Directive".

E. D. Martino, *EU Bank Governance and Bail-In*, EBI Studies in Banking and Capital Markets Law,
https://doi.org/10.1007/978-3-032-20699-2_4

An extensive amount of literature highlighted the peculiar mechanisms of corporate governance in banks.[3] In particular, this literature questions the conventional wisdom in corporate governance, according to which maximising shareholders value leads to a socially optimal outcome. The very nature of banking activities shifts this paradigm and generates incentives towards excessive risk-taking.[4]

In contrast, bondholders are, in principle, interested in limiting the risk-taking policies of their borrower, so that their value at risk decreases and, conversely, expected return on their investment increases. Therefore, in the banking sector, their incentives have been considered more aligned with the socially optimal outcome than the shareholders' one. The BRRD should have reinforced this mechanism, at least according to the policymaker wishes.[5]

The policy goal of ending the too-big-to-fail problem led, among many other things, to the creation of a category of bail-inable creditors, whose claims can be written down or converted into equity to recapitalise distressed institutions. The resulting incentives of bail-inable creditors should match the social objective, i.e., avoiding, or at least preventing and mitigating, bank distress.[6] The BRRD itself makes it clear that a renewed push towards market discipline represents a cornerstone of the regulatory architecture: "The bail-in tool will therefore give shareholders and creditors of institutions a stronger incentive to monitor the health of an institution during normal circumstances".[7]

Beyond these intuitive arguments, the ability of bail-inable creditors to actually influence managers' risk-taking attitude represents an open

[3] See, among many others, Marco Becht, Patrick Bolton and Ailsa Röell, 'Why Bank Governance Is Different' (2011) 27 Oxford Review of Economic Policy 437.

[4] John Armour and others, 'Bank Governance' (2016) ECGI Law Working Paper 316/2016.

[5] Within the Euro Area, the Single Resolution Mechanisms Regulation (SRMR) discipline the powers of Resolution Authorities. Nonetheless, since the resolution tools, the resolution objectives and the condition for resolution are identical in the BRRD and the SRMR, there is no need for differentiation. This approach has been widely applied, see for instance Alex Kunde, 'Legal Constraints on Resolution Measures and the Application of the Bail-in Tool under BRRD and SRMR', *ECB Legal Conference 2015—From Monetary Union to Banking Union, on the way to Capital Markets Union* (2015).

[6] Jianping Zhou and others, 'From Bailout to Bail-in: Mandatory Debt Restructuring of Systemic Financial Institutions' [2012] Journal Issue 3.

[7] Recital 67 BRRD.

and heavily discussed issue. Specifically, this chapter intends to tackle a narrower question: within the BRRD framework, are bail-inable creditors provided with appropriate incentives to engage in efficient monitoring?

This does not merely represent a theoretical exercise, as the answer to this question has relevant consequences for the extent to which the new resolution framework can enhance the resilience of the banking system, decreasing the risk-taking appetite of financial institutions.

Many have cast doubts on the ability of bail-inable creditors to discipline bankers. So far, the literature has only focused on exogenous impediments preventing creditors from exerting market discipline. These mainly stem from two factors: the lack of credibility of the bail-in tool,[8] and the high level of unpredictability of the resolution process, due to the high complexity of the legal design and the considerable discretion granted to supervisory and resolution authorities.[9] This chapter aims at testing the following hypothesis: the legal design of the BRRD inherently dilutes the incentives for creditors to engage in monitoring activities.

In so doing, this chapter goes beyond the standard critiques, showing that, even assuming a world of certainty and full predictability the outcome in terms of creditors' monitoring, would not be efficient because of the legal design of resolution. In turn, this is ultimately rooted in the competing policy objective pursued by the Directive.[10]

This chapter discusses the theoretical expectations on the disciplining role of bail-inable creditors and discusses the relevant legal rules shaping the status of bail-inable creditors, highlighting how they should impact on creditors' ex-ante incentives. Given this background, the smooth functioning of both the resolution and the market for bail-inable securities is assumed, so that the legal design of the BRRD remains the only element affecting the incentives of creditors. Thereafter, the rules on creditors' treatment are conceptualised in terms of ex-ante incentives towards monitoring, highlighting that the legal design itself dilutes monitoring incentives for bail-inable creditors.

[8] Charles Goodhart and Emilios Avgouleas, 'A Critical Evaluation of Bail-in as a Bank Recapitalisation Mechanism' in Franklin Allen, Elena Carletti and Joanna E Gray (eds), *Bearing the Losses from Bank and Sovereign Default in the Eurozone* (FIC Press 2014).

[9] Tobias Tröger, 'Why MREL Won't Help Much' (2019) 20 Journal of Banking Regulation.

[10] See Article 31(2) BRRD. For further explanation on resolution objectives see Sect. 3.

2 A Review of Market Discipline in Banking. Theory and Regulation

Market Discipline is a complex and multifaceted concept. Hence, a preliminary and comprehensive definition may be of use, since such a concept might be ambiguous, especially in the legal domain.[11] Lane defined market discipline as the ability of financial markets to provide signals that leads borrowers to engage in projects consistent with their solvency.[12] Market discipline is not a bank-specific concept.[13] Market discipline means the ability of the investors to influence the decision-making of the companies they invest in by adjusting the price to the risk profile of the company. Price adjustment is not the only disciplining mechanism in banking, although it is the most prominent one. For instance, contractual clauses can have disciplining effects,[14] as well as debt governance through voice.[15]

Price adjustment, contracts and voice can be seen as complementary mechanisms.[16] This chapter focuses on market discipline through price adjustment. This has been seen as the dominant channel, especially in the

[11] There are many channels for disciplining behaviours; this analysis solely focuses on the price adjustment according to the risk profile of bank activities.

[12] Lane (n 1) 55.

[13] Ibid. 54. The clearest example is the disciplining effect of bankruptcy that imposes a budget constraint on the entrepreneur shifting the control rights of the corporation to creditors contingent on the event of default. See János Kornai, 'Hardening the Budget Constraint: The Experience of the Post-Socialist Countries' (2001) 45 European Economic Review 1573; Philippe Aghion and Patrick Bolton, 'An Incomplete Contracts Approach to Financial Contracting' (1992) 59 The review of economic Studies 473. This optimises, at least theoretically, the ex-ante cost of finance. See, Alan Schwartz, 'A Contract Theory Approach to Business Bankruptcy' (1998) 107 The Yale Law Journal 1807.

[14] On the ability of financial contracting over bail-inable securities to discipline banks behaviours see Chapter 5.

[15] This represents a heavily understudied aspect, especially in the European legal domain. For a general framework on that matter see John Armour and Jeffrey N Gordon, 'Systemic Harms and Shareholder Value' (2014) 6 Journal of Legal Analysis 35; Steven L Schwarcz, 'Misalignment: Corporate Risk-Taking and Public Duty' (2016) 91 Notre Dame L. Rev. 1.

[16] The complementarity between exit and voice in influencing decision-making is well established in the literature, stemming from the seminal work by Hirschman. See Albert O Hirschman, *Exit, Voice, and Loyalty: Responses to Decline in Firms, Organizations, and States*, vol 25 (Harvard University Press 1970).

policy discourse. In its financial connotation, the underlying mechanisms on which the disciplining power of the market relies are the Efficient Capital Market Hypothesis (ECMH)[17] and the ability of prices to embed information.[18]

Nonetheless, in the context of financial institutions, market discipline is something different as well as something more than the stock market monitoring for non-financial firms,[19] even though these mechanisms share the same fundamentals. Market discipline in financial institutions does not only cope with the efficiency of prices given the available information. It also interplays with regulatory discipline for minimising the threats to financial stability.[20] Thus, it is not by chance that the literature, especially in the last three decades, focused prominently on banking since the information produced can be used for supervisory purposes, potentially acting as a complement of prudential regulation.

Accordingly, in the specific context of the banking industry, Sironi defines market discipline as the ability of financial markets to discipline banks' behaviour by pricing their borrowings according to their risk profile.[21] This definition relies on two underlying assumptions, as pointed

[17] Eugene F Fama, 'Efficient Capital Markets: A Review of Theory and Empirical Work' (1970) 25 The journal of Finance 383.

[18] Sanford Grossman, 'On the Efficiency of Competitive Stock Markets Where Trades Have Diverse Information' (1976) 31 The Journal of finance 573. This view has been heavily challenged, for instance, by Hellwig. See Martin F Hellwig, 'On the Aggregation of Information in Competitive Markets' (1980) 22 Journal of economic theory 477, where the author incorporates "noise" in the analysis of financial information and Robert E Verrecchia, 'Information Acquisition in a Noisy Rational Expectations Economy' [1982] Econometrica: Journal of the Econometric Society 1415, where the author considers the case in which information costs are positive. In both those scenarios, the ability of market prices to reflect firm's information efficiently is impaired.

[19] Bengt Holmstrom, 'Understanding the Role of Debt in the Financial System' (2015) No. 479.

[20] Mark J Flannery and Robert R Bliss, 'Market Discipline in Regulation: Pre-and Post-Crisis' in Allen N Berger, Philip Molyneux and John OS Wilson (eds), *Oxford Handbook of Banking* (3rd edn, Oxford Handbook of Banking (3rd edition), Oxford University Press, 2018).

[21] Andrea Sironi, 'Testing for Market Discipline in the European Banking Industry: Evidence from Subordinated Debt Issues' (2003) 35 Journal of Money, Credit, and Banking 443.

out and critically discussed by Bliss.[22] First, bond yields spreads reflects the risk of individual banks; second, the payoff matrices of debtholders and regulator closely resemble one another. The latter assumption highly depends on both the institutional set-up and the type of debt instrument held by the investor. Hence, when discussing the new regulatory framework, the arguments about its impact on market discipline are going to question whether such assumptions hold true.

In the realm of banking, market discipline must be considered as a governance device, as it represents the mean through which creditors impact managers' behaviour.[23] Indeed, as Pacces and Heremans pointed out: "all aspects of behaviour of financial firms can be ultimately understood as Corporate Governance issue".[24] Building on our working definition, the remainder of the section discusses the channels through which market discipline impacts on bankers' behaviours, the conditions for making market discipline effective and the different regulatory approaches towards market discipline.

The economic literature disentangled various aspects of market discipline and identified several conditions under which debtholders can effectively impinge upon bank governance. In particular, Kwast et al. disentangled a direct and indirect channel of influence.[25] On the one hand, investors can directly push managers towards activities with lower risk profile increasing the cost of funds for riskier banks. At the same time, the movement of market prices may indirectly attract the attention of the supervisor, feeding it with new relevant information. Consistently with the motivation and the goal of this research, the direct channel is going

[22] Robert R Bliss, 'Market Discipline and Subordinated Debt: A Review of Some Salient Issues' (2001) 25 Economic Perspectives 24.

[23] On the agency conflict between shareholders and creditors and the peculiar shape it assumes in banking, where high leverage magnifies the incentives to shift the risk to unsecured creditors, see extensively Becht, Bolton and Röell (n 32) 459.

[24] Alessio M Pacces and Dirk Heremans, 'Regulation of Banking and Financial Markets', *Encyclopedia of Law and Economics—Volume 9* (Edward Elgar 2012) 33. Corporate governance has been defined as: "the ways in which supplies of finance assure themselves of getting a return on their investment". See Andrei Shleifer and Robert W Vishny, 'A Survey of Corporate Governance' (1997) 52 The journal of finance 737, 3.

[25] Myron L Kwast and others, 'Using Subordinated Debt as an Instrument of Market Discipline' (1999) 172 Report of a Study Group on Subordinated Notes and Debentures, M. Kwast, Chair. Board of Governors of the Federal Reserve System, Staff Study.

to be the most considered; nonetheless, it is essential to bear in mind that also the indirect disciplining channel works in the background.

Four key conditions ought to hold for both the direct and indirect channels of discipline to effectively work.[26] First, the relevant market must be open and freely accessible to make interest rates sensitive to borrowers' risk profile.[27] Second, lenders need to have access to all relevant information about borrowers' debt.[28] Third, market participants should have no bailout expectations. This condition consists of two distinct aspects: the commitment of the government not to bail out a failing firm and the credibility that such a commitment generates towards the market.[29] Finally, the borrower needs to be able and willing to respond to the market signal and adjust its risk profile accordingly.[30] Increasing the interest rate represents an efficient answer to risk-taking only up to a certain level of risk, beyond such a level, the borrower runs out of funding opportunities and is out of the market. This latter prospect is clearly not in line with safeguarding the solvency of the firm.[31]

Regarding the openness of the market, despite some specific and minor foreclosures, the market has to be considered open so that no impediments to market discipline arise from this perspective.[32] On the contrary,

[26] On those conditions, see extensively Lane (n 1).

[27] See also Hal S Scott, 'Market Discipline for Financial Institutions and Sovereigns' in Claudio Borio (ed), *Market Discipline across Countries and Industries* (MIT Press 2004).

[28] Andrew Crockett, 'Market Discipline and Financial Stability' (2002) 26 Journal of Banking & Finance 977.

[29] For an analysis on the conditions of a credible bail-in tool, see Giulio Velliscig and others, 'The Bail-in Credibility: Barking Dogs Seldom Bite' (2024) 25 Journal of Banking Regulation 1.

[30] David T Llewellyn, 'Inside the 'Black Box'of Market Discipline' (2005) 25 Economic Affairs 41.

[31] In the context of banking, and especially in the context of the latest financial crisis, this point proved to be highly problematic and crucially linked with the (lack of) liquidity available in the market. On this specific aspect see Brunnermeier and Pedersen (n 35); whereas the specific case of perverse effect of market discipline through the latest financial crisis is detailed at the end of this section.

[32] An instance in which market foreclosure can impair market discipline is the geographical segregation of banking activities that were common before the liberalization wave of the 90s both in Europe and in the U.S. After the crisis, some new foreclosures have been proposed and debated, as, for instance, a ban on retail sale of subordinated debt. See Martin R Götz and Tobias Tröger, 'Should the Marketing of Subordinated Debt Be Restricted/Different in One Way or the Other? What to Do in the Case of Mis-Selling?'

the other three conditions raise delicate problems. The full availability of information is impaired by the very design of commercial bank business model, involving the maturity and liquidity mismatched of bank assets and liabilities.[33] As for the second condition, the bank is better positioned than any other investors in monitoring and screening the quality of its own assets because of their inherent opacity.[34] This impairs the ability of bank creditors to impose efficient discipline on bank management.

The third condition—i.e., lack of bailout expectations—has also been proven to be problematic in banking.[35] The State, historically, has implicitly guaranteed bank solvency to avoid massive systemic externalities stemming from bank failures.[36] Therefore, investors expect not to suffer losses in case of bank distress; accordingly, their sensitivity to the risk profile of the borrowing bank decreases. This impairs their ability to price debt according to the risk profile of the borrowing bank.[37] Crucially,

(2016). Nevertheless, this kind of foreclosure seems to be socially desirable and, at the same time, preserve market discipline from more severe impairments. In the 2019 reform package, the EU legislator inserted the Article 44a which regulates the sale of bail-inable securities to retailers, including a mandatory suitability test ex art 25(2) of the Directive 2014/65/EU of the European Parliament and of the Council of 15 May 2014 on markets in financial instruments and amending Directive 2002/92/EC and Directive 2011/61/ EU. OJ L 173 (MiFID II).

[33] John Armour and others, *Principles of Financial Regulation* (Oxford University Press 2016). Tri Vi Dang, Gary Gorton and Bengt Holmström, 'The Information View of Financial Crises' (2020) 12 Annual Review of Financial Economics 39.

[34] Douglas W Diamond, 'Financial Intermediation and Delegated Monitoring' (1984) 51 The review of economic studies 393.

[35] Between 2008 and 2017, the European Commission approved over 5 trillion euro of State Aid towards the banking sector to cope with the latest financial crisis. Data is retrievable at http://ec.europa.eu/competition/state_aid/scoreboard/index_en.html (accessed on 30/09/2025).

[36] Marco Bodellini, 'Corporate Governance of Banks and Financial Stability: Critical Issues and Challenges Ahead' (2018) 39 Business Law Review 160. On top of those arguments, Avguleas and Cullen introduced into the analysis also behavioural features, arguing that—in line with the behavioural economics stream of literature—shareholder and stakeholders are not able to exactly convey and process the complex amount of information they are provided with. See Emilios Avgouleas and Jay Cullen, 'Market Discipline and EU Corporate Governance Reform in the Banking Sector: Merits, Fallacies, and Cognitive Boundaries' (2014) 41 Journal of Law and Society 28.

[37] João AC Santos, 'Evidence from the Bond Market on Banks' 'Too-Big-To-Fail'Subsidy' [2014] Economic Policy Review 29.

the resolution framework was supposed to smoothen market discipline by eliminating, or at least minimising, bailout expectations.[38]

Finally, banks have a limited ability to promptly adjust the risk profile in response to market signals, mainly because of the inherent maturity mismatch between assets and liabilities. On the one hand, this can be a merely theoretical problem in times of economic expansions when the markets are liquid and the bank can adjust the composition of its assets and liabilities at low cost.[39] On the other hand, in times of economic and financial turmoil, when liquidity dries up, adjusting the balance sheet to react to market signals might be disruptive. Fire-sales may be needed, and funding opportunities might not be available for any reasonable price. This proved to be a decisive element in spreading and worsening the latest financial crisis.[40]

If the assumptions hold and creditors can discipline their borrowing bank, the next question to be answered is what this implies in terms of regulatory policy. Three main approaches to the debt-discipline narrative are worth mentioning, as they entail radically different approaches from a regulatory perspective.

The first can be labelled as the "substitutability approach". The market is considered to be in a better position than the supervisor to discipline managers' behaviour because of the higher quantity and quality of available information.[41] Thus, the direct disciplining channel is the most relevant one. The normative consequence of such an approach is financial deregulation and less stringent capital requirements[42] complemented by pervasive regulation on disclosure and transparency to overcome the

[38] Zhou and others (n 6). More details, especially for the European resolution framework, are provided in Sect. 3.

[39] Pistor defines liquidity as "the ability to sell any asset for the other assets or cash at will". Katharina Pistor, 'A Legal Theory of Finance' (2013) 41 Journal of Comparative Economics 315, 316.

[40] Markus K Brunnermeier, 'Deciphering the Liquidity and Credit Crunch 2007–2008' (2009) 23 Journal of Economic perspectives 77.

[41] See, theoretically, Charles W Calomiris and Charles M Kahn, 'The Role of Demandable Debt in Structuring Optimal Banking Arrangements' [1991] The American Economic Review 497.

[42] Charles W Calomiris, 'Blueprints for a New Global Financial Architecture' in Leonardo Auernheimer (ed), *International Financial Markets: The Challenge of Globalization* (The University of Chicago Press 1998).

inherent information asymmetry problem.[43] This approach was *en vogue* in the 90s and the early 2000s and now it is widely discredited.

A different, moderate, approach looks at market discipline mostly as a complement to supervisory activities. In such a complementary approach, the literature commonly differentiates two channels through which market discipline operates. On the one hand, thus, market discipline can be defined as the combination of "mere" market monitoring and market influence,[44] the first being the ability of investors to screen, detect changes in firm's condition and incorporate them into the price of the security. On the other hand, "market influence" defines the investors' impact on banks behaviour,[45] pushing them towards "sustainable policies".[46] Following this approach, direct and indirect disciplining channels are equally relevant.

A third, more radical, approach denies the aptness of financial markets to discipline banks managers. Particularly, Admati and Hellwig argue that the discipline of short-term debt in banking is "little more than a myth".[47] Following their claim for high equity-capital requirements as the only credible method to enhance systemic resilience,[48] these authors contrast the narrative according to which debtholders can discipline the behaviour of bank management. On the contrary, they explain the reliance on short-term debt as an equity avoidance strategy, seeking a government subsidy on debt.

The prevalence of any of these approaches in the policy debate has shaped the regulatory approach to market discipline. Since the effectiveness of the market discipline, as well as its efficiency, highly depends on the incumbent regulatory framework, it is useful to briefly examine the regulatory context where market discipline operated in the last decades.

[43] Erlend Nier and Ursel Baumann, 'Market Discipline, Disclosure and Moral Hazard in Banking' (2006) 15 Journal of Financial Intermediation 332.

[44] Bliss (n 22).

[45] Mark J Flannery, 'The Faces of "Market Discipline"' (2001) 20 Journal of Financial Services Research 107.

[46] Lane (n 1) 56.

[47] Anat R Admati and others, 'Fallacies, Irrelevant Facts, and Myths in the Discussion of Capital Regulation: Why Bank Equity Is Not Socially Expensive' (2013) 23.

[48] Anat Admati and Martin Hellwig, *The Bankers' New Clothes: What's Wrong with Banking and What to Do about It* (Princeton University Press 2014).

The deregulatory wave of the 80s and 90s and the increasing academic attention to market discipline in the banking sector marked its first cornerstone in the regulatory landscape with the Basel II Accords. Following Calomiris[49] and Meyer,[50] the Basel Committee for Banking Supervision issued a consultative paper on capital adequacy stating that: "supervisors have a strong interest in facilitating effective market discipline as a lever to strengthen the safety and soundness of the banking system".[51] Afterwards, market discipline was structurally embedded as a Pillar, together with minimum capital requirements and supervisory review of capital adequacy, of the prudential regulation in the final version of Basel II Accords.[52] In the end, the channel through which the Pillar III rules aimed at strengthening market discipline was through regulation about transparency and disclosure of information. This testifies that, especially in the early 2000s, the substitutability approach won over the others.

In the aftermath of the financial crisis, the new version of the Basel Accords has maintained the overall regulatory framework. However, the role of the supervisor has increased, and the regulation became stricter, leaning towards the complementary approach. Indeed, despite the academic and regulatory desiderata, market discipline mechanisms massively failed both in the period leading up to and during the financial crisis. In particular, it failed to detect and prevent the build-up of systemic risk during good times, relying too much on the information provided by Credit Rating Agencies (CRAs) and Credit Default Swaps (CDSs).[53] On the contrary, during the crisis, disciplining mechanisms functioned even too much, tightening the credit sources for risky institutions, with adverse repercussions in the overall market confidence.[54] The required haircut for short-term secured funding, such as repos, represents a paradigmatic case in this regard. Haircuts remained negligible until the

[49] Calomiris (n 41).

[50] Laurence H Meyer, 'Market Discipline as a Complement to Bank Supervision and Regulation', *Speech before the Conference on Reforming Bank Capital Standards, Council on Foreign Relations, New York, June* (1999).

[51] BCBS (n 1).

[52] Jose A Lopez, 'Disclosure as a Supervisory Tool: Pillar 3 of Basel II' (Federal Reserve Bank of San Francisco 2003) 22.

[53] Constantinos Stephanou, 'Rethinking Market Discipline in Banking: Lessons from the Financial Crisis' (2010) 5227 11.

[54] Ibid. 9.

beginning of the financial crisis and skyrocketed as it began, failing to constrain the excessive risk-taking in good times and impeding market participants to access funding at reasonable conditions once liquidity dried up.[55] In other words, markets played an ex-post role which was neither informative nor disciplining. The effects were not in line with the ultimate goal of preserving banks' solvency ex-ante, and the market did not act as a gatekeeper of financial stability.

In the aftermath of the financial crisis, the framework in which market discipline operates has changed. The Green Paper on Corporate Governance in financial institutions and remuneration policies, issued by the EU Commission,[56] focuses on a market-based approach to corporate governance, highlighting the role of monitoring both from shareholders and debtholders. Moreover, the reforms focused not only on providing the (allegedly) efficient quantity and quality of information, as it is under Pillar III rules but also on incentivising creditors to exert market influence. In this same vein, the Financial Stability Board, in its Key Attributes for Effective Resolution,[57] states that an effective resolution regime should "be credible, and thereby enhance Market Discipline and provide incentives for market-based solutions". The EU legal implementation of the Key Attributes and the legal rules affecting market discipline represent, therefore, the next building block of the analysis.

In line with the approach advocated by Admati and Hellwig, this chapter—and more generally the whole book—argues that short-term debt discipline is a myth; and when imposed can be even dangerous. However, expanding Admati and Hellwig's approach, the disciplining effects of long-term, bail-inable creditors carry more potential.

[55] Gary Gorton and Andrew Metrick, 'Securitized Banking and the Run on Repo' (2012) 104 Journal of Financial economics 425. For a more sophisticated setting where the perverse incentives provided by bankruptcy remoteness to short-term secured creditors is taken into account, see Rafael Matta and Enrico C Perotti, 'Insecure Debt' (Centre for Economic Policy Research 2015) No. 1050.

[56] European Commission, 'Corporate Governance in Financial Institutions and Remuneration Policies'.

[57] Financial Stability Board, 'Principles on Loss-Absorbing and Recapitalisation Capacity of G-SIBs in Resolution—Total Loss Absorbency Capacity' (2011).

3 Market Discipline and the Resolution Framework

Since the first draft of the BRRD came out,[58] many authors have criticised it because of its excessive complexity and lack of clarity.[59] Nevertheless, the European Legislator, even without directly addressing the issue, made a point crystal-clear: in the new regulatory environment the channel for creditors to discipline banks' behaviour has to be through bail-inable securities.[60] This view is opposed to the narrative about short-term debt discipline that was mainstream in the early 2000s.[61]

Thus, before analysing the role of bail-inable creditors in disciplining their borrowers, it is worth describing the rationale and the main rules on resolution procedures in the BRRD (Sect. 3.1) and the specific rules governing the position of creditors (Sect. 3.2).

3.1 A Glance at Resolution and Bail-In

The Bank Recovery and Resolution Directive entered into force in its entirety on the 1st of January 2016. Its main goals are, generally speaking, twofold: to protect taxpayers' money by limiting the too-big-to-fail problem and to harmonise bankruptcy procedure for financial institutions throughout the European Union.

The first goal is not a European peculiarity.[62] Back in January 2010, presenting the Dodd-Frank Act, President Obama affirmed: "Never again

[58] While writing this chapter a proposal for reforming the BRRD is pending. In this piece, the current version of the BRRD is solely considered insofar as the fact that the proposed modifications do not hamper, and maybe even reinforce, the argument proposed. The text of the proposal for the so-called BRRD2 can be retrieved at https://data.consilium.europa.eu/doc/document/ST-6290-2019-INIT/en/pdf.

[59] Emilios Avgouleas and Charles Goodhart, 'Critical Reflections on Bank Bail-Ins' (2015) 1 Journal of Financial Regulation 3. For an analysis of the implementation of the first resolution cases in Italy and the relevant decision-making mechanisms, see Lorenzo Stanghellini, 'The Implementation of the BRRD in Italy and Its First Test: Policy Implications' (2016) 2 Journal of Financial Regulation 154.

[60] Flannery and Bliss (n 20).

[61] Thomas M Eisenbach, 'Rollover Risk as Market Discipline: A Two-Sided Inefficiency' (2017) 126 Journal of Financial Economics 252.

[62] Peter Sester, 'Towards a Transnational Bank Restructuring Law-The Attempt of G20 to Initiative and Monitor Regulatory Responses to the Too Big To Fail Problem' (2010) 7 ECFR 512.

will the American taxpayer be held hostage by a bank that is too big to fail".[63] One year later, the Financial Stability Board issued the Key Attributes for Effective Resolution,[64] stating in its preamble that: "An effective Resolution regime should [...] not rely on public solvency support and not create an expectation that such support will be available".

On the one hand, the BRRD represents, to a certain extent, the European implementation of the Key Attributes.[65] Indeed, consistently with the Financial Stability Board viewpoint, it immediately states that: "The objective of a credible recovery and resolution framework is to obviate the need for such action [bailouts] to the greatest extent possible".[66]

On the other hand, the goal of harmonising resolution procedure is European-specific and aimed at addressing the severe problem faced in resolving cross-border banks during the financial crisis.[67] The lack of a common toolkit caused delays and inefficiencies in handling failing cross-border banks, such as the cases of Fortis and Dexia.[68]

The cornerstone of the BRRD is that bank insiders ought to bear losses arising from bank distress, at least at first, shifting the paradigm from bailout to bail-in.[69] This is in line with the Burden-Sharing rule imposed by the European Commission in the Banking Communication in 2013,

[63] On the too-big-to-fail problem and its legal implication in the European context see Rolef de Weijs, 'Too Big to Fail as a Game of Chicken with the State: What Insolvency Law Theory Has to Say about TBTF and Vice Versa' (2013) 14 European Business Organization Law Review 201.

[64] Financial Stability Board, 'Key Attributes of Effective Resolution Regimes for Financial Institutions' (2011).

[65] Peter G Brierley, 'Ending Too-Big-To-Fail: Progress Since the Crisis, the Importance of Loss-Absorbing Capacity and the UK Approach to Resolution' (2017) 18 European Business Organization Law Review 457.

[66] Recital 1 BRRD.

[67] Jens-Hinrich Binder, 'Cross-Border Coordination of Bank Resolution in the EU: All Problems Resolved?', *Research Handbook on Cross-Border Bank Resolution* (Edward Elgar Publishing 2019).

[68] M Cihak and Erlend Nier, 'The Need for Special Resolution Regimes for Financial Institutions-The Case of the European Union' [2012] Harv. Bus. L. Rev 395. The necessity to avoid fragmentation and establish a common framework for bank insolvency was highlighted, unsuccessfully, also before the financial crisis. See, in particular, Eva HG Hüpkes, 'Insolvency—Why a Special Regime for Banks?', *Current developments in monetary and financial law, Vol. 3* (International Monetary Fund 2002).

[69] Paul Calello and Wilson Ervin, 'From Bailout to Bail-In' 30 *The Economist* (2010); Jeffrey N Gordon and Wolf-Georg Ringe, 'Bank Resolution in the European Banking

according to which aids to failing banks comply with the EU State Aid framework only if the investors in bank capital bear part of the losses.[70]

The BRRD provides the resolution authority with four main tools to implement resolution: the sale of business tool,[71] the bridge-bank tool,[72] the asset separation tool,[73] and the bail-in tool.[74] The bail-in tool represents the archetype of the new resolution framework[75] as it provides the resolution authority to write down or convert into equity some part of the banks' liabilities to set off the losses and restore regulatory capital.[76] To assure that resolution is at any time possible, the Resolution Authority has the power to determine a tailor-made Minimum Requirement for Own Funds and Eligible Liabilities (MREL) to be held by any individual bank at any time.[77]

Union: A Transatlantic Perspective on What It Would Take' (2015) 115 Colum. L. Rev. 1297.

[70] Communication from the Commission on the application, from 1 August 2013, of State aid rules to support measures in favour of banks in the context of the financial crisis ('Banking Communication'). 2013/C 216/01.

[71] Article 38 BRRD.

[72] Article 40 BRRD.

[73] Article 42 BRRD.

[74] Article 43 BRRD.

[75] Avgouleas and Goodhart (n 58); Wolf-Georg Ringe, 'Bank Bail-In between Liquidity and Solvency' (2016) 92 Am. Bankr. LJ 299. For a recent assessment of bail-in shortcoming, see Christos Hadjiemmanuil, 'Bail-in's Unfulfilled Promise' (2025) 26 European Business Organization Law Review 89. For a far-fetched proposal of reform, see Urs B Lendermann, 'Automated Bail-in: Eliminating Regulatory Restraints' [2025] Journal of Banking Regulation.

[76] Karl-Philipp Wojcik, 'Bail-in in the Banking Union' (2016) 53 Common Market Law Review 91, 107. Ibid. 113. For deeper details on eligible liabilities and the application of the bail-in see Sect. 3. The power to write down and convert capital instrument can be used also outside resolution pursuant to Article 63 BRRD, yet liabilities that are not part of regulatory capital can suffer losses through write down of principal amount and/or conversion only in resolution.

[77] Wojcik (n 75) 113. On the problems specific to MREL design and calibration see Tröger (n 9). On the differences between MREL and the Total Loss Absorbency Capacity (TLAC) mandated by the FSB to the Globally Systemic Institutions see Ashley Lee, 'TLAC Conundrums' (2015) 34 Int'l Fin. L. Rev. 17; Tom Young, 'Why TLAC and BRRD Discrepancies Will Fade' [2015] Int'l Fin. L. Rev. The MREL regime was modified in 2019 to align it with TLAC requirements. For an analysis of the legislative updates, see Edoardo D Martino and Katarzyna M Parchimowicz, 'Go Preventive or Go Home–the Double Nature of MREL' (2021) 18 European Company and Financial Law Review 608.

A resolution procedure begins when the competent authority designates a bank to be "failing or likely to fail".[78] Moreover, there should be no reasonable prospect of alternative private solutions and, the resolution authority shall deem the resolution to be in the public interest.[79]

The Resolution Authority has no absolute power on the implementation of the resolution procedure. Indeed, it has to pursue the specific resolution objectives set out in Article 31(2). Namely, the Resolution Authority must have regard to (1) ensure the continuity of critical functions; (2) avoid adverse effects on the financial system; (3) preserve market discipline; (4) protect public funds and protect insured depositors. Importantly, the Directive states that the resolution objectives are of equal significance and should be balanced as deemed appropriate.[80] Intuitively, balancing broad objectives that might be even competing one another can create significant implementation issues.

If the Resolution Authority decides to apply the bail-in tool,[81] the Authority has to calculate the amount of liabilities that must bear losses.[82] Such an assessment needs to follow the preliminary valuation of assets and liabilities carried out pursuing Article 36. The amount of bailed-in liabilities should be enough to cover all the losses and restore the level of required capital.[83]

After such a determination, Articles 47 and 48 determine the loss-absorbing waterfall: first, the shareholders bear the losses; subsequently, other creditors can suffer losses if capital instruments have a lower value than the one calculated pursuant to Article 46. The creditors suffer

[78] Article 32(1)(a) BRRD. For more details, see the guidelines of European Banking Authority. EBA, 'Guidelines on the Interpretation of the Different Circumstances When an Institution Shall Be Considered as Failing or Likely to Fail under Article 32(6) of Directive 2014/59/EU. EBA/GL/2015/07' (2015).

[79] Article 32(5) BRRD. See Jens-Hinrich Binder, 'Proportionality at the Resolution Stage: Calibration of Resolution Measures and the Public Interest Test' [2019] European Business Organization Law Review 1. The public interest test proved to be crucial in the cases involving Banca Popolare di Vicenza, Veneto Banca and ABLV. The non-confidential material on these cases is available at https://srb.europa.eu/en/content/banca-popolare-di-vicenza-veneto-banca (accessed on 30/09/2025).

[80] Article 31(3) BRRD.

[81] The proceeding of the argument would be functionally identical for other resolution tools.

[82] Article 31(2) BRRD.

[83] Article 46 BRRD. See Wojcik (n 75) 110.

losses in accordance with the seniority of their claim as provided by the national insolvency laws. The expected outcome of the procedure is to make the institution, which was "failing or likely to fail", viable again.[84] Furthermore, Articles 73–75 BRRD provide for ex-post safeguards for the claimholders involved in the resolution process.[85]

3.2 A New Channel for Market Discipline (?)

Over time, the increasing awareness of the peculiar nature of banking firms made it clear that depositors were unable to monitor and discipline their banks and had to be fully insured.[86] In the same way, trying to impose market discipline through other types of creditors turned out to be unsatisfactory and, sometimes, disruptive.

What conceptually is closer to bail-inable securities, in terms of loss-absorbing capacity,[87] are Subordinated Notes and Debentures (i.e., subordinated debt). Indeed, these kinds of securities were widely employed in studying market discipline in the banking sector after 2000.[88] Nonetheless, the category of subordinated debt differs from

[84] It is possible, and likely, that the bail-in tool is used together with other resolution tools (Articles 38–42) so that the resulting bank is not the same legal entity that entered in resolution. Nonetheless, the outcomes are functionally identical.

[85] Wojcik (n 75) 122.

[86] A clear and spectacular example of the need for full deposit insurance is the Northern Rock run, back in 2007; the first physical bank run since the collapse of City of Glasgow Bank in 1878. At that point in time, the UK deposit insurance scheme was covering only the 90% of the deposited amount, on the assumption that depositors would have monitored more and better having some skin in the game. On this issue see extensively Dalvinder Singh and John Raymond LaBrosse, 'Northern Rock, Depositors and Deposit Insurance Coverage: Some Critical Reflections' (2010) 2010 Journal of Business Law 55.

[87] This expression is here used *ante litteram*, as the concept arose in the regulatory arena after the financial crisis, see Financial Stability Board (n 63). Loss-absorbing capacity indicates the ability of capital and debt instruments of a bank to absorb losses. Therefore, that is conceptually correct even for the pre-crisis environment.

[88] See, for instance, Sironi (n 21). A review of the empirical literature on the disciplining effect of debt yields is provided by Flannery and Bliss (n 20) 11. Reading through this review makes clear how a clear-cut empirical answer is far from being reached, since the evidences are mixed and highly depend on the design and assumptions of each model. There are also few preliminary empirical studies on market discipline and bail-inable securities, see, with different designs and slightly different results Fabrizio Crespi, Emanuela Giacomini and Danilo V Mascia, 'Bail-in Rules and the Pricing of Italian Bank Bonds' (2018) 25 European Financial Management 1321; Jannic Alexander Cutura, 'Debt Holder

bail-inable securities as for the nature and origin of their markets. Subordinated bonds are an entrepreneurial invention based on legal provisions. Bail-inable securities reverse this paradigm. The regulator, through law, builds on corporate finance practices and generates a new class of securities. Therefore, the market for bail-inable securities is primarily meant to serve the interests of the regulator.

The Legal Theory of Finance, and its main building blocks, provides a suitable theoretical background.[89] Financial markets are a rule-bound system made up of a network of enforceable contractual obligations linking the market participants. The network is inherently hierarchical, meaning that the distance from the apex, where political power and discretion play a major role, is different. In times of crisis, the closer a contractual obligation is to the apex, the higher the ex-ante probability that stability consideration will lead to a relaxation of those obligations.[90]

Within this framework, the BRRD can be seen as an attempt to move the crisis management of banks towards the periphery of the financial system, thereby decreasing the discretion of governments and central banks in terms of timing and methods to address failing institutions. On the contrary, the path of bail-inable securities followed the opposite direction: from a peripheral contractually regulated market,[91] the BRRD has imposed rules governing these kinds of instruments and granted the power to resolution authorities to "relax" contractual obligation in times of crisis.[92]

To sum up, the market for bail-inable securities originates from legal provisions and is tailored to a specific goal—i.e., making distressed banks

Monitoring and Implicit Guarantees: Did the BRRD Improve Market Discipline?' (SAFE 2018) 232.

[89] Pistor (n 38) 321. The Legal Theory of Finance has been successfully used as a framework to assess the European Banking Union and, specifically, the resolution framework. See, for instance, Biljana Biljanovska, 'Aligning Market Discipline and Financial Stability: A More Gradual Shift from Contingent Convertible Capital to Bail-in Measures' (2016) 17 European Business Organization Law Review 105.

[90] What Pistor calls "elasticity of the law". Pistor (n 38) 320.

[91] The enforcement of contractual obligation "imposing" MD in distressed banks had been a problematic issue in term of systemic stability during the crisis, as pointed out by Stephanou (n 52) 9.

[92] Ansgar Walther and Lucy White, 'Rules versus Discretion in Bank Resolution' (2019) CERP Discussion Paper 14048.

resolvable.[93] The primary channel, at least chronologically, to address banking crises is the "Private Sector Involvement", meaning that when resolution is triggered (some of) the private creditors of the distressed bank bear the losses.[94] This should allow for sufficient recapitalisation of the bank, avoiding any public intervention.

Therefore, the payoff matrix of the regulator/supervisor should be—theoretically—aligned with the payoff matrix of the bail-inable debtholders, so that the theoretical assumption discussed in Sect. 2 should hold.[95] This, in turn, would facilitate the alignment of bank insiders with the public interest, through market discipline channels. The necessary condition to trigger resolution is that the institution is "failing or likely to fail".[96] This means that the holders of bail-inable securities will suffer losses once the institution crosses this threshold. Thence, this latter instance is what both supervisors/regulators and debtholders should strive, ex-ante, to avoid.

Given these regulatory expectations, one would expect the related rules to be consistently in line with providing bail-inable creditors with suitable incentives to engage in monitoring and allowing long-term investors to appreciate the risk profile of the instruments and behave accordingly. Nonetheless, the interplay between multiple policy goals pursued hampers the possibility to provide bail-inable creditors with optimal incentives. In particular, the protection of property rights of creditors and the preservation of financial stability necessitates norms that deviate from the market discipline objective.

[93] Bail-inable debt can be seen as a class of securities, which is in turn made up of subclasses according to the seniority of individual securities. Nonetheless, it is highly doubtful that bail-inable creditors can be treated as a class, i.e., interests are not homogeneous and therefore behaviours can be highly divergent. For the purpose of this study, as it aims to assess the reliability of regulator's *desiderata*, the homogeneity of creditors is assumed as the regulator does.

[94] Christos Hadjiemmanuil, 'Bank Stakeholders' Mandatory Contribution to Resolution Financing: Principle and Ambiguities of Bail-In', *ECB Legal Conference 2015—From Monetary Union to Banking Union, on the way to Capital Markets Union* (2015).

[95] Bliss (n 22).

[96] Article 32(1)(a) BRRD.

4 The Market for Bail-Inable Securities and Its Rules

The BRRD shapes the market for bail-inable securities. Therefore, the analysis of the relevant provisions provides a good perspective on its functioning mechanisms and the resulting incentives for bail-inable creditors. Two main aspects deserve specific attention. On the one hand, the BRRD rules can allocate a high degree of discretion to the supervisor or the resolution authority, generating ex-ante uncertainty for the investor. On the other hand, legal provisions may hinge on investors' incentives, even outside of any discretionary considerations. The two instances are often concurrent; still, disentangling them is crucial for explanatory purposes.

The relevant norms can be categorised into three broad groups.[97] The first group of norms defines the borders of the market for bail-inable securities (Sect. 4.1); the second states the principles on the bail-inable creditors' treatment (Sect. 4.2). These two groups set the baseline of the analysis. The third group of provisions, instead, squeezes overlapping policy goals into the analysis of the market for bail-inable securities. Those overlaps modifying creditors' incentives towards monitoring by shielding their claims from losses (Sect. 4.3).

4.1 The Scope of the Market

Article 44 (1) of the BRRD states that, in principle, all the liabilities of the institution are bail-inable, allowing resolution authorities to re-engineer the whole liability side of the bank's balance sheet.[98] Nevertheless, several exceptions and exemptions restrict the scope of application of the bail-in tool.

[97] One additional element of complication is the complex group structure of banks, making the allocation of losses opaque and complex to compute. For the sake of simplicity, this aspect is not part of the scope of the analysis of this chapter. See Ilya Kokorin, 'The Rise of "Group Solution" in Insolvency Law and Bank Resolution' (2021) 22 European Business Organization Law Review 781.

[98] Tröger (n 9) 16.

Article 44 (2) and (3) define the claims that are not to be written down or converted into equity if the resolution is triggered.[99] Specifically, Article 44 (2) legally exempts from bail-in some classes of liabilities. The rationale behind the exemption of certain liabilities is, unsurprisingly, to safeguard financial stability.[100] Hence, the law exempts the deposits covered by Deposit Guarantee Schemes, the short-term claims by other banks or backstop mechanisms and the secured claims.

Differently, Article 44 (3) lists the "exceptional" factual instances in which, once the resolution is triggered, the Resolution Authority can discretionally decide to exclude from the bail-in. The other cases of legal exemptions follow two additional rationales. On the one hand, the Directive aims to avoid de facto bailouts, i.e., the use of public money to recapitalise the distressed banks even through the bail-in mechanism. Therefore, the BRRD exempts liabilities arising from mandatory contribution to Deposit Guarantee Schemes (DGSs)[101] and Tax and Social Security Authorities. The Directive also exempts those liabilities whose very nature falls outside the resolution purposes, such as retail and employment-related liabilities. Additionally, the Resolution Authority retains the power not to bail-in, totally or partially, those liabilities necessary to ensure the continuity of critical functions (e.g., payment systems, IT infrastructure). The same goes for the liabilities whose bail-in might

[99] Anna Gardella, 'Bail-in and the Financing of Resolution within the SRM Framework' in Guido Ferrarini and Danny Busch (eds), *European Banking Union* (Oxford University Press Oxford, UK 2015) para 11; Wojcik (n 75) 109.

[100] Zhou and others (n 6) 13. On the specific EU case, see Jonathan Bauerschmidt, 'Financial Stability as the Objective of the Banking Union' (2020) 17 European Company and Financial Law Review 155.

[101] The public nature of the DGSs contributions have been questioned by the General Court of the European Union in the so-called "Tercas Case". In that case, the Commission prevented the Italian DGS, "Fondo Interbancario di Tutela dei Depositi ('the FITD')" from covering Tercas negative equity, claiming that it would result in a State Aid. The General Count annulled that decision, stating that the intervention of the FITD would have not resulted in State Aid; see Judgment of the General Court of 19 March 2019—Italy and Others v Commission (Joined Cases T-98/16, T 196/16 and T-198/16). Such case does not hamper, per se, the argument proposed above, since the contribution due to the DGSs is still exempted for the same ratio. Moreover, the outcome of the case is still uncertain, as the appeal is now pending in front of the ECJ. Finally, it is worth noting that the Italian case might not be prone to general application throughout all Member States. The FITD is *de jure a* private consortium, whereas the vast majority of other DSGs are public entities.

provoke the risk of contagion or run (e.g., SMEs deposits larger than the covered amount, as expressly stated in the Directive).

The BRRD allocates further discretion to the Resolution Authority which is entitled to exempt from bail-in on a case-by-case basis some classes of liabilities. Among them, it is worth mentioning the liabilities that are impossible to bail-in promptly or whose bail-in would provoke value destruction greater than in the scenario where they would not be bailed-in.[102]

Concerning deposits, in Articles 108 and 109, the Directive further specifies their special status. Indeed, Article 108 mandates that non-covered deposits eligible for bail-in[103] ought to be senior in comparison with unsecured, non-preferred claims.[104] Moreover, Article 109 holds the Deposit Guarantee Schemes liable for the number of covered deposits that would have been written down,[105] making them an additional player that should, theoretically, exert market discipline.[106]

Table 1 summarises the interplay between the resolution objectives, as stated in Article 31, and the rationales behind the provision of Article 44. The exemptions and exceptions of Article 44 directly serve the resolution objectives, as the match between the two is striking.

[102] Wolf-Georg Ringe and Jatine Patel, 'The Dark Side of Bank Resolution: Counterparty Risk through Bail-In' [2019] European Banking Institute Working Paper Series 2019—no. 31; Oxford Legal Studies Research Paper; Benjamin Bernard, Agostino Capponi and Joseph E Stiglitz, 'Bail-Ins and Bailouts: Incentives, Connectivity, and Systemic Stability' (2022) 130 Journal of Political Economy 1805.

[103] Those are deposits from natural persons and SMEs greater than 100.000 €, pursuing Article 6 of the Directive 2014/49/EU.

[104] Excluding eligible deposits, those are to be considered the most senior bail-in eligible liabilities.

[105] Article 108(b)(ii) ranks this liability as senior compared to any other eligible liability, including eligible deposits.

[106] Maria Nieto, 'Bank Resolution and Mutualization in the Euro Area' (2016) 2 European Economy, Banks, Regulation, and the Real Sector 138. The role of Deposit Guarantee Schemes in Resolution might sharply changed after the General Court of the European Union annulled a decision of the European Commission that forbid the Italian Deposit Guarantee to provide aid to Banca TERCAS, forcing it into liquidation. The decision, in the moment I am writing, has still to be published in the official journal, an unofficial version has been published in the form of press release on 19 March 2019 and can be retrieved at: https://curia.europa.eu/jcms/upload/docs/application/pdf/2019-03/cp190034en.pdf.

Table 1 Article 44 BRRD and the resolution objectives

	Resolution objectives (Article 31 BRRD)			
	Continuity of critical function	*Avoid adverse consequences*	*Protect public funds and deposits*	*Protect client funds and assets*
Safeguard financial stability	– Ensure the continuity of critical functions Article 44(3)(b)	– Original maturity less than 7 days Article 44(2)(e) and (f) – Secured claims Article 44(2)(b) – Avoid contagion and risk of run Article 44(3)(c)	– Covered deposits Article 44(2)(a)	
Avoid public subsidy			– Preferred claim of tax and social security authorities Article 44(2)(g) and (m)	
Other policy goals				– Clients assets and money Article 44(2)(c) – Fiduciary relationships Article 44(2)(d)
Implementation issues		– Practical impossibility Article 44(3)(a) – Avoid value destruction Article 44(3)(d)		

Only the exemptions of the liabilities towards employees can be considered exogenous to resolution objectives.[107] All the other cases are a direct application of the provision of Article 31.[108]

4.2 Creditor's Treatment in Resolution

The Article 34 BRRD lists the general principles governing resolution. The general principle is that shareholders shall bear first losses. Thereupon, the Directive tackles the status of bail-inable creditors, regulating their treatment under resolution in three different directions. First, the loss-absorbing waterfall (hierarchy principle); second, the treatment of creditors belonging to the same class (equitable treatment principle); third, the treatment of creditors in resolution a hypothetical normal insolvency proceeding (No-Creditors-Worse-off principle).[109]

According to the hierarchy principle, in resolution, any class of creditors must suffer losses according to the order of priority of their claim under normal insolvency procedures.[110] At the same time, within each class, creditors shall be treated in an equitable manner.[111] Even though the idea behind those two principles appears to be straightforward, their actual functioning is likely to generate more friction than expected because of the complexity of the legal issues tackled by the Directive.[112]

Article 48 disciplines the condition for moving from one class of holders to the following one.[113] A senior class can be bailed-in if and

[107] Art. 44(2)(g)(i) and (ii).

[108] For the purpose of the present analysis, i.e., assessing the impact of the BRRD on the functioning of External Governance mechanisms through market discipline, voting shares fall out of the scope of the analysis as well. Note that, there is no parallel between voting rights and capital class, as even CET1 instruments can be issues without voting rights attached to the capital ones, as expressly state by Article 32(4) Regulation (EU) 575/2013—CRR.

[109] No creditors worse-off, see Sect. 4.3.

[110] Article 34(1)(b) BRRD.

[111] Article 34(1)(f) BRRD.

[112] For a detailed analysis of the implementation issues in relation to national insolvency laws, see Lynette Janssen, 'Bail-In from an Insolvency Law Perspective' (2017) 26 Norton Journal of Bankruptcy Law and Practice.

[113] See Article 47(3) (b) and (c).

only if the bail-in of the previous class was insufficient to smooth out the losses and restore a sufficient level of regulatory capital.[114]

Nonetheless, the bail-in tool cannot be plainly applied only according to the level of loss absorbency. Indeed, for any of the rationales listed in Table 1, it can happen quite the opposite, as the dashed line in Fig. 1 aims at symbolising. For instance, imagine two liabilities A and B, belonging to the same class. When the resolution is triggered, the Resolution Authority appraises that is practically infeasible to promptly bail-in Liability A.[115] Therefore the authority writes-down or converts only Liability B, while Liability A suffers no losses. The same can happen even if Liability A is junior to Liability B. In the first case, where A and B belong to the same class, Articles 44 relaxes the Equitable Treatment principle. In the second case, where A is junior to B, Article 44 relaxes the Hierarchy principle.

As noted earlier, the exemptions and exceptions contemplated by Article 44 are closely tied to the objectives of resolution themselves, as stated in Article 31.[116] Therefore, in the practical implementation of

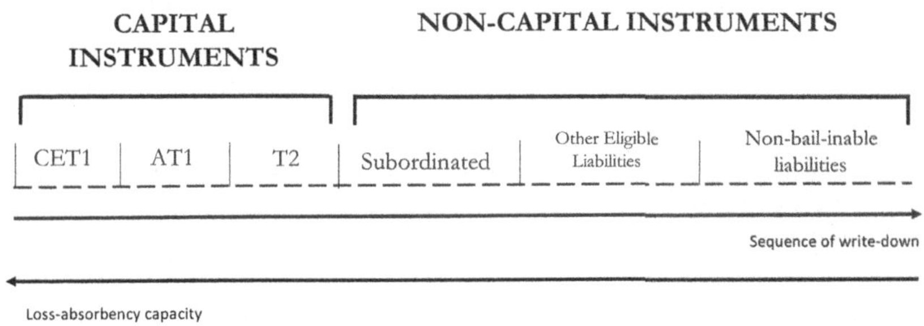

Fig. 1 Article 48 BRRD: Sequence of write down and conversion

[114] Pursuant the provisions about capital requirements embedded in the CRR-CRDIV package.

[115] Article 44(3)(a).

[116] The resolution objectives referred to in paragraph 1 are:

(a) to ensure the continuity of critical functions;
(b) to avoid a significant adverse effect on the financial system, in particular by preventing contagion, including to market infrastructures, and by maintaining market discipline;
(c) to protect public funds by minimising reliance on extraordinary public financial support;

the bail-in tool unequal treatment may become the rule rather than the exception.[117] This, in turn, decreases the predictability of the resolution outcome, impacting the incentives of the holders of bail-inable securities to monitor.[118]

4.3 The No-Creditor-Worse-Off (NCWO) Principle

The NCWO principle postulates that, within any resolution procedure, creditors cannot incur greater losses than those they would have incurred if the institution had been liquidated.[119] Accordingly, creditors who suffer greater losses are entitled to compensation equal to the shortfall they have suffered.[120] Intuitively, this rule impacts on the incentives of bail-inable creditors to discipline bankers. As noted by Professor Chiu: "no creditor worse off principle could also convince bail-inable debt holders that taking a back seat in monitoring would make no difference".[121]

Functionally, the NCWO principle mandates that investors in bail-inable securities have to be indifferent, between resolution and liquidation.[122] Nevertheless, this constraint is not enforced through an ex-ante

(d) to protect depositors covered by Directive 2014/49/EU and investors covered by Directive 97/9/EC;
(e) to protect client funds and client assets.

[117] Jens-Hinrich Binder, 'The Position of Creditors Under the BRRD', *Commemorative Volume in memory of Professor Dr. Leonidas Georgakopoulos* (Bank of Greece's Center for Culture, Research and Documentation 2016) 45.

[118] Tobias H Tröger, 'Too Complex to Work: A Critical Assessment of the Bail-in Tool under the European Bank Recovery and Resolution Regime' (2018) 4 Journal of Financial Regulation 35, 21.

[119] Article 34(1)(g) BRRD.

[120] VPG de Serière, 'No Creditor Worse Off in Case of Bank Resolution. Food for Litigation' (2016) 31 Journal of International Banking Law and Regulation 376, 376.

[121] Iris HY Chiu, 'Corporate Governance: The Missing Paradigm in the Mandatory Bail-in Regime for Creditors of Banks and Financial Institutions' [2014] Journal of business law 611, 627.

[122] This goes under the assumption of perfect compensation in case of detrimental treatment in the implementation of the resolution tool and of absence of judicial costs. See Binder, 'The Position of Creditors Under the BRRD' (n 115) 44.

property entitlement, but rather through an ex-post liability rule.[123] The BRRD allocates to the Resolution Authority the power to impact on the claim of bail-inable investors without granting them any procedural or substantive rights during resolution, as opposed to normal insolvency proceedings.[124] Therefore, the property rights embedded in the bailed-in claims cannot be protected through ex-ante rights preventing the Resolution Authority to cause unjustified harm to bail-inable debtholders. However, the Directive provides for ex-post protection through compensation in case of violation of the NCWO principle.[125]

The rationale is twofold and reflects the interplay between competing policy objectives. On the one hand, the Directive aimed to avoid obstacles to prompt resolution by waiving all the procedural rights that creditors have in normal bankruptcy procedures.[126] On the other hand, the NCWO represents a way to protect the creditors' rights through compensation so to respect the right to property.[127]

In a nutshell, NCWO principle should theoretically guarantee the protection of property rights so that creditors have no incentives to engage in disruptive runs in the proximity of resolution.[128] At the same

[123] Pursuing Guido Calabresi and A Douglas Melamed, 'Property Rules, Liability Rules, and Inalienability: One View of the Cathedral' [1972] Harvard law review 1089.

[124] See, for instance, Articles 38(1), 40(1), 42(1) and 85 BRRD.

[125] Those different approaches in protecting the entitlements of creditors fit the Calabresi and Melamed framework. The first approach, where creditors can prevent the Resolution Authority to impose excessive losses, is a property rule: "An entitlement is protected by a property rule to the extent that someone who wishes to remove the entitlement from its holder must buy it from him in a voluntary transaction in which the value of the entitlement is agreed upon by the seller". Calabresi and Melamed (n 121) 192. On the contrary, the NCWO rule, where creditors are only entitled to an ex-post compensation for the breach of their property entitlements is a liability rule. "Whenever someone may destroy the initial entitlement if he is willing to pay an objectively determined value for it, an entitlement is protected by a liability rule". Ibid. 192.

[126] On the ontological difference between bank resolution and insolvency law see Hadjiemmanuil (2015, p. 232).

[127] Wojcik (n 75) 116. On the compatibility of burden-sharing exercise in bank distress with the right to property the ECJ delivered a preliminary ruling for a Slovenian Case, in which European Judges deemed that the right to property can be interpreted as not precluding burden sharing of losses. See Case C-526/14 *Tadej and Others v Državni zbor Republike Slovenije* [2016]. For a more extensive legal reasoning on the point, see the opinion of Advocate General Wahl, delivered on 18 February 2016 on the same case.

[128] Ibid. 120.

time, it provides resolution authorities with some degree of flexibility to promptly implement a resolution.[129]

Indeed, the salient aspect of the NCWO legal design is that the European Legislator has not provided any procedural rights to bailed-in creditors, as opposed to normal insolvency procedures. This allows for the speeding up the resolution process, which represents a crucial aspect of the success of any bank resolution.

As previously mentioned, the maximum amount of losses that investors can bear is equal to the amount of losses that they would have borne in case of liquidation. This can be seen as a safety net for the Resolution Authority,[130] allowing it to promptly implement any resolution leaving any other order of consideration, as creditors' treatment, to an ex-post valuation. Nevertheless, this design poses considerable legal challenges, so that many commentators doubt whether this tool can deliver the desired goal.[131]

In applying the bail-in tool, the Resolution Authority has to adhere to the valuation of assets and liabilities carried out ex Article 36.[132] Such a procedure consists of a fair, prudent, and realistic valuation carried out by a person independent from any public authority before the Resolution Authority takes any resolution action. The Authority can carry out a provisional evaluation following a simplified procedure if, as it is likely to be, the urgency of the situation does not allow to perform the independent valuation.[133]

Article 36(8) requires the independent expert to include in the valuation an estimate of the treatment that each class of creditors would have been expected to receive under normal insolvency procedure.[134] Therefore, in applying the bail-in tool, the Resolution Authority ex-ante complies with the general principle of NCWO by adhering to the preliminary valuation of the counterfactual insolvency scenario.

[129] Thomas Huertas, 'European Bank Resolution: Making It Work!' (2016).

[130] Zhou and others (n 6).

[131] Gardella (n 97); George Jacobs and David Mitchell, 'The No-Creditor-Worse-Off Principle from a Valuation Perspective: Standing in the Shoes of a Hypothetical Liquidator' (2014) 28 Journal of International Banking and Financial Law 233.

[132] Article 46(1) BRRD.

[133] Article 36(2) and (9).

[134] The same paragraph clarifies that such an estimate "shall not affect the application of the 'no creditor worse off' principle to be carried out under Article 74".

Nevertheless, given the opaqueness and complexity of banks' assets and liabilities and considering the large array of material impediments that the resolution process can face, it is possible and likely that the ex-ante valuation differs from the real value of bank's assets and liabilities.[135]

After the resolution has taken place, an independent expert must carry out an ex-post valuation.[136] Ex-post safeguards counterbalance the lack of ex-ante procedural rights. Article 75 states that, after the ex-post valuation, worse-off creditors have the right to compensation.[137] The resolution financing arrangements must pay out these compensations.

From a functional perspective, the NCWO represents an (uncertain)[138] ceiling to expected losses that creditors might have suffered in a hypothetical world where resolution does not exist. This means that NCWO also impacts on ex-ante incentives towards monitoring: it caps the level of expected losses. Therefore, the incentives to monitor are altered.

The NCWO can become an impediment to resolvability of distressed banks mainly through three legal channels.[139] First, the application of exclusions and exemptions provided by Article 44(2) and (3) of the Directive. By definition, exemptions and exclusions generate a mismatch between the treatment of the other creditors under resolution and under insolvency.[140]

[135] Martin F Hellwig, 'Valuation Reports in the Context of Banking Resolution: What Are the Challenges?' (2018) 2018/06.

[136] Article 74 BRRD.

[137] The same applies to DGSs in the case of Article 109(2).

[138] To make it certain, one should assume that the preliminary valuation exactly matches the final valuation ex Article 74 BRRD and that investors have ex-ante information about the preliminary valuation. On the assumptions necessary for a smooth functioning of the bail-in mechanisms see Sect. 4.

[139] For detailed examples on how each of these channels can result in impediments to resolvability because of the NCWO principle see the Appendix.

[140] For the interaction of Article 44 and NCWO principle see Hadjiemmanuil (2015, p. 236 and ff.). For a concrete application of the NCWO principle to the exclusion from bail-in of liabilities covered by netting arrangements, see Geoffrey Davies and Marc Dobler, 'Bank Resolution and Safeguarding the Creditors Left Behind' (2011) 51 Bank of England. Quarterly Bulletin 213.

Second, aspects related to bankruptcy law may come into play.[141] For instance, consider the case, massively discussed in the literature, of contractual or statutory clawback provisions on executives' remuneration.[142] In a nutshell, the competent authority can require the restitution of bonuses and performance-related components of the remuneration packages in case of managerial misconduct. Especially in idiosyncratic crises, the case for managerial misconduct is likely to materialise. In this case, the (potentially non-trivial) amount of money recovered from the clawback would enrich the amount of assets devoted to creditors under normal insolvency procedure.

Third, theoretically eligible liabilities may not be bailed-in for cross-jurisdictional issues.[143] The Article 55 BRRD foresees this problem and mandates the issuers of bail-inable liabilities to include a contractual clause for third-country recognition of the power of Resolution Authorities to bail them in, third-country investors, as well as third-country authorities, are not prone to accept such clauses.[144]

[141] Clawback is a term used in bankruptcy law to indicate any repayment, to receivers of a company in bankruptcy, any preference payments, or monies deemed to have bene ted one party at the expense of others during the period of financial distress. Functionally is a way to attract further assets for distribution to the mass of creditors under the condition that those assets were not meant to be allocated elsewhere in the first place because of bankruptcy norms. In this situation, the party whose assets are clawed back becomes a creditor ranked as it would have been if the unlawful repayment would have never happened. It is worth noting clawbacks can be bank specific. See J Hill, 'Regulating Executive Remuneration after the Global Financial Crisis: Common Law Perspectives' [2012] Research Handbook on Executive Pay 219.

[142] As the one introduced in Section 304 of the Sarbanes–Oxley act in the U.S., on which see Rachael E Schwartz, 'The Clawback Provision of Sarbanes–Oxley: An Underutilized Incentive to Keep the Corporate House Clean' [2008] The Business Lawyer 1. Another typical case is the clawback of executive remuneration, see Johanna Stark, 'Clawback Provisions in Executive Compensation Contracts' (2021) 18 European Company and Financial Law Review 669.

[143] Matthias Lehmann, 'Bail-in and Private International Law: How to Make Bank Resolution Measures Effective across Borders' (2017) 66 International & Comparative Law Quarterly 107.

[144] This obstacle to resolvability has been directly acknowledged by the European Commission Explanatory memorandum to the proposal for amending Article 55—Proposal for a DIRECTIVE OF THE EUROPEAN PARLIAMENT AND OF THE COUNCIL amending Directive 2014/59/EU on loss-absorbing and recapitalization capacity of credit institutions and investment firms, 23 November 2016—COM (2016) 852 final.

All these cases show, along with many studies,[145] that determining the counterfactual scenario under liquidation is to say the very least, doubtful and will result in long-lasting and costly litigation.[146] It is, nonetheless, unclear how courts are going to decide these cases. Namely, the extent to which courts will, implicitly or explicitly, consider the recovery rates in similar cases. For example, the anecdotal evidence of Lehman Brothers[147] shows that NCWO could become extremely burdensome to the resolution financing arrangements. The senior creditors of Lehman Brothers' German and UK subsidiaries recovered 100% of their exposure.[148]

So far, the only application of a resolution procedure at European level, the Banco Popular case,[149] somehow confirmed the fear that the NCWO principle can act as a disincentive towards monitoring ex-ante given the expectation of ex-post safeguards. Several cases were litigated in front of the European Court of Justice challenging the decision of the Single Resolution Board.[150] Many of those sought for compensation for the breach of the NCWO safeguard.[151]

[145] See, for instance, Chris Bates and Simon Gleeson, 'Legal Aspects of Bank Bail-Ins' (2011) 5 Law and Financial Markets Review 264; Hadjiemmanuil (n 94).

[146] De Serière (n 118). For an analysis of the judicial review process in the Banco Popular case, see Marco Lamandini and David Ramos Muñoz, 'Bank Resolution and Judicial Review: Lessons of the Banco Popular Litigation' [2025] European Business Organization Law Review.

[147] Michael J Fleming, Asani Sarkar and others, 'The Failure Resolution of Lehman Brothers' [2013] Economic Policy Review 175.

[148] Jens-Hinrich Binder, 'The Banking Union and the Governance of Credit Institutions: A Legal Perspective' (2015) 16 European Business Organization Law Review 467.

[149] Isabel Fernández Acín, 'Caso Banco Popular (Banco Popular Case)' (2018) <https://papers.ssrn.com/sol3/papers.cfm?abstract_id=3132293>.

[150] The decision and other relevant disclosed material can be retrieved at https://srb.europa.eu/en/node/315.

[151] See, for instance, the Case T-570/17, Algebris (UK) and Others v Commission, still pending in front of the ECJ where the plaintiff claim: the valuation of Banco Popular, which formed the basis for the resolution action taken under the Resolution Scheme, was not fair, prudent or reliable, and was inconsistent with the 'no creditor worse off principle'; it did not therefore constitute accurate and reliable and consistent evidence on which to base the Resolution Scheme; and it was not capable of supporting the contested decision. Further and for the same reasons, the Resolution Scheme (and so the Decision) was manifestly disproportionate by going beyond the measures necessary to secure the resolution objectives.

4.4 *The Residual Possibility of Granting Public Funds in Resolution*

In line with the burden-sharing policy imposed by the Banking Communication in 2013,[152] the Directive conditions any public support[153] to distressed institutions to a minimum amount of Private Sector Involvement.[154] Accordingly, Article 37(10)(a) sets the amount of burden-sharing at the 8% of total liabilities (including own funds), measured following the valuation of Article 36.[155] Indeed, it is unlikely that the bail-in tool will ever be able to do the whole work on itself. Therefore, the Banking Communication in 2013 and, eventually, the BRRD tried to strike a balance between the instances of financial stability, competition in the banking sector and safeguard of public finances.

Furthermore, Article 44 (4) and (5) refer to the possibility of granting public funds when the losses that should have been born by excluded liabilities cannot be passed fully on other creditors. Again, the Directive conditions this possibility to the 8% burden-sharing requirement.[156] This represents a way to deal with insufficient eligible funds. Under Article 44, the presence of "very extraordinary situation of a systemic crisis" is not required for granting public aid.

From the perspective of bail-inable creditors, assuming a consistent application of the Directive, those provisions increase the expectations that creditors will some public relief if and only if their claim is senior to at

[152] Communication from the Commission on the application, from 1 August 2013, of State aid rules to support measures in favour of banks in the context of the financial crisis ("Banking Communication") (2013/C 216/01).

[153] In the forms provided by Articles 56–58 BRRD.

[154] Christos Hadjiemmanuil, 'Limits on State-Funded Bailouts in the EU Bank Resolution Regime' [2016] European Economy 91.

[155] For a detailed analysis of the changes in the proposed CMDI reform, see Ioannis G Asimakopoulos and Tobias H Tröger, 'Reform of the CMDI Framework—Driving Off With the Brakes On' (2025) 21 European Company and Financial Law Review 53.

[156] Article 44(8) contemplates a situation in which even the 8% contribution is waived, subject to a series of conditions among which the contribution of at least 20% of Risk Weighted assets (RWA) and assets below 900 billion EUR on a consolidated basis. Those requirements mean that this further flexibility in granting public funds is reserved to non-systemically relevant institutions with high quality assets.

least 8% of bail-inable eligible liabilities.[157] The way this instance impacts on investor's incentives is clear: junior claimers have, on paper, full skin in the game so that they should have optimal incentives to monitor banks' behaviours.

Nonetheless, the resolution procedure may move away from the 8% requirement in some cases of public intervention. For instance, this is the case of precautionary recapitalisation[158] and liquidation aid.[159] In these cases, public funds can directly or indirectly cover the losses that should have been allocated to the private sector according to the bail-in rule.

In particular, precautionary recapitalisation allows for direct injection of capital "necessary to address capital shortfall established in the national, Union, or SSM-wide stress tests".[160] The measure can be applied only to solvent institutions and is conditional on the approval under EU State Aid framework.[161] In this case, the burden-sharing according to the Banking Communication of 2013 still requires the mandatory involvement of private sector actors, but the involvement can be lower than the 8% threshold to have clearance under State Aid law.

So far, the fourth-largest Italian bank, MontePaschi Spa, in 2017 applied for and obtained a precautionary recapitalisation.[162] The Italian government injected 5.4 billion euro of capital and guaranteed 15 billion

[157] This outcome consists in the combination of Article 37(10), Article 34(1)(b) about the Hierarchy Principle, and 44(2) and (3) exemptions and exception in applying the bail-in tool.

[158] For a critical analysis of precautionary recapitalization in practice, see Edoardo D Martino and Andrea Perini, 'Rescued Banks Back to the Market?' (2025) 22 European Company and Financial Law Review 267.

[159] This is a peculiar contingency that materialises in the case of Veneto Banks and will be discussed in Sect. 5.3.

[160] Article 32(4)(d) BRRD.

[161] Marco Bodellini, 'Greek and Italian "Lessons" on Bank Restructuring: Is Precautionary Recapitalisation the Way Forward?' (2017) 19 Cambridge Yearbook of European Legal Studies 144.

[162] Precautionary recapitalization is one of the options currently on the table also to deal with the distress of Banca Carige Group. See Cristina S Dias and Jerome J Deslandes, 'Recent Measures for Banca Carige from a BRRD and State Aid Perspective' (2019) PE 624.413.

of subordinated debt.[163] In the decision of the European Commission on State Aid,[164] the Commission approved the recapitalisation acknowledging the burden-sharing happened in the form of a swap between subordinated debt and ordinary shares.[165] The decision states that: "there is sufficient burden-sharing by shareholders and also subordinated debt holders".[166] Therefore, creditors below the 8% threshold can expect to be at least partially shielded by public interventions via precautionary recapitalisation of solvent but distressed banks.[167]

[163] Martin Götz, Jan Pieter Krahnen and Tobias Tröger, 'Taking Bail-in Seriously: The Looming Risks for Banking Policy in the Rescue of Monte Paschi Di Siena' (SAFE Policy Letter 2017).

[164] European Commission, C (2017) 4690 final. State Aid SA.47677 (2017/N)—Italy New aid and amended restructuring plan of Banca Monte dei Paschi di Siena. Retrievable at http://ec.europa.eu/competition/state_aid/cases/270037/270037_1951496_149_2.pdf.

[165] European Commission, C (2017) 4690 final, paragraph 17(iv): "In the specific case of MPS, burden sharing is implemented by means of a conversion of subordinated debt instruments in ordinary shares at pre-defined conversion rates. Out of 11 issuances subject to conversion, one is converted at a rate of 18% of the nominal value (a Floating Rate Equity-linked Subordinated Hybrid or "FRESH"), three at a rate of 75% of the nominal value (Tier 1 issuances) and seven at a rate of 100% of the nominal value (Tier 2 issuances)".

[166] Paragraph 103.

[167] In all the Italian cases, there are several problems of ex-post restitutions to retail investors in case of mis-selling. See Filippo Fiordiponti, 'Le Aspettative Restitutorie Di Azionisti e Creditori Ai Tempi Del Bail-In' (2016) 15 Analisi Giuridica dell'Economia 527; Raffaele Lener, 'Profili Problematici Delle Nuove Regole Europee Sulla Gestione Delle Crisi Bancarie' (2018) 37 Banca Impresa Società 13. The application of precautionary recapitalization tool is critically discussed in Nicolas Véron, 'Precautionary Recapitalisation: Time for a Review?' (Bruegel 2017) 21. For similar cases related to Ireland, see Elise Lefeuvre, 'The Strategic Importance of Public Recapitalisation in Banking Resolution, What Ireland Can Tell' (2024) 21 European Company and Financial Law Review 104.

5 Market Discipline and Effort in Monitoring in an Ideal Environment

What prevents market discipline from effectively working is twofold. In the first place, the implicit guarantee is still in place, given the impracticability of the resolution framework.[168] Moreover, even assuming that resolution is always applied and delivers efficient outcomes, scholars have argued that the high level of ex-ante unpredictability of the resolution process would endanger the ability of investors to discipline the risk-taking behaviours of their borrowers.[169]

As discussed in Sect. 4, I test the hypothesis that the BRRD's legal design inherently dilutes the incentives towards monitoring regardless of complexity and uncertainty. To test this hypothesis, this section builds an ideal environment where the exogenous impediments to resolution are ruled out by assumption, so as to assess the impact of the legal design in itself. This allows us to introduce and explain the basic incentive structure to monitor provided by the Directive's legal design. Eventually, Sect. 5.2 introduces the NCWO principle and the 8% rule, discussing how these dilute the investors' incentives to monitor.

5.1 The Ideal Resolution Environment

A smooth and credible resolution is what the EU financial regulator dreams of. In more hopeful words, the medium-term objective to be pursued. For the sake of this analysis, I assume that this holds true. To this end, two general assumptions are necessary.

(a) smooth functioning of the resolution procedure, i.e., bail-in is always and consistently applied in case of bank distress[170];
(b) smooth functioning of the market for bail-inable securities, i.e., investors are able to screen and monitor the risk-taking behaviours of the bank and adjust the price accordingly.

[168] Many problematic instances have been arisen from this perspective. The most discussed and serious one is the inability of resolution to deal with systemic crises.

[169] Tröger (n 116).

[170] This broad assumption is made up of several narrower ones discussed in the literature. See, for instance, Avgouleas and Goodhart (n 58); Bernard, Capponi, and Stiglitz (n 100).

The latter assumption can be further disentangled into further assumptions necessary for (b) to hold. Namely: (1) the bail-in commitment is ex-ante credible[171]; (2) the market for bail-inable securities is liquid, and a secondary market exists so as to continuously monitor the risk profile of the bank's behaviours[172]; (3) investors have perfect information in determining the outcome of the application of the rules disciplining the market of bail-inable securities; (4) the supervisory and the resolution authorities exercise their discretionary powers consistently so that investors can anticipate the outcome of the resolution procedure; (5) bail-inable creditors have homogeneous interests; hence, they can be treated as a class; (6) the Minimum Amount for Own Fund and Eligible Liabilities (MREL) is adequate, and the banks comply with it.[173]

Given these assumptions, a (fully rational) investor faces the rules discussed so far and responds accordingly. That is to say, as long as the return on their investment is subject to the viability of their borrower, investors will take every efficient action to maintain such viability. Investors will undertake those actions as long as the marginal cost of exerting monitoring is lower than the marginal benefit investors' gains, in expected terms.

Indeed, monitoring is not a costless activity since gathering and computing relevant information about the risk profile and sustainability of the borrowing bank involves activities that come at a cost, e.g., employing a team of analysts to take the investment decision and to determine the investor's willingness to pay for bail-inable securities.

Within this framework, the bank is entering in resolution with an attached probability known by assumption. Investors decide, accordingly, the level of effort in monitoring that maximises their return. Indeed, the assumptions assure that the investors can impact on the probability of the bank entering in resolution.

[171] This is the direct consequence of point (a); for a setting in which bail-in commitments are credible see Bernard, Capponi and Stiglitz (n 100).

[172] If such a secondary market does not exist, a further assumption has to be taken; namely, the risk profile of each security is stable over time, so that once it has been priced and sold in the primary market the disciplining activity is concluded. On the dynamic nature of the risk profile of bail-inable securities see Tröger (n 116) 36.

[173] Mathias Dewatripont, 'European Banking: Bailout, Bail-in and State Aid Control' (2014) 34 International journal of industrial organization 37.

The level of effort crucially depends on the costs and benefits of monitoring. The critical aspect is the amount of losses, in expected terms, investors are going to suffer in case of resolution (i.e., the bank reaches the point of non-viability).

The investor aims to minimise expected losses; accordingly, she faces actual costs for engaging in monitoring activities (e.g., conveying information). Conversely, the benefits stemming from exerting monitoring activities consists of the decrease in the probability of entering in resolution.

In this framework, each creditor engages in monitoring as long as benefits (i.e., reduction in expected losses consequent to the reduction in resolution probability) outweigh the costs (i.e., costs to exert monitoring). Throughout the analysis, the cost of monitoring will be stable so that the level of discipline that is efficient for investors varies according to the benefits stemming from monitoring.

To substantiate this construct, think of Investor "*i*" who faces a loss of 100 in case of resolution. The probability of resolution, which is here known by assumption, is 10%. Expected losses are 10 in this scenario. The investor knows, by assumption, that exerting monitoring activities that cost 2 would discipline bank managers, driving down the probability of resolution decrease to 7.5%. Expected losses are now 7.5 so that it is efficient for the investor to engage in monitoring. The investor can also put more effort into their monitoring, decreasing the probability of resolution to 6.5% for a cost of 4. In this case, the Investor will decide not to engage in costlier monitoring. The cost of monitoring plus the expected losses the investor still faces amount to 10.5 and outweigh the expected losses with no monitoring (10).

The underlying criterion to carry out the analysis is to understand what and who shield creditors from bearing losses. According to this criterion, the rules shaping the incentive structure of investors can be divided into two categories: (i) "contractual shielding" mechanisms; (ii) "external shielding" mechanisms. The first category of provisions encompasses all the rules clarifying the contractual entitlements of bail-inable debtholder, such as the hierarchy and the equitable treatment principles. In contrast, the NCWO rule and the 8% rule belong to the second category as they do not directly pertain to the contractual entitlement of the bondholder but rather to the pursuit of other regulatory goals.

The rules on "contractual shielding" represent the baseline scenario. The hierarchy and equitable treatment principles describe how losses are allocated, shaping the basic incentive structure of bail-inable creditors and pertaining to their contractual entitlement. For instance, the contractual entitlement of an investor in senior unsecured bonds shields her from losses by investors in subordinated debt. In the same vein, the contractual entitlements of two investors in senior unsecured debt treat those in an equitable manner.

Figure 2 depicts the baseline scenario where the resolution works smoothly and the probability of resolution to be triggered depends on the level of monitoring. The y-axis represents the amount of expected losses; while, the x-axis represents the liability side of the bank balance sheet, ordered according to the seniority of each class.

The expected losses are decreasing in seniority and are stable within each class, complying with hierarchy and equitable treatment principles. In this scenario, the seniority (Hierarchy principle) of bail-inable creditors guides the allocation of expected losses. Losses are constant within each class of creditors (Equitable Treatment principle).

Specifically, the Hierarchy principle, from the investor's perspective, means that the higher the seniority of a claim is, the lower the expected

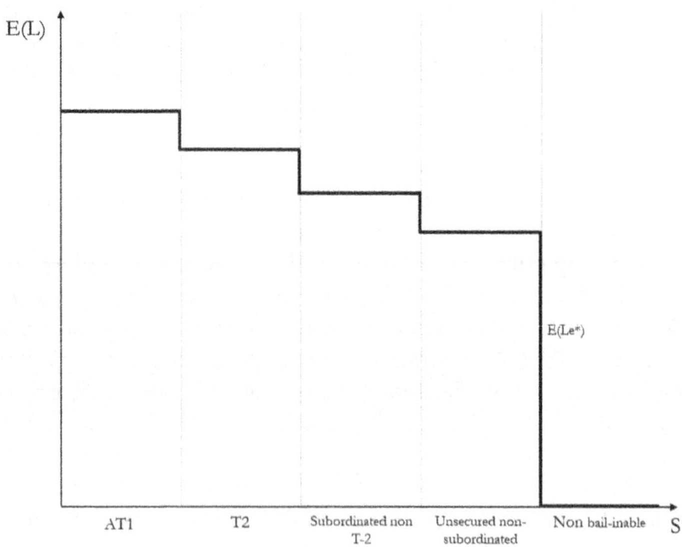

Fig. 2 Basic incentive structure of bail-inable creditors

losses are. Therefore, the optimal level of effort in monitoring is lower for senior unsecured creditors than for subordinated ones. The Equitable Treatment principle implies that expected losses are not decreasing linearly, but in a staggered way so that the level of expected losses is constant for the creditors with the same seniority.

The assumptions allow us not to consider, at this stage of the analysis, the impact of the exemptions and exclusions of Article 44(2) and (3). Investors who know in advance which liabilities fall under those provisions embed the information in their behaviours. The consequences of such an instance are twofold: on the one hand, the creditors that will be excluded or exempted will exert no monitoring.[174] On the other hand, the exemption/exclusions do not directly affect investors' incentives, but only the level of expected losses.[175]

If the heroic assumptions stated at the beginning of this section holds, private incentives of single investors are aligned with social welfare, at least from a microprudential perspective. Investors engage in monitoring as long as the magnitude to which expected losses decrease outweigh the cost of monitoring. This means that creditors' monitoring minimises the probability of resolution.

5.2 *External Shielding and Effort in Monitoring*

If a regulator was daydreaming, she would dream of the baseline scenario depicted in Fig. 2: distressed bank internally recapitalised in a going-concern without adverse spillovers. No credibility issues, information asymmetries nor any other external factors that can threaten such a dreamlike environment.

Nonetheless, the dreamlike resolution can easily turn into a nightmare even without opting out of the assumptions designed in Sect. 5.1. It suffices to embed the rules stemming from competing policy goals. In pursuing these competing goals, the Directive provides for "external

[174] The counter-intuitive consequence of this stream of argumentation is that, in the real-world scenario, a non-trivial level of uncertainty in this respect increases the ex-ante incentives to monitor of at least this part of creditors.

[175] This means that, if—for instance—junior creditors are expected to be exempted, the expected losses for senior creditors are going to be higher, increasing the Marginal Benefit of exerting monitoring.

shielding" mechanisms for creditors which alters the incentive structure and result in inherent dilution of incentives towards monitoring.

To understand how the NCWO rule 8% rule alters the baseline scenario, it is important to focus on the structural difference between "contractual shielding" and "external shielding". The former implies that investors whose claim have different seniority will exert different levels of discipline.[176] The latter implies that investors, despite their seniority, can reduce their exposure in case of resolution via external mechanisms (i.e., the counterfactual liquidation scenario and the State intervention).

To appreciate the fundamental difference between the two categories of rules considered, think of the simple numerical example described in Sect. 5.1. When only "contractual shielding" rules are in place (the baseline scenario), the investor is facing losses in case of resolution and can influence the probability of resolution if she exerts costly monitoring.

If "external shielding" rules play a role, the situation might dramatically change. For instance, the investor may expect to recover 25% of their exposure under normal liquidation because of any of the external shielding mechanisms discussed in Sect. 4.3. Now, the investor expects to bear losses for 75 in resolution and if the probability of resolution is 10%, the expected losses are 7.5. The investor still has to choose whether to engage in costly monitoring (cost of 2) to decrease the probability of resolution from 10% to 7.5%. Now, given the non-contractual expectation of being shielded, exerting monitoring is not rational for the investor. Monitoring costs 2 and the benefit from monitoring is the difference between expected losses with and without monitoring (7.5 – 5.6 = 1.9). It is worth noting that whether the NCWO actually applies is irrelevant, as what is relevant is the reasonable expectation of being partly shielded via NCWO.[177] This represents a step forward as compared with previous analysis and adds to the understanding of market discipline in the context of bank resolution.[178]

[176] For a formal explanation of how debt contracts shield creditors by allocating to them control rights upon specific contingencies, see Philippe Aghion and Patrick Bolton, 'An Incomplete Contracts Approach to Financial Contracting' (1992) 59 The review of economic Studies 473.

[177] This can happen both ex-ante, when applying the resolution tool, or ex-post through compensation ex Article 75.

[178] As compared, for instance, to Tröger (n 116).

The Impact of the No-Creditor-Worse-Off Principle

The NCWO principle imposes that resolution has to consist of a welfare-neutral procedure from the creditors' perspective.[179] This was deemed necessary to protect the investors' property rights, so to comply with their constitutional rights.[180] From the eye of the investors, this means that, despite the level of expected losses stemming from the resolution procedure, they cannot bear actual losses greater than in the insolvency counterfactual scenario. Therefore, they can foresee to be shielded by this external mechanism.

In turn, this affects the incentives of the investors towards monitoring. The counterfactual insolvency scenario artificially shields investors from losses.[181]

The basic incentive structure showed that investors would be able to re-calculate the expected losses they are going to incur, under the assumption that investors know ex-ante which liabilities will be exempted and excluded from the bail-in procedure. Nevertheless, those exemptions/exclusions hinge upon investors' incentives through the NCWO principle, since they increase the spread between the investors' treatment under resolution and in the alternative insolvency scenario.[182]

In Fig. 3, the NCWO conceptualisation is added to the basic incentive structure: the dashed line represents an example of such a conceptualisation, thus representing the level of losses in the alternative liquidation scenario. This calibration considers a parsimonious scenario, as both AT1 and T2 instruments are assumed to bear full losses in the counterfactual

[179] Diego Valiante, 'Harmonising Insolvency Laws in the Euro Area' (2016) 153.

[180] In their legal understanding, as enucleated by Article 1 of the 1st protocol to the ECHR: "*Every natural or legal person is entitled to the peaceful enjoyment of his possessions. No one shall be deprived of his possessions except in the public interest and subject to the conditions provided for by law and by the general principles of international law*". See Case C-526/14 *Tadej Kotnik and Others v Državni zbor Republike Slovenije* [2016].

[181] As Sect. 4.3 discussed, the impact of the NCWO principle can derive from different channels, some of which are endogenous to resolution; namely the exemptions/exclusion of Article 44. To an extent, the same argument goes for theoretically eligible securities, which are issue under a third country who is not accepting the contractual recognition ex Article 55. On the other hand, there are instances where NCWO can play a role, such as ex-post clawback, which cannot be anticipated at all even assuming ex-ante perfect information.

[182] In the cases in which exemptions/exclusions would be treated differently under the two scenarios. This is, for instance, the case of Article 44(3)(a) [practical impossibility to implement the bail-in].

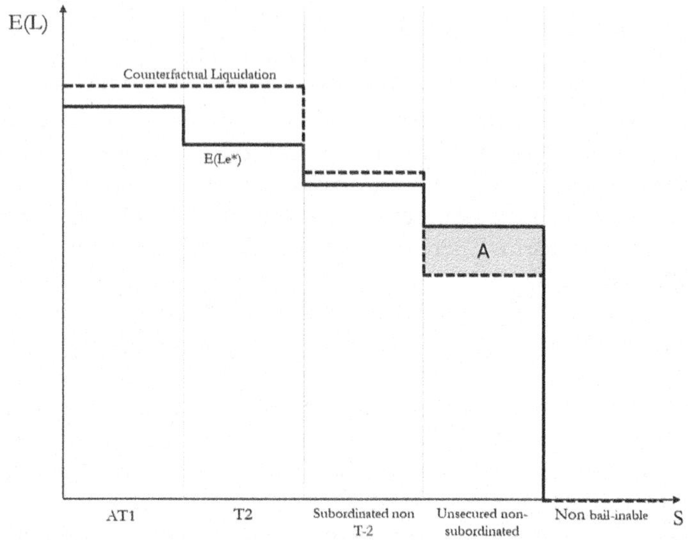

Fig. 3 Incentive structure of bail-inable creditors when the NCWO principle is in place

insolvency scenario. It is worth noting that if the dashed line (NCWO) intercepts the solid line, the expected losses are capped, consequently diluting incentives to monitor. This is exemplified by the grey area "A" in the Figure.

In conclusion, the NCWO can dilute incentives by way of capping losses creditors can incur in resolution. The channel through which this can concretely happen consist of the rules applied in resolution whose spillovers affect the counterfactual insolvency scenario.

The Impact of the 8% Threshold

The BRRD did not eradicate the governmental guarantee on banks' solvency once and for all. Indeed, as discussed back in Sect. 4.4, the BRRD itself recognises the possibility of using public funds during resolution to prevent spillovers. Thus, even in the ideal setting plotted here, it is reasonable to expect public interventions once there has been an 8% contribution of insiders.

From the investors' perspective, this exogenously impacts their payoff structure, altering the level of losses they expect to bear. For instance, if the claim of Investor A has seniority above the threshold of 8% of total liabilities (including own funds), he can reasonably expect to be, at least partially, shielded by public intervention.

For such a process to happen, the assumption of a smooth market for bail-inable securities needs to be specified. In particular, the investors need to have complete information about whether their claim is junior or senior to the 8% of eligible liabilities out of the total amount of liabilities. This has two implications: first, the investors need complete information on the capital structure of their borrower; second, they also need complete information about exemptions/exclusion of liabilities according to Article 44 and their impact in reaching the 8% threshold.

Figure 4 graphically depicts the situation. For the sake of simplicity, we assume that the 8% threshold falls at the end of T2 instruments. As expressed before, the expectation to be shielded by public intervention lowers the expected losses. Hence, the graph highlights a discontinuity between the expected losses in the basic scenario (vertical line) and the resulting incentives in the case of public intervention. The grey areas "A" and "B" represent the incentive dilution corresponding to the public shielding of senior investors.

To sum up, the flexibilities embedded in the BRRD generate a discontinuity in the investors' incentive structure lying above or below the threshold of 8% of eligible liabilities out of total liabilities. Indeed, creditors above such a threshold can reasonably expect to be bailed-out. Moreover, considering the precautionary recapitalisation detailed in Sect. 4.4, the threshold required for burden-sharing can be lower than 8%. Therefore, more investors expect the shielding effect of public intervention, worsening the ex-ante incentives towards monitoring.

Finally, in terms of the effect of both NCWO rule and the state intervention rules, the expected result is to lower the sensitivity of interest rates to the actual risk profile of the borrower, decreasing the level of discipline imposed on managers' behaviours. Overall, both the rules lower the expected losses of investors so that the return on investment (interest rate) required diminishes.[183]

[183] It is important to notice that this does not mean that the cost of funding for the bank has not increased after the BRRD entered into force, but that such an increase is not tightly linked with the behaviour of the individual bank, so that its discipline effect is limited.

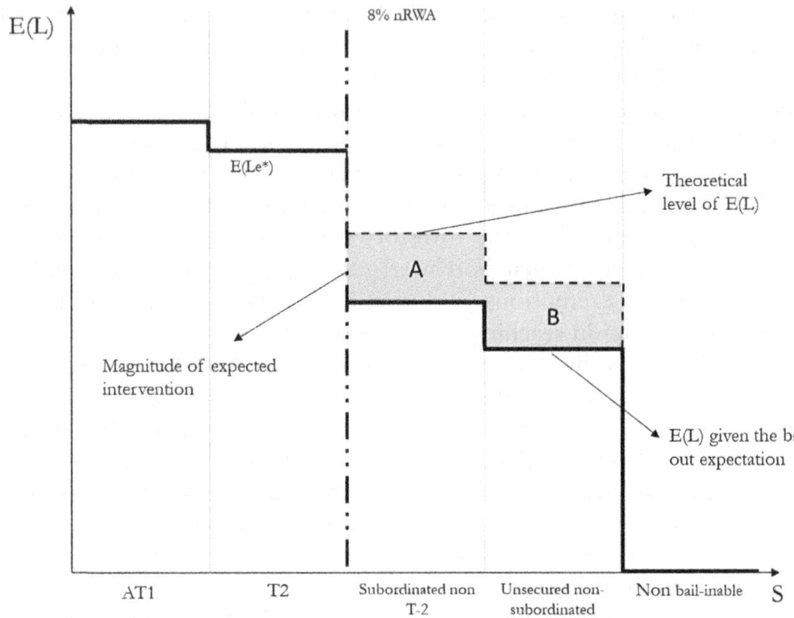

Fig. 4 Incentive structure of bail-inable creditors when the 8% threshold is in place

5.3 *A Reality Check*

Even though it is not possible to evaluate all the cases of resolution in light of the theory proposed so far, it is crucial to provide at least some anecdotal evidence showing the inability and/or unwillingness of investors to discount future losses. Some cases, such as the resolution of Banco Popular and the precautionary recapitalisation of Monte Paschi Bank, have already been briefly analysed and support my findings.[184]

[184] A wider review of resolution cases can be found in World Bank, *Understanding Bank Recovery and Resolution Directive in EU: A Guideline to the BRRD* (Word Bank 2016); T Philippon and A Salord, 'Bail-Ins and Bank Resolution in Europe: A Progress Report. Geneva Reports on the World Economy Special Report 4' [2017] International Center for Monetary and Banking Studies (ICMB), Geneva (Switzerland). For an up to date analysis of cases, see Marco Ventoruzzo and Giulio Sandrelli, 'O Tell Me the Truth About Bail-In: Theory and Practice' (2019) 13 The Journal of Business, Entrepreneurship & the Law 187.

On the Banco Popular case, several cases of violation of the NCWO rule are raised both in front of the ECJ and the SRM Board of Appeal.[185] This hints at the fact that investors relied on the NCWO protection, or that at least they opportunistically tried to get some ex-post compensation.[186] All the cases were dismissed, which can hopefully provide guidance to limit strategic litigation in future cases. On the MontePaschi Bank case, the Italian State stepped in before resolution after shareholders and junior creditors borne some losses outside resolution, in the form of share dilution and debt swap.[187]

The investors in Contingent Convertible instruments issued by Deutsche Bank[188] provided a further paradigmatic case of the inability of investors to ex-ante discount future losses in pricing their instruments.[189] Deutsche Bank reported losses for the fiscal year 2015 and, once the news became public, the price of the shares fell, eroding the capital position of the bank and coming close to breaching the so-called "combined buffer requirement".[190] According to the existing regulation, if the capital ratio of a (still solvent) bank breaches such "combined buffer requirements" distributions on Contingent Convertible instrument (i.e., payment of the 6% coupon) can be cancelled, so that the investors somehow bear the costs

[185] See, for instance Case T-570/17, Algebris (UK) and Others v Commission. Among other pleas, the claimants argue that the NCWO rule was breached in the resolution decision.

[186] In line with the argument proposed by de Serière (n 118).

[187] See European Commission, C (2017) 4690 final. State Aid SA.47677 (2017/N)—Italy New aid and amended restructuring plan of Banca Monte dei Paschi di Siena. Retrievable at http://ec.europa.eu/competition/state_aid/cases/270037/270037_1951496_149_2.pdf.

[188] Contingent Convertible instruments (CoCos) are bail-inable instruments that are also part of regulatory capital. In this case, they were part of Additional Tier 1 capital pursuing Article 51 and 54 of the Capital Requirement Regulation (CRR).

[189] An extensive description and analysis of the case can be found in Paul Glasserman and Enrico Perotti, 'The Unconvertible CoCo Bonds' in Douglas D Evanoff and others (eds), *Achieving Financial Stability: Challenges to Prudential Regulation*, vol 61 (World Scientific 2017).

[190] Articles 131 and 141 of the Capital Requirement Directive (CRDIV). The Combined Buffer Requirements consists in normal minimum capital requirements (Article 92 CRR), institution specific additional capital requirements (Article 97 CRD IV) and additional buffers (Articles 131 and ff. CRD IV).

of early distress. This is in line with the new philosophy underpinning the resolution framework, i.e., private sector involvement.[191]

The market panic that stemmed from the fear of missing a coupon testifies that investors did not internalise the probability of future losses on their investment. The price of the instrument dropped, losing almost 30% of their value in one month and recovering only after the regulator intervened exploiting a legal loophole for allowing lawful distribution of the coupon in 2016.[192]

Skipping the payment of a coupon is a mild way of bearing losses as opposed to a fully fledged bail-in or a going-concern conversion. However, market participants were unable to discount such a possibility in pricing the instruments and only reacted retrospectively once the problem materialised. One would expect an efficient market discipline regime to work precisely in the opposite direction. This, anecdotally, confirms the soundness of the findings of the qualitative model developed in the previous sections.

6 Conclusion

This chapter has tackled the long-lasting debates on the ability of creditors to discipline banks' behaviours from the perspective of the post-crisis stream of reforms and the alleged alignment between the interests of bail-inable debtholders and of regulators/supervisors.

The rules shaping the market for bail-inable securities hinge upon features external to the status of investors under resolution, i.e., counterfactual insolvency situation and the possibility of granting public money to the bank. The analysis showed that the overall outcome of these rules dilutes the incentives to monitor banks' risk-taking behaviour. This is

[191] For more information about the underlying legal mechanisms and the ambiguities existing in the EU law and supervisory practices, see B Mesnard and M Magnus, 'What to Do with Profits When Banks Are Undercapitalized: Maximum Distributable Amount, CoCo Bonds and Volatile Markets' [2016] European Parliament (Briefing, PE 574.399) 1.

[192] The legal point was the stacking order of Pillar 2 requirements imposed by the supervisor. The new praxis is to differentiate between Pillar 2 requirements and Pillar 2 Guidance, where only the first is binding and counts for breaching the "combined buffer requirements". See, finally, EBA Guidelines on common procedures and methodologies for the supervisory review and evaluation process (SREP), EBA/GL/2014/13, 19 July 2018.

because investors rationally expect to be shielded from losses due to mechanisms beyond their contractual entitlements. The inherent dilution in incentive derives from the co-existence of a plurality of policy objectives.

"Maintaining market discipline"[193] and "minimising reliance on extraordinary public financial support" are expressly mentioned by Article 31(2) as resolution objectives. The protection of property rights is implicitly part of those objectives as it represents a pillar of the legal system, protected by national constitutions as well as at European level.[194] Even though the BRRD explicitly states that "the resolution objectives are of equal significance",[195] the actual legal design and the foreseeable resolution practice lean towards the primacy of investor and property protection considerations. In a nutshell, the co-existence and the interplay of multiple policy goals addressed by the BRRD impede the provision of bail-inable creditors with optimal incentives to monitor their borrower. Even though conflicting objectives in resolution have been heavily understudied, it seems unreasonable that an alternative design could fix the incentive dilution towards monitoring, allowing for the same level of flexibility and protection of property rights.

The enthusiasm for the disciplining capacity of the resolution framework appears to be misplaced, or at least overemphasised. Expecting bail-inable creditors to carry out an optimal level of monitoring and adjust the price of securities accordingly is little more than a dream. Neither theory nor current practices support such an expectation. Therefore, at least in the current regulatory framework, the effectiveness of resolution to improve bank corporate governance and hence help prevent future crises cannot solely rely on the disciplining capacity of bail-inable creditors through price adjustment.

[193] Even though this research made clear that the word "maintaining" associated to the concept of Market Discipline in the banking industry is, to say the least, misleading.

[194] As enshrined by Article 1, Protocol 1 of the European convention of Human Rights. Whether or not the NCWO is the apt mean to efficiently protect PRs falls beyond the scope of this research. On that see Tröger (n 9); Wojcik (n 75).

[195] Article 31(3) BRRD. An identical provision can be found in the SRMR, Article 14(3).

Appendix: A Stylised Application of the NCWO Principle

The principle of NCWO has been heavily criticised for its vagueness and complexity: beyond the appealing idea and the underlying rationales, it is difficult to grasp how it is supposed to concretely work. Therefore, building on the previous legal analysis, it is useful to provide some easy and simplified numerical examples. This allows for a better understanding of how the NCWO principle alters the incentive structures of investors. Moreover, this example shows that the NCWO is not just a theoretical safeguard, but it can have a concrete impact on the resolution process and investors in bail-inable securities.

"Bank A" in normal times own assets worth 100, wholly made up of loans. Bank A's funding consists of capital, two layers of debt and deposits (Fig. 5—Panel 1). For the sake of simplicity, we assume that the equity ratio (Total Assets/Equity) of Bank A is 8% of total assets and it matches the regulatory requirements.

Baseline scenario (Panels 3 and 4). An idiosyncratic shock happens and Bank A's loans now worth only 70, with a total amount of losses of 30 (Panel 2). Bank A is now failing, and The Resolution Authority decides to apply the bail-in tool to restore a net asset value equal to zero and sufficient capital, pursuing Article 46.

To cover the losses capital holders are completely wiped out. Junior creditors are, then, partly wiped out [22] so that losses are fully covered and partly converted into new equity [3]. Moreover, senior claims are partly converted into equity [3] to restore the appropriate level of regulatory capital (Panel 3). In this case, no creditor is worse-off, as in the counterfactual scenario of liquidation both depositors and senior creditors fully recover their investments and junior creditors have a recovery rate of 12%.[196] In such a situation NCWO has no impact on the resolution process and, hence, in investors' ex-ante incentives, as shown in Fig. 5.

Let us now consider two alternatives in which the scenario depicted so far is altered. The first alternative scenario implies that during the liquidation procedure liabilities are clawed back; the second considers the case in

[196] This goes under the assumption that the debt-equity swap follows the rate of conversion of 1:1. The amount of converted capital remains approximately the 8% of total assets.

(1) NORMAL TIMES			
ASSETS		LIABILITIES	
Loans	100	8	Capital
		25	Junior Debt
		17	Senior Debt
		50	Deposits
Total assets	100	100	Total Liabilities

(2) IDYOSINCRATIC SHOCK			
ASSETS		LIABILITIES	
Loans	70	8	Capital
		25	Junior Debt
		17	Senior Debt
		50	Deposits
		-30	Losses
Total assets	70	70	Total Liabilities

(3) APPLICATION OF BAIL-IN			
ASSETS		LIABILITIES	
Loans	70	6	Capital
			(converted 3 junion + 3 senior)
		14	Senior Debt
		50	Deposits
Total assets	70	70	Total Liabilities

(4) COUNTERFACTUAL LIQUIDATION			
ASSETS		LIABILITIES	
Loans	70	3	Junior debt
		17	Senior Debt
		50	Deposits
Total assets	70	70	Total Liabilities

(5) COUNTERFACTUAL LIQUIDATION WITH CLAWBACK			
ASSETS		LIABILITIES	
Loans	70	8	Junionr
Clawed back assets	5	17	Senior Debt
		50	Deposits
Total assets	75	75	Total Liabilities

(6) APPLICATION OF BAIL-IN TOOL WITH EXEMPTED CREDITORS			
ASSETS		LIABILITIES	
Loans	70	6	Capital
DGS contribution	1	15	Junior Debt (excluded)
		0	Senior
		50	Deposits
Total assets	71	71	Total Liabilities

Fig. 5 Application of NCWO to the stylised balance sheet of Bank A

which some of the liabilities are considered to be ineligible by the Resolution Authority, for any of the reasons provided by Article 44 (2) and (3). The main difference between those two scenarios is that in the first the assessment of the counterfactual liquidation changes, while in the second what changes is the bail-in outcome.

Clawback Scenario (Panel 5). During the liquidation procedure, the Court orders the clawback of capital whose value is 5. Imagine, for instance, that the directors unlawfully distributed dividends in a time of financial distress instead of increasing the bank's reserves. This alters the counterfactual liquidation scenario since the amount of distributable assets increases accordingly, and junior creditors recover a larger share of their investment, with a recovery rate of 32%. In this scenario, junior creditors are worse-off, as depicted in Panel 3. Figure 6 shows that junior creditors suffer higher losses under bail-in than under liquidation. Thus, they are entitled to compensation pursuant Article 75 BRRD.

Non-eligible liabilities scenario (Panel 6). For any of the reasons listed in Article 44 (2) and (3), the Resolution Authority decides that a fraction of junior debt [15] cannot be bailed-in. This can happen for a wide number of reasons. Imagine junior securities issued under the law of a third country that is not promptly bail-inable; or an even more compelling case in which the exempted junior liabilities are held by a distressed bank that cannot bear that kind of losses without becoming failing. In this situation, for covering the losses [30], both capital [8] and the part of eligible junior debts left [10] are wiped out. Moreover, a part of senior debt is wiped out as well [12] to cover the reaming losses and the other is converted into equity [5]. Finally, to restore the regulatory capital, the Deposit Guarantee Scheme has to step in and make a subrogated contribution ex Article 109(1)(a). In fact, there are no other eligible liabilities: thus, the Deposit Guarantee Scheme is liable for the amount by which covered deposits would have been written down.

Figure 8 shows that both junior and senior creditors suffer higher losses under bail-in than under liquidation. Thus, they are both entitled to compensation pursuant to Article 75 BRRD. Moreover, since covered depositors would have incurred losses, the Deposit Guarantee Scheme has to step in to bear them, meaning that the array of actors involved in the bail-in process is larger under these circumstances (Figs. 7 and 8).

Level of losses		
	Bail-in	Liquidation
Capital	100%	100%
Junior Debt*	88,00%	88,00%
Senior Debt*	0,00%	0,00%
Depositors	0,00%	0,00%

* Under the bail-in scenario, in determining the level of level of losses, we assume a 1:1 rate of conversion between equity and junior/senior debt

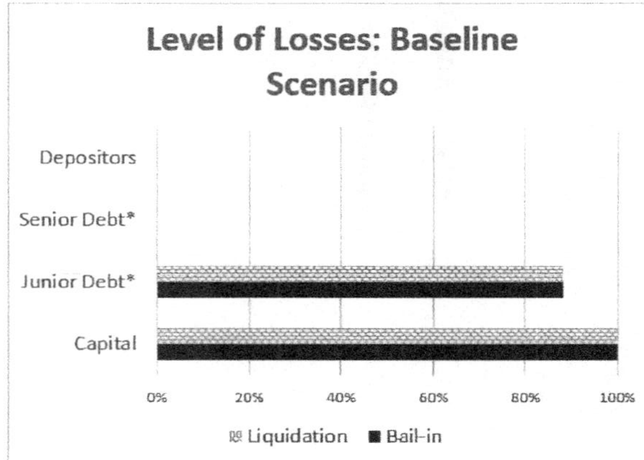

Fig. 6 Level of losses under bail-in and liquidation regime in the baseline scenario

Level of losses		
	Bail-in	Liquidation
Capital	100%	100%
Junior Debt	88,00%	68,00%
Senior Debt	0,00%	0,00%
Depositors	0,00%	0,00%

* Under the bail-in scenario, in determining the level of level of losses, we assume a 1:1 rate of conversion between equity and junior/senior debt

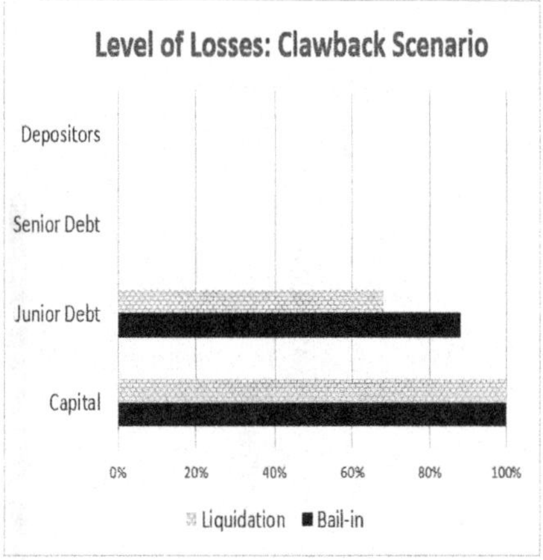

Fig. 7 Level of losses under bail-in and liquidation regime in the clawback scenario

Level of losses		
	Bail-in	Liquidation
Capital	100%	100%
(Eligible) Junior Debt	100,00%	88,00%
Senior Debt	70,50%	0,00%
Depositors (via DGS)	2,00%	0,00%

* Under the bail-in scenario, in determining the level of level of losses, we assume a 1:1 rate of conversion between equity and junior/senior debt.

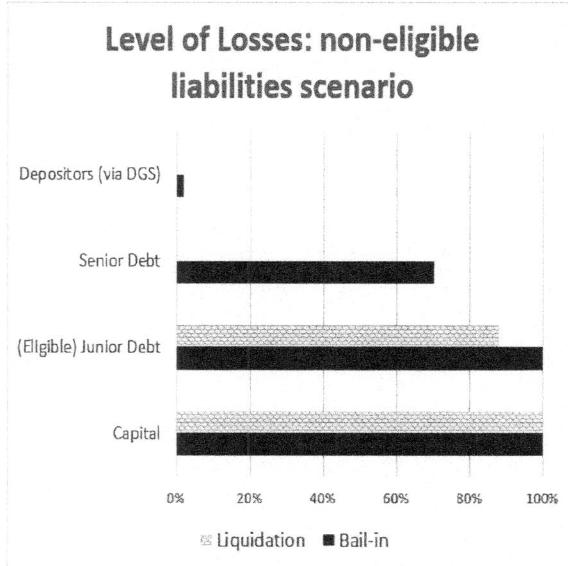

Fig. 8 Level of losses under bail-in and liquidation regime in the non-eligible liabilities scenario

CHAPTER 5

Financial Contracting in Bail-Inable Securities and Debt Governance

1 Introduction

Can investors discipline bankers through contracts? To address this question, it is important to go back to the fundamental features of bank governance, the resolution framework and its ex-ante potential.

Corporate governance failures and excessive risk-taking have often been blamed as two major drivers of the latest financial crisis.[1] These failures are ultimately rooted in the existing trade-off between financial stability policies and moral hazard.[2] The easiest exemplification of such a trade-off is the implicit guarantee of the State on the solvency of financial institutions, especially the "systemically relevant" ones, leading creditors not to exert appropriate monitoring and softening the budget constraints

This chapter heavily draws from Edoardo D Martino, 'Bail-Inable Securities and Financial Contracting: Can Contracts Discipline Bankers?' (2019) 10 European Journal of Risk Regulation 164.

[1] See, Jacques De Larosière and others, 'Report of the High-Level Group on Financial Supervision in the EU' [2009] European Commission. Brussels para 23.

[2] See William A Allen and Geoffrey Wood, 'Defining and Achieving Financial Stability' (2006) 2 Journal of Financial Stability 152, 160.

E. D. Martino, *EU Bank Governance and Bail-In*, EBI Studies in Banking and Capital Markets Law,
https://doi.org/10.1007/978-3-032-20699-2_5

of bank managers.[3] Many doubts surround the efficiency and effectiveness of the resolution regime.[4] The previous chapter highlighted the inherent limitation of the resolution regime to efficiently incentivise bail-inable creditors to monitor their borrowing bank and adjust price accordingly. In this chapter, we take a step forward, looking at the role of contracts.

As made clear by the analysis of previous chapters, the role of creditors in disciplining the risk appetite of banks results from the interplay between the governance channels and the financial structure of the bank, where the latter is a function of regulatory constraints. From this starting point, this chapter analyses financial contracting as a potential channel to discipline bankers. In other words, it aims to answer the following question: given the regulatory framework, can private solutions (i.e., contracts) provide adequate incentives towards optimal risk-taking?

This chapter fills a relevant gap in the literature on bank governance. The economic and financial literature extensively discussed contracts as

[3] For a wider discussion of the rationale and key principles underpinning the regulatory response after the financial crisis, see Chapter 3. It is here worth recalling that the financial crisis hit particularly hard on the EU Member States, and the existing regulatory framework was unprepared to face it. The EU has answered with a massive wave of reforms leading up to the European Banking Union, which was welcomed by Commissioner Barnier as "nothing less than a revolution: the most ambitious project since the creation of the euro". The recovery and resolution framework represents one of the pillars of the Banking Union, providing EU-wide uniform rules for the recovery and resolution of distressed banks. This chapter focuses on the Bank Recovery and Resolution Directive (BBRD)—Directive 2014/59/EU of the European Parliament and of the Council of 15 May 2014 establishing a framework for the recovery and resolution of credit institutions and investment firms [2014] *OJ L 173*. Among the tools provided by the Directive, the bail-in tool has drawn substantial policy and academic attention as a regulatory innovation having the potential to disrupt the discourse on financial stability. A bank bail-in consists in the power of the resolution authority to impose losses of failing banks on both shareholders and creditors through write down or conversion, carried out in an administrative procedure. On this point, see Karl-Philipp Wojcik, 'Bail-in in the Banking Union' (2016) 53 Common Market Law Review 91, 95.

[4] Regarding efficiency, see Charles Goodhart and Emilios Avgouleas, 'A Critical Evaluation of Bail-in as a Bank Recapitalisation Mechanism', in Douglas Evanoff et al. (ed), *The New International Financial System: Analyzing the Cumulative Impact of Regulatory Reform* (World Scientific, 2015). Regarding effectiveness, see Tobias H Tröger, 'Too Complex to Work: A Critical Assessment of the Bail-in Tool under the European Bank Recovery and Resolution Regime' (2018) 4 J.Financ.Reg, 35. Note, also, that the resolution objectives listed in Art. 31 BRRD do not take into account any *ex-ante* benefit.

a mechanism for disciplining the behaviours of the borrowing corporations.[5] The distinctive features of banking and especially the extensive reliance on short-term debt led both the legal and economic literature to focus on price adjustment as the only channel for creditors' influence.[6] This chapter complements the analysis on monitoring and price adjustment, analysing (bail-inable) debt contracts as the means to discipline banks.

Debt contracts of bail-inable securities are generally unable to discipline bank risk-taking because of the peculiarities of bank activities that restrain debt contracts from performing as well as in the non-financial industries. Nonetheless, this chapter argues that specific contractual arrangements imposed on contingent convertible (CoCo) debt can enhance discipline both before and after the event of a bail-in.[7]

2 Bail-Inable Securities: An Incomplete Contracts View

2.1 Debt and Incomplete Contracting

The role of debt and debt contracts is one of the focal points in corporate finance. Thus, going through the main theoretical explanations of debts and the role of financial contracting is crucial for understanding the role of new bail-inable instruments.

[5] Starting from Philippe Aghion and Patrick Bolton, 'An Incomplete Contracts Approach to Financial Contracting' (1992) 59 The review of economic Studies 473.

[6] Mark J Flannery, 'Debt Maturity and the Deadweight Cost of Leverage: Optimally Financing Banking Firms' (1994) 84 The American Economic Review 320.

[7] For a comprehensive survey, see Mark Flannery, 'Contingent Capital Instruments for Large Financial Institutions: A Review of the Literature' (2014) 6 Annu.Rev.Financ.Econ. 225. On the limis of these instruments, see See Paul Glasserman and Enrico Perotti, 'The Unconvertible CoCo Bonds' in Douglas D Evanoff and others (eds), *Achieving Financial Stability: Challenges to Prudential Regulation*, vol 61 (World Scientific 2017). However, CoCos' governance impact is, to the best of the author's knowledge, heavily understudied, especially in Europe. In the US some attention has been devoted to the topic, see John Coffee Jr, 'Systemic Risk after Dodd-Frank: Contingent Capital and the Need for Regulatory Strategies beyond Oversight' (2011) 111 Colum.L.Rev. 795. Besides, the policy recommendation by Coffee would be unavailable according to the EU regulatory framework. For an analytical framework highlighting the importance of contingent actions to promt bank recovery, see Edoardo D Martino and Enrico C Perotti, 'Containing Runs on Solvent Banks: Prioritizing Recovery over Resolution' (2025) 7 Journal of Financial Crises 1.

Corporate finance scholars firstly approached the debt from the perspective of the firm, investigating its optimal capital structure, i.e., which combination of equity and debt financing maximises the value of the firm. Modigliani and Miller[8] demonstrated that, under a certain set of assumptions,[9] the choice between equity and debt does not affect the overall value of the firm (irrelevance proposition).[10]

This basic yet revolutionary idea was later refined, questioning its assumptions. For what is here of interest, the refinements related to agency and incomplete contract theory deserve further discussions. The agency theory, among other features, explains the fundamentals of debtholders role in the corporation; while, incomplete contract theory takes a step forward, explaining the rationale for lending.

Jensen and Meckling, relaxing the assumption of symmetric information, showed that shareholders partially shift the risk (and costs) of bankruptcy to bondholders (risk-shifting).[11] Therefore, being shareholders in charge of decision-making, risk-taking tends to be excessive since shareholders bear only a small fraction of expected bankruptcy costs.[12] "Gambling for resurrection" incentives represent the extreme consequence of this phenomenon: once financial distress approaches, shareholders are rationally prone to undertake negative net present value

[8] Franco Modigliani and Merton Miller, 'The Cost of Capital, Corporation Finance and the Theory of Investment' (1958) 48 The American economic review 261.

[9] Absence of bankruptcy costs, symmetric information, and absence of taxes.

[10] This approach represents the theoretical background for proposals to sharply increase regulatory capital of banks. See, Anat Admati and Martin Hellwig, *The Bankers' New Clothes: What's Wrong with Banking and What to Do about It* (Princeton University Press 2014).

[11] Michael C Jensen and William H Meckling, 'Theory of the Firm: Managerial Behavior, Agency Costs and Ownership Structure' (1976) 3 Journal of financial economics 305.

[12] This issue is amplified in banking, given their inherently highly levered nature. The fraction of bankruptcy costs borne by shareholders is smaller and incentives towards risk-taking increase. This represents a standard argument for capital regulation, as explained in the continuing of the section. See John Armour and others, *Principles of Financial Regulation* (Oxford University Press 2016) ch 16.

projects, yielding high returns with low probabilities, since they would fully gain the benefits without bearing any costs.[13]

Building on the agency theory, the "costly contracting hypothesis"[14] of debt argues that controlling bondholder-shareholder conflicts can increase the value of the firm. In other words, creditors can play a positive role in the governance of the firm. Although financial contracting is costly, parties are willing to bear these costs—e.g., to draft, monitor, and enforce a covenant—as long as the benefits deriving from financial contracting outweigh the bargaining and enforcement costs, at the margin.

The literature analysed so far explains the role of debt for the value of the firm, but it fails to explicate the rationale for debt contracting. This link is crucial, as corporate governance has been defined as the ways in which suppliers of finance (including creditors) to corporations ensure themselves of getting a return on their investment.[15] Aghion and Bolton modelled debt contracts as a mechanism to allocate control contingently on future situations that are difficult or impossible to describe *ex-ante*.[16] Accordingly, the capital structure of a firm is relevant for managerial incentives as long as contracts are incomplete, i.e., their enforcement is constrained by the lack of compelling provisions for each and every possible course of action. Contingent allocation of control evokes, first and foremost, statutory bankruptcy, where the ability of the shareholders to retain control is contingent on meeting the debt obligation. Besides, one can think of debt covenants restricting the courses of action available to the firm and thus limiting the control power of shareholders.[17] Again, secured debt allocates control over specific assets to a creditor, contingent on default on contractual obligation.

[13] For a simple numerical exemplification, see Marco Becht, Patrick Bolton and Ailsa Röell, 'Why Bank Governance Is Different' (2011) 27 Oxford Review of Economic Policy 437.

[14] Such hypothesis builds mainly on Stewart Myers, 'Determinants of Corporate Borrowing' (1977) 5 J.Financ.Ec. 147; Clifford Smith Jr and Jerold Warner, 'On Financial Contracting: An Analysis of Bond Covenants' (1979) 7 J.Financ.Ec. 117.

[15] Andrei Shleifer and Robert Vishny, 'A Survey of Corporate Governance' (1997) 52 J. Financ. 737.

[16] Philippe Aghion and Patrick Bolton, 'An Incomplete Contracts Approach to Financial Contracting' (1992) 59 Rev.Financ.Studies 473.

[17] For a complete taxonomy of covenants, see Michael Bradley and Michael Roberts, 'The Structure and Pricing of Corporate Debt Covenants' (2015) 5 Q.J.Financ.

2.2 *The Special Case of Bank Debt*

In the specific context of banks, the understanding of contingent allocation of control needs to be broadened. Debt is excessively difficult to restructure,[18] and short-term debt is an (inefficient) way of allocating control.[19] Parties agree on short-term exposures with the perspective of rolling them over as long as the condition of the firm situation does not deteriorate.[20] Considering this peculiarity, one could wonder whether, and to what extent, the theory of debt previously discussed applies to banks. Banks are special for a wide array of reasons, among which at least two are crucial here.[21]

First, banks perform maturity transformation of their assets, as they borrow money short term and lend long term, exposing banks to (retail and wholesale) runs.[22] This provides a sound argument for deposit guarantees which, in turn, begs for intrusive regulation substituting for the lack of monitoring by depositors.[23] As a by-product, banks implicitly rely on public bailouts, strengthening the moral hazard problem. Second, big and interconnected banks generate systemic risk, meaning that the failure of a financial institution results in much bigger costs than the ones borne by the institution, as the effects of one failure propagate to the rest of the financial system (e.g., contagion risk, trust issues, etc.).[24]

[18] Patrick Bolton and Olivier Jeanne, 'Structuring and Restructuring Sovereign Debt: The Role of a Bankruptcy Regime' (2007) 115 J.Polit.Ec. 901.

[19] Technically: an inefficient equilibrium derived by the impossibility of differently allocation control. See Douglas Diamond and Raghuram Rajan, 'A Theory of Bank Capital' (2000) 55 The Journal of Finance 2431.

[20] On the relevance of short-term contract in bank financing, see Flannery, 'Debt Maturity and the Deadweight Cost of Leverage: Optimally Financing Banking Firms' (n 10). Short-term funding also implies funding and liquidity risk, that have been blamed as the main driver of the latest financial crisis, on this matter see Markus Brunnermeier, 'Deciphering the liquidity and credit crunch 2007–2008' (2009) 23(1) JEP 77.

[21] For a comprehensive explanation, se e Markus Brunnermeier et al., *The Fundamental Principles of Financial Regulation*, vol 11 (ICMB, Internat Center for Monetary and Banking Studies 2009).

[22] Douglas Diamond and Philip Dybvig, 'Bank Runs, Deposit Insurance, and Liquidity' (1983) 91 J.Polit.Ec. 401.

[23] The so-called "representation hypothesis", as proposed by Mathias Dewatripont and Jean Tirole, '*The Prudential Regulation of Banks*' (MIT Press 1994).

[24] On systemic risk see extensively, Steven Schwarcz, 'Systemic Risk' (2008) 97 Geo.LJ 193.

The post-crisis wave of reforms has confronted both issues introducing the concept of loss-absorbing capacity of the bank's liabilities. This means that banks should bear in their balance sheet sufficient instruments for internal recapitalisation, minimising the impact of a potential default on financial stability.[25] Those instruments can be either capital, as defined by the Basel III accords,[26] or non-capital instruments that are apt to absorb losses.[27] What makes an instrument apt to absorb losses are its qualitative characteristics, i.e., contractual arrangements.

In the European Union, the regulatory framework for loss-absorbing instruments is composed by the Capital Requirement Regulation (CRR),[28] laying down qualitative and quantitative requirements for capital instruments; and the BRRD, dealing with the qualitative requirements for non-capital instruments, considered "eligible" to be counted as bail-inable liabilities.[29] Once the bank goes into financial distress and becomes "failing or likely to fail",[30] the resolution authority can decide to write-down or convert bail-in eligible claims through the so-called bail-in mechanism, recapitalising the bank without the need for a State bailout.[31]

Therefore, from an ex-ante perspective, loss-absorbing instruments are designed to work as a buffer against the risk of financial distress, insofar as the losses arising from financial distress are allocated to investors in bail-inable securities and not on the general public. In a world of complete contracts,[32] this should also optimise risk-taking incentives of bankers,

[25] Financial Stability Board, 'Key Attributes of Effective Resolution Regimes for Financial Institutions' (2011).

[26] BCBS, 'Basel III: A Global Regulatory Framework for More Resilient Banks and Banking Systems' (2010).

[27] See Financial Stability Board, 'Principles on Loss-Absorbing and Recapitalisation Capacity of G-SIBs in Resolution—Total Loss Absorbency Capacity' (2011).

[28] Regulation (EU) No 575/2013 of the European Parliament and of the Council of 26 June 2013 on prudential requirements for credit institutions and investment firms [2015] OJ L 176.

[29] Quantitative requirements for bail-inable securities are not set down in primary legislation but are individually determined by the resolution authority together with the supervisory authority, pursuing Art. 45(6) BRRD.

[30] Art. 32(1)(a) BRRD.

[31] On the doubt over the efficiency and effectiveness of these mechanisms, see supra note n. 8.

[32] The ideal situation in which each and every future course of action can be *ex-ante* forecasted and disciplined.

since each future course of action would be governed in a way consistent with the fulfilment of contractual obligations attached to bail-inable securities, i.e., not becoming "failing or likely to fail" so as to avoid losses for bail-inable debtholders.[33]

In contrast, in a world of incomplete contracts such an outcome is dubious. Even more so, considering that the qualitative requirements on loss-absorbing instruments and the administrative discretion of the resolution authority further constrain the possibility of contingently allocating control. The proceeding of this chapter discusses the qualitative requirements for bail-in eligible liabilities from the perspective of the investor, i.e., as a set of constraints to contractual possibilities.

3 Regulatory Constraints as a Limit to Contractual Freedom

The qualitative requirements for bail-inable instruments ensure that, in the event of financial distress, the bank can absorb losses, according to the seniority of its liabilities. The more junior a liability is, the stricter the requirements are. Hence, the primary objective of qualitative requirements is to preserve financial stability and minimise the need for public bailouts.

From the perspective of an investor, strict qualitative requirements mean constraints on the ability to bargain on the terms of the investment. This implies, in turn, limited chances for contractual solutions to efficiently allocate contingent control and more reliance on the role of regulators and supervisors in disciplining the manager's behaviour.[34] Moreover, as discussed in the previous chapter, the discretion of the Resolution Authority in imposing losses in the event of distress additionally hampers the condition of investors in bail-inable securities, resulting in uncertainty about the return on their investment.[35]

The proceeding of the section outlines the qualitative requirements of capital and non-capital bail-inable securities (Sect. 3.1). Afterwards,

[33] See, for instance, Jianping Zhou and others, 'From Bailout to Bail-in: Mandatory Debt Restructuring of Systemic Financial Institutions' [2012] Journal Issue 3.

[34] Consistently with the Representation Hypothesis, see supra note n. 29.

[35] On the ambiguity in the interpretation and the application of the "public interest" principle in bank distress cases in Europe see Wolf-Georg Ringe, 'Bank Bail-In between Liquidity and Solvency' (2016) 92 Am. Bankr. LJ 299, 29.

this chapter discusses the compliance of control allocation mechanisms with such requirements. This allows to understand the channels, if any, through which an investor can efficiently allocate control and bargain out of supervisory discretion (Sect. 3.2).

3.1 A Brief Overview of Qualitative Requirements[36]

The BRRD[37] requires institutions to meet at all times a Minimum Requirement for Own Funds[38] and Eligible Liabilities (MREL).[39] In the first version of the BRRD, MREL quantitative calibration was set as a tailor-based requirement. In the 2019 iteration of the BRRD, the quantitative requirements were aligned to the international standards for systemic banks, including clear quantitative requirements; while for smaller banks the tailor-made decision still applies.[40] In contrast, the CRR statutorily set the required amount of own funds (Fig. 1).

Before individually addressing each class of items, three general features deserve some attention. First, to absorb losses, eligible instruments must provide a genuine contribution of wealth; thus, they cannot be owned by, secured by, funded by, or guaranteed by the issuing institution. If that happened, the losses would be indirectly borne by the issuer itself. Second, eligible instruments rank below all the others and, within eligible

[36] This section focuses partly on Additional Tier 1 instruments and mainly on Tier 2 instruments, as Common Equity Tier 1 instruments fall out of the scope of this research.

[37] Art. 45 BRRD. In this contribution, MREL is preferred over TLAC as a regulatory standard on which to base the analysis given its Eurocentric perspective. Nonetheless, the core of the arguments proposed would not vary significantly. On the inter-relation between MREL and TLAC see, EBA, 'Final Report on MREL' (2016).

[38] The aim of MREL requirement is to make the bank able to absorb losses and restore their capital position, allowing it to continuously perform their critical economic functions during and after a crisis. As a first approximation, it consists of the sum of Tier 1 and Tier 2 capital, see Art. 71 CRR.

[39] Bank liabilities that are not exempted *ex* Art. 44(2) and complies with the requirements of Art. 45(4).

[40] Edoardo D Martino and Katarzyna M Parchimowicz, 'Go Preventive or Go Home—the Double Nature of MREL' (2021) 18 European Company and Financial Law Review 608.

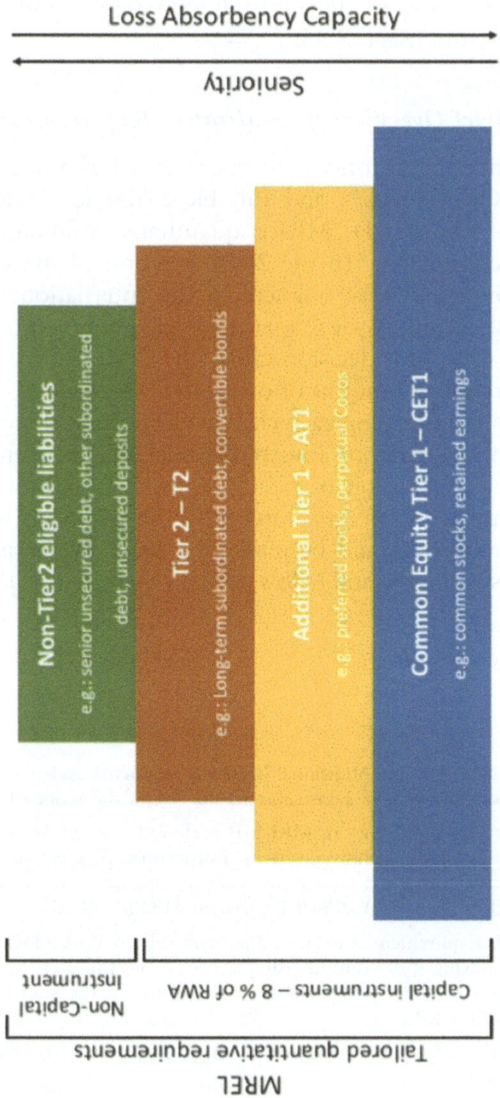

Fig. 1 Capital and bail-in eligible liabilities waterfall

instruments, each class of instruments has different seniority.[41] Third, Article 48 BRRD regulates the sequence of subordination, allocating the losses to CET1 holders first, then AT1, T2 and eventually other eligible liabilities, as described in Table 1. Specifically, the analysis covers the requirements on maturity, loss absorption, repayment of the principal amount, and distribution of interests/dividend.

For explanatory purposes, non-Tier 2 instruments are analysed first and, subsequently Tier 2 and Additional Tier 1. Indeed, to be eligible, junior liabilities should comply with the requirements set for senior instruments, and with further requirements specific to the senior class. Table 1 summarises all the requirements.

MREL-eligible instruments must have a remaining maturity of at least one year.[42] Hence, for instance, a bond whose maturity is 31 January 2025 will be fully counted as MREL eligible until 31 January 2024. Moreover, Article 44(2) BRRD exempts from the application of bail-in some classes of liabilities that are incompatible with the aim of the tool, such as covered deposits.[43] MREL-eligible instruments are not required to comply with specific rules on repayments of principal amount and distribution of interests.

Coming to capital instruments, Tier 2 liabilities must be issued with an initial maturity of at least five years.[44] The instrument can be redeemed (called, repurchased or repaid) in advance after five years from the issuance and with prior supervisory approval.[45] Besides, no contractual provisions can provide incentives for early repayment[46]; as well as no contractual

[41] To cope with potential problems with different bankruptcy waterfall across different jurisdiction, in 2019 it was introduced a requirement of 'structural subordination' of all MREL-eligible liability vis-à-vis all non-eligible ones. See Article 72b(1)(d) CRR.

[42] Art. 45(4)(d) BRRD. Note that liabilities with more than 7 days to maturity can still be bailed-in in resolution, but they do not count for MREL compliance.

[43] For an in-depth analysis of exemptions of Art. 44(2), see Tröger (n 8).

[44] Art. 63(1)(g) and 64 CRR. In the last 5 years before maturity, the liability is linearly amortised so that only a fraction can be counted as Tier 2 capital. Nonetheless, it is still full MREL eligible. On the other hand, the full instrument is not MREL eligible anymore when has less than 1-year maturity even though a fraction of the instrument can still be counted as regulatory capital. Such inconsistency does not hamper the overall argument of this contribution.

[45] Art. 63(1)(j) and 77 CRR.

[46] Art. 63(1)(h),(i),(k).

Table 1 Outline of the main qualitative requirements for bail-in eligible liabilities

	Main legal source	*Maturity*	*Loss absorbtion/ subordination*	*Distributions*	*Repayments*
Non-Tier 2 bail-in eligible	Articles 44, 45 and 48 BRRD	At least 1 reaming year	**BRRD framework** After Tier 2 instrument	No specific requirements	No specific requirements
Tier 2	Articles 62–65 CRR	– At least 5y at issuance – Callable after 5y with supervisory permission – Linear amortisation in the last 5y	**BRRD framework** After AT1 instruments	No specific requirements	– No contractual incentives to redeem or repay in advance – Call option at sole discretion of the issuer – Instruments are callable or redeemable after 5 years upon supervisory approval – No contractual indication of anticipated repurchase or repayment – No contractual provision for repayment acceleration

	Main legal source	*Maturity*	*Loss absorbtion/ subordination*	*Distributions*	*Repayments*
Additional Tier 1	Articles 51–55 CRR	Perpetual, callable after 5 years with supervisory permission	**CRR framework** Rank below Tier 2; Principal write down or conversion upon a trigger event **BRRD framework** After CET1 instrument	– Paid out of distributable assets – Full discretion for the issuer to cancel distribution	– No contractual incentives to redeem or repay in advance – Call option at sole discretion of the issuer – Instruments are callable or redeemable after 5 years upon supervisory approval – No contractual indication of anticipated repurchase or repayment – No contractual provision for repayment acceleration

clause can give the holder the right to accelerate the repayment of interests and the principal amount of the instruments.[47] Whereas AT1 and T2 items share the provisions governing redeemability, and constraints on contractual clauses, the main difference between the two lies in the contingent convertibility of AT1 items. Moreover, distributions should be paid out of distributable items (profits, retained distributable earnings) and the issuer has full discretion in cancelling distributions.

Loss-bearing provisions outside of a resolution procedure complement the principle of seniority in resolution.[48] According to the CRR framework, AT1 items must be written down or converted into CET1 when the level of CET1 falls below 5.125% of RWA, allowing the institution to have new equity when that would be difficult or too expensive to raise. The trigger event for write down or conversion can be higher than the statutory one if provided in the contract.[49]

3.2 *Contractual Discipline and Qualitative Requirements*

This section demonstrates that many of the usual contractual devices are largely unavailable in banking because such devices do not comply with existing regulation. On the one hand, it is easy to rule out the possibility of complying with capital and MREL requirements through short-term or secured debt for financial stability purposes. Short-term exposures are prone to run in case of idiosyncratic or systemic turmoil. On the other hand, the stability of financial institutions, as well as the feasibility of resolution procedures, beg for long-term non-runnable items on which other short-term investors, depositors, and the market as a whole can rely. In a similar vein, eligible liabilities need to absorb losses. Therefore, secured items are radically incompatible with the aim of capital regulation, and the principles of resolution, as the loss-absorbing capacity would only be fictional as the institution would still bear the losses.

The situation is more entangled when it comes to covenants. The salience of covenants can be grasped by referring to Patrick Bolton: "In short, the area where the issue of contractual incompleteness perhaps

[47] Art. 63(1)(l) CRR.

[48] Art. 52(1)(n) and 54 CRR.

[49] This specific aspect is crucial. Section 4 discusses it widely.

matters most, when it comes to debt contracts, is the design and enforcement of debt covenants".[50]

First, for the sake of financial stability and public trust, using a covenant breach as an event of default to force debt renegotiation represents an unavailable option.[51] Contractually granting the opportunity to force a financial institution into bankruptcy in case of a breach would provide the creditor with disproportionate powers, putting them in the position to generate significant negative externalities for the whole economy. Covenants can also have other functions. For instance, covenants are used to speed up the repayment in case of a breach, allowing to end a risky exposure. Again, covenants can be used to impose behavioural remedies upon a breach.[52]

As previously described, covenants speeding up repayments are unavailable for capital instruments, while there are no constraints for non-capital eligible items. The regulator has extensive control over capital items both through regulatory tools, such as the ban on the acceleration of repayment, and supervisory tools, such as the necessary permission to call items earlier than the original maturity.

Behavioural covenants (e.g., restriction on payment of dividends) are, in principle, compliant with the requirements of both capital and non-capital items. However, covenants are costly to draft and enforce. Therefore, it might well be that, even if available, their costs outweigh the benefits. Banks' assets and operations are, by definition, opaque, so that monitoring costs are higher than in non-financial firms.

Besides, there is a set of rules mimicking the possible behavioural covenants that could be imposed.[53] For instance, Article 141 of the Capital Requirement Directive restricts the possibility of paying dividends and coupon on capital instruments if the Combined Buffer Requirements

[50] Patrick Bolton, 'Corporate Finance, Incomplete Contracts, and Corporate Control' (2013) 30 The Journal of Law, Economics, & Organization i64, 75.

[51] This solution is widely employed and desirable in corporate debt. See empirical evidence furnished in Greg Nini, David C Smith and Amir Sufi, 'Creditor Control Rights, Corporate Governance, and Firm Value' (2012) 25 The Review of Financial Studies 1713.

[52] Restriction on investments (e.g., mergers), on financing (e.g., future senior debt issuances) and on dividends, as categorised in Bradley and Roberts (n 23).

[53] See back in Sect. 2 about the theory of banking regulation and the Representation Hypothesis (n 29).

(CBR) is breached.[54] After the 2019 reform, also the BRRD imposed a similar limitation on coupon distribution on MREL-eligible liabilities if the MREL or CBR is breached.[55] Thus, on the one hand, in comparison with non-financial firms, imposing covenants would be costlier, because of the higher cost of compliant drafting, monitoring, and enforcement. On the other hand, the benefits, if any, would amount to the marginal increase of mismanagement deterrence that a tailored-made covenant can yield on top of the supervisory rules.[56]

Finally, some attention has to be devoted to the hypothesis of statutory bankruptcy and the special ways in which it materialises for banks. Once the bank reaches the point of non-viability, there are two main options: liquidation (gone concern) and resolution (going-concern).[57] For what is here of interest, we do not consider gone concern options, as the procedure of bank liquidation has no governance implication, i.e., no contingent shift in control, since it is usually controlled by national administrative authorities driving the insolvent bank out of the market. On the contrary, in a going-concern scenario, investors can have a potentially relevant governance impact when the resolution authority decides to convert eligible liabilities into shares.[58]

[54] Directive 2013/36/EU of the European Parliament and of the Council of 26 June 2013 on access to the activity of credit institutions and the prudential supervision of credit institutions and investment firms [2013] *OJ L 176*. For a deeper analysis of the governance provisions contained in the CRD IV that might mimic potential covenants, see Luca Enriques and Dirk Zetzsche, 'Quack Corporate Governance, Round III? Bank Board Regulation Under the New European Capital Requirement Directive' (2015) 16 Theoretical Inquiries in Law 211.

[55] Article 16a BRRD.

[56] The risk of redundancy and conflicts for covenants on bail-inable securities and existing regulation has been highlighted also in Fiona Mann and others, 'Market Discipline and UK Bank Bondholders' (2017) 57 Bank of England Quarterly Bulletin 26.

[57] In the liquidation scenario, the bank is shut down according to national insolvency and the legal entity cease to exist. In the resolution scenario, the critical functions of the bank continue, as provided by Art. 31(2)(a) BRRD, and the distress of the bank is coped with an administrative procedure employing one or more resolution tools provided in the BRRD. The result can be either full going-concern scenario, where the original legal entity is made viable and continues to operate (e.g., bail-in tool) or a scenario where the original legal entity ceases to exist (e.g., bridge institution tool).

[58] Using the power provided by Art. 63(1)(f) BRRD, while the power to write down provided by Art. 63(1)(e) is not here considered for the reasons discussed above in the case of gone concern solutions.

Some authors have argued that converting debtors into shareholders may influence the incentives of managers towards risk-taking: creditors are thought to be more risk-averse than shareholders so that they would influence the management in that direction.[59] Moreover, the conversion of other instruments likely follows the substantial dilution or even the complete write-off of outstanding shares.[60] Hence, a radical shift in control would happen. Some preliminary observations are worth discussing.

First, the governance characteristics of converted shares are not clearly regulated. Indeed, eligible items ought to be converted into common shares, as preferences in distributions and repayment are not allowed under the subordination requirement of CET1.[61] On the contrary, neither the CRR nor the BRRD cover the issue of governance rights of the converted items.[62]

Second, the conversion would happen at the point of non-viability, so that the incentives of new shareholders would not sharply differ from the old ones' in terms of risk-shifting and gambling for resurrection.[63] No rational reasons, indeed, lead one to believe that allegedly risk-averse

[59] This is the underlying idea in Coffee Jr (n 13).

[60] See Recital n. 77 BRRD: "Losses should first be absorbed by regulatory capital instruments and should be allocated to shareholders either through the cancellation or transfer of shares or through severe dilution".

[61] Differential rights in the magnitude of distributions are allowed in case of shares have limited or no voting rights, as provided by Art. 28(4) CRR.

[62] According to the CET1 requirements shares can have limited or no voting rights. See supra note n 65.

[63] This view is antithetical with the one proposed by some authors, claiming under the assumption that creditors structurally more risk-averse than shareholders are. See, for instance, Coffee Jr (n 13); Zhou and others (n 39).

bondholders will stick to their risk appetite in the event of conversion. Risk appetite cannot be assumed to be immutable,[64] as it changes according to the investor's payoffs.[65]

Ultimately, the decision of public authorities over the most desirable course of action to undertake, i.e., the probability of conversion, remains discretionary. Nonetheless, contracts might come at hand once again. It is possible to write contractual clauses for the conversion of eligible liabilities into CET1 items once a pre-established trigger event materialises (contingent convertibles or CoCos). Therefore, theoretically, investors can bargain out of regulatory discretion, assuming that CoCos are always and consistently written down or converted.

4 Bargaining out of Discretion: Contingent Convertibles

4.1 Rationale and Design Features

Contingent Convertibles represent an academic invention dating back to the early 2000s.[66] They became popular in the aftermath of the financial crisis, as they seemed to be innovative items that could potentially disrupt the discourse on financial stability.[67] CoCos are financial instruments that are written down or converted into equity, depending on their contractual

[64] Here, the assumption on constant preference still holds and given the risk preference, the appetite towards risk varies according to the specific context. This conservative approach is sufficient for the argument. Nonetheless, one could go further and drop off the assumption of constant preference, leaning towards the behavioural literature on context-specific preferences. See, Amos Tversky and Itamar Simonson, 'Context-Dependent Preferences' (1993) 39 Management science 1179.

[65] This line of reasoning is reinforced by the fact the under the MiFID II framework bail-inable securities are classified as a "complex instruments", that makes highly complex for retail investors to buy them. Guidelines on complex debt instruments and structured deposits, 04 February 2016|ESMA/2015/1787.

[66] Mark J Flannery, 'No Pain, No Gain. Effecting Market Discipline via Reverse Convertible Debentures' [2005] Capital Adequacy Beyond Basel: Banking, Securities, and Insurance 171. The published version is based on a working paper delivered in 2002. For a comprehensive literature review, see Philippe Oster, 'Contingent Convertible Bond Literature Review: Making Everything and Nothing Possible?' (2020) 21 Journal of Banking Regulation 343.

[67] See, among many other, Mark J Flannery, 'Stabilizing Large Financial Institutions with Contingent Capital Certificates' (2016) 6 Quarterly Journal of Finance 1650006.

design, when a contractually predetermined event (trigger) occurs, with the immediate consequence of recapitalising a bank that is going towards financial distress.[68] After a few years of limited attention, the discussion on CoCos surged again following the write-down of Credit Suisse CoCos.[69] A specific analysis of the Credit Suisse demise and the role of CoCos thereof is carried out in Chapter 9.

In the EU, CoCos count for regulatory capital as long as their characteristics comply with qualitative requirements for specific classes, as discussed in Sect. 3. Hence, they count as AT1 if they are perpetual and distributions are discretionary, or as T2 if those are long-term. CoCos can even count as non-capital bail-in eligible if their maturity is shorter than five years or they embed covenants that are incompatible with capital instruments.[70] However, issuing non-capital CoCos would make little sense since the bank would need to issue costly instruments twice. Thus, it is reasonable to argue that CoCos are either AT1 or T2, depending on their characteristics,[71] with the additional constraint that the trigger event of AT1 cannot be lower than 5.125% of CET1 over RWAs.[72]

Looking closer at the literature, "contingent convertible" represents an umbrella concept that comprehends a wide variety of items, whose goal and main characteristics are similar while sharply differing in their design.

[68] Patrick Bolton and Frederic Samama, 'Capital Access Bonds: Contingent Capital with an Option to Convert' (2012) 27 Economic Policy 275.

[69] For an in-depth analysis, especially in relation to the EU regime, see Edoardo D Martino and Tom Vos, 'Fixing CoCos in Bank Prudential Regulation—A Life-Cycle Approach' (fortchoming) European Business Organization Law Review. For an analysis of the EU law position vis-à-vis the Credit Suisse AT1 saga, see Sjur Swensen Ellingsæter, 'Could It Happen in the EU? An Analysis of Loss Distribution between Shareholders and AT1 Bondholders under EU Law' (2024) 10 Journal of Financial Regulation 194.

[70] The Swiss regulator adopted a sharply different approach, where CoCos are the only instruments that count as regulatory capital other than CET1. Swiss regulation requires large banks to issue CoCos amounting to at least 9% of RWAs, of which at least two-third with a trigger point higher than 7% of capital over RWAs. For the Swiss regime on Capital Adequacy of banking institutions, see the Verordnung über die Eigenmittel und Risikoverteilung der Banken und Wertpapierhäuser, entered into force on 1 January 2013. On the impact of Swiss regulatory framework, see Georg Junge and Peter Kugler, 'Quantifying the Impact of Higher Capital Requirements on the Swiss Economy' (2013) 149 Swiss Journal of Economics and Statistics 313.

[71] Besides, for tax shielding purposes, most likely CoCos issuances take the form of bonds even if they could in principle be preferred stocks.

[72] Art. 54(1) CRR.

A comprehensive survey of all the possible CoCos' designs is beyond the scope of this analysis, but some crucial aspects ought to be introduced.

First, setting the correct trigger event is crucial for efficient design. This represents a conundrum that financial economists are heavily discussing. Here it is sufficient to emphasise that there are two main policy options: CoCos with high or low triggers. High trigger indicates the fact that the triggering event is relatively far from the point of non-viability,[73] while low trigger means the opposite. Second, CoCos can contractually provide both for conversion and write-down of their principal amount once the event is triggered.[74] Third, a further variation is to design reconvertible items, i.e., contractually establish a second event that, if triggered, converts back the shares into CoCos. The reconversion can be automatic or in the form of an option in favour of the converted shareholders. As Sect. 4.3 illustrates, the design with a reconversion option can have beneficial effects from a corporate governance perspective.

4.2 CoCos and Risk-Taking

There is no consensus in the economic literature about the impact of CoCos on risk-taking.[75] The overall effect on risk-taking appetite encompasses three main dimensions. First, the immediate consequence of converting CoCos into ordinary shares is to deleverage the balance sheet

[73] The market value of shares represents the crucial variable, as when multiplied by outstanding shares and divided by the assets as indicated by latest available accounting data provide a proxy for the market value of banks equity and the level of financial distress.

[74] For mutual banks, only the principal write-down option is available, as they do not have common shares to exchange with convertible bonds. Thus, for instance, Rabobank in 2010 issued convertible bonds providing for writing their principal amount down once the event is triggered.

[75] This directly descends from the lack of a generalised view on how to approach the issue and the outcome is highly dependent on the assumptions of the various models. Some papers argue for risk-reduction effect while some others claim the exact opposite. See, respectively, Natalya Martynova and Enrico Perotti, 'Convertible Bonds and Bank Risk-Taking' [2018] Journal of Financial Intermediation; Tobias Berg and Christoph Kaserer, 'Does Contingent Capital Induce Excessive Risk-Taking?' (2015) 24 Journal of Financial Intermediation 356. For an opposite analysis, claiming that AT1 CoCo loss absorbtion should always come after shareholders being wiped out, irrespective of the contractual design of the instrument, see Javier Paz Valbuena and Horst Eidenmüller, 'Bailout Blues: The Write-Down of the AT1 Bonds in the Credit Suisse Bailout' (2023) 24 European Business Organization Law Review 409.

of the bank which, in turn, reduces the incentives for "risk-shifting" and "gambling for resurrection" behaviours. This can be a persistent effect only if the bank is profitable. If the value of shares keeps decreasing, the beneficial effect of deleveraging will not last. Second, there is an effect on incentives towards monitoring. CoCo holders bear losses with relatively high probability, so that their incentives to monitor banks activities, in general, and the trigger event-related issues in particular, increase.[76] Third, and most relevant for our purposes, there might be "pure" governance effects, i.e., the contractual design of convertible items positively affects the agency problems among corporate constituencies, providing for ways to assure a return on investment better aligned with risk-decreasing attitude.[77] The remainder of the section discusses the potential for beneficial governance effects and the necessary contractual features for it to materialise.

4.3 *Governance Features of CoCo Design*

The crucial issue in assessing the governance benefits deriving from contingent convertibles rests upon the type of shares CoCos would be converted in.[78] As a first approximation, one can think of two main possibilities. First, converting CoCos into plain ordinary shares that do not differ from the pre-existing ones in the voting and economic rights; second, converting CoCos into different kind of shares with different voting and economic rights.

As discussed in Sect. 4.1, if the converted shareholders have the same position of the pre-existing ones, there is no rational ground for arguing that their risk incentives are going to act as more risk-averse just because

[76] Note that the increase on monitoring incentives may well be suboptimal, because the costs still outweigh the expected benefits or because of the complex and unpredictable legal framework. On the suboptimality of market discipline through monitoring, see Emilios Avgouleas and Jay Cullen, 'Market Discipline and EU Corporate Governance Reform in the Banking Sector: Merits, Fallacies, and Cognitive Boundaries' (2014) 41 Journal of Law and Society 28.

[77] See the definition of corporate governance by Shleifer and Vishny (n 20).

[78] For explanatory purposes, this section assumes that the troubled bank has only one class of shares providing one vote to each share. A complex structure with multiple share classes would not hamper the overall argument, even though can make more difficult the shift in control (for instance in case of multiple voting shares).

they were bondholders beforehand. However, designing financial instruments for banks is all but straightforward and unrestricted, so it is issuing CET1 instruments. Thus, for qualifying as CET1, shares should not be in any way preferred to other CET1 items in neither distribution of dividends nor liquidation.[79] This instance limits, at least in the EU framework, the argument put forward by Coffee about positive governance effects if CoCos convert into preferred stocks with considerable voting rights.[80] Within equally subordinated shares, the CRR allows differentiating the quantity of voting and economic rights. Banks, in principle, can issue multiple, restricted or non-voting shares if the jurisdiction of issuance allows so.[81] The economic rights can be adjusted accordingly, i.e., higher economic rights can be attached to shares with fewer or no voting rights.[82]

Given this framework, governance effects arise both before and after conversion. In good times, shareholders are averse to conversion if that means a considerable dilution of their voting or economic rights.[83] Moreover, and most importantly, once the bank runs into financial distress and the conversion happens, CoCo holders are playing an active governance role whose content is highly dependent on the contractual design of converted shares. If risk appetite is context-dependent so that one cannot rationally expect that CoCo holders are sticking to their risk-averse attitude once converted, this is also true for contractual entitlements that vary the context and so the appetite towards risk.

The governance role of converted shareholders varies according to the design of convert shares. We discuss three possibilities.

[79] Art. 28(1)(h)(i) CRR. This implies that preferred stocks would not count as CET1 but as AT1 instruments.

[80] See Coffee Jr (n 13).

[81] For a review of the multiple voting share literature in Europe, see Klaus J Hopt and Susanne Kalss, 'Multiple-Voting Shares in Europe-A Comparative Law and Economic Analysis' [2024] European Corporate Governance Institute-Law Working Paper.

[82] Art. 28(4) CRR.

[83] This is also an argument in favour of large conversions that can *ex-ante* threaten shareholders. Moreover, as discussed supra (note 82), if the banks have a complex dual class structure the *ex-ante* effect could be weakened. An immediate follow-up of this argument is that high-trigger CoCos amplify the aversion to conversion. This is also a powerful argument against non-dilutive CoCos, including principal write-down instruments; see Stefan Avdjiev, Anastasia Kartasheva and Bilyana Bogdanova, 'CoCos: A Primer' [2013] BIS Quarterly Review 43, 44.

1) No voting rights: in this scenario, converted shareholders have no say in the decision-making process of the bank, so that their direct governance impact is negligible, whereas the "deleveraging effect" stays the same. Anyhow, higher economic rights, compliant with CET1 requirements, could be attached to non-voting shares so that the *ex-ante* aversion of pre-existing shareholders to conversion can be slightly amplified.

2) Same voting and economic rights: in this situation, the argument about context-dependent risk appetite applies; hence, converted shareholders have the same risk incentives as the pre-existing ones. However, if controlling shareholder extracts detrimental private benefits from control,[84] the conversion can still have beneficial governance consequences. If the amount of converted shares and the conversion ratio alter the existing control powers, converted shareholders can push for a more shareholder's value-oriented management, for instance, substituting the incumbent managers. Moreover, the conversion scenario in this situation would amplify the *ex-ante* aversion towards the conversion of controlling shareholders that may opt for limiting the private benefit extracted from the bank. Nevertheless, being absent regulatory requirements to issue CoCos, a more straightforward solution is not to issue them in the first place.

Even outside of the latter scenario, an option to reconvert can modify the incentive parallelism. In this scenario, new shareholders may decide to reconvert to CoCos once a second event is triggered. So, in case of a high-trigger CoCo that converts into shares, once the turmoil has passed, the converted shareholders have the opportunity to opt for reconversion to a relatively safer asset, undercutting the shift towards larger risk appetite. This would elicit risk preferences of converted shareholders so that the genuinely risk-averse ones will push for a more cautious approach to get out of distress and reconvert to bonds. Thus, if the trigger is high enough not to provide "gambling for resurrection" incentives and the amount of converted shares is big enough to impact on the control of the bank significantly, the reconversion option can be a powerful tool.

3) Limited voting rights: it is relatively common for companies to issue classes of shares whose voting rights are limited to specific issues (usually strategic decision, such as mergers) or contingent to some event

[84] On private benefits of control and the cases in which it is harmful to firm's value see Alessio Pacces, *Rethinking Corporate Governance: The Law and Economics of Control Powers* (Routledge 2013).

(e.g., dividends are not distributed for two years in a row). In our context, limited voting rights seem more likely to occur. In such a scenario, most of the arguments proposed for (unrestricted) voting shares are applicable, including the beneficial effect of an option for reconversion.

What sharply differs from the latter design is that restricted voting shares are not apt to perform a shift in control, since they do not usually provide for voting rights in the election of the board. Therefore, the magnitude of the beneficial impact is more limited than for the previous design, especially with regard to limiting rent extractions Finally, limited voting shares can provide enhanced economic rights, which *ex-ante* increase the aversion towards the conversion of pre-existing shareholders.

Beyond the three main CoCo designs discussed above, one can think of a wide variety of more "exotic" variations. For instance, converting CoCos into a class of shares that have the specific right to appoint one or more directors or, again, the case for multiple voting rights shares. However, the feasibility of such designs is jurisdiction dependent. In fact, not only qualitative requirements impose restrictions on the rights that can be attached to shares, but also national corporate laws. For instance, it is relatively easy to issue multiple voting shares in Anglo-Saxon jurisdictions, while that is not the case in Civil law-oriented ones, where the principle one-share-one-vote is harder to opt out of for companies that are already listed.[85] The same argument goes for the specific rights to elect directors: it could be relatively simple in Italy, where the slate voting procedure for board election represents a well-established legal tool, while it may turn out to be virtually impossible in Germany, where the code-termination principle makes the composition of the board a particularly delicate equilibrium.[86]

[85] This represents, nowadays, an oversimplification of the composite landscape offered by national corporate laws. For a comprehensive and problematised overview, see Marco Ventoruzzo, 'The Disappearing Taboo of Multiple Voting Shares: Regulatory Responses to the Migration of Chrysler-Fiat' [2015] Bocconi Legal Studies Research Paper; Guido Ferrarini, 'One Share–One Vote: A European Rule?' (2006) 3 European Company and Financial Law Review 147. For the latest development on multiple voting shares and the distinction between already listed and yet-to-be-listed companies, see Claire A Hill and Alessio M Pacces, 'The Neglected Role of Justification under Uncertainty in Corporate Governance and Finance' (2018) 3 Annals of Corporate Governance 276, 320.

[86] Paul L Davies and Klaus J Hopt, 'Corporate Boards in Europe—Accountability and Convergence' (2013) 61 The American Journal of Comparative Law 301. For an empirical

In conclusion, assuming that CoCos are consistently written down or converted at the trigger point, the contractual design of CoCos matters for corporate governance. Design features that differentiate the incentives of pre-existing and converted shareholders are potentially able to decrease the overall risk appetite of the bank. This holds as long as the trigger event for the conversion is set relatively high, and the amount of converted shares is significant enough to impact on corporate decision-making. This markedly differentiates CoCos from other bail-inable securities. The latter category, given the current regulatory framework, is unfit to discipline risk-taking behaviours of managers.

5 Conclusion

This chapter analyses the trade-off between financial stability and market discipline through the lenses of financial contracting, evaluating the possibility to contractually designing bail-inable securities that could discipline bankers. The analysis reveals that financial stability considerations prevail both in the pre-crisis and post-crisis regulatory framework, being absent compelling arguments to drop off and strongly favour market discipline imposed through contracts.

Given the current regulatory framework, this chapter explores the room left to investors to impact on banks stability through contractual arrangements, focusing on contingent allocation of control and looking at financial regulation as constraints to contractual freedom. Traditional contractual devices are typically unavailable because of either capital regulation or the recovery and resolution framework. Moreover, even when contractual devices are compliant with existing regulation, room for actually impacting on bankers' behaviour is limited, also because of the risk of redundancy with other pieces of legislation and the supervisory activities.

One key avenue for disciplining bankers through contracts is to manipulate the design of contingent convertible (CoCo) instruments. From the perspective of financial stability, CoCos represent a powerful buffer, especially if the trigger event is far from the point of non-viability. Moreover, the available contractual characteristics of CoCos, if properly designed, can have an impact on the *ex-ante* and *ex-post* risk appetite of banks that

evaluation of board composition and choice, see Martin Gelter and Mathias Siems, 'Letting Companies Choose between Board Models: An Empirical Analysis of Country Variations' (2021) 43 U. Pa. J. Int'l L. 137.

decide to issue them. In particular, the crucial design features consist of voting rights, economic rights, and reconversion options, so to diversify the incentives of original shareholders from the ones of CoCo holders. The analysis highlights that CoCos' contractual design can improve bank governance, under the assumption that conversion or write down consistently happen at the trigger point. The first decade of application clearly showed that this assumption does not hold.[87] However, the finding of this chapter shows that reforming CoCos, making them more credible, represents an important avenue for future reforms.

[87] For an analysis of why this is the case see Martino and Vos (n 69).See also Sjur Swensen Ellingsæter, 'Could It Happen in the EU? An Analysis of Loss Distribution between Shareholders and AT1 Bondholders under EU Law' (2024) 10 Journal of Financial Regulation 194.

CHAPTER 6

The Composition Bail-Inable a Debtholders and Debt Governance

1 Introduction

The resolution regime aims to shift losses stemming from bank failures from society to insiders. Hence, studying the specific role of the counterparties of bank bail-inable securities seems a natural approach to the problem of efficiency and effectiveness of the new framework. Despite such an intuition, both regulators and academics have overlooked and almost neglected the issue.[1]

The FSB states that an effective resolution regime should, among other objectives, "be credible, and thereby enhance market discipline and

[1] With the notable exception of a working paper by Wolf-Georg Ringe and Jatine Patel, 'The Dark Side of Bank Resolution: Counterparty Risk through Bail-In' (2019) 31. In this working paper, the authors approach the issue from the perspective of systemic risk creation through counterparty risk. See also Carlo Altavilla and others, 'Bank Bond Holdings and Bail-in Regulatory Changes: Evidence from Euro Area Security Registers' (ECB Working Paper 2022).

This chapter heavily draws from Edoardo D Martino, 'Towards an Optimal Composition of Bail-Inable Debtholders?' (2021) 21 Journal of Corporate Law Studies 321.

E. D. Martino, *EU Bank Governance and Bail-In*, EBI Studies in Banking and Capital Markets Law,
https://doi.org/10.1007/978-3-032-20699-2_6

provide incentives for market-based solutions".[2] Similarly, in the BRRD,[3] the European legislator affirms: "The bail-in tool will [therefore] give shareholders and creditors of institutions a stronger incentive to monitor the health of an institution during normal circumstances".[4]

This latter statement hints at the fact that an allegedly credible resolution framework in place should enhance the quality of bank governance. In this perspective, bail-inable creditors play a crucial role, as their incentives are in line with the regulatory goal to maintain the bank's stability and solvency. Nevertheless, it is not clear whether investors who are theoretically more willing and capable of disciplining the risk-taking of their borrowers pose greater stability concerns. This chapter studies this manifestation of the trade-off between financial stability and market discipline.[5]

The role of creditors is salient given the requirement, contained in the BRRD, of issuing enough bail-in eligible liabilities (MREL).[6] Such a requirement is set by the resolution authority for each individual bank.[7]

[2] Financial Stability Board, 'Key Attributes of Effective Resolution Regimes for Financial Institutions' (2011).

[3] Bank Recovery and Resolution Directive (BBRD)—Directive 2014/59/EU of the European Parliament and of the Council of 15 May 2014 establishing a framework for the recovery and resolution of credit institutions and investment firms [2014] *OJ L 173*.

[4] Recital n. 67 BRRD.

[5] Andrew Crockett, 'Market Discipline and Financial Stability' (2002) 26 Journal of Banking & Finance 977; Markus Konrad Brunnermeier and others, ***The Fundamental Principles of Financial Regulation***, vol 11 (ICMB, Internat Center for Monetary and Banking Studies 2009).

[6] Minimum Requirement for Own Funds and Eligible Liabilities (MREL). On MREL see Chapter 3, Sect. 3.2.

[7] For Globally Systemic Important Banks (G-SIBs), more specific quantitative requirements are required at a supranational level, according to the Total Loss Absorbency Capacity (TLAC) framework. See Financial Stability Board, 'Principles on Loss-Absorbing and Recapitalisation Capacity of G-SIBs in Resolution—Total Loss Absorbency Capacity' (2011). In 2019, the European legislator modified the BRRD and the CRR to align these piecies of legislation to the TLAC requirements. For an in-depth analysis of how MREL is set and its preventive potential, see Edoardo D Martino and Katarzyna M Parchimowicz, 'Go Preventive or Go Home–the Double Nature of MREL' (2021) 18 European Company and Financial Law Review 608.

However, on average, the required MREL capacity should amount to 26% of RWAs, and European Banks are far from reaching this goal.[8]

These preliminary remarks underline two salient features at the core of the analysis. First, an enormous amount of bail-inable securities needs to be issued and, consequently, held. This might appear a trivial observation. The remainder of the analysis shows that, on the contrary, that is dense with relevant consequences. Throughout this chapter, this is labelled as the "existence constraint". Second, who holds those debt instruments matters because of the different investment strategies of the holders as well as the different willingness and ability to discipline the issuing banks. Nonetheless, the analysis of the corporate governance role of bail-inable creditors has remained superficial and unsatisfactory in both the benevolent and critical approach to the matter.[9]

Most of the contributions on the new resolution framework state, correctly, that neither bank crossholdings nor substantial household holdings are desirable. What remains unsatisfactory is the lack of in-depth analysis of the concrete channels through which creditors are supposed to influence their borrowers, scrutinising the impact of the new regulatory framework on those channels. Indeed, this aspect of the new resolution framework has only been tangentially touched upon by several authors who took different focal points.

On the contrary, who owns bail-inable securities represents one of the key aspects to make the system more resilient and resolvable. In addressing this gap in the literature, this chapter discusses the discrete impact on corporate governance of different types of investors in bail-inable securities and, building on such a discussion, proposes some potential toward resolvability.

[8] Dominique Laboureix, speech at 6th Industry Dialogue: 2017 MREL Policy, accessible at https://srb.europa.eu/sites/srbsite/files/20171120_6th_industry_dialogue_item_2_mrel_dominique_laboureix.pdf (accessed 30/09/2025). The MREL shortfall was estimated in 117 billion euro.

[9] Following professors Pacces and Heremans who argued: "all aspects of behaviour of financial firms can be ultimately understood as Corporate Governance issues". See Alessio M Pacces and Dirk Heremans, 'Regulation of Banking and Financial Markets', *Encyclopedia of Law and Economics—Volume 9* (Edward Elgar 2012). With specific regard to bail-in, professor Armour and co-authors claimed that: "This [the use of bail-in tool] has both financial and governance consequences for the bank [...] as the former debt-holders become equity holders", John Armour and others, *Principles of Financial Regulation* (Oxford University Press 2016) 359.

The rest of this chapter unfolds as follows. Section 2 pinpoints the policy and academic relevance of the matter and sets some methodological specifications. Section 3 builds a benchmark of a theoretically perfect buyer, drawing from the existing literature on the holders of bail-inable securities. Section 4 describes available data, their limitations, and provides a snapshot of the limited knowledge that is currently available, supplying some descriptive statistics. Section 5 discusses the pros and cons of each category of investors from both a corporate governance and a financial stability perspective. Section 6 moves to normative considerations, discussing which mix of investors can positively impact bank governance and preserve financial stability. Section 7 concludes.

2 Bail-Inable Creditors Composition: Why and How to Study It

The corporate governance and corporate finance literature has extensively discussed mechanisms through which debtors can act as governance actors and their potential for disciplining influence to contain the risk-taking of credit institutions.[10] In the context of banks, one can mainly think of three main channels: price adjustments (i.e., trading or threat of trading), contractual design of debt securities and "private engagement" of investors (see Fig. 1).

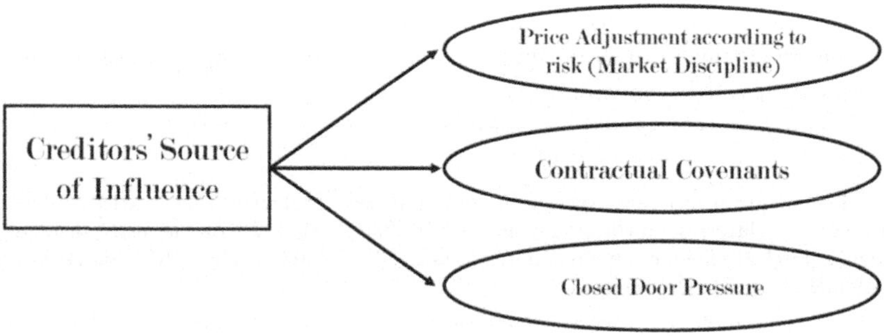

Fig. 1 Channels for creditors' influence

[10] For a comprehensive overview, see Jean Tirole, *The Theory of Corporate Finance* (Princeton University Press 2006) ch 1.6.

Previous chapters critically addressed the case for market discipline through price adjustments[11] and the case for contingent allocation of control through contracts,[12] pointing out the impediments posed by the legal design of the existing regulation. Hence, even assuming the credibility of the resolution framework, the market for bail-inable securities cannot smoothly work. Therefore, the generality of holders is not able to use market-based or contractual based arrangements to discipline the risk-taking of their borrower. This chapter adds a further layer of complexity to the analysis, decomposing the category of bail-inable creditors, and highlighting the different incentives and abilities of different bail-inable securities holders.

The case of bail-inable securities held by households as compared to hedge funds is a straightforward example in this regard. The difference is clear in terms of sophistication, business models, investment strategy, portfolio diversification, ability to convey and process available information, etc.[13] Despite its relevance for resolution and supervision, the regulator has remained neutral about the matter, and little is known about the actual composition of bail-inable debtholders and even less about the "optimal" composition of holders.

In searching for optimal composition, corporate governance considerations must complement financial stability ones and, more precisely, the "adverse spillovers" different investors might generate. This tension will be better illustrated in Sect. 6. Suffice to say that a composition that assures the maximum level of benefits in terms of corporate governance and, at the same time, creating considerable concerns from a financial stability perspective is far from optimal.

[11] This is the point on which the current literature mostly focus, See, with different arguments and perspectives, Avgouleas and Cullen (n 5); Tröger (n 5); Mark J Flannery and Robert R Bliss, 'Market Discipline in Regulation: Pre-and Post-Crisis' in Allen N Berger, Philip Molyneux and John OS Wilson (eds), *Oxford Handbook of Banking* (3rd edn, Oxford Handbook of Banking (3rd edition), Oxford University Press, 2018). On the specific impact on market discipline of the BRRD legal design, see also Chapter 4.

[12] See Chapter 5.

[13] The fact that different holders of the same security behave in different ways and pursue different objective has been acknowledge long ago in equity-related research, as exemplified by the gigantic amount of research on shareholder activism. For a broad introduction to the matter, see Stuart L Gillan and Laura T Starks, 'The Evolution of Shareholder Activism in the United States' (2007) 19 Journal of Applied Corporate Finance 55.

The (limited) literature on the topic focused mainly on who should not buy bail-inable debt for financial stability purposes. On the contrary, to the best of the author's knowledge, no thorough analysis of the consequences of different compositions has been carried out. This specific aspect is particularly relevant for supervisors and resolution authorities. If different compositions yield different outcomes in terms of market discipline, the activities of supervisors and the resolution planning should adjust accordingly, relying more (or less) on the market information.[14] Moreover, it would make a remarkable difference in resolution planning, especially in relations to the exclusions and exemptions provided by Article 44 (3) of BRRD, influencing the ex-ante credibility of the bail-in itself.[15]

For the purpose of the present study, the impact on corporate governance[16] of the bail-inable securities holders should be disentangled into four main aspects, graphically summarised in Table 1[17]:

(1) the incentives and the capability of monitoring bank activities ex-ante;
(2) the investment strategy and consequent risk appetite of the holder;
(3) the ability to influence the decisions of the borrower[18];

[14] For the difference between direct and indirect effect of market discipline see Mark J Flannery, 'The Faces of "Market Discipline"' (2001) 20 Journal of Financial Services Research 107.

[15] For a deeper analysis of the exemptions from bail in see Chapter 4. Here it suffices to notice that in case of high levels of crossholdings among banks, the resolution authority might exempt a large part of the debt from bearing losses to avoid contagion, pursuing Article 44(3)(c) BRRD. Taking into account the composition of bail-inable debtholders beforehand, such an outcome can be anticipated, and the resolution plan adjust accordingly.

[16] On shareholders' apathy see Wolf-Georg Ringe, *The Deconstruction of Equity: Activist Shareholders, Decoupled Risk, and Corporate Governance* (Oxford University Press 2016) 9.

[17] Following the definition given by professors Shleifer and Vishny back in 1997: "Corporate governance deals with the ways in which suppliers of finance to corporations assure themselves of getting a return on their investment". Andrei Shleifer and Robert W Vishny, 'A Survey of Corporate Governance' (1997) 52 The journal of finance 737.

[18] The differentiation between monitoring and influence is consistent with the economic literature on market discipline. See Flannery (n 19).

Table 1 Dimension to consider for analysing the impact of different holders of bail-inable securities

Corporate governance	*Spillovers*
(1) Ex-ante incentives and capability to monitor (2) Investment strategy & Risk preference (3) Ability to influence decision-making (4) Holding Concentration of Bail-inable Debt *SENIORITY OF THE CLAIM* *EXISTENCE CONSTRAINT*	(1) Contagion Risk (2) (Other) Adverse Economic Consequences

(4) holdings of bail-inable debt should be relatively concentrated to avoid rational apathy.[19]

Notably, the ability to influence management for creditors represents a black box and shading light into it is all but straightforward.[20] The main channel one can think of is the so-called "private engagement"[21]: the growing tendency of investors to directly address management and directors out of the official channels, in the shadow of corporate law powers. For instance, Michelle Edkins, the Global Head of BlackRock's Investment Stewardship Team, stated: "In our experience (private engagement) has a fair degree of traction with management, we can raise (an) issue without having to dictate how management should address it".[22]

[19] Another crucial element that falls beyond the scope of this chapter is the trading activity close to conversion: who steps in and who opts out once probability of default increase? Unfortunately, there is no available data on such flows.

[20] In a broader view, the influencing mechanisms of all the investors represent a sort of black box, especially when it comes to analysing the corporate governance role of institutional investors. In this respect, a growing literature is attempting to investigate on private engagement strategies. See Joseph A McCahery, Zacharias Sautner and Laura T Starks, 'Behind the Scenes: The Corporate Governance Preferences of Institutional Investors' (2016) 71 The Journal of Finance 2905.

[21] See 'Shareholder Engagement: A New Era in Corporate Governance' https://deloitte.wsj.com/riskandcompliance/2013/10/01/shareholder-engagement-a-new-era-in-corporate-governance/ (accessed 30/09/2025).

[22] Barry B Burr, 'Money Managers Increasing Activism on Governance—But Quietly, Pension and Investments'. https://www.pionline.com/article/20120319/PRINT/303199980/money-managers-increasing-activism-on-governance-but-quietly (accessed 30/09/2025).

Assessing the governance role of individual classes of investors accounts for only one side of the story. Hence, when it comes to adverse spillovers, two main components ought to be considered: the first can be labelled as "Contagion Risk" and the second as "Adverse economic consequences".

"Contagion risk" relates to the risk that financial distress of one bank spills over to counterparties or the whole financial system. In the context of the new resolution framework, the contagion risk is easy to conceptualise.[23] Think, for instance, of the case of crossholding, where a Bank A holds in its portfolio a substantial amount of bail-inable instruments of Bank B. If Bank B enters into financial distress and the Resolution Authority decides to allocate losses on bail-inable instruments, the value of Bank A's assets will decrease accordingly. Such losses might, consequentially, result in Bank A's distress. Contagion can also indirectly materialise from institutions that get their leverage from banks, such as hedge funds. The trade-off between more concentration to enhance incentives to intervene and more dispersion to decrease the risk of contagion needs no further explanations.

"Adverse economic consequences" represent a sort of residual category, i.e., negative externalities whose direct channel is not contagion. Adverse spillovers can arise from aspects not directly related to financial stability. Think, for instance, of the case in which households hold a considerable stake of bail-inable debt. When losses materialise and the resolution authority allocates them to bail-inable creditors, the fact that households bear losses does not directly imply contagion risk. However, it shrinks the spending capacity of households, yielding adverse consequences on the real economy. A similar argument applies to other categories of investors, such as pension funds.[24]

Beyond corporate governance and adverse spillovers, a third dimension, which horizontally influences the magnitude of effects on both governance and spillovers, is the seniority of the bail-inable claim. It is clear that the more junior the holding position, the higher the probability of actually bearing losses. Consequentially, the more junior a liability is,

[23] See Avinash D Persaud, 'A Ticking Time Bomb: TLAC and Other Attempts to Privatise Bank Bailouts' [2016] Butterworths Journal of International Banking and Financial Law 160. See also Dirk Schoenmaker, *Contagion Risk in Banking* (LSE Financial Markets Group 1996).

[24] Persaud (n 28).

the higher the ex-ante incentives to monitor and the higher the probability of adverse spillovers to materialise. Given the complexity of the framework, the proceeding of the analysis will mainly focus on the first two dimensions (i.e., governance and spillovers), while considerations on the seniority of the holding positions will be limited and strictly functional to the other two.

Finally, taking the regulatory framework as a given, the analysis must cope with the "existence constraint". At first sight, this statement might appear little more than a tautology. Nonetheless, to grasp the enormous role it plays, it suffices to consider a few figures. First, at the beginning of 2017, the amount of Risk-Weighted assets of the 20 top European banks amounted to over 6 trillion euros.[25] For the same period, Dominique Laboureix, Board member of the Single Resolution Board, estimated that the average MREL target, applying the SRB 2017 MREL policy,[26] was on average 26% of RWA.[27] The same estimate prudentially forecasts an aggregate shortfall of 117 billion euros, of which 47 billion are in subordinated instruments. This implies that, willingly or unwillingly, an enormous amount of bail-inable securities must be issued and, consequently, held by investors.

3 The Anatomy of a Perfect Buyer

In exploring the role of investors in bail-inable securities, a first necessary step is to set out a benchmark. It is not possible to assess the role different investors play without having in mind an "ideal buyer". The definition of the "ideal buyer" of bail-inable securities constitutes the focus

[25] See Jan Schildbach, 'Where Do European Banks Stand? 10 Years after the Start of the Financial Crisis. 10 Years after the Start of the Financial Crisis' (2017) <https://www.dbresearch.com/PROD/RPS_EN-PROD/PROD0000000000450356/Where_do_European_banks_stand%3F_10_years_after_the_.PDF>.

[26] SRB, Minimum Requirement for Own Funds and Eligible Liabilities (MREL) SRB Policy for 2017 and Next Steps. Available at https://srb.europa.eu/sites/srbsite/files/item_1_-_public_version_mrel_policy_-_annex_i_-_plenary_session.pdf (accessed 30/09/2025).

[27] Dominique Laboureix, speech at 6th Industry Dialogue: 2017 MREL Policy, accessible at https://srb.europa.eu/sites/srbsite/files/20171120_6th_industry_dialogue_item_2_mrel_dominique_laboureix.pdf (accessed 30/09/2025). The estimation considers a sample of 76 banks, accounting for almost 80% of total assets of the banks subject to SRB authority.

of this section. In the proceeding of this chapter, the "ideal buyer" will represent the benchmark against which to assess the corporate governance impact of investors' categories and their adverse spillovers. Therefore, the desirability of the burden-sharing policy[28] and the resolution principles in allocating losses is not part of the analysis.

To begin with, it is useful to highlight some of the partial paradigms proposed in the literature. Even though no detailed analysis of the desirable holding composition exists, some authors have tangentially discussed the desirable characteristics of the holders of bail-inable securities. Krahnen and Moretti[29] mainly focus on minimising the risk of contagion, advocating in favour of institutional investors pursuing a long-term strategy, such as pension funds, life insurance companies, and private bankers. The authors also propose a stringent limit to access the market for bail-inable securities to long-only investors. Gotz and Tröger,[30] in arguing against household holdings, propose that the ideal investor in bail-inable debt must have three main characteristics: (1) being a sophisticated investor, (2) not being part of the banking sector, and (3) having a business model without an asset/liability maturity mismatch. Such a paradigm considers aspects of both governance and stability. The sophistication requirement looks at the ability to convey and compute information and, therefore, at market discipline.

On the other hand, other elements look at financial stability, such as the ban on both the banking sector and other investors performing maturity transformation activities.[31] Cross holdings increase bank interconnectedness, thus generating contagion risk. Avoiding maturity transformation would increase the loss absorbency capacity of investors whose risk of running into liquidity issues in case of substantial losses is lower.[32] Such a

[28] European Commission, Communication from the Commission on the application, from 1 August 2013, of State aid rules to support measures in favour of banks in the context of the financial crisis ('Banking Communication' (2013/C 216/01).

[29] JP Krahnen and L Moretti, 'Bail-in Clauses' [2015] Financial Regulation. Cambridge University Press, Cambridge.

[30] See Götz and Tröger (n 14).

[31] On maturity transformation and its implication for the fragility of banks, see Armour and others (n 13) 278.

[32] Brunnermeier and others (n 9) 32.

description fits insurance companies, pension funds, and high-net-worth individuals.[33]

Persaud[34] considers both "contagion risk" and "adverse economic consequences" among the negative spillovers stemming from investing in bail-inable debt. The author argues that neither banks and leveraged investors nor long-term investors should invest in bail-inable securities. The doubts about the first category mimic the arguments already put forward by the majority of the literature, i.e., crossholding is a threat to financial stability. In addition to this standard remark, Persaud adds a layer of complexity, juxtaposing to contagion risk other potential economic downsides. The author criticises the superficial view according to which long-term investors should own bail-inable securities since their investment strategy focuses on assets whose risk falls over time, while bail-inable securities are the exact opposite.[35]

These approaches are, in principle, not mutually exclusive: each of them points out relevant aspects of investing in bail-inable debt for specific classes of investors. Nonetheless, taking the current regulatory framework as a given, these approaches compete with each other and turn out to be incomplete. As mentioned beforehand, one has to consider the "existence constraint": bail-inable securities must be issued and, consequently, held.

Comparing the theoretical constructs on "who should invest in bail-inable debt" and the amount of securities that needs to be issued a paradox arises: on the one hand, nobody should, for different and reasonable rationales, buy bail-inable securities; on the other hand, the amount of bail-inable securities that need to be marketed is stunning.

In facing such a paradox, the analytical framework proposed in Sect. 2 comes in handy for two main reasons. First, it considers potential benefits that specific classes of holders can bring to the borrowing bank in terms of corporate governance impact. Second, it represents a framework apt to perform a maximisation exercise, given the "existence constraint".

[33] Benjamin Bernard, Agostino Capponi and Joseph E Stiglitz, 'Bail-Ins and Bailouts: Incentives, Connectivity, and Systemic Stability' (2017) wp23747.

[34] Persaud (n 28).

[35] The probability of a bank running in financial distress and facing the need for resolution in the short term is relatively low in good times, while it increases sharply in the long term.

The bail-in represents a way to redistribute losses of bank distress from taxpayers to investors.[36]

Therefore, building on the theoretical framework depicted so far, this chapter discusses the optimal mix of investors, i.e., the mix of investors ensuring the best result in terms of maximising the governance benefit while minimising adverse spillovers. In other words, this chapter focuses on marginal improvements that different compositions of bail-inable debtholders yield. On the contrary, it steers clear of the discussion on the efficiency of the new regulatory regime as compared with the old one or other possible regimes.[37]

As I mentioned, on the one hand, achieving an optimal composition of bail-inable debtholders implies maximising the positive impact of investors on corporate governance and, at the same time, minimising adverse spillovers.[38] On the other hand, maximising beneficial corporate governance impact means that investors should be capable and willing to monitor the borrower's activities, have risk appetite that is compatible with socially desirable levels of risk-taking (i.e., a relatively low-risk appetite) and willing and capable to influence the decisions of their borrowers. Minimising adverse spillovers means that investors should have as little interconnection as possible among them. Interconnectedness can be both sectorial and geographical. So, for instance, it is not desirable to have a high proportion of domestic holding, while it is desirable to have a considerable amount of holdings out of the Euro Area countries.[39] Moreover, the probability of being bailed-in must be consistent with the loss absorbency capacity of each investor, i.e., investors with highly mismatched balance sheet should opt for senior holdings. Finally, investors should not have holdings accounting for too-high of a share of their portfolio, especially if their preferred investment strategy seeks assets whose risk decreases over time.

[36] In this respect, one may consider the expression "loss absorbency capacity" as misleading, since losses are not plainly absorbed, but just allocated to other counterparties that are hopefully able to bear them without getting into trouble.

[37] On the efficiency of new EU regimes see, for instance, Avgouleas and Goodhart (n 4).

[38] A formal exercise, where such a maximisation problem is modelled, falls out of the scope of this contribution that, instead, focus on the relevant institutional characteristics.

[39] Martijn A Boermans and Sweder van Wijnbergen, 'Contingent Convertible Bonds: Who Invests in European CoCos?' [2017] Applied Economics Letters 1.

By way of a preliminary conclusion, no bulletproof investor in bail-inable securities exists. No one can satisfy all of the relevant conditions: maximising corporate governance benefits, minimising the threat to financial stability and other adverse spillovers and, at the same time, satisfying the existence constraint.

If no specific category of investors can efficiently hold bail-inable securities, it is necessary to look at a solution where a mix of different, individually suboptimal, investors can yield the best workable outcome.

Section 4 provides some data about holders of bail-inable securities, in order to understand whether the current composition reflects the theoretical considerations discussed so far. Should that not be the case, the analysis discusses the exogenous factors impeding the matching of such a benchmark.

4 Bail-Inable Debt Holder Competition: The State of the Art

This section aims to show the relevant information on the holders of bail-inable securities that is, at the time of writing, publicly available. The analysis is based on the data provided by "Security Holding Statistics" (SHS), a database compiled by the ECB statistic services.[40] The SHS provides data on the holders of an array of securities issued by EU credit institutions (i.e., banks) since 2013. It computes the amount of securities held by different categories of investors. Section 4.1 further discusses the specificities and the limitations of the data.

Before moving to the description of the dataset, it is important to stress how this empirical evaluation represents a necessary step to understand whether and how market forces are adapting to the new regulatory environment as well as to detect factors that potentially impede an efficient

[40] Established by the Regulation (Eu) No 1011/2012 Of The European Central Bank of 17 October 2012 concerning statistics on holdings of securities (ECB/2012/24) as lastly amended by Regulation (EU) 2018/318 of the ECB of 22 February 2018 amending Regulation (EU) No 1011/2012 concerning statistics on holdings of securities (ECB/2018/7), OJ L 62, 5.3.2018, p. 4. Reporting methodology has been furtherly developed in the Guideline of the ECB of 22 March 2013 concerning statistics on holdings of securities (ECB/2013/7), OJ L 125, 7.5.2013, p. 17, as lastly amended by Guideline (EU) 2018/323 of the ECB of 22 February 2018 amending Guideline ECB/2013/7 concerning statistics on holdings of securities (ECB/2018/8), OJ L 62, 5.3.2018, p. 38.

adjustment. Even though the available data do not allow for comprehensive statistical exercise, which would fall outside the scope of the analysis in any case, having a clear picture of the current aggregate composition and trends will prove to be insightful. Section 4.1 describes the data, discusses the related literature, and highlights the scope and limitation of the analysis.

4.1 Data and Limitations

The analysis is based on the "Security Holding Statistics" (SHS), a database compiled by the ECB statistic services. The publicly available data consist of only a fraction of the data collected and are aggregated at country level. Thus, we only know the category of investors holding bail-inable securities issued by the banks of each Euro Area Countries. Moreover, these data are collected on a security-by-security basis, according to the mandatory reporting of the holders. For this reason, only the holdings of EA investors are part of the dataset.[41] Data on investors' holdings, which represent the focus of the analysis, have been collected from the fourth quarter of 2013.[42]

Among the available classes of securities, the SHS provides data on the holders[43] of "non-covered debt securities", issued by European Banks and with initial maturity longer than one year. The analysis focuses on this class of securities and their holders.[44]

A few examples may clarify the cases covered by the available data. The data cover the case of a German household holding non-covered debt issued by a Spanish bank; whereas the data does not cover the case in which a US investor holds non-covered debt issued by the same Spanish bank[45]: the SHS data cover only investors resident in the Euro Area. The

[41] Accessible at http://sdw.ecb.europa.eu/browse.do?node=9689727 (accessed 30/09/2025).

[42] For a comprehensive overview, see ECB, 'Who Holds What? Nwe Information on Securities Holdings' [2015] ECB Economic Bullettin 72.

[43] The data capture only holders that are residents in the Euro Area or non-resident holders whose securities are deposited with Euro Area custodians.

[44] Consistent with MREL requirement set out in Article 45(4)(d), pursuing which only securities with remaining maturity of at least 1 year can count to meet MREL.

[45] Unless the securities are deposited with a Euro Area (for instance, French) custodian.

data do not cover the case in which an Italian pension fund holds non-covered debt issued by a Danish bank: the data cover only securities issued by Euro Area banks.

The data, and consequently the analysis, suffers from two main limitations. First, the scope of the analysis is limited. In this regard, the previous examples highlight the limitation of the analysis. It is not possible to have a complete view of the holders of all the outstanding debt of a bank, but only the distribution among sectors of the holders located in one of the Euro Area countries, since those are the only ones having a legal obligation to report their holdings to the ECB. In the same vein, it is not possible to provide a comprehensive assessment of the exposure of each sector in bail-inable securities, since the data include only the securities issued by banks located in Euro Area countries.

Second, the data does not exactly match "bail-inable securities" but only proxies them.[46] In this respect, two main aspects ought to be considered. First, in the real world, understanding, ex-ante, which securities are bail-inable according to Article 44(2) and (3) of the BRRD is not straightforward, since the Resolution Authority retains considerable discretionary power.[47] Moreover, specifically on SHS data, it is only possible to extrapolate non-covered debt issuances whose initial maturity is longer than one year. However, no specific information is available on the main characteristics, including the seniority of the claim.

Despite these limitations, the (limited) literature[48] on the matter consistently relied on this proxy since non-covered debt securities mirrors to a large extent the instruments that constitute banks' "own funding and

[46] According to the BRRD, all banks liabilities that are not exempted *ex* Art. 44(2) [e.g., insured deposits] are bail-inable.

[47] On these issues, see back Chapter 4 where such complications where ruled out by assumption so to being able to discuss the effects of the legal design. See also, Tröger (n 5).

[48] See, mainly, Claudia Pigrum, Thomas Reininger and Caroline Stern, 'Bail-in: Who Invests in Noncovered Debt Securities Issued by Euro Area Banks?' (2016) 32 Financial Stability Report 101; Anne-Caroline Hüser and others, 'The Systemic Implications of Bail-in: A Multi-Layered Network Approach' [2017] Journal of Financial Stability; Mr Giovanni Dell'Ariccia and others, ***Trade-Offs in Bank Resolution*** (International Monetary Fund 2018). See also, ECB, 'Financial Stability Review—November 2016' (2016). In Box 7 there is the analysis: "The evolution of Sectoral holding of bail-inable debt".

eligible liabilities" other than CET1 instruments.[49] Hence, this represents a "state-of-the-art" proxy for bail-inable securities. Given that the analysis refrains from any causal interpretation of the data, such a proxy can be prudently used. In what follows, the phrases "bail-inable securities" and "non-covered debt" will be used as synonyms.

The holders of bail-inable securities are split into five main categories: (1) households[50]; (2) Monetary financial institution (other than Central Banks), which encompass banks and money market funds[51]; (3) Insurance Firms and Pension Funds; (4) Non-Financial Corporations; (5) Other financial institutions (OFIs), such as private bankers, hedge funds, investment funds (other than pension funds), and mutual funds.[52]

As the description of the data and the sample of reference made clear, no causal interpretations can be inferred; therefore, the rest of this section will focus on providing a snapshot of the current composition of bail-inable debtholders and showing some of the relevant trends over the last five years. In so doing, the proceeding of the section will partly rely on previous studies and partly on original and updated data processing, depending on the public availability of relevant data. Specifically, Sect. 4.2 focuses on the available data on the geographical distribution of holders, relying on previous studies; Sect. 4.3 discusses the distribution of bail-inable debts across sectors of Euro Area investors, presenting original data processing; Sect. 4.4 provides limited evidence on the distribution of holders according to seniority, relying on previous studies.

[49] Pigrum, Reininger and Stern (n 54). See, with a different design and slightly different data used, Ringe and Patel (n 2).

[50] Together with Non-Profit Institutions Serving Households (NPISH), such as trade unions; professional or learned societies; consumers' associations.

[51] This clearly implies some issues in separately assessing the two categories. Nonetheless, previous empirical evidence shows that the amount of MMF exposures is less the 1/6 as compared with banks and these exposures are particularly concentrated in the Netherlands, France, and partially Germany. Therefore, in the amount of crossholdings that will be displayed in the proceeding of the section such overestimation shall be considered for those countries.

[52] On the methodology employed in aggregating the data on the basis of sector holders see, Jose Cartas and Qi He, 'Issuance and Holdings of Securities in a "From-Whom-to-Whom" Framework', *Handbook on Securities Statistics* (International Monetary Fund) ch 8.

4.2 Geographical Distribution: EA vs Non-EA

As mentioned beforehand, the actual geographical distribution of holders represents one of the limitations of the available data. Nonetheless, it is possible to discuss some crucial aspect of such a dimension whose relevance encompasses both systemic risk considerations and adverse economic consequences. On the contrary, geographical distribution seems not to have direct governance consequences.

The geographical distribution of investors on bail-inable debt has a twofold impact on systemic risk: on the one hand, high concentration of holders in the same jurisdiction increases the level of interconnectedness[53] among local actors, intensifying both the contagion risk and potential adverse economic spillovers. On the other hand, if investors in bail-inable debt are located worldwide, potential losses propagate to a larger part of the global financial system.[54] Small shocks can be efficiently absorbed globally, while large shocks might trigger a domino effect worldwide generating a regulatory appetite for ring-fencing against foreign risks.[55]

Nonetheless, if one takes into consideration not only contagion risk but also the adverse consequences on the economy at large, a greater geographical diversification seems to be desirable. Indeed, allocating most of the bank losses on domestic households, pension funds, or banks would mean to harm the spending capacity of the population and tighten to a massive extent the ability of access to bank credit.

From the perspective of Euro Area (EA) stability, a substantial amount of non-EA holding is therefore desirable[56] even though, looking at the data, is far from being reached in many EA countries. This part mostly

[53] On the so-called "Too-Interconnected-to-fail" problem see, among many others, Anne-Caroline Hüser, 'Too Interconnected to Fail: A Survey of the Interbank Networks Literature' (SAFE 2016) 91.

[54] Geographical diversification also entails more cross-border issues in implementing resolution. Even though this aspect falls out of the scope of the analysis, the literature has monotonically insisted on cross-border issues as one of the main elements in arguing against the credibility of the new resolution regime. See, for instance, Federico Lupo-Pasini and Ross P Buckley, 'International Coordination in Cross-Border Bank Bail-Ins: Problems and Prospects' (2015) 16 European Business Organization Law Review 203.

[55] Katia D'Hulster and Inci Ötker-Robe, 'Ring-Fencing Cross-Border Banks: An Effective Supervisory Response?' (2015) 16 Journal of Banking Regulation 169.

[56] Boermans and van Wijnbergen (n 44).

relies on data published on previous studies, since not all the relevant data are publicly available.[57]

Figure 2 shows the distribution of holders of non-covered debt issued by banks, distinguishing between EA and non-EA holders. Conceptually, this represents a proxy of the ability of each banking sector to attract international investors. On average, the holders of non-covered debt issued by EA banks are mostly resident within EA (61%), while 39% are non-EA investors.[58] Beyond such an aggregate figure, what immediately attracts the attention of the observer is the massive cross-country variation. For instance, Italian (95%)[59] banks heavily rely on the EA market for bail-inable debt; while other countries have a much more balanced situation, and some others lean toward a non-EA majority of holdings. German banks are among the "balanced" ones, with 47% of EA holdings, while the reliance on EA investors of Dutch (39%) and Finnish (36%) banks is particularly limited.

The case of Italian banks reflects the hardship of the country in having a strong and attractive position in international financial markets, suggesting that the link between banks and their sovereign debt has not been severed[60] or, at least, that path dependency plays a major role. On the contrary, the figures on non-EA holdings of "more virtuous" countries as the Netherlands and Germany signal a greater capacity to attract foreign funds. Finally, these data are less significant in the case of EA countries with traditionally strong economic and financial ties to non-EA countries. This is the case, for instance, of Finnish banks, whose non-covered debt is mainly held by non-EA investors. This result is probably driven by the close ties with the Swedish and Danish financial system, accounting for a large proportion of the banking market share.

[57] Specifically, Fig. 3 is taken from ECB (n 54). Figure 4 is taken from Pigrum, Reininger, and Stern (n 54). The choice of relying on other studies is due to the fact that relevant data, even when available, suffered from category mismatches between relevant databases (specifically, Security Holding Statics Database and Balance Sheet instruments database) and reporting inconsistencies. All data on this section refers to the fourth quarter of 2015.

[58] There is a 2% of non-covered debt whose holding is unreported.

[59] But also Greek (90%) and Spanish (71%) banks with, respectively, 90% and 71% of Euro Area holdings. See Table 3 in the Appendix.

[60] Valerie De Bruyckere and others, 'Bank/Sovereign Risk Spillovers in the European Debt Crisis' (2013) 37 Journal of Banking & Finance 4793.

Fig. 2 Geographical distribution (within or outside Euro Area) of holders of non-covered debt securities. Own calculations

A closer analysis of data on domestic and EA investors reinforces the previous argument (Fig. 3): here, it is clear that high stakes of EA investor holdings are associated with considerable domestic biases (in Italy, Spain, and Greece). On the other side of the spectrum, Benelux countries show an almost negligible amount of domestic holdings, steadily below 10%, with the Netherlands leading the group with only 3% of domestic holdings.

Finally, EA holding can be further disentangled. Figure 4 shows the geographical distribution of non-covered debt held in the EA, distinguishing between "Domestic holdings", "non-domestic holding of the Top 3 holding countries", and "non-domestic holding of the other than Top 3 holding countries". The figure shows that most of non-domestic EA holdings are located within the "Top 3 holding Countries", with the partial exception of Luxemburg, the Netherlands, and Ireland where around 20% of non-covered bank debt is held throughout the rest of Eurozone.

This overview showed that, generally, within the Euro Area, the domestic bias in non-covered debtholding is deeply rooted. Moreover, the high cross-country heterogeneity hampers the "level playing field" in the

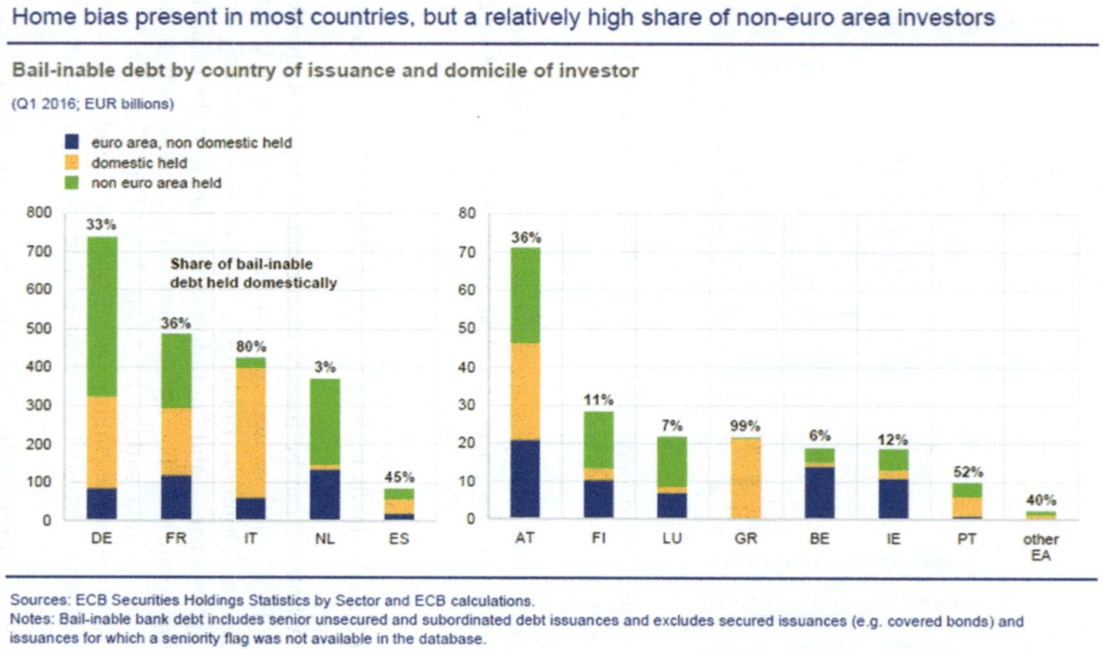

Fig. 3 Geographical distribution of holders according to the country of issuance (domestic, Euro Area, Non-EA)

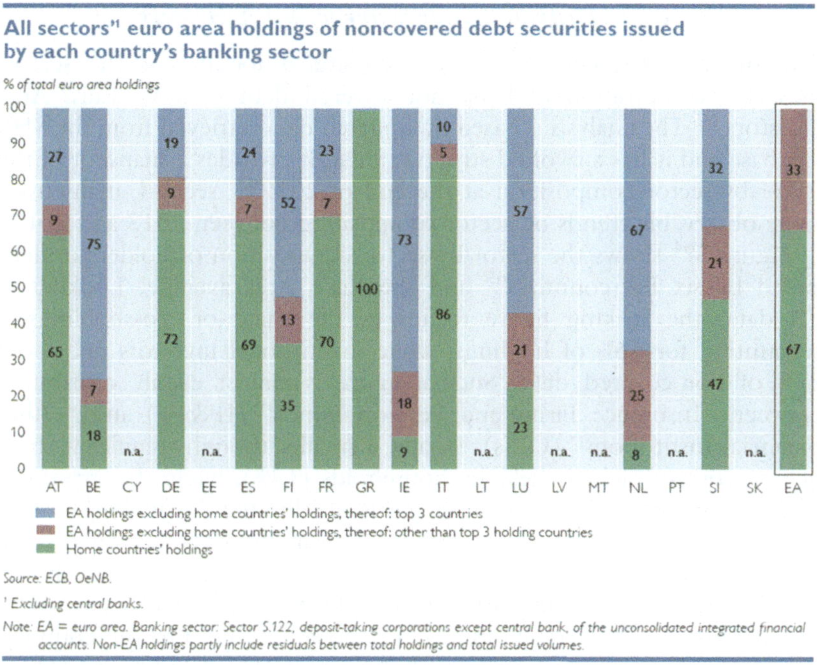

Fig. 4 Geographical distribution of non-covered debt securities holders within Euro Area

internal market, which represents one of the primary goals of the entire resolution framework.[61] Indeed, the domestic effects of implementing a resolution procedure in Italy or the Netherlands will be sharply different.

[61] See Recital 108 BRRD: "Ensuring effective resolution of failing institutions within the Union is an essential element in the completion of the internal market. The failure of such institutions has an effect not only on the financial stability of the markets where it directly operates but also on the whole Union financial market. [...] Ensuring effective financing of the resolution of those institutions across Member States is not only in the best interests of the Member States in which they operate but also of all the Member States in general as a means of ensuring a level competitive playing field and improving the functioning of the internal financial market".

4.3 *Distribution by Sector with EA Holders*

The situation becomes even more entangled looking at the sector-by-sector composition of bank non-covered debt held by Euro Area investors.[62] The analysis is based on updated data retrieved from the SHS database and it has a twofold structure: first, it provides a snapshot of the sector-by-sector composition at the end of 2017[63]; second, it discusses some observable trends on sector composition between 2013 and 2017.

Figure 5[64] shows the sector-by-sector composition of holders of debt issued by six EA countries[65] and the Euro Area average. Looking at EA data, the striking figure relates to the share of crossholdings,[66] accounting for 46% of holdings, while institutional investors only hold 37% of non-covered debt. Such a figure is almost evenly distributed between "Insurance Firms and Pension Funds" (IF&PF) and "Other Financial Institutions" (OFIs). Finally, a smaller though significant share of non-covered debt is held by households (13%), while the exposures of governments and non-financial firms are limited (cumulatively 4%). Nevertheless, compositions at country level vary considerably. First, some countries rely on crossholdings much more than the EA average shows. Notably, Spain (61%) and Portugal (79%) lead the way, while Italy (50%) and Germany (54%) crossholdings are above average. On the contrary, French and Dutch banks exhibit a shallow level of crossholdings (31%).

Institutional investors, on the other hand, clearly act as substitutes for crossholdings. Indeed, the countries with lower amounts of crossholdings show, conversely, high holdings by IF&PF and OFIs. That is the case

[62] As discussed earlier, available data do not allow for having the same information for non-EA investors. Therefore, the proceeding of the analysis captures only a limited share of outstanding debt that varies county by county depending on the percentage of EA holding. For instance, sector-by-sector data cover 95% of non-covered debt issued by Italian banks, but only the 53% of debt issued by German banks. This might lead to overestimate the amount of Households holdings that is reasonable to assume as mainly domestic, for the countries with a high stake of non-EA holdings, such as Germany, the Netherlands, etc.

[63] Table 3 in the Appendix shows the percentage amount of holding for 11 EA countries and its evolution between 2013 (Q4) and 2017 (Q4).

[64] In the Appendix shows the same statistics for all the EA countries.

[65] Namely the countries with higher level of outstanding non-covered debt.

[66] See the caveat on the possible overestimation back at note 56.

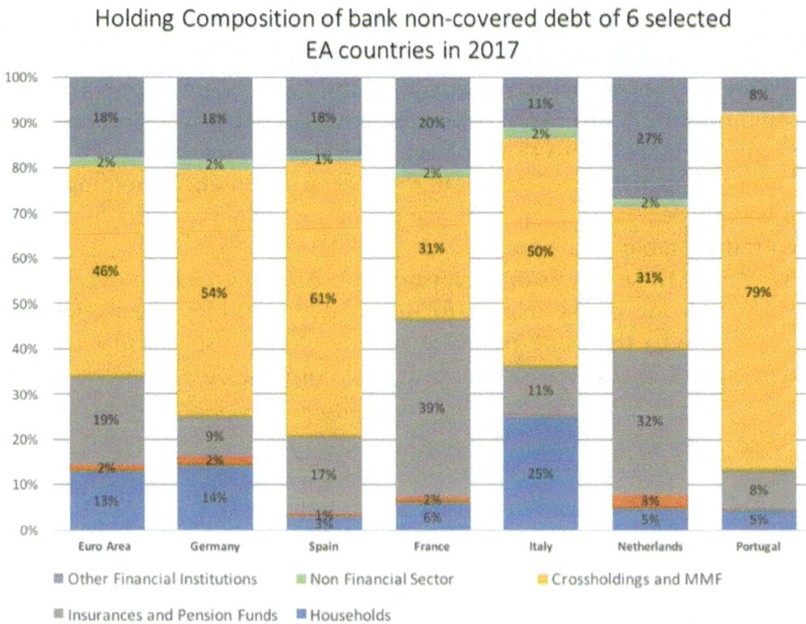

Fig. 5 Sector composition of non-covered debt held by EA investors 2017Q4 in selected EA countries. Own calculations

for French and Dutch banks whose non-covered debt is held by institutional investors for 59%, well above the EA average. On the contrary, the other countries show a reverse picture, with low institutional investors' holdings.

Finally, the majority of the countries considered show a low stake of household holdings, with the notable exceptions of Italy and Germany. Italy, in particular, shows 25% of households holding.

From this snapshot, one can see how holders of non-covered debt are mostly sophisticated investors, with the notable exceptions of Italy and, to a certain extent, Germany. Moreover, data show a high degree of substitutability between crossholdings and institutional investors' holdings.

This is where the market for bail-inable securities stands now; yet it is important to understand how it has arrived here. In other words, has the demand-side of the market for bail-inable securities evolved over time? Fig. 6 shows percentage changes in sector holdings between 2013 and

2017, taking 2013 as a benchmark. The red line indicates the entrance into force of the bail-in tool, as of 1 January 2016.[67]

The graph shows a sharp increase in institutional investors' holdings throughout the Euro Area bank non-covered debt. The increase was particularly relevant for OFIs in 2017 (+15% as compared with 2015 and +31% as compared with 2013). On the contrary, household holdings have consistently decreased during the sample period, while crossholdings have been rather stable over time.

However, these trends only capture Euro Area aggregate movement of the demand-side of the market for bail-inable securities. Again, looking more closely to the same trends at country level, a spectacular level of heterogeneity arises. For instance, Fig. 7 compares the same trends in

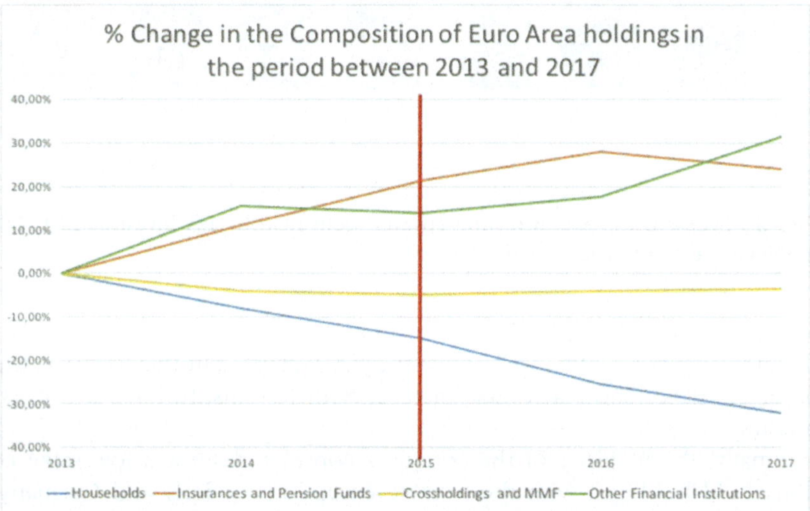

Fig. 6 % variation of sector holdings as of 2013. Own calculations

[67] Article 130 BRRD. Since the data takes into account the end of each year, the 2015Q4 observation coincides with the entrance into force of bail-in. It is worth remembering that, given the nature of the available data the analysis cannot infer any kind of casual relationship between the bail-in entering into force and changes in holding composition. Moreover, such an inference would be particularly difficult to prove even with granular data as the investors were likely to anticipate it, since the first drafts of the BRRD dates back to 2012 and the final version was promulgated in May 2014.

sector holdings for non-covered debt issued by Italian and Dutch banks. The differences between the two are striking both quantitatively and qualitatively.

On the one hand, holding composition has been relatively stable for Dutch banks, where the stake of institutional investors has increased mainly in the last two years of the sample period, while crossholdings and household holdings have decreased in the same time frame. On the other hand, the holding composition of non-covered debt issued by Italian banks experienced a sort of revolution, in which institutional investors almost doubled their holdings (from 11.07% to 21.87%), while households nearly halved them (from 41.2% to 25.3%). Notably, crossholdings overall increased by 10% in the sample period, although in the first part of the period crossholdings were decreasing. This may be deemed a transitional trend, in which crossholdings substitute for the sharp decrease in household holdings in the wake of the latest turmoil with Italian failing banks.[68]

Given the stunning cross-country variation in both trends and compositions, Sect. 5 will discuss specific data for each sector in assessing its governance and stability impact. Before moving to that analysis, Sect. 4.4 briefly surveys available data on the seniority of claims and the relative holders by sector.

4.4 *Sector Holding and Seniority*

As mentioned before, publicly available data do not allow for analysing the sectoral preferences for bail-inable securities with different seniority. The category of "non-covered debt" encompasses both Additional Tier,[69] Tier 2, subordinated, and senior unsecured instruments. Moreover, existing evidence based on studies carried out with proprietary datasets is extremely limited.[70]

In the Financial Stability Review of November 2016,[71] the ECB showed a significant shift in security holdings according to their seniority

[68] For a deeper analysis about the Italian case, see Edoardo Martino, 'Subordinated Debt under Bail-in Threat' (2017) 2 University of Bologna Law Review 252.

[69] As long as they are not issued in the form of preferred stocks.

[70] With the notable exceptions of Boermans and van Wijnbergen (n 44); ECB (n 54).

[71] See ECB (n 54) 100. Chart C.

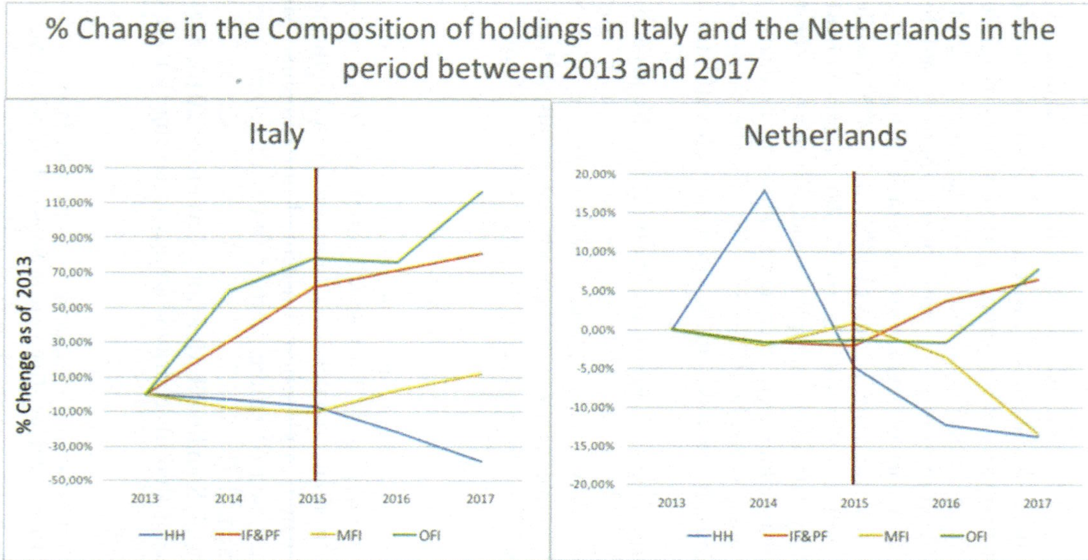

Fig. 7 % variation of sector holdings as of 2013 in Italy and the Netherlands. Own calculations

between 2013(Q4) and 2016(Q1). Specifically, crossholdings exposures shift toward senior positions, while households exhibit a preference for junior, and thence riskier and more remunerative, bank assets. The same shift toward junior exposures has been observed for Insurance Firms and Pension Funds and, especially, for Investment Funds.

Consistent with those findings, Boermans and van Wijnbergen analysed the market for contingent convertibles (CoCos) issued by European banks between 2009 and 2015. They found that the market is steadily growing and that CoCo holders mainly reside outside the Euro Area (74%). The investment funds (78%) located in the EA's biggest financial hubs dominated the share of EA holdings: Luxembourg (46%) and Ireland (28%).

5 Different Holders: Divergent Incentives and Specific Spillovers

It is now time to piece together the insights of the theoretical framework, and the empirical evidence discussed earlier. Therefore, this section will address the role of each investor class in terms of both corporate governance and financial stability.

In so doing, the proceeding of the section introduces and discusses the specific trends of non-covered debtholdings in the sample period, highlighting abnormal variations that might be interpreted, at least partly, as a response to the new resolution framework. This allows for a discussion of the desirability of market adjustments and the necessity for further regulatory interventions. The analysis only considers the five European countries with the largest banking sector and the highest level of non-covered debt issued (France, Germany, Italy, The Netherlands, Spain).[72]

The categorisation that follows is somewhat artificial, while a functional approach could have been more useful in answering the research question. Labelling an investor as a Pension Fund or Mutual Fund is neither necessary nor sufficient for arguing about the business model and the corporate governance role of each investor. Nonetheless, that is not possible at this stage of research: aggregated data do not allow for a functional approach. Despite such a limitation, it is still informative for the

[72] At the end of 2017, the banking sectors of these 5 countries issued 86.94% of the outstanding non-covered debt with original maturity longer than 1 year.

reader to grasp the fundamental characteristics of each class of investors as reported by the SHS published by the ECB. Section 6, building on the arguments developed through such an artificial categorisation, attempts to provide a functional interpretation of the state of the art and its desirable developments.

In analysing specific investor classes, the discussion will encompass relevant pieces of regulation contributing to shaping the holding composition (especially when it comes to households and crossholdings).

5.1 Households

A. Corporate governance role and adverse spillovers. As already mentioned, many authors[73] have already argued against retail investors holding bail-inable securities. Such a general and intuitive scepticism about household holdings is consistent with the framework of this research since they contribute neither to enhancing corporate governance nor in minimising adverse spillovers.

On the one hand, households lack the necessary sophistication for collecting and processing the relevant information on the risk-taking of their borrowers. Moreover, and perhaps more fundamentally, households radically lack the ability to influence the decision-making process of the borrowing banks.

On the other hand, in case of bank distress, imposing losses on household brings about significant negative spillovers that, in the categorisation proposed back in Sect. 2, can be labelled as "adverse economic consequences". In case of distress, if bank losses are allocated to households, whose portfolios are likely to be relatively undiversified, their spending capacity shrinks, harming the real economy and posing issues of social justice, and making the option to "bail-in" politically unviable.[74]

[73] Both tangentially in articles about resolution framework in general and with specific pieces discussing households' holdings. For the former see Avgouleas and Goodhart (n 4). For arguments against households investing in bail-inable securities see Simone Alvaro and others, 'The Marketing of MREL Securities after BRRD Interactions between Prudential and Transparency Requirements and the Challenges Which Lie Ahead' (2017) 15 CONSOB Legal Research Papers (Quaderni Giuridici).

[74] A paradigmatic example in this regard is represented by the Resolution of four small Italian Banks in November 2015, where losses where widely born by retail consumers that had often been victim of mis-selling. Such a resolution decision ("Decreto Salva Banche") opened up the floor for massive political debate and social opposition as well as for indirect

Consequently, a high level of household holdings might increase bailout expectations ex-ante, since bailing in households implies high societal costs.

The EU legal framework is no longer completely agnostic to retail investors holding bail-inable securities. The European Securities and Market Authority (ESMA)[75] included debt instruments eligible for bail-in among the "complex" instruments under MIFID II,[76] imposing stringent information duties on investment firms. Specifically, investment firms have the legal obligation to control the specific knowledge of the client on the products she is willing to invest in. Additionally, if the client shows insufficient knowledge about the risk of the financial product, investment firms have the legal obligation to warn the client that she is not in a position to judge whether to invest or not in the instrument.[77] This mainly aims to prevent mis-selling.[78]

In conclusion, households should hold a negligible amount of bail-inable instruments since they cannot act as effective investors in corporate governance and, at the same time, high societal costs stem from their bearing of losses in the case of a bail-in. In this vein, MIFID II tightened the duty of investment firms to inform households about the riskiness of the product appropriately.

B. Trends. Panel A of Fig. 8 shows a heterogeneous path when it comes to the percentage of bank non-covered debt held by households, while Panel B shows a somewhat similar trend in the percentage change of non-covered debt held taking 2013 as the reference year, with a sharp but not uniform decrease.

bailout expenditures in the form of reimbursement of the losses born by retail investors. On this issue, see Bank of Italy, 'Financial Stability Report No. 1' (2016) <https://www.bancaditalia.it/media/notizia/financial-stability-report-no-1-2016/>. Specifically on legal and economic consequences of "Decreto Slava Banche", see Martino (n 74).

[75] Guidelines on complex debt instruments and structured deposits, 04 February 2016 | ESMA/2015/1787. Bail-in eligible instruments are included among the "Debt instruments incorporating a structure making it difficult for the client to understand the risk" at paragraph 13.g.

[76] Directive 2014/65/EU of the European Parliament and of the Council of 15 May 2014 on markets in financial instruments. OJ L 173, 12.6.2014.

[77] Article 25(3) and 25(4)(iii) MiFID II.

[78] On the miss-selling, with specific analysis of the Italian and Portuguese case, see Götz and Tröger (n 14).

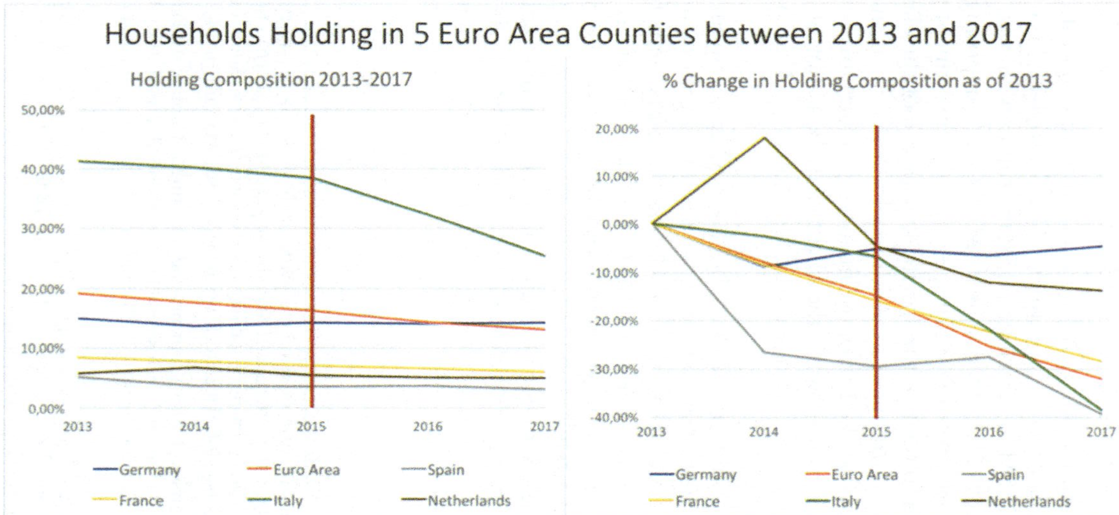

Fig. 8 Households Holdings trend between 2013 and 2017. Own calculations

In this diversified but somehow converging scenario, German banks represent a peculiar case. The amount of household holdings has remained stable throughout the sample period, around 14% of non-covered debt issued by banks, which is now higher than the EA average. This appears to signal that German households firmly believe in the resilience of their banks. It is also possible that households dismissing their investment in bank debt in other countries have migrated to debt from German banks.

To sum up, the market forces seem to converge toward a low amount of household's holdings, which is in line with the theoretical expectations, with the considerable exception of German bank debtholders. Nonetheless, significant legacy issues and path-dependent behaviours still have to be overcome.

5.2 *Bank Crossholdings*

A. **Corporate Governance Role and Adverse Spillovers.**

Bank crossholdings of bail-inable instruments have also received widespread opposition in the literature since they increase the interconnectedness of banks and correlate counterparty risks.[79] Despite such a predominant consensus, policymakers did not regulate counterparties since it would be difficult to do so and might have severe unintended consequences as well.[80]

Unlike household holdings, the analysis partly departs from the consensus against bank crossholdings because of the "existence constraint" of bail-inable securities. Moreover, as stated in Sect. 3, policymakers face a minimisation problem: systemic risk should be as low as possible but cannot be eliminated since it is somehow inherent to

[79] Bernard, Capponi and Stiglitz (n 38). In a more general setting, see Xavier Freixas, Bruno M Parigi and Jean-Charles Rochet, 'Systemic Risk, Interbank Relations, and Liquidity Provision by the Central Bank' [2000] Journal of money, credit and banking 611.

[80] See Wolf Wagner, 'Diversification at Financial Institutions and Systemic Crises' (2010) 19 Journal of Financial Intermediation 373. For a more general argument on anti-herding regulation, Ian Ayres and Joshua Mitts, 'Anti-Herding Regulation' (2015) 5 Harv. Bus. L. Rev. 1.

banking. Reducing interconnection too much would increase the cost of funding and reduce the amount of credit available to the real economy.

The legal framework is not entirely agnostic when it comes to bank crossholdings: ex-ante, the Financial Stability Board (FSB) and the Basel Committee on Banking Supervision (BCBS) modified Basel III standards to account for crossholdings.[81]

In the TLAC Term Sheet,[82] the FSB provided for the necessity to deduct from one bank's TLAC the exposures to TLAC instruments issued by other banks.[83] This means that if a bank massively invests in other bank's bail-inable securities (crossholdings), that bank must issue more capital or eligible securities to comply with TLAC requirements.

The Basel Committee for Banking Supervision[84] implemented the FSB provision by modifying some of the Basel III provisions on capital definition. For what is of strict interest, on the one hand, holdings exceeding 10% of TLAC instruments of the issuer must be deducted from Tier 2 Capital for the investing bank. The same regime applies to non-regulatory capital TLAC-holdings exceeding 5% of the investing bank's common equity. On the other hand, MREL regulation does not provide for such

[81] This applies in relation to Total loss Absorbency Capacity (TLAC) representing a minimum requirement for "loss-absorbing" liabilities that since 1 January 2019 onwards will be applied to systemically relevant institutions (G-SIBs). Conceptually, TLAC and MREL are similar and pursue the same objective, even though they are not completely overlapping. On differences and similarities between TLAC and MREL, Jose Carlos Pardo and Victoria Santillana, 'The European MREL: Main Characteristics and TLAC Similarities and Differences' [2014] European Regulation Watch. On the perspective of reform to harmonise MREL with TLAC for the implementation of TLAC by European G-SIBs, see European Banking Authority, 'Final Report on MREL—Report on the Implementation and Design of the MREL Framework—EBA-Op-2016-21' (2016) 154.

[82] Total Loss Absorbency Capacity, Financial Stability Board (n 11). See back Chapter 3, Sect. 3.2.

[83] Ibid. Section 15: "In order to reduce the risk of contagion, G-SIBs must deduct from their own TLAC or regulatory capital exposures to eligible external TLAC instruments and liabilities issued by other G-SIBs in a manner generally parallel to the existing provisions in Basel III that require a bank to deduct from its own regulatory capital certain investments in the regulatory capital of other banks. The Basel Committee on Banking Supervision (BCBS) will further specify this provision, including a prudential treatment for non-G-SIBs".

[84] BCBS, 'Standard. TLAC Holdings. Amendments to the Basel III Standard on the Definition Capital' (2016).

deductions for non-G-SIBs.[85] In a nutshell, if the 13 European bigger banks (the ones designated as G-SIBs) want to have TLAC instruments issued by other banks in their portfolio, will need to hold more capital to account for the increase in contagion risk this pose.

Also, the BRRD recognises that bailing-in crossholdings might trigger a domino effect. Therefore, the BRRD grants the Resolution Authority the power to exclude or partially exclude, in exceptional circumstances, liabilities whose bail-in would give rise to widespread contagion.[86] This provision, although desirable in principle, might have an unwanted consequence: banks might be strategically incentivised to keep a high level of interconnection and reduce the likelihood of being bailed-in and, more generally, the credibility of the new resolution framework.[87]

These two pieces may appear as somehow contradictory. On the one hand, crossholdings are penalised ex-ante by means of deduction in the capital and eligible liabilities holdings. On the other hand, the BRRD grants the resolution authority with the discretionary power of exempting crossholdings from bail-in in case of risk of contagion, giving rise to potential opportunistic behaviours.[88]

On the governance side of the story, the discussion on crossholdings can be relatively short and clear-cut: no positive impact can be derived from banks that compete one with another and are not willing to convey and compute relevant information to enhance the decision-making of other banks.

Therefore, the efficient level of crossholdings considerably differs from zero, especially if one considers the "existence constraint" (i.e., that a gigantic quantity of bail-inable instruments has to be issued and, consequently, held). Nonetheless, the discretion of the resolution authority, which appears reasonable from an ex-post perspective, is likely to generate

[85] A proposal of Directive amending the BRRD is still pending in the moment I am writing. See, Proposal for a DIRECTIVE OF THE EUROPEAN PARLIAMENT AND OF THE COUNCIL amending Directive 2014/59/EU on loss-absorbing and recapitalisation capacity of credit institutions and investment firms, COM (2016) 852 final.

[86] Article 44(3)(c) BRRD.

[87] This is the main point put forward in Ringe and Patel (n 2).

[88] In this sense, ibid. 15. argues that banks have incentives to hold others banks' bail-inable debt and increase systemic risk so to reduce the likelihood of an actual resolution happening; i.e., hamper the ex-ante credibility of the entire resolution framework.

opportunistic behaviours ex-ante, especially for the majority of banks that will not be subject to TLAC deduction as of January 2019. For this reason, the arguments proposed so far root in favour of the application of a deduction system beyond G-SIBs, with slightly laxer threshold so as not to impose excessive burdens on smaller banks.

Furthermore, on the one hand, bank crossholdings should move toward senior positions[89] so that the interconnectedness among banks lies at a lower level of the loss absorbency capacity cascade and the actual probability of bearing losses is limited. On the other hand, junior positions that are more likely to bear losses should be held by investors raising lower systemic concerns and that are more willing and capable of monitoring and influencing the borrowing bank. In this sense, modulating the threshold and the level of deduction according to the seniority of the crossholdings, making junior crossholdings considerably more costly, should provide optimal incentives.

Before moving to the other categories of investors, an important caveat is worth discussing. Banks are not the sole highly leveraged investor performing transformation activities. The whole shadow banking sector does so, without being subject to the whole banking regulation.[90] The proceeding of the analysis discusses some paradigmatic cases of shadow banking if a subset of the category considers performing shadow banking activities.[91]

B. Trends. The scenario of bank crossholdings reflects, to a certain extent, the theoretical expectations. The level is high relatively stable throughout the sample period: 48% in 2013 as compared with 46.26% in 2017.

Given the available data, it is not possible to clearly understand whether such a situation represents the result of strategic behaviours or whether the relatively constant overall amount is hiding a shift toward senior

[89] As noted in Sect. 4.4 limited evidence suggests that this shift is happening. See, ECB (n 54) 100. Chart C.

[90] Hossein Nabilou and Alessio M Pacces, 'The Law and Economics of Shadow Banking', *Research Handbook on Shadow Banking* (Edward Elgar Publishing 2018).

[91] Namely, Insurance Firms promising a rate of return and allowing for redeemable policies; money market mutual funds guarantee redemption value, bond funds tracking in index synthetically, through futures and warrants, without investing in the underlying assets.

positions.[92] Therefore, the explanatory power of the data is particularly low for this category of holders. Moreover, since significant reforms are entering into force as of 1 January 2019, current levels might not represent a reliable indicator for future developments.

Despite all of the above, it appears clear that countries belong to two different groups: with a very high level of crossholdings and with a relatively low level of crossholdings. Germany and Spain belong to the first group, laying well above the EA average but expose divergent trends: crossholdings in German banks are slightly decreasing over time (−11% between 2013 and 2017), on the contrary, Spanish crossholdings have increased in the sample period (+3%) (Fig. 9).

On the other side of the spectrum, "only" 31% of French and Dutch non-covered debt is held by other banks, with a notable decreasing trend, especially for the Netherlands in the last two years of the sample period (−13%). The high level of institutional investors' holdings balances this relatively low figure (see Sects. 5.3 and 5.4). Generalising this observation, highly concentrated banking systems are also better able to position themselves in the international financial market and, consequently, need to rely less on crossholdings to satisfy the "existence constraint".

In such a scenario, Italy still plays a peculiar role, laying in the middle of the two groups. Italian banks' crossholdings seemed to sharply decrease in the first half of the sample period but, eventually, the figure increases again, with an overall net change of +11% between 2013 and 2017. This might be partly due to the sudden decrease in household holdings in the same portion of the sample period.

5.3 *Pension Funds and Insurance Firms (PF&IFs)*

Unlike previous categories, this Section is affected by a further layer of limitation. Available data are even more aggregated, displaying in one figure the combination of different kinds of investors: pension funds and insurance companies. Therefore, the proceeding of the analysis will firstly discuss theoretical expectations on Pension Funds and Insurance Firms, highlighting the extent to which they overlap, and sketch the aggregate trends without being able to distinguish the "Pension Funds" and "Insurance Firms" components.

[92] This represents the main claim in Ringe and Patel (n 2).

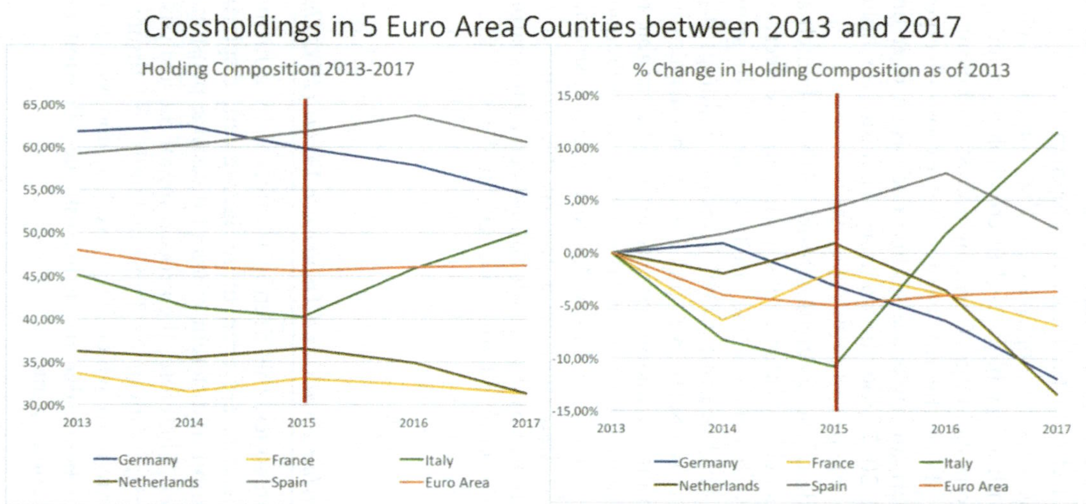

Fig. 9 Crossholdings trend between 2013 and 2017. Own calculations

It is important to note a common trait between the two investors included in this category. Indeed, both pension funds and insurance firms are types of institutional investors whose investments are funded by the contributions of clients and are functional to realise future goals defining the objective of the business, i.e., paying out compensation in case the insured harmful event happens and paying out pensions when the time is due. Another characteristic justifying the union of these two investor categories is the fact that, unlike "Other Financial Institution" (Sect. 5.4), for PF&IFs investing is not the core business of their activities, rather the natural consequence of their core activities according to which they hold liquid assets today against future payments.

Pension Funds

Pension funds are financial institutions whose primary source of funding is the contributions of employees and employers and whose liabilities consist of the future entitlement of employees to receive their pension when the time comes due. Pension funds invest the contribution of the participants to the pension scheme with a medium-term perspective, so as to maintain and marginally increase the value of its assets and be able to meet obligations toward pensioners in the future.

To shield against investment risk, pension funds retain highly diversified portfolios and as long-term sophisticated investors, they should exert considerable monitoring over their investments. Moreover, pension funds pose little concerns from a financial stability perspective since they do not usually resort to high leverage in their activities, and they do not face the risk of a run.[93] Therefore, many commentators have imagined pension funds as desirable holders of bail-inable securities.

Nonetheless, bail-inable securities contrast with the optimal investment strategies of a pension scheme,[94] since they seek assets whose risk falls over time. On the contrary, by their very design, the risk of bail-inable securities does not fall over time, since they are prone to bear losses in case of distress that might materialise in the future. Such a contingency is likely to refrain pension funds from massively investing in bail-inable securities as long as they consider the resolution framework credible (i.e., the regulator will actually impose losses in case of distress).

[93] See, Armour and others (n 13) ch 22.4.

[94] See Persaud (n 28).

Besides this, imposing losses on pensioners might be economically inefficient and politically unviable. In this respect, there is evidence that pension funds are often shielded from losses in bankruptcy.[95] In other words, it is more likely that the regulator will avoid or delay to take the necessary resolution decisions if that would endanger the solvency and stability of a pension scheme.[96] Taking also these arguments into consideration, one might go as far as arguing that bail-inable securities held by pension funds are likely to have, de facto, low loss absorbency capacity, thereby endangering the credibility of the resolution regime.

Overall, pension schemes should not invest massively in bail-inable securities even though they have, in theory, a positive potential impact on corporate governance. Moreover, it is desirable that, when investing in bail-inable securities, they invest in relatively senior instruments whose probability of suffering losses is lower.

Insurance

Insurance firms are financial institutions that shield economic actors from risky events, allowing them to undertake activities that they would not have undertaken, by pooling such risk.[97] To do so, an insurance firm accepts the payment of a premium in exchange for the promise to make payment in the future if the risky event materialises.[98] Consequently, insurance firms invest premia against future pay-outs.

Before considering the corporate governance role and the potential adverse spillovers of investing in bail-inable securities, it is essential to preliminary define the scope of "insurance firms". This section considers the case for "traditional" insurance companies and does not take into consideration pathological cases where financial institutions are only labelled as "insurance firms" while de facto acting as shadow banks or broker-dealers.[99] The mind goes to the case of AIG, an insurance

[95] See, for the case of bankruptcy beneficial treatment in the U.S., David A Skeel Jr, 'The Empty Idea of Equality of Creditors' (2017) 166 U. Pa. L. Rev. 699.

[96] Remember that Article 44(3)(d) BRRD allow the Resolution Authority to exempt on a case by case ground liabilities that would generate a disproportionate value destruction in case of a bail-in.

[97] Armour and others (n 13) 493.

[98] Armour and others (n 9) Ch 22.3

[99] This is consistent with regulatory reforms striving for impeding shadow banking activities to insurance firms.

company that acted as a dealer in the CDS market and needed a government bailout during the 2008 financial crisis.[100]

On the one hand, given the narrow definition of Insurance Firms provided above, the adverse spillovers of them being bailed-in are somewhat limited. Insurance firms perform no maturity or liquidity transformations and are not likely to experience runs on their liabilities that are due when a probabilistic event materialises.[101] This latter characteristic also implies that the insurer's risk has a limited correlation with the financial cycle.

On the other hand, insurance firms are sophisticated investors with medium-term orientation, can monitor their investments, and are willing to influence their borrowers. Nonetheless, as with pension funds, insurance companies still suffer from some sort of incompatibility between their investment strategies and the design of bail-inable securities: the risk profile of the investments in bail-inable instrument does not fall over time.

Nonetheless, bailing-in an insurance firm is not as politically unviable as with pension funds. One can, therefore, argue that the moral hazard problem does not affect insurance companies investing in bail-inable securities since it is far less likely that the regulator will avoid imposing losses on insurance than on pension funds. Moreover, Solvency II[102] already regulates capital requirements for insurance firms, mandating them to hold capital against their investment risk.

[100] On the role of CDS in the latest financial crisis and, specifically the AIG case, see René M Stulz, 'Credit Default Swaps and the Credit Crisis' (2010) 24 Journal of Economic Perspectives 73.

[101] For a simple definition of maturity and liquidity transformation activities see Armour and others (n 13) 277. Insurance receives premia from clients to insure them against future risks. Premia, unlike bank deposits, cannot be withdrawn on demand; thence the risk of run is minimal. As for the correlation with the financial cycle, the probabilistic, future, events can be correlated with the cycle. A spectacular example of correlation in the financial crisis were the CDS issued by insurance firms. Yet, as specified in the main text, this kind of insurance, performing de facto shadow banking activities, are not part of the narrow definition employed here. Moreover, the insurance group should be able to pool its risks by insuring also non-cyclical events (e.g., hazardous activities, car insurance, etc.).

[102] Directive 2009/138/EC of the European Parliament and Of the Council of 25 November 2009 on the taking-up and pursuit of the business of Insurance and Reinsurance (Solvency II). OJ L 335, 17.12.2009, p. 1.

In conclusion, insurance companies should invest in the whole spectrum of bail-inable securities, also the junior ones. They are well-positioned to play a positive governance role while posing relatively low concerns in terms of adverse economic spillovers in case of losses. Regulation can make the investment in bail-inable securities relatively cheaper for insurance firms through risk-weighting regulation so as to increase their willingness to buy.

Data and Trends

As mentioned above, given the highly aggregated nature of the available data, it is almost impossible to highlight reliable trends, especially because the expectations over the two components of the data, pension funds and insurance firms, diverge.

It is still possible to notice a general increase in PF&IFs holdings, consistent with the general decrease in households' holdings and crossholdings. The Euro Area average at the end of the sample period was about 20%, experiencing a considerable increase throughout the period (+24.05%). Again, such a figure lies between two groups of countries (Fig. 10).

Countries like France and the Netherlands have a high level of PF&IFs holdings, respectively 38.90% (+10.01%) and 32.16% (+6.43%) at the end of the sample period. Consistently with the Euro Area trend, the share of PF&IFs increased, but the relative increase is lower than other countries whose PF&IFs is well below EA average. These are Germany (8.61%) and Italy (10.42%). In relative terms, the figure on Italian bail-inable securities holdings is striking: the share of PF&IFs holdings almost doubled in 5 years (+80.75%). This figure is likely to partly offset the sharp decrease in households' holdings that Italy experienced in the same period.

Overall, path dependence and country heterogeneity play a major role in PF&IFs holdings, even though it is reasonable to imagine that in the coming years the gap between countries with high and low PF&IFs holdings must be drastically reduced.

The general trend, throughout the Euro Area, shows a considerable increase in PF&IFs holdings. However, this trend is difficult to assess in terms of efficiency since the two components of such category, though sharing fundamental traits, differ quite dramatically when it comes to investing in bail-inable securities.

In conclusion, although an increase in professional investors' holding is overall desirable, the extent to which this trend can yield efficient

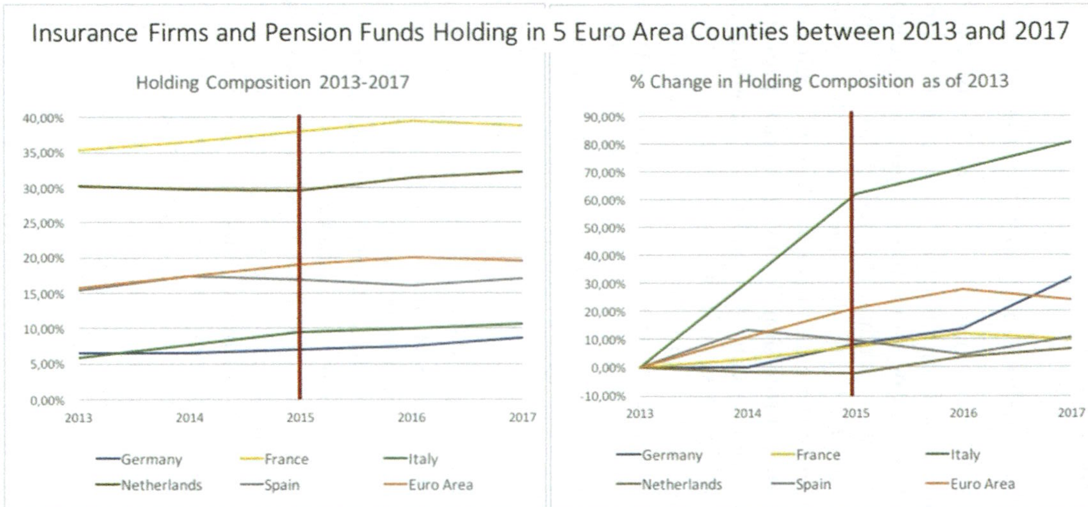

Fig. 10 Insurance Firms & Pension Funds holdings trend between 2013 and 2017. Own calculations

outcomes is unclear, especially in terms of credibility of the new resolution framework and, consequently, on the corporate governance role of bail-inable instrument holders.

5.4 *Other Financial Institutions*

In the ECB Dataset, "Other Financial Institutions" represents a residual category: it indicates those financial actors that are neither credit institutions nor PF&IFs. On the one hand, this category is increasingly highly heterogeneous. Therefore, data have limited ability to explain what is going on in the real world. On the other hand, the institutions that are part of this category share an important feature: their core business is to, broadly speaking, professionally invest money provided by their clients or borrowed (for leveraged institutions) according to different legal entitlements and business models.

Since it is impossible here to review all the instances falling into the category, the proceeding of this section focuses on two prominent examples that are useful for the purpose of the analysis given their potential qualitative and quantitative impact: mutual funds, and activist hedge funds.

Mutual Funds

The category of Mutual Funds includes diversified and heterogeneous investment funds where an asset manager invests the money provided by clients while the latter retains investment risk. These funds can act as "passive" and "active" investors. Passive funds are getting increasingly popular among investors as they are characterised by very low fees[103] and an investment strategy that mimics a benchmark or an index. Therefore, the decisions to enter or exit are not dictated by specific investment strategies and opportunities but by the value of the underlying shares and bonds composing the benchmark. On the contrary, active funds charge higher fees to their customers; these are justified by a more elaborated activity of market screening and asset picking. Section 6 discusses this differentiation and explains the different roles that those investors have in the mix of bail-inable debtholders.

[103] As low as 3 basis points for the S&P500 trackers offered by Vanguard. See https://investor.vanguard.com/etf/profile/VOO (accessed 30/09/2025).

From the perspective of adverse spillovers, mutual funds have a limited impact on contagion risk, since leverage in these institutions is limited if not prohibited. Nonetheless, in high-yield bond funds, such as those investing in bail-inable securities, there is a moderate incentive to run.[104] If investors want to exit the funds in times of stress, they can redeem their share in the fund, with variable time windows and constraints depending on contractual arrangements.[105] When the market for the underlying instruments (in this case: bail-inable securities) is illiquid, then the first to exit will have an advantage while the others will face the risk of a discount sale of the asset manager to match the demand for redemption.[106]

This holds true for the "traditional" mutual funds; whereas, the so-called Money Market Mutual Funds (MMFs), performing shadow banking activities, pose peculiar risks in terms of financial stability.[107] However, this analysis can largely neglect the role of MMFs. After the latest reforms,[108] "Constant Net Asset Value" MMFs cannot invest in instruments such as bail-inable securities anymore and, therefore, are out of the market.[109] Therefore, the analysis can be limited to the Mutual Funds regulated under UCTIS Directives.[110]

From the perspective of Corporate Governance, the difference between active and passive funds matters. On the one hand, Active funds should proactively engage in the governance of the investee companies. Indeed,

[104] Armour and others (n 9) 481.

[105] Some funds issue shares that can be traded, such as ETF, while other funds offer more limited possibility to exit. Mark Mobius, *Mutual Funds: An Introduction to the Core Concepts* (John Wiley & Sons 2007).

[106] Douglas W Diamond and Philip H Dybvig, 'Bank Runs, Deposit Insurance, and Liquidity' (1983) 91 Journal of political economy 401.

[107] For an overview of the problems related to MMFS and the possible regulatory strategies to address those, see Jeffrey N Gordon and Christopher M Gandia, 'Money Market Funds Run Risk: Will Floating Net Asset Value Fix the Problem' [2014] Colum. Bus. L. Rev. 313.

[108] Regulation (EU) 2017/1131 of the European Parliament and of the Council of 14 June 2017 on money market funds (Text with EEA relevance. OJ L 169, 30.6.2017, pp. 8–45.

[109] See Article 24 of the MMF Regulation.

[110] Directive 2009/65/EC of the European Parliament and of the Council of 13 July 2009 on the coordination of laws, regulations and administrative provisions relating to undertakings for collective investment in transferable securities (UCITS). OJ L 302, 17.11.2009, p. 32.

the higher fees allow them to engage in costly monitoring. They can play a twofold disciplining role: exiting their exposure or trying to influence the decision-making process of the bank. On the other hand, passive funds have been seen as inert players from a corporate governance perspective in order to save costs.[111] Nonetheless, a new trend of the literature[112] shows that also passive investors are, from a governance standpoint, active and privately engage the management.

For all those reasons, the investment in bail-inable securities by mutual investment funds is highly desirable since it poses a relatively low risk for financial stability and has a potential to play a positive role in corporate governance, especially since assets managers can specialise in this type of investment. Both active and passive approach to bail-inable securities holdings can play a positive role, for different reasons, as Sect. 6 will detail more precisely. Finally, it is worth noting that the more liquid the secondary market for bail-inable securities is, the more incentivised mutual funds will be to invest in such securities since the risk of "redemption run" is minimised.

Activist Hedge Funds

Hedge Funds are financial institutions that engage in a variety of activities following diverse investment strategies, which make "Hedge Fund" little more than a label. To cope with such heterogeneity, both EU and US laws define them in a negative way. The EU Alternative Investment Funds Directive (AIFD)[113] defines Hedge Funds as investment funds that do not qualify as retail funds (UCITS)[114] under the relevant legislation.

[111] On this debate, with convincing empirical analysis pointing at the active engagement of passive investment, see, Ian R Appel, Todd A Gormley and Donald B Keim, 'Passive Investors, Not Passive Owners' (2016) 121 Journal of Financial Economics 111.

[112] McCahery, Sautner and Starks (n 25).

[113] Directive 2011/61/EU of the European Parliament and of the Council of 8 June 2011 on Alternative Investment Fund Managers and amending Directives 2003/41/EC and 2009/65/EC and Regulations (EC) No 1060/2009 and (EU) No 1095/2010. OJ L 174, 1.7.2011, pp. 1–73.

[114] Directive 2014/91/EU of the European Parliament and of the Council of 23 July 2014 amending Directive 2009/65/EC on the coordination of laws, regulations and administrative provisions relating to undertakings for collective investment in transferable securities (UCITS) as regards depositary functions, remuneration policies and sanctions. OJ L 257, 28.8.2014.

While it is impossible to account for all the possible variations and investment strategies of hedge funds, for the purpose of the present study, some features are crucial. First, hedge funds are highly sophisticated investors whose services are directed to clients with a high level of sophistication either. Second, the client's funds are, to different extents, locked up and withdrawal on demand is not possible. Third, most of the hedge funds are highly leveraged institutions, though not as much as banks are. Fourth, hedge funds often try to intrude in the governance of the firm they invest in to gain profits by reselling the securities at a premium at a later stage.[115] These are the so-called "Activist Hedge Funds" and, due to their peculiar relevance they have for this study. This section mainly focuses on them.

On the one hand, the contractual lock-in of client's funds minimises the risk of run. On the other hand, being leveraged, hedge funds face a fire-sale risk when they hold illiquid assets, as bail-inable securities may become in times of financial turmoil. Moreover, hedge funds may contribute to increasing systemic risk through interconnection with other financial institutions. In this respect, the standard regulatory response has been to indirectly tackle the issue by requiring capital requirements and limit large exposure of banks towards leveraged funds.[116]

The fourth characteristic, i.e., target investments for profiting from future selling after some corporate reorganisation has taken place, is instead crucial for assessing the impact hedge funds might have on the governance of targeted banks.

First of all, it is worth remarking that activist hedge funds are highly sophisticated investors that are specialised in corporate governance engagement. Nonetheless, their intervention is not necessarily desirable. Back in Sect. 3, the impact on corporate governance was defined not only by the ability and willingness of monitoring and influencing the borrower but also by the preferences of the investor. In a sense, this represents a particular feature of the long-lasting debate on hedge fund

[115] For an introduction of the impact of hedge funds activism on corporate governance, see John C Coffee Jr and Darius Palia, 'The Wolf at the Door: The Impact of Hedge Fund Activism on Corporate Governance' (2016) 1 Annals of Corporate Governance 1.

[116] On the desirability of indirect regulation, see Hossein Nabilou and Alessio M Pacces, 'The Hedge Fund Regulation Dilemma: Direct vs. Indirect Regulation' (2015) 6 Wm. & Mary Bus. L. Rev. 183.

short-termism.[117] In time of distress a suitable strategy for a hedge fund is to lobby for diminishing the leverage of the bank by shrinking assets and, thus, reducing available credit for the real economy. Such a critique is grounded, though it might understate the actual potential of hedge funds.

Hedge fund activism usually does not work in isolation but in combination with passive investors that "decide" whether hedge funds' claims are worth supporting.[118] Moreover, in the specific case of banks close to financial distress, the role of a supervisor might actually constrain the possibility of hedge funds to implement deleverage via asset shrinking in a socially detrimental way.

Furthermore, on the governance side of the story, having hedge funds investing in bail-inable securities can enhance market discipline based on price adjustment, thanks to their, often times, contrarian investment strategy. Indeed, it can reduce market volatility and enhance the quality of price discovery. Nonetheless, being the law as it is, hedge funds might have limited incentives to invest in bail-inable securities since the room they have for engaging with the management is rather limited. On the contrary, a normative shift somehow including bail-inable creditors in the internal governance dynamic may provide hedge funds with powerful incentive to enter the market for bail-inable securities.[119]

A different, and arguably more important, limitation of hedge funds as bail-inable debtholders comes from their investment strategy. Hedge-funds actively investing in debt instruments are usually late-comers: these invest in debt instruments whose price already dropped considerably. This way, the funds aim at realising a profit by selling back debt instruments at a higher price at a later stage.[120] This decreases the potential

[117] On short-termism and corporate governance, see Mark J Roe, 'Corporate Short-Termism—in the Boardroom and in the Courtroom' [2013] The Business Lawyer 977. Empirically, many studies have showed how activism yield long-term improvement in the profitability and value of the targeted corporations. See Marco Becht and others, 'Returns to Hedge Fund Activism: An International Study' (2017) 30 The Review of Financial Studies 2933; Lucian A Bebchuk, Alon Brav and Wei Jiang, 'The Long-Term Effects of Hedge Funds Activism' (2015) 115 Colum. L. Rev. 1085.

[118] Alessio M Pacces, 'Exit, Voice and Loyalty from the Perspective of Hedge Funds Activism in Corporate Governance' (2016) 9 Erasmus L. Rev. 199.

[119] See Chapter 8.

[120] Michelle M Harner, 'The Corporate Governance and Public Policy Implications of Activist Distressed Debt Investing' (2008) 77 Fordham L. Rev. 703.

of hedge funds to positively impact corporate governance in good times but, conversely, increases such potential once the banks' stability deteriorates. This latter consideration highlights a further layer of complexity in analysing bail-inable debtholders, which is the discrete role of different investors over the lifecycle of the issuing bank.

In conclusion, from a social welfare standpoint, it is desirable to have hedge funds investing in bail-inable securities. They pose limited risks of adverse spillovers and they have the ability and willingness to impact the corporate governance of the borrowing bank, even though the desirability of such impact is ambiguous, especially in times close to distress. In this respect, the relevance of a smart mix of investors in bail-inable securities supported by effective supervision becomes clear.

Data and Trends

The available data for this category of investors is particularly uninformative. "Other Financial Institutions" is a residual category, and the impact of different investors included in this category might sharply differ, as the discussion of two prominent investor categories (Mutual Funds and Activist Hedge Funds) clearly showed.

Nonetheless, the data still provide some limited insights. Throughout the sample period, OFIs' holdings (+31.30%) significantly increase in the Euro Area. The increase was relatively modest in countries that had already a considerable share of OFIs' holdings at the beginning of the sample period, such as the Netherlands (+7.80%). This might signal that, given current legislation and the incentive structure, the share of holdings is close to what is privately efficient for the investors falling under such category (Fig. 11).

On the contrary, the increase is higher in countries where the initial amount of OFIs' holdings was below the Euro Average, such as Germany (+37.34%). Again, Italy (+116.73%) represents a somehow unique case of adjustment toward more sophisticated investors holding bail-inable securities, even though the share of OFIs' holdings is still below the Euro Average.

Overall, cross-country heterogeneity and path dependence play a significant role also for this category of investors. However, a clear route toward greater convergence in the Euro Area has started and it is in its early stages.

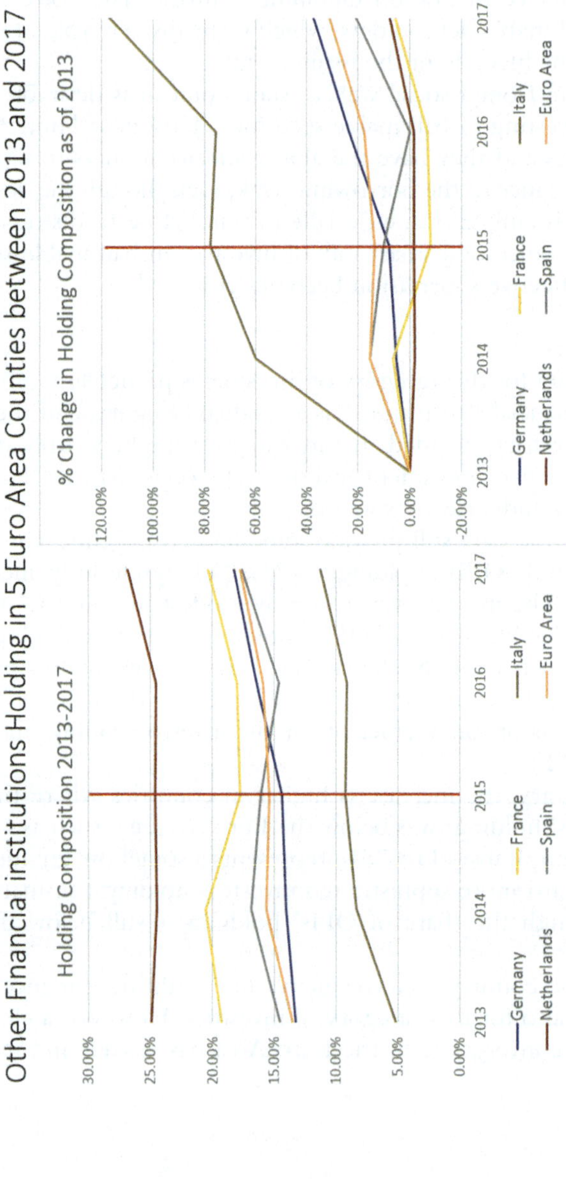

Fig. 11 Other Financial Institution holdings trend between 2013 and 2017. Own calculations

6 Towards an Optimal Composition

Before moving to the discussion of what a balanced mix of bail-inable investors might look like, it is worthwhile summing up the main findings of Sect. 5. Table 2 summarises the impact of different kinds of investors in terms of both governance and spillovers. Upward arrows indicate a positive effect or, in the case of spillovers, the minimisation of negative effects. Given their impact on governance and negative spillovers, Table 2 indicates the seniority of the instruments that investors should hold.

As argued throughout the analysis, households are the worst performers both in terms of financial and economic stability, closely followed by credit institutions. The residual amount of households holdings is better allocated to more senior positions. A similar argument goes for banks, with the difference that banks should continue to invest in senior bail-inable securities so as to fulfil the "existence constraint".

Moving to "institutional investors", insurance firms, mutual funds and hedge funds, all for different reasons and with different specifications, pose relatively low concerns in terms of adverse spillovers and are well-positioned to play a positive role in corporate governance. It is therefore desirable that they invest in junior, high yield, bail-inable positions. A somewhat different story can be told for pension funds, since the crucial social and economic function they perform might encourage the regulator to grant them special protection, shielding them from losses even beyond

Table 2 Summary of the impact of different investors' category

Investor's category	*Governance*	*Economic stability*	*Seniority*
Households	↓↓	↓↓	Senior
Crossholdings	↓	↓↓	Senior
Insurance Firms	↑	↑	Junior and Senior
Pension Funds	↑↓	↓	Senior
Mutual Funds (active and passive)	↑	↑	Junior and Senior
Hedge Funds	↑	↑	Junior

the letter of the BRRD. It is therefore advisable they only undertake senior bail-inable position, helping to fulfil the existence constraint.

Bearing these conclusions in mind, the proceeding of this section attempts to generalise the arguments that have been proposed so far and suggests what a mix of bail-inable investor should look like. In so doing, the analysis shifts from an approach focused on the labels of investor's categories as provided by the SHS dataset, to a more functional approach, discussing the salient feature of investors building up the best possible mix of investors.[121]

Bail-inable instruments are grossly divided into "junior" and "senior" positions. For explanatory purposes, one can take the 8% threshold of shareholders and bail-inable creditors as a reference point, as they have to suffer losses before any state intervention can be allowed according to the State aid framework.[122]

A. Junior positions. Junior bail-inable instruments, i.e., instruments that are more likely to suffer losses in the case of distress, should be held by investors that are both sophisticated and pose low risks of adverse spillovers if losses materialise. This way, the positive impact on corporate governance would be maximised while the risk of adverse spillovers would be minimised.

Throughout this study, both theoretical arguments and data showed that there is no bulletproof investor; i.e., there is no investor (or investor category) that, at the same time, fulfils three conditions. Namely:

(1) investors raising no risks of adverse spillovers;
(2) investors capable of and willing to influence the risk-taking incentives of the borrowing bank toward social optimality;
(3) investors with such deep pockets to satisfying herself the "existence constraint".[123]

[121] The analysis that follows is mainly based on social optimal outcome, while privately optimal investment strategies, and therefore market willingness to adjust to social optimum is not here considered. As I will argue in Chapter 8, investors can be incentivised toward socially optimal outcome through corporate governance adjustments granting them some ex-ante governance role.

[122] See Banking Communication (2013), cit., para 9; Articles 37(10)(a) and 44(5)(a) BRRD. Note that this differentiation is theoretical as it is ex-ante unclear who the marginal creditor below the 8% threshold is. For an in-depth analysis of this matter, see back Chapter 4, Sect. 4.4.

[123] See Sects. 3 and 5 in this chapter.

The limited literature on the topic has proposed valid arguments against the investment in bail-inable securities for almost all the possible categories of investors. However, upon closer scrutiny, two salient elements arose: some investors can perform the task better than others, and a mix of investors, combining their business models, investment strategies and risk preferences, has the potential to positively interact with each other.

Building on the description of various categories of investors in Sect. 5 that provided some glimpse on such smart mix, from a functional perspective three types of investors can positively interact with each other and yield good results in terms of corporate governance impact, while adding few adverse spillovers.

1) Targeted Investment: highly sophisticated and specialised investors screen the market and detect undervalued and poorly managed firms. These investors invest in companies to reverse the trend and earn a big premium in the resale price once the resilience and profitability of borrowing bank have been enhanced. This function is usually undertaken by the so-called active investors, especially activist hedge funds.

2) Specialised active funds: investment funds (e.g., mutual funds) that are specialised and actively invest in a vast array of bail-inable securities. This has two main advantages as compared with an atomistic investor: first, the fund is specialised in bail-inable securities, being able to pick them in the market and to have the ability to influence the management while they are holding these securities. Second, the risk to bear losses is two-way pooled: among the clients of the funds and along the securities issued by a diversified sample of banks held by the fund.

3) Indexed investing: funds that invest horizontally in all outstanding (listed) bail-inable securities.[124] This type of investment enjoys the same pooling characteristic of the specialised funds described above. Moreover,

[124] There is a growing U.S. based literature showing that passive investors that horizontally invest in corporations listed in one index have incentive to horizontally maximise their investment, meaning that they do not have profit maximising incentives in each and every corporation they invest in but rather profit maximising incentive of the network of investment they have. It is easy to raise a suggestive argument in the banking industry, since the case for horizontal maximisation implies stability and resilience way more than the case for individual profit maximisation. Although, this still represents nothing more than a suggestive idea, future research should focus on the positive potential of horizontal investment in specific industries such as the banking one. On costs and benefits of horizontal shareholders, see Alessandro Romano, 'Horizontal Shareholding: The End of Markets and the Rise of Networks' (2018) Available at SSRN 3255948.

indexed, passive, funds do not usually engage directly and officially in the governance of the corporations they invest in, but rather privately engage the management (closed-door pressure) and/or can support the claim of more active investors, playing the role of an arbiter.

B. Senior Positions. One of the pillars of the new resolution framework is to establish a sufficient buffer of bail-in eligible liabilities (MREL) so to allow the Resolution Authority to ordinarily resolve institutions in case of distress and, ex-ante, to reinforce the resilience of institutions in good times. In so doing, an enormous amount of eligible liabilities needs to be issued, generating the "existence constraint" as defined in Sect. 2. Therefore, it is likely that not enough "good" investors are willing to buy bail-inable securities so that some other categories with deep pockets have to step in.

In this scenario, an optimal mix of investors in bail-inable instruments requires that such investors hold senior positions. Holding senior positions, such investors are shielded by more junior ones and probably also by the State that can, at least partially, step in after the burden-sharing of at least 8% of nRWA.[125] This minimises both the negative economic spillovers of them bearing losses and the negative effect of their inability/unwillingness to engage in corporate governance.

Therefore, in a smart mixed composition of bail-inable instrument holders, senior positions should be covered with the "good" investors described in Panel A to the extent that this is possible. Then, other investors posing considerable contagion risk (such as other banks) or generating the risk of considerable adverse consequences for the real economy (such as pension funds and retail investors) should step in, so long as the existence constraint has not yet been satisfied.

For this reason, the deduction of crossholdings from TLAC/MREL should be contingent on seniority, i.e., for banks it should be cheaper to invest in senior positions in other banks' bail-inable debt as compared with more junior positions.

[125] See Banking Communication (2013), cit., para 9; Articles 37(10)(a) and 44(5)(a) BRRD.

7 Conclusions

This chapter discusses the optimal composition of bail-inable securities holders, highlights the lack of a bulletproof category of investors, shows the relevant trends pinpointing how investors are adjusting to the new resolution framework, and, eventually, suggests some functional characteristics of an optimal mixed composition of investors in bail-inable securities.

In building the benchmark of an ideal investor in bail-inable securities, I argue that an ideal holder should maximise the positive corporate governance impact by reducing excessive risk-taking behaviours as well as minimise the adverse impact on the economy, in terms of both financial stability and other spillovers. On top of these two dimensions, an "existence constraint" has to be also satisfied, i.e., since the required amount of outstanding eligible securities has been estimated to be around 26% of banks' RWA, an enormous amount of securities has to be issued, and thus held. This constraint, though frequently neglected, plays a crucial role in seeking an optimal composition.

The analysis showed that no category of investors matches such an ideal benchmark; i.e., there is no bulletproof investor that can yield efficient outcomes in terms of both corporate governance and stability while having a sufficiently deep pocket to fulfil the "existence constraint".

Thereupon, the rest of the analysis seeks a mix of holders whose combined impact mimics the benchmark as closely as possible. In so doing, I first investigate the current composition of bail-inable debtholders in the EA and its evolution from 2013 to 2018, relying on aggregated data published in the Security Holding Statistics Dataset. Such an exercise showed that investors are adjusting to the new resolution framework, with an increasing share of institutional investors, a rather stable involvement of other banks, and a sharp decline in retail investors' holdings. Nonetheless, data show considerable cross-country heterogeneity where path dependence hinders the creation of a level playing field among European banks.

Finally, this chapter attempts to generalise its findings and highlight some functional characteristics of investors that should compose the optimal mix. In so doing, bail-inable securities are grouped according to the seniority of the claim: senior claims can be held by categories with deep pockets, even though they might pose considerable stability concerns (such as banks). In contrast, junior positions should be held by investors that are able and willing to influence bank management and pose relatively low stability concerns.

This research highlights how the composition of bail-inable debtholders affects the outcome of any possible resolution decision and is, therefore, dense with policy-relevant implications. Even more so from an ex-ante perspective: a composition of bail-inable debtholders that would yield suboptimal outcomes in the case of a resolution would make the decision to resolve a failing bank particularly difficult, endangering the overall credibility of the entire resolution framework.

As the functional argument of this chapter suggests, granting (some) ex-ante governance rights to (some) bail-inable debtholders might provide the correct incentives toward an optimal mix. Therefore, future research should critically scrutinise the desirability and feasibility of explicitly linking bail-ins and corporate governance.[126]

Appendix

See Table 3 and Fig. 12.

[126] This is consistent with the argument proposed by Iris HY Chiu, 'Corporate Governance: The Missing Paradigm in the Mandatory Bail-in Regime for Creditors of Banks and Financial Institutions' [2014] Journal of business law 611; John Armour and Jeffrey N Gordon, 'Systemic Harms and Shareholder Value' (2014) 6 Journal of Legal Analysis 35.

Table 3 Sector-by-sector non-covered debt holding in 11 EA countries

	Sector	*AT (%)*	*BE (%)*	*DE (%)*	*FI (%)*	*FR (%)*	*IE (%)*	*IT (%)*	*LU (%)*	*NL (%)*	*PT (%)*	*ES (%)*	*EA (%)*
2013	HH	24.45	35.96	14.96	10.47	8.28	8.11	41.19	13.34	5.67	9.66	5.09	19.09
	Gov	2.77	0.93	1.43	5.26	1.10	1.60	0.34	0.56	1.56	6.75	4.42	1.68
	IF&PF	13.12	16.09	6.54	14.69	35.36	11.45	5.88	13.50	30.22	12.37	15.38	15.70
	MFI	44.42	19.27	61.83	43.98	33.68	41.47	45.05	49.37	36.23	66.50	59.25	48.00
	Non-Fin	3.03	2.22	1.97	1.59	2.32	2.16	2.33	2.30	1.38	0.46	1.32	2.03
	OFI	12.11	25.52	13.27	23.93	19.25	35.19	5.19	20.92	24.94	4.25	14.55	13.50
2014	HH	26.32	24.48	13.63	8.45	7.57	7.63	40.11	9.94	6.68	12.18	3.73	17.58
	Gov	2.56	0.77	1.46	5.38	1.66	1.13	0.40	0.78	1.96	3.42	0.54	1.31
	IF&PF	14.18	14.76	6.54	15.04	36.45	11.38	7.67	13.47	29.75	12.66	17.44	17.42
	MFI	41.46	30.15	62.38	47.46	31.54	41.59	41.33	50.38	35.51	62.61	60.29	46.07
	Non-Fin	3.56	1.46	1.98	1.50	2.22	2.13	2.18	1.55	1.47	0.55	1.19	1.99
	OFI	11.92	28.38	14.00	22.02	20.52	36.13	8.30	23.80	24.53	8.58	16.80	15.61
2015	HH	25.62	18.99	14.19	6.97	6.96	5.34	38.38	9.58	5.39	5.19	3.58	16.25
	Gov	3.50	1.83	1.78	5.60	1.77	1.02	0.28	1.25	2.31	4.02	0.67	1.50
	IF&PF	15.53	15.74	7.07	15.16	38.07	9.63	9.51	15.26	29.59	13.14	16.83	19.03
	MFI	39.10	35.46	59.91	48.34	33.11	44.94	40.19	49.36	36.55	72.57	61.79	45.62
	Non-Fin	3.86	1.21	2.68	1.46	2.37	1.72	2.39	2.09	1.55	0.25	1.1	2.22
	OFI	12.39	26.77	14.37	22.47	17.72	37.34	9.23	22.46	24.61	4.83	16.03	15.37
2016	HH	27.70	11.94	13.99	3.09	6.42	4.71	32.16	7.13	4.98	3.54	3.69	14.23
	Gov	3.80	2.58	1.84	5.98	1.69	0.90	0.30	1.81	2.70	4.20	0.76	1.60
	IF&PF	16.68	16.77	7.43	15.83	39.56	10.96	10.06	14.35	31.33	10.20	16.09	20.07
	MFI	32.95	37.95	57.85	52.62	32.35	47.27	45.86	57.19	34.93	78.28	63.73	46.08
	Non-Fin	4.13	3.36	2.50	0.96	2.00	1.43	2.48	1.19	1.51	0.21	1.16	2.13
	OFI	14.75	27.40	16.39	21.52	17.97	34.73	9.12	18.32	24.55	3.58	14.57	15.89
2017	HH	27.34	8.03	14.26	2.94	5.91	3.35	25.30	4.77	4.89	4.63	3.08	12.96
	Gov	4.07	3.43	2.24	6.56	1.61	0.85	0.34	1.87	3.06	0.25	0.73	1.57
	IF&PF	16.77	11.97	8.61	14.70	38.90	10.95	10.62	11.93	32.16	8.30	17.01	19.47
	MFI	31.84	32.57	54.46	52.97	31.38	46.00	50.21	55.94	31.35	78.85	60.60	46.26
	Non-Fin	4.05	2.62	2.20	0.81	1.87	1.12	2.26	1.78	1.65	0.34	1.01	2.00
	OFI	15.94	41.37	18.23	22.01	20.33	37.73	11.25	23.71	26.89	7.64	17.57	17.73

HH: Households; **Gov**: Government; **IF&PF**: Insurance Firms and Pension Funds; **MFI**: Monetary Financial Institutions (Crossholdings and MMF); **Non-Fin**: Non-Financial Sector; **OFI**: Other Financial Institutions

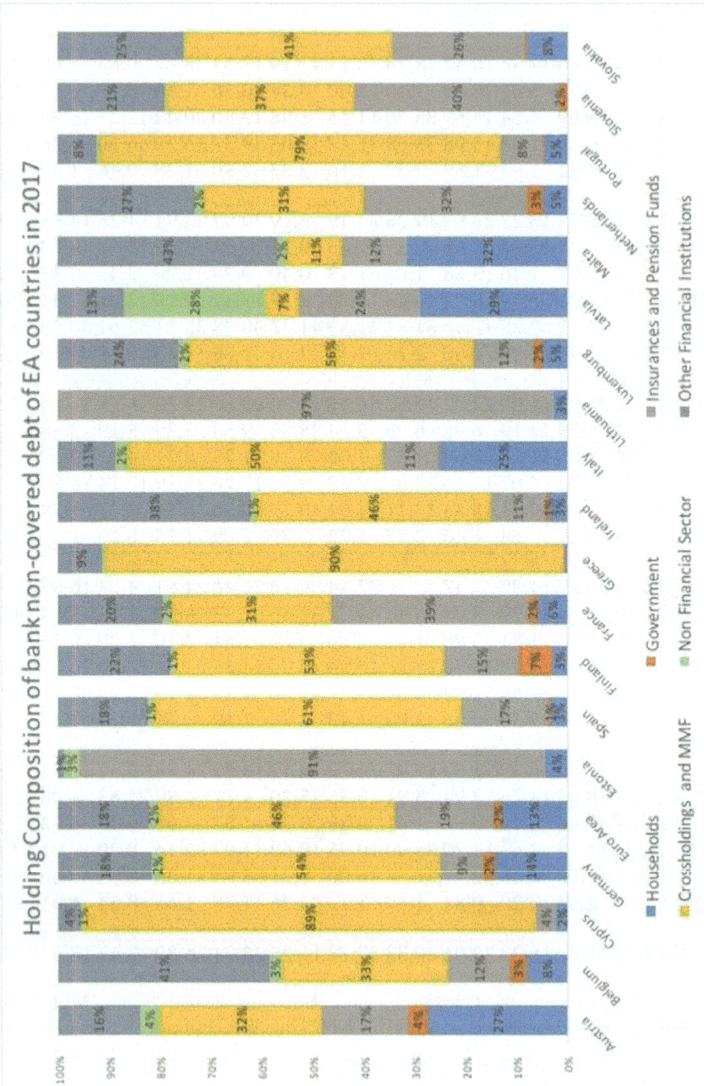

Fig. 12 Sector composition of non-covered debt held by EA investors 2017Q4 for each EA country

CHAPTER 7

Enabling Debt Governance: Bail-Inable Debt and Remuneration

1 Introduction

The remuneration of executives represents one of the most debated and divisive topics in the corporate governance literature, especially in financial institutions, given its political sensitivity. Indeed, it comes as no surprise that the spectacular magnitude of remuneration of many bank managers attracted media commotion and public rage during the latest crisis, including the not uncommon cases of spectacular remuneration awarded to bank managers whose banks went underwater only a few months later. The former CEO of Lehman Brothers, Mr. Richard Fuld, provides the most prominent example of the matter: Lehman filed for bankruptcy in September 2008. However, in 2007 Mr. Fuld received

This chapter heavily draws from Edoardo D Martino, 'Fine-Tuning Bank Governance and Resolution: The Case for Remunerating Bankers through Bail-Inable Debt' (2020) 31 European Business Law Review 845.

E. D. Martino, *EU Bank Governance and Bail-In*, EBI Studies in Banking and Capital Markets Law,
https://doi.org/10.1007/978-3-032-20699-2_7

total compensation of over 22 million dollars, of which almost 17 million awarded in stocks.[1]

Unsurprisingly, regulating bank managers' remuneration became a politically sensitive matter in the aftermath of the global financial crisis.[2] This, on the one hand, gave stimulus to policy innovation. On the other hand, political calculus often drove the reform, rather than efficiency and effectiveness considerations. Therefore, more than a decade later, the regulation on bankers' pays not only failed to achieve the desired objectives but even created unintended negative consequences.

Intending to fix such shortcomings, this chapter proposes to award part of bank managers' remuneration in the form of bail-inable debt, so as to exploit the potential for positive synergies between bank governance and the resolution framework. The idea of remunerating executives and high-profile employees with debt is controversial and might seem naïve. In standard corporate governance models for non-financial firms, remuneration packages represent a reward strategy to align managerial and shareholders' incentives and ultimately foster social welfare,[3] so that the role played by debt is by definition very limited.[4] However, as widely discussed in Chapter 2, bank governance is rather special, and substantive adjustments might be warranted.

To this end, the interplay between bank governance, pay regulation, and the resolution framework for failing banks represents the focus of this chapter. Indeed, the latter establishes the category of "bail-inable debt", i.e., debt instruments that can be wiped out or converted into equity in the case of bank distress, before bankruptcy. Therefore, if managers received bail-inable instruments, they would be the first in line to bear losses in the case of distress. Consequently, managers would have ex-ante

[1] Lucian A Bebchuk, Alma Cohen and Holger Spamann, 'The Wages of Failure: Executive Compensation at Bear Stearns and Lehman 2000–2008' (2010) 27 Yale J. on Reg. 257. It has been estimated that between 1993 and 2007, while serving as CEO, Mr. Fuld received almost half a billion dollars.

[2] In this chapter, the expression "bank managers" and "bankers" will both indicate the identified staff subject to the CRD pay regulation. For a more precise definition, see fn n. 128.

[3] John Armour and others, *Principles of Financial Regulation* (Oxford University Press 2016) 139.

[4] Nevertheless, it shall be noted that debt-like elements of remuneration are a long-lasting overlooked practice, especially in the form of pension schemes. Only recently, the effect of remuneration through debt has started to be taken into account, see Sect. 2.2.

incentives not to take on excessive risk in order to preserve the value of the awarded instruments.

This chapter adds to the extensive literature on bank managers' remuneration. The proposal for mandatory regulation of bank managers' remuneration stems from the necessity to fine-tune bank governance and the resolution framework. This represents the originality of the research. Regulating the cash flow rights of managers is not an end in itself. Rather, it represents a means to adjust the governance of financial institutions to the specificities of bank governance[5] and, at the same time, to enhance the credibility of the resolution framework and the resolvability of individual banks. Hence, using also bail-inable debt in bank managers' remuneration packages would prove beneficial for both financial stability and corporate governance and, besides, would generate positive spillovers for bank resolvability.

This chapter proceeds as follows. Section 2 scrutinises the theoretical arguments on remuneration in both financial and non-financial firms. It highlights the elements of specificity of bank governance that justify the departure from the conventional wisdom on bankers' remuneration (2.1); discusses the theoretical justification and empirical evidence on remuneration through debt (2.2); and analyses early experiences of remuneration through debt in banking (2.3). Section 3 introduces the main policy proposals put forward in the aftermath of the financial crisis, as well as the main international documents discussing regulatory standards and good practices on remuneration in banking. Subsequently, Sect. 4 focuses on the regulation on bank managers' remuneration in the EU, critically discussing the structural regulation imposed at European level, and pointing out the extent to which such regulation departs from the theoretical background set earlier, and fails to achieve its policy objectives. Section 5 discusses the case for remuneration through bail-inable debt in the European Union, describing the current regulatory environment (5.1) and proposing a detailed modification to fine-tune regulation on remuneration and bank regulation with the specificities of bank governance (5.2). Eventually, Sect. 6 discusses two possible strategies for implementing the proposal to remunerate high-profile employees with bail-inable debt. Section 7 concludes.

[5] Marco Becht, Patrick Bolton and Ailsa Röell, 'Why Bank Governance Is Different' (2011) 27 Oxford Review of Economic Policy 437.

2 Remuneration and Bank Risk-Takers. A Review of Theory and Evidence

2.1 *The Agency Framework and Bank Specialty*

The debate over executives' compensation has been one of the most vibrant and contentious in corporate governance for the last 40 years.[6] This strand of research lies, pre-eminently, on the quintessential elements of modern corporations: the separation of ownership and control[7] and the agency costs arising therefrom.[8]

Once the agency theory of the firm reached a certain degree of consensus, studying the optimal compensation structure to handle the agency conflict between shareholders and managers represented a natural step forward.[9] The standard setting of the mainstream theory on executive compensation assumes an all-equity, widely held corporation with weak shareholders and aims to align the CEO's long-term objectives with shareholders' ones. In such a setting, rewarding executives with stock-based compensation can provide managers with the correct incentives.[10]

Therefore, the idea of aligning executives' incentives with shareholders' interests became one of the foundations of the compensation practice

[6] The load of academic research in the field of law, economics, finance, and business management arose in the early 1980s; nonetheless there were previous pioneering studies on the matter. See, notably, David R Roberts, 'A General Theory of Executive Compensation Based on Statistically Tested Propositions' (1956) 70 The Quarterly Journal of Economics 270. (The paper already recognises the role of executive compensation in incentivising managers as a response to the separation of ownership and control, advocating for variable remuneration tailored on the specificities of each firm). For a review of the early studies on executives compensation, see Kevin J Murphy, 'Executive Compensation' (1999) 3 Handbook of labor economics 2485.

[7] Adolf Augustus Berle and Gardiner Coit Means, *Modern Corporation and Private Property* (Transaction Publishers 1932).

[8] Michael C Jensen and William H Meckling, 'Theory of the Firm: Managerial Behavior, Agency Costs and Ownership Structure' (1976) 3 Journal of financial economics 305.

[9] Murphy (n 5).

[10] Bengt Holmström and Jean Tirole, 'Market Liquidity and Performance Monitoring' (1993) 101 Journal of Political Economy 678.

for modern corporations.[11] This allows, in theory, to tackle two critical issues. First, remuneration should incentivise executives to seek all the positive net present value opportunities. Executives tend to be risk-averse since their capital, monetary as well as human, is disproportionately invested in the company.[12] Second, well-designed compensation packages that align the remuneration of executives with long-term interests of shareholders would limit the rent extraction of entrenched managers.[13] In order to limit rent extraction, academic research and corporate practice have enucleated a series of new tools for controlling the quality of pay packages, such as the remuneration committee[14] and "say on pay" procedures.[15]

The idea of rewarding good managerial performance through compensation packages composed of a fixed part and a stock-based part is soundly grounded on financial theory. Following the efficient capital market hypothesis,[16] stock prices can be conceptualised as an unbiased estimate of the fundamental value of the firm. Therefore, tying managerial incentives to stock prices means fostering long-term value creation

[11] For early empirical evidence on CEO sensitivity to share prices, see Michael C Jensen and Kevin J Murphy, 'Performance Pay and Top-Management Incentives' (1990) 98 Journal of political economy 225.

[12] Michael C Jensen and Kevin J Murphy, 'Remuneration: Where We've Been, How We Got to Here, What Are the Problems, and How to Fix Them' (2004) ECGI Finance Working Paper N°. 44/2004.

[13] Lucian Arye Bebchuk, Jesse M Fried and David I Walker, 'Managerial Power and Rent Extraction in the Design of Executive Compensation' (National bureau of economic research 2002). (The paper highlights the risk that powerful executives might capture the design of compensation packages).

[14] Brian GM Main and James Johnston, 'Remuneration Committees and Corporate Governance' (1993) 23 Accounting and Business Research 351. The Cadbury Code already suggested to let a remuneration committee deal with executives compensation packages: "Executive directors' pay should be subject to the recommendations of a remuneration committee made up wholly or mainly of non-executive directors", Adrian Cadbury, 'Cadbury Report: The Financial Aspects of Corporate Governance' [1992] Tech report, HMG, London.

[15] Jeffrey N Gordon, 'Say on Pay: Cautionary Notes on the UK Experience and the Case for Shareholder Opt-In' (2009) 46 Harv. J. on Legis. 323; Randall S Thomas and Christoph Van der Elst, 'Say on Pay around the World' (2014) 92 Wash. UL Rev. 653.

[16] Eugene F Fama, 'Efficient Capital Markets: A Review of Theory and Empirical Work' (1970) 25 The journal of Finance 383.

of the company.[17] In this sense, in an influential review on managerial compensation, Murphy stated that: "Stock ownership provides the most direct link between shareholder and CEO wealth".[18]

After this brief and necessarily incomplete review of the main economic arguments behind the current practices on executive compensation,[19] one might wonder whether and to what extent this plainly applies in banking.

Indeed, the idea that bank governance is special reached a fair degree of consensus in the aftermath of the Global Financial Crisis.[20] However, the implications of such a specialty remain somehow nebulous insofar as the approach to the corporate governance of banks resembles the mainstream paradigm used for the corporate governance of non-financial firms.[21] In other words, the specialty of banks is accounted for by embedding some adjustments of specific governance tools and stricter regulations[22] and not by adjusting the corporate governance paradigm to the specific nature of banks.

Especially in the last decade, both the legal and economic literature has highlighted the peculiar shape of incentives that banks and, for what

[17] This represents the baseline to advocate a strong sensitivity of pay to corporate performance. On this issue see the early study by Jensen and Murphy (n 6). See also Lucian A Bebchuk and Jesse Fried, *Pay without Performance* (Harvard University Press Cambridge, MA 2006), where the authors critique the remuneration packages of bankers showing the lack of sensitivity of pay and performance.

[18] Murphy (n 5) 2532.

[19] For a review of the theory and current challenges on the matter, see Guido Ferrarini and Maria Cristina Ungureanu, 'Executive Remuneration. A Comparative Overview' in Wolf-Georg Ringe and Jeffrey N Gordon (eds), *Oxford Handbook of Corporate Law and Governance* (Oxford University Press Oxford, UK 2018).

[20] See, among many others, John Armour and others, 'Bank Governance' (2016) ECGI Law Working Paper 316/2016; Becht, Bolton and Röell (n 4); Jonathan R Macey and Maureen O'Hara, 'The Corporate Governance of Banks' [2003] FRBNY Economic Policy Review 91.

[21] See, for instance, BCBS, 'Principles for Enhancing Corporate Governance' [2010] Basel Committee; European Commission, 'Corporate Governance in Financial Institutions and Remuneration Policies'. In these policy documents both the Basel Committee and the European Commission insights mainly rely on the standard corporate governance best practices already established in other governance codes. In addition, acknowledging the specialty of banks, they suggest adopting sophisticated monitoring mechanisms especially for remuneration packages and risk governance.

[22] Christoph van der Elst, 'Corporate Governance and Banks: How Justified Is the Match?' (2015) ECGI-Law Working Paper 284/2015.

matters here, bank managers face.[23] This is mainly due to three elements: bank leverage, moral hazard, and systemic externalities. Banks are more leveraged than any other non-financial institution so that the problem of risk-shifting[24] from equity to debtholders is more acute, especially in good times, piling up risks that might abruptly explode once the credit cycle moves downwards,[25] as it happened during the latest financial crisis. Moreover, highly leveraged institutions have to face the debt-overhang problem,[26] where bank shareholders are not willing to finance positive net present value projects since the benefit of these would mainly go to creditors, leading to worsening the situation of a credit crunch that is likely to arise when the credit cycle is weak.[27] Therefore, if the compensation packages are perfectly aligned with shareholders' interests, bank managers will be particularly sensitive to risk-shifting and debt-overhang too.

On top of the incentive effects of bank leverage, moral hazard exacerbates the problems of tying managerial incentives to shareholders' interests because of an implicit state guarantee on banks' solvency. Despite one of the cornerstones of the new resolution framework is to end the too-big-to-fail policy, there are reasons to argue that a bailout has not been permanently and rigidly ruled out. Thus, the moral hazard problem might have been partially alleviated, but for sure not entirely handled.

Finally, and tightly related to the former argument, shareholders do not internalise all social costs of their decisions: the failure of a bank might mean relatively little to a diversified shareholder, whereas it has disruptive consequences for the economy as a whole, sometimes even on a global scale.[28]

[23] Jeffrey N Gordon, 'Executive Compensation and Corporate Governance in Financial Firms: The Case for Convertible Equity-Based Pay' [2010] Columbia Law and Economics Working Paper; Lucian A Bebchuk and Holger Spamann, 'Regulating Bankers' Pay' (2009) 98 Geo. LJ 247.

[24] Jensen and Meckling (n 7).

[25] David Aikman, Andrew G Haldane and Benjamin D Nelson, 'Curbing the Credit Cycle' (2015) 125 The Economic Journal 1072.

[26] Stewart C Myers, 'Determinants of Corporate Borrowing' (1977) 5 Journal of financial economics 147.

[27] Filippo Occhino, 'Debt-Overhang Banking Crises: Detecting and Preventing Systemic Risk' (2017) 30 Journal of Financial Stability 192.

[28] Steven L Schwarcz, 'Systemic Risk' (2008) 97 Geo. LJ 193.

So far, the discussion has converged on the theoretical arguments showing the link between management incentives, executive pay, and excessive risk-taking in banking. However, the role of allegedly flawed pay packages in causing the bolstering of the global financial crisis is, in the end, an empirical matter. Thus, it is worth reviewing and critically commenting on the main pieces of empirical literature linking remuneration of bank managers and risk-taking incentives.

Beltratti and Stultz[29] investigate the determinants of bank performance during the crisis using a worldwide sample of large banks. The authors found no evidence that corporate governance failures caused the crisis. However, they found that banks that, by the traditional definition, had a better corporate governance perform worse during the crisis: "Our results show that no evidence exists that banks with a better alignment of the CEO's interests with those of the shareholders had higher stock returns during the crisis. Some evidence shows that banks led by CEOs whose interests were better aligned with those of their shareholders had worse stock returns and a worse return on equity".[30]

Fahlenbrach and Stultz[31] looked more closely to CEO incentives and bank performance during the crisis. They found no evidence that CEOs whose incentives were better aligned with shareholders' interests performed better whereas the contrary might be true: "Our results show that no evidence exists that banks with a better alignment of the CEO's interests with those of the shareholders had higher stock returns during the crisis. Some evidence shows that banks led by CEOs whose interests were better aligned with those of their shareholders had worse stock returns and a worse return on equity".[32]

Finally, Tung and Wang[33] analysed the compensation structure of 83 bank CEOs looking at their debt-equity ratio. The authors found

[29] Andrea Beltratti and René M Stulz, 'The Credit Crisis around the Globe: Why Did Some Banks Perform Better?' (2012) 105 Journal of Financial Economics 1.

[30] Ibid 16.

[31] Rüdiger Fahlenbrach and René M Stulz, 'Bank CEO Incentives and the Credit Crisis' (2011) 99 Journal of Financial Economics 11.

[32] Ibid.

[33] Frederick Tung and Xue Wang, 'Bank CEOs, inside Debt Compensation, and the Global Financial Crisis' [2012] Boston Univ. School of Law Working Paper.

evidence supporting the hypothesis that CEO's inside debt[34] decreases risk-taking incentives, highlighting how the magnitude of inside debt in director remuneration has potential to enrich the standard literature whose focus has almost exclusively been on equity compensation.

These pieces of evidence are not conclusive, though they clearly show an unsurprising wedge between the common wisdom on executives' compensation in non-financial firms and what happened in banking. This might have two interpretations, not necessarily mutually exclusive. First, the traditional wisdom is wrong, and what is good governance for non-financial corporations is not good governance for banks.[35] Second, factors other than governance better explain risk-taking incentives and bank performances during the crisis.[36]

Given the theoretical arguments and the empirical hints provided, it is difficult to rule out the role of governance and managers' incentives in piling up risk in the period before the financial crisis erupted. Therefore, the overarching objective of using compensation packages for achieving socially optimal outcomes will stay the same. However, the peculiarities of incentives in banking need to be acknowledged and taken into account in the policy proposals.

Indeed, nowadays there is a fair degree of consensus on the fact that tying too tightly remuneration packages with stock prices incentivised to engage in excessively risky activities so that the compensation in banking must be somehow different from non-financial firms. There is also a widespread consensus on the fact that, given banks' specialties, there is a serious case for regulation, since market forces are unable to reach an efficient output themselves.[37]

[34] In the form of pension schemes. For more extensive discussion of inside debt, its possible forms and implications, see Sect. 2.2.

[35] As suggested by Renée Birgit Adams, 'Governance and the Financial Crisis' (2012) 12 International Review of Finance 7.

[36] In this sense, the claims of many policy reports blaming flawed corporate governance as a primary causing factor of the Global Financial Crisis might be seen as exaggerated. For instance Kirkpatrick and the OECD claimed that: "the financial crisis can be to an important extent attributed to failures and weaknesses in corporate governance arrangements", see Grant Kirkpatrick, 'The Corporate Governance Lessons from the Financial Crisis' (2009) 2009 OECD Journal: Financial Market Trends 61.

[37] Bebchuk and Spamann (n 22). On the contrary, professor Ferrarini argues against regulating bankers pays, especially when it comes to pay structure. See Ferrarini and Ungureanu (n 18).

Nonetheless, the proposals for regulating bank managers' pay are countless, sharply divergent and often focuses on different aspects. Among many possible approaches, the proceeding of the analysis considers four crucial issues in addressing compensation structures and regulation.

First, in banking, it is not sufficient to talk about executive remuneration. Indeed, executives do not determine themselves the risk-taking appetite of their bank since many middle-to-high-level employees with special responsibilities (e.g., traders, loan officers, etc.) have a considerable impact on that.[38] Therefore, talking about remuneration and incentives in banking means talking both about executives' and, more broadly, risk-takers' remuneration.

Second, this chapter focuses on ex-ante incentives provided by remuneration packages rather than on an ex-post assessment of actual losses born by bank's directors. Indeed, if the overarching goal is to induce a correct risk-taking attitude through remuneration, the only sensible approach is to analyse the incentives that remuneration packages provide to bank managers. This goes in an opposite direction compared to some commentators who pointed out how many executives suffered tremendous losses after their bank went bankrupt, arguing against the fact that compensation packages were flawed.[39] The fact that ex-post losses happened says very little about the decision that those managers took and that lead to bankruptcy. It only means that, in expected terms, managers were willing to take on excessive risk, bearing the risk of suffering losses in the case of default.

Third, related to the latter point, it is essential to consider the overall portfolio of a manager and not only on the structure and amount of yearly compensation. Professor Bebchuck and co-authors showed how executives at Bearn Stern and Lehman Brothers were able to cash out over two billion dollars in the period between 2000 and 2008.[40] This makes clear that focusing only on yearly remuneration and clawbacks in case of

[38] See Article 92(2) Capital Requirement Directive—Directive 2013/36/EU of the European Parliament and of the Council of 26 June 2013 on access to the activity of and the prudential supervision of credit institutions and investment firms [2013] OJ L 176.

[39] Bebchuk and Spamann (n 22) 268.

[40] Bebchuk, Cohen and Spamann (n 1). The authors estimate that "top executive teams of Bear Stearns and Lehman Brothers derived cash flows of about $1.4 billion and $1 billion, respectively, from cash bonuses and equity sales during 2000–2008".

distress is insufficient to rule out the role of compensation packages in piling-up systemic risk.[41]

Fourth, in case of substantial equity investment of the CEO and the top management of a distressed bank, there might be a disincentive towards prompt recapitalisation since that would severely dilute their position. A CEO with substantial equity investment would suffer a greater net wealth loss compared with a diversified shareholder. Therefore, in the absence of mechanisms to force early recapitalisation, high equity stakes in the bank might induce top management to pass on recapitalisation opportunities, making the position of their bank less sound. Professor Gordon first highlighted this set of incentives. In his study, the disincentives towards early recapitalisation are labelled as the "Fuld problem" from the name of the last CEO of Lehman Brothers and speculating about the fact that he might have unduly delayed any attempt to recapitalise to avoid any dilution of his equity position.[42]

The present study lies in this stream of literature and attempts to link optimal remuneration with the new resolution framework, proposing to use bail-inable securities for remunerating bank managers. This would have two main benefits: on the one hand, it is important to build a coherent financial regulation framework; on the other hand, the present proposal aims at directly tackling the specificity of banks. To substantiate such a proposal, the following section reviews the theoretical arguments in favour and against remuneration through debt.

2.2 *Remuneration Through Debt and Risk Incentives*

The idea of remuneration through debt is, at least, as old as the agency theory of the firm. Indeed, its first formulation dates back to the seminal paper by Jensen and Meckling itself.[43] Back then, the authors admitted that remuneration through inside debt[44] would allow to "eliminate to a large part (perhaps all) of the agency costs of debt". Nonetheless, as shown in the previous section, the academic debate almost exclusively

[41] Johanna Stark, 'Clawback Provisions in Executive Compensation Contracts' (2021) 18 European Company and Financial Law Review 669.

[42] Gordon (n 22).

[43] Jensen and Meckling (n 7) 353.

[44] For inside debt is meant the debt or debt-like instrument owned by executives and high-profile employees.

focused on remuneration through stock, stock-like instruments and cash payments. One of the potential reasons for such gap in legal, economic, and financial scholarship is that, as Jensen and Meckling pointed out, "for large diffuse owner corporations the practice [of remuneration through debt] does not seem to be common".[45] On the contrary, as more recent scholarship has started to show,[46] the practice of remunerating through debt-like instruments is more common than we thought, primarily through pension schemes.

The situation drastically changed when the Security and Exchange Commission (SEC) reformed the disclosure regime applicable to executive compensation, including pension plans among the information that must be publicly available.[47] Data availability and increased awareness of the significance of inside debt remuneration is leading to a growing body of both legal and economic literature on the role and the efficiency of remuneration through debt-like instruments.

Edmans and Liu,[48] in their seminal contribution, provide a sound theoretical framework for the analysis demonstrating that inside debt (i.e., remuneration through debt-like instruments) is a superior solution to bonuses and salaries in handling the agency cost of debt. Inside debt makes managers not only willing to avoid bankruptcy but also sensitive to liquidation value.

The authors proved that inside debt, as long as it is not secured, hampers the incentives to gamble for resurrection close to insolvency since managers are sensitive to the liquidation value of the firm.[49] This argument is particularly attractive in the domain of financial regulation.

[45] Jensen and Meckling (n 7) 354.

[46] See, among the firsts, Lucian A Bebchuk and Robert J Jackson Jr, 'Executive Pensions' (2005) 30 Journal of Corporation Law 823.

[47] Security Exchange Commission (SEC), Regulation S-K, Item 402. Nonetheless, Bebchuk and Robert advocated for more transparency based on anecdotal evidence and hand-collected financial data.

[48] Alex Edmans and Qi Liu, 'Inside Debt' (2011) 15 Review of finance 75. The published paper is based on a previous influential working paper that was already widely cited in the related growing empirical literature. See Alex Edmans, 'Inside Debt' (2006).

[49] Following this intuition Yiar Listokin proposed to compensate CEOs with debt in bankruptcy, since—in his view—only compensation though debt would tie compensation to executive's performance in bankruptcy. See, Yair Listokin, 'Paying for Performance in Bankruptcy: Why CEOs Should Be Compensated with Debt' [2007] University of Pennsylvania Law Review 777. The proposal has been heavily criticised since it would

Making managers more sensitive to liquidation value and effectively disincentivising them to gamble for solvency, not only better protects creditors but also has positive spillovers on financial stability.

Finally, the authors highlight that the structure of remuneration matters so that the optimal remuneration consists of a mix of fixed salary, equity, and debt. The optimal mix is firm- and industry-specific; yet, there should always be a bias towards equity to incentivise managers to maximise the value of the corporation adequately.

A growing body of empirical literature seems to support these theoretical predictions. Sundaram and Yermack[50] analysed CEO compensation in 237 large corporations from 1996 to 2002 and showed that *ceteris paribus* the higher debt-based compensation, the lower the incentives towards risk-shifting.[51] Consistently, Anantharaman and co-authors[52] found that, as long as inside debt is not secured, higher debt-like compensation lead creditors to require lower yield and impose fewer covenants, i.e., decrease the cost of capital. This additional finding stresses a crucial issue: compensation through debt can handle the agency cost of debt only if the debt-like instruments are concretely prone to bear losses in the same way of other unsecured creditors.

Within this theoretical and empirical framework, the special set of incentives discussed in Sect. 2.1 should shape the proposal for remunerating bankers with bail-inable securities. Indeed, such proposal aims

bring about more costs than benefits. The agency costs of debt in bankruptcy can be quite low, whereas structuring incentive compatible pay structure through debt.

[50] Rangarajan K Sundaram and David L Yermack, 'Pay Me Later: Inside Debt and Its Role in Managerial Compensation' (2007) 62 The Journal of Finance 1551.

[51] The authors test for this implication using firm's "distance-to-default", i.e., the number of standard deviations decreases in the firm's value that are required for the firm to default so that a higher distance-to-default indicates a lower likelihood of default. The empirical results show that as the CEO's pension value increases relative to his equity value, risk-taking as measured by distance-to-default declines. Specifically, a firm's distance-to-default is 0.3 to 0.4 standard deviations higher when the CEO's personal debt-to-equity ratio exceeds his company's debt-to-equity ratio.

[52] Divya Anantharaman, Vivian W Fang and Guojin Gong, 'Inside Debt and the Design of Corporate Debt Contracts' (2014) 60 Management Science 1260.

at aligning the incentives of managers and unsecured creditors with the long-term viability of the institution.[53]

To this end, the perverse incentives provided by aligning managers' and bank shareholders' interests should be limited and managerial incentives should be re-aligned with financial stability goals when the situation of the banks deteriorates. This latter feature can be further disentangled: first, incentivising managers to maximise liquidation value reduces the room for contagion in case of bank distress. Moreover, as noted in the previous section, more inside debt decreases the dilution effect of early recapitalisation, at least partially handling the "Fuld Problem".[54] Besides, so far research prominently focused on executive pensions as the only form of inside debt, whereas this proposal goes beyond pension plans and suggests including bail-inable securities in remuneration packages as part of variable remuneration.

On top of a general scepticism due to the traditional wisdom on executive compensation, inside debt faces some specific critiques. In a pioneering study on executive pensions, Bebchuk and Jackson[55] strongly attack the praxis of granting generous pension packages to executives of large U.S. corporations arguing that it substantially weakened the link between pay and performance. The authors rebut any possible efficiency arguments in favour of inside debt, claiming that the main and almost exclusive purpose of such retirement benefits was to hide a conspicuous amount of resources to executives in a way that is not transparent to shareholders.[56]

Bebchuk and Jackson examined the alignment of managers and creditors as a possible efficiency rationale behind inside debt. However, for the purpose of their argument, they reject such possibility focusing on three main points. First, making managers too conservative implies efficiency losses; second, retirement benefits are often senior to unsecured

[53] With similar arguments, see Gordon (n 22); Frederick Tung, 'Pay for Banker Performance: Structuring Executive Compensation for Risk Regulation' (2011) 105 Nw. UL Rev. 1205.

[54] As labelled by Gordon (n 22).

[55] Bebchuk and Jackson Jr (n 44). The underlying argument derives from Lucian Bebchuk and Jesse Fried, *Pay without Performance*, vol 29 (Cambridge, MA: Harvard University Press 2004).

[56] Therefore, their main policy proposal, that has been implemented by the SEC in 2007, was to increase transparency and disclosure duties.

debt in bankruptcy; third, the alignment of managers and creditors could be achieved "by providing executives with compensation consisting of a mix of equity and debt securities".[57] This first line of critique does not hamper the normative claim of this proposal and, if any, it even reinforces it. The importance of reducing risk-taking incentives in banking has been already widely discussed. As for the second and third critiques, the present proposal expressly aims at providing executives with a mix of equity and debt securities that rank as other bail-inable securities in resolution.

Alces and Galle put forward a more radical set of critiques.[58] The authors argue that designing executive's compensation to reduce risk incentives is a false promise, stressing the role of bounded rationality both on the side of executives and investors that are unable to fully operationalise and discount the incentive structure of complex pay packages.

First, the authors criticise the use of inside debt for aligning managers' interests with creditors, arguing that imposing covenants on debt contracts represents a more efficient solution. However, at least in the context of EU banking regulation, such a criticism does not apply. Indeed, even accepting that covenants represent a more efficient way to handle agency cost of debt in non-financial firms,[59] previous research showed that given existing regulation, standard covenants are largely unavailable for instruments that qualify as capital or bail-inable instruments.[60]

Second, the authors argue that inside debt excessively misaligns the incentives of the management, shielding them from the cost of their decisions, since equity bears losses first and hence would protect managers from losses. Leaving aside potential problems of seniority in the bankruptcy waterfall, this critique still represents a contentious matter. Nonetheless, as previously specified, the purpose of this chapter is to provide ex-ante incentives towards optimal risk-taking whereas the

[57] Bebchuk and Jackson Jr (n 44). This idea has been, later, developed specifically for the financial sector in Bebchuk and Spamann (n 22).

[58] Kelli A Alces and Brian D Galle, 'The False Promise of Risk-Reducing Incentive Pay: Evidence from Executive Pensions and Deferred Compensation' (2012) 38 J. Corp. L. 53.

[59] Such argument is at odds with the empirical findings by Anantharaman, Fang and Gong (n 50).

[60] See Chapter 5, Sect. 3.2. With a similar argument, see also Fiona Mann and others, 'Market Discipline and UK Bank Bondholders' (2017) 57 Bank of England Quarterly Bulletin 26.

amount of losses that materialises ex-post is not decisive, as long as they are in line with ex-ante expectations. The extreme losses that bank executives of troubled banks suffered during the Global Financial Crisis did not prevent those from taking hazardous decisions that, in expected terms, were profitable for them.

Finally, Alces and Galle highlight that the calibration of the remuneration package with inside debt would be overly complex to design. On this final point, one must agree with the critique. Yet, Sects. 3 and 4 will outline how many other policy proposals and existing regulation present a high degree of complexity. Therefore, for the purpose of this study, this does not represent an insurmountable critique but rather a warning: designing a policy proposal that, at the very least, does not complicate the situation further and, ideally, marginally simplifies it.

2.3 Remuneration Through Debt: Early Cases

The previous section showed how debt has always been an important aspect of pay packages even though it received no policy and scientific prominence until recently. Such inattention is rooted in the lack of disclosure of the debt component of remuneration and, perhaps, on some inattention of the academic community, disproportionately focused on equity and cash as the only two components of pay packages.

The debt component of remuneration in both financial and non-financial institutions before the crisis was mainly composed of pension schemes. Nonetheless, some early examples of remuneration through debt other than pension schemes exist and it is worth briefly reviewing those before moving on. There are two groups of cases: the cases of temporary remuneration through debt because of legacy issues and the case of permanent and structural remuneration through debt implemented, to the best of my knowledge, so far only by UBS AG.

In the aftermath of the Global Financial Crisis, some of the banks more harshly harmed engineered forms of remuneration through debt for handling the severe losses experienced in previous years. For instance, in 2009 Lloyds and Royal Bank of Scotland, which at the time were nationalised, offered their top employees subordinated debt to pay the deferred part of the bonus.[61] Both banks offered a commercial loan scheme so that

[61] See "RBS to pay bonuses worth up to £950 m", Financial Times, 17 February 2009, retrievable at https://www.ft.com/content/81d2f4b8-fd08-11dd-a103-000077b07658;

employees could borrow against the deferred portion of compensation in subordinated debt. This, de facto, heavily weakened the effectiveness of such deferral. This subordinated debt scheme was reverted to more traditional pay packages shortly after, once the banks went back to the market.

A more interesting case, still within the category of remuneration through debt to handle legacy issues, is provided by Credit Suisse Group. In 2008 Credit Suisse designed a radical bonus scheme called PAF (Partner Asset Facility) to transfer some risks from the bank to employees. This constituted an internal employee fund where the parent undertaking transferred junk-grade loans and commercial-mortgage-backed bonds. The bank moved the risks off its books and allowed employees to benefit from the recovery on those instruments.[62] The experiment demonstrated to be an enormous success and the bank decided to launch the PAF2 programme in 2012. For what is of interest here, the main shortcoming of schemes such as PAF is their scope of application. Indeed, these schemes are mainly thought for, and sometimes reserved to, high-profile investment bankers.[63] After the CRD III entered into force, the programme ended as it became non-compliant with the European regulation on remuneration through instruments other than shares. More details on these points are provided later on in this chapter (Sect. 5).

Finally, UBS AG, the largest Swiss bank, provides the most interesting and structural example of remuneration through debt in the financial industry. Since 2012, UBS pays a significant part of its bonuses through Additional Tier 1 instruments.[64] The initiative was strongly proposed by Mr. Alex Weber, the former president of the Bundesbank who became the chairperson of UBS in 2012.

"Lloyds and RBS to offer loans as staff bonuses", Financial Times, 16 April 2009. Retrievable at https://www.ft.com/content/7b932404-2ab4-11de-8415-00144feabdc0.

[62] See "At Credit Suisse, Toxic Bonuses Turn into Gold", Bloomberg, 27 January 2012, retrievable at https://www.bloomberg.com/news/articles/2012-01-26/at-credit-suisse-toxic-bonuses-turn-into-gold.

[63] See "Credit Suisse plans new asset-backed bonus scheme", Reuters, 4 January 2013, retrievable at https://www.worldfinance.com/contributors/want-your-bonus-youll-have-to-wait-says-credit-suisse.

[64] See "Credit Suisse replaces radical bonus scheme", Financial Times, 5 February 2013, retrievable at https://www.ft.com/content/47d6e2ae-6ee9-11e2-9ded-00144feab49a.

The original Deferred Contingent Capital Plan (DCCP)[65] counted for 50% of variable compensation. Managers were awarded Additional Tier 1 (AT1) instruments that paid market-based coupons; moreover, such instruments embed a contractual clause for writing down their principal amount to zero in case the capital ratio (CET1/RWAs)[66] fell below 7%. The year after, the scheme was revised, and the Deferred Contingent Capital Plan counted for 37.5% of the deferred compensation whereas equity-based bonus increased to 62.5%.[67] The threshold for writing down Awarded AT1 instruments increased from 7 to 10%, making the write-down much more likely and, consequently, impacting incentives more effectively.[68] Figure 1 reports the structure of remuneration packages for 2012 and 2013.

The vesting period of the DCCP Program is five years; instruments only vest if CET1 remains higher than the write-down threshold, and the bank delivers a before-tax profit. Likewise, annual interests are paid only if the bank delivers a before-tax profit. Moreover, employees forfeit 20% of the contingent instruments awarded for each loss-making year, which means that in case of five years straight of losses no instruments will vest, this represents a further risk of losses for high-level employees, on top of the risk of write-down.

Currently, the structure of remuneration packages closely resembles that of 2013, showing satisfaction with such remuneration practice. In the 2018 Remuneration Report, UBS officials state: "Over the last five years, USD 2.0 billion of DCCP was issued, contributing to the Group's total loss-absorbing capacity (TLAC). Therefore, DCCP awards not only support competitive pay but also provide a loss absorption buffer that

[65] Moritz Seiler and Damian Fischer, '"Bonus Bonds" for Bankers: A New Type of Debt-Based Remuneration in the Financial Industry' (2015) 425 ECFR 461. For a broader context, see Peter Laaper and Danny Busch, 'How to Behave Like a Good Banker?' (2022) 18 European Company and Financial Law Review 899.

[66] The Ration between Common Equity (CET1) and Risk Weighted Asset (RWA) represents the standard ratio in all Basel Accord for Minimum Capital Requirements.

[67] An equity bias when remuneration (also) through debt is consistent with the theoretical findings in Edmans and Liu (n 46).

[68] See UBS, 2013 compensation highlights and key changes. Retrievable at https://www.ubs.com/global/en/investor-relations/financial-information/annual-reporting/ar-archive/2013.html.

Total compensation for GEB members for the performance years 2013 and 2012

CHF, except where indicated[1]

Name, function	For the year	Base salary	Immediate cash[2]	Annual performance award under EOP[3]	Annual performance award under DCCP[4]	Benefits[5]	Contributions to retirement benefit plans[6]	Total
Sergio P. Ermotti, Group CEO	2013	2,500,000	1,000,000	4,530,000	2,370,000	127,300	202,822	10,730,122
Sergio P. Ermotti, Group CEO (highest-paid)	**2012**	2,500,000	0	3,660,000	2,440,000	69,500	201,088	**8,870,588**
Andrea Orcel (highest-paid)	2013	1,500,000	1,000,000	5,300,000	2,700,000	727,048	202,822	11,429,870
Aggregate of all GEB members who were in office at the end of the year[7]	2013	16,873,360	9,949,062	33,894,646	18,790,161	1,548,784	1,347,784	82,403,796
	2012	16,273,460	0	31,355,592	20,903,728	640,683	1,233,719	**70,407,181**
Aggregate of all GEB members who stepped down during the year[8]	2013	0	0	0	0	0	0	0
	2012	1,593,288	0	0	0	105,865	14,799	**1,713,952**

Fig. 1 UBS remuneration structure for 2012 and 2013

protects the firm's capital position".[69] Given such success, one might wonder why nobody followed the virtuous example provided by UBS AG. The remainder of the analysis will show the regulatory obstacles to such a paradigm shift and why a regulatory intervention is warranted for spreading the remuneration through bail-inable securities through the European banking industry.

2.4 A Simple Numerical Example

This section provides a simple numerical example to substantiate the claim of remuneration through debt and link systemic externalities to bankers' moral hazard. For the sake of simplicity, the example assumes that the required rate of return on both debt and equity is zero and that the market value of assets and liabilities equals accounting values.

The example highlights a case of risk-shifting, where the risks of a negative NPV project are shifted from shareholders to bail-inable creditors. In this setting, different remuneration arrangements matter for the final decision of the bank management on the risky project.

Consider "Bank A" with a balance sheet as shown in Table 1. Depositors are covered by deposit guarantee.

An investment opportunity materialises. It costs 10 and yields 90 in the case of success and 0 in the case of default. The project will succeed with 10% probability whereas with 90% probability it will default. The project has negative Net Present Value, since in expected terms, its value is -1, as shown in Table 2.

Table 1 "Bank A" balance sheet

Bank A			
Asset		*Liabilities*	
Risky loans	90	Deposits	90
Cash	10	Bail-inable debt	5
		Equity	5

[69] UBS Compensation Report for 2013, 14. Retrievable at https://www.ubs.com/content/dam/assets/cc/investor-relations/annual-report/2018/epaper/comp/en/index.html.

Table 2 Project opportunity

Project			
Cost		*10*	
Probability of success	0,1	Value if success	90
Probability of default	0,9	Value if default	0
NPV	−1	Project should not be undertaken	

Table 3 Risk-shifting incentives

Risk-shifting incentives			
	Success	*Failure*	*E(V)*
E(V) of equity	85	0	8.5
E(V) of bail-inable debt	5	0	0.5

Shareholders are willing to undertake the projects since they have limited liability, and shift part of the risk of the investment to creditors, in this case bail-inable creditors. Therefore, the bank decides to deplete its cash component of assets and undertake the project.

If the investment succeeds, the value of assets becomes 180, which means that the value of equity (Assets–Debt) increases to 85. On the other hand, if the investment defaults, the value of assets becomes 90, which is barely able to repay depositors so that losses are born by equity as well as bail-inable debtholders. In expected terms, given the probability of success and default, the expected value of equity increases from 5 to 8.5. This represents the typical situation of risk-shifting in highly leveraged institutions.

Now suppose that a "decision-maker" decides whether to undertake the investment. Such "decision-maker" is an agent of shareholders and can be rewarded for her services in two different ways:

(1) Awarding to her 2 in equity;
(2) Awarding to her 2 of which 1,1 in equity and 0,9 in bail-inable debt.

In the first scenario, the incentives of the decision-maker are aligned with the other equity holders (Table 4): her welfare increases with undertaking the risky project and, therefore, the decision will still shift the risk to bail-inable creditors. In case of success, the value of equity increases to 32. In the case of failure, the value goes to 0 and also bail-inable debtholders bear losses.

In the second scenario, the mix of instruments awarded changes the incentives of the "decision-maker". She enjoys the upside of her risk-taking through the equity component of remuneration but also bears the downside, through debt. In particular, in case of success, the value of her equity goes to 17.6 and to 0 in case of failure. Whereas, the debt component remains 0.9 in case of success and goes to 0 in case of default. Unlike equity, debt is a fixed claim against the institution that does not change with the value of assets. As shown in Table 5, the welfare of the decision-maker decreases, in expected terms, under this type of reward mechanism. Therefore, the negative NPV project would not be undertaken.

Table 4 Remuneration through equity

Two remuneration scenarios			
Scenario 1: the decision-maker, as a result of remuneration policy, holds 2 in equity			
	Success	Failure	E(V)
E(V) for the decision-maker	32	0	3,2
Comment: the welfare of the decision-maker increases in expected terms. The project will be undertaken, and the risk will be shifted to bail-inable creditors			

Table 5 Remuneration (also) through bail-inable debt

Two remuneration scenarios			
Scenario 2: the decision-maker, as a result of remuneration policy, holds 1,1 in equity and 0,9 in bail-inable debt			
	Success	Failure	E(V)
E(V) for the decision-maker (equity part)	17.6	0	1.76
E(V) for the decision-maker (debt part)	0.9	0	0.09
Comment: the welfare of the decision-maker decreases in expected terms (1.85 < 2). The project will not be undertaken			

Finally, it is worth noting that equity holders would choose the first remuneration scenario since it is potentially welfare-enhancing for them. Therefore, the second scenario, in which the negative NPV project is not undertaken, can be reached only through regulation.

3 The International Debate Over Remuneration in Banking

As widely discussed beforehand, the negative externalities stemming from pay packages provide a strong argument for regulation.[70] Indeed, in the aftermath of the Global Financial Crisis, new international standards, guidelines, and regulation were issued under substantial political pressure. Thus, these did not always respond to the economic rationale underpinning bank managers' remuneration but often compromised efficiency with political rent-seeking of policymakers.

The proceeding of this section briefly analyses the international standards and the main policy proposals on remuneration. The analysis will be, to the larger extent possible, functional to our main claim, i.e., remunerating banks' material risk-takers (also) with bail-inable securities. Consequently, this cannot be considered a comprehensive analysis of the legal implications related to the regulation on bank managers' remuneration.

Financial Stability Forum drafted the leading policy document that informed the post-crisis discussion in 2009.[71] The document highlights the crucial principle of long-term orientation in remuneration policy as the primary tool to ensure sound practices.[72] In so doing, it poses three

[70] Bebchuk and Spamann (n 22).

[71] Financial Stability Board, 'Principles for Sound Compensation Practices' (2009).

[72] This is closely mirrored by the position taken OECD on which see Kirkpatrick (n 35) 13–15. If any, the OECD position is even more conservative, making clear that the main objective should be to align managers' and long term shareholders' interests, grounding the fallacies of previous remuneration packages only on the wedge between pay and performance.

general principles of effectiveness in regulating pay[73]: effective governance of compensation,[74] effective supervisory oversight,[75] and effective alignment with prudent risk-taking.

The principles regarding the "effective alignment with prudent risk-taking" (Principles 4–7) are of particular interest since they pertain to the regulation of the structure of bankers' pay. Principles 4 and 5 focus on the alignment of compensation outcomes and risk, enriching the concept of "performance" in the financial sector. Reaching the same outcome in terms of short-term profit, while engaging in less risky activities, represents a superior performance and must be rewarded accordingly. Eventually, principles 6 and 7 go to the core of regulating pay suggesting that pay-out schedules be made more and more sensitive to time horizons[76] and aligning the mix of cash, equity and "other forms of compensation" with risk-taking.[77]

A broad academic consensus on regulating pay structure arose in the aftermath of the Global Financial Crisis. Nonetheless, the proposals on the type of structural regulation have been numerous and so different from one another that it is impossible to reconcile them in a "consensus

[73] The choice of the dimension of effectiveness instead of efficiency or soundness is, in itself, indicative of the new approach of regulators towards bankers' compensation, looking for an intrusive and interventionist role despite any possible efficiency argument, which is consistent with an attitude of political rent seeking.

[74] Principles 1–3: Strengthening the stewardship role of the Board of Directors in designing, overseeing, and reviewing the compensation system and assuring the independence of the staff engaged in financial and risk control.

[75] Principles 8–9: Strengthening the role of supervisors in reviewing compensation packages and increasing the disclosure duties of financial firms regarding their compensation policies.

[76] Following academic proposal and best practices on restricted stock option and deferred compensation. See, for instance, Sanjai Bhagat and Roberta Romano, 'Reforming Executive Compensation: Focusing and Committing to the Long-Term' (2009) 26 Yale J. on Reg. 359.

[77] As Sect. 4 will detail the EU went well beyond what suggested by this principle in regulating the mix of cash and equity in bankers' pay. For a critique of the EU approach, see Guido Ferrarini, 'CRD IV and the Mandatory Structure of Bankers' Pay' (2015) ECGI-Law Working Paper 289.

view" on pay structure. For instance,[78] in Romano and Bhagat[79] the main policy proposal is here to design compensation packages made of only restricted stock and restricted stock option that can be sold or exercised by managers only a considerable period after their last day of office. Bebchuk and Spamann[80] suggest tying bank managers' remuneration not only to share prices but to a basket of equity, hybrid and debt security so to decrease risk-taking incentives. Again, Bolton and his co-authors[81] suggest tying executive remuneration to CDS spread. This represents the only proposal expressly including debt in the remuneration package. Compared to CDS spreads, the proposal put forward in this chapter has two key advantages. First, CDS tend to be procyclical and are not thought to provide early signals of distress.[82] Therefore, tying remuneration to CDS spreads would not alleviate the problem of excessive risk-taking in good times. Second, tying remuneration to CDS spread would have no positive spillovers in the resolvability of the institution and the credibility of resolution.

On the contrary, professor Ferrarini argued against any kind of structural regulation[83] arguing that governance and disclosure regulation would suffice to align managerial incentives with optimal risk-taking. However, structural regulation quite often implies translating current best practices into law, creating a rigid framework that does not fit each and every financial institution. I will come back to this important aspect in Sect. 5, arguing why and how the proposal of remuneration through bail-inable debt circumvent such critique.

[78] This list has the only aim to provide prominent examples of sharply different policy proposals on regulation of pay structure and has not intent of being complete and comprehensive. For a survey see Raghavendra Rau, 'Executive Compensation' (2017) 10 Foundations and Trends® in Finance 181.

[79] Bhagat and Romano (n 74).

[80] Bebchuk and Spamann (n 22).

[81] Patrick Bolton, Hamid Mehran and Joel Shapiro, 'Executive Compensation and Risk-taking' (2015) 19 Review of Finance 2139.

[82] On the procyclicality of CDS spreads and their inability to provide early warnings of distress, see Hyun Song Shin, *Procyclicality and the Search for Early Warning Indicators* (International Monetary Fund 2013) 5.

[83] See Guido Ferrarini and Maria Cristina Ungureanu, 'Economics, Politics, and the International Principles for Sound Compensation Practices: An Analysis of Executive Pay at European Banks' (2011) 64 Vand. L. Rev. 429.

4 Regulating Bankers Pay in the EU

In the aftermath of the Global Financial Crisis, the EU firstly adopted a supervisory approach to remuneration[84] mirroring to a large extent the direction laid down by the FSB via the principles on remuneration policy issued by the Committee of European Banking Supervisors (CEBS).[85] However, specific shortcomings due to fragmented implementation and a growing pressure from media and politicians steered the debate towards a new regulatory approach, more focused on direct regulation than on supervisory oversight.

Such a change in the approach of the EU policymakers emerged in 2010 with the enactment of the Capital Requirements Directive III (CRD III).[86] It is not here possible to review all relevant norms on remuneration policy included in the CRD III.[87] To provide the reader with a flavour of the new attitude towards remuneration it suffices to mention that the Directive required that at least 50% of variable remuneration to be in the form of shares or equivalent ownership interests and to defer at least 40% of the variable remuneration for a period no shorter than three years.

This intrusive regulatory trend continued and reached a new peak with the reform package of 2014 and the new version of the Capital Requirement Regulation (CRD IV). The proceeding of the section critically analyses the provisions, embedding the limited innovation provided by the fifth version of the CRD. Section 4.1 introduces the rules on governance, supervision, and disclosure of remuneration policies, whereas

[84] Commission Recommendation on remuneration policies in the financial sector, C (2009) 3159, (April 2009).

[85] Committee of European Banking Supervisors (CEBS), High-Level Principles for Remuneration Policies (April 2009). This committee no longer exist and, functionally, can be considered the predecessor of the European Banking Authority and (partly) of the Single Supervisory Board before the Banking Union was implemented. Yet, the committee had limited powers and mainly focused on cooperation and coordination of national policies on supervision.

[86] Directive 2010/76/EU of the European Parliament and of the Council of 24 November 2010 Amending Directives 2006/48/EC and 2006/49/EC As Regards Capital Requirements for the Trading Book and for ReSecuritisations, and the Supervisory Review of Remuneration Policies, Official Journal of the European Union 2010, L329/3.

[87] For a comprehensive overview, see Eilís Ferran, 'New Regulation of Remuneration in the Financial Sector in the EU' (2012) 9 European Company and Financial Law Review 1.

Sect. 4.2 provides an in-depth analysis of the substantive rule pertaining to the structure of remuneration packages. Eventually, Sect. 4.3 critically assess the current regulation focusing on whether and to what extent it addresses the specific of bank governance and the other economic considerations carried out in Sect. 2.

4.1 Governance, Supervision, and Disclosure

Article 92 of the CRD mainly deals with governance provisions on remuneration policies; these provisions can be divided into two groups. The first group comprises general principles that should inform remuneration policies, whereas the second group comprises more stringent norms on the governance of remuneration.

Starting from the general principles, the remuneration policy should promote sound and effective risk management and not encourage excessive risk-taking.[88] Moreover, such policy should be in line with the long-term interests of the institution, taking into consideration its business strategy, objectives, and values.[89]

The truthful application of such principle, in the CRD architecture, must necessarily pass through the implementation of some governance best standards. Therefore, the Directive entrusts the management body of each institution to adopt a yearly review, and oversee the implementation of general principles of the institutions' remuneration policy.[90] On top of the oversight of the management body, the implementation of such principles must be subject to independent internal review at least annually.[91] Finally, the Directive requires significant institutions to establish a remuneration committee.[92] The committee must take responsibility for the preparation of all the decisions regarding remuneration[93] as well as for directly overseeing the remuneration of senior officers employed

[88] Article 92(2)(a) CRDIV.

[89] Article 92(2)(b) CRDIV.

[90] Article 92(2)(c) CRDIV.

[91] Article 92(2)(d) CRDIV.

[92] Article 95(1) CRDIV.

[93] Article 95(2) CRDIV.

in risk management and compliance functions.[94] Crucially, the Directive mandates that "when preparing such decisions, the remuneration committee must take into account the long-term interests of shareholders, investors, and other stakeholders in the institution and the public interest",[95] widening the objective function of the committee beyond the mere shareholder interest approach.

The governance provisions discussed above are complemented by a wide mandate to the competent authority to supervise remuneration policies and their implementation. The competent authority shall supervise the application of all the relevant regulations in terms of remuneration policy.[96] The mandate is particularly wide and encompasses the level of the group, parent undertakings and subsidiaries, including branches and subsidiaries established in third countries. Moreover, and most importantly, in order to make effective the supervision over remuneration policy and compliance, as part of the supervisory review and evaluation process,[97] the competent authority can limit variable remuneration as a percentage of net revenues to assure the maintenance of a sound capital basis.[98] If the situation further deteriorates and distributions need to be limited,[99] the payment of variable remuneration is among the types of distributions that must be limited or wholly voided.[100]

Finally, the CRR requires strengthened disclosure requirements to assure both effective supervision and the enhancement of market oversight on remuneration policy. Specifically, a large set of disclosure duties intends to provide the competent authority with all the relevant information to carry out the evaluation process and to generally oversight the safety and soundness of the institutions' business model, strategies, and goals.[101] For instance, institutions must disclose information on the link between pay and performance, the criteria used for risk adjustment,

[94] Article 92(2)(f) CRDIV.

[95] Article 95(2) CRDIV.

[96] Recital 67 and Article 92(1) CRD IV.

[97] Articles 97-101 CRD IV.

[98] Article 104(1)(g) CRD IV.

[99] This happens if the Combined Buffer Requirement of Article 128 CRD IV is breached.

[100] Article 141(2)(b).

[101] Article 450(1) CRR.

the ratio between fixed and variable remuneration, aggregate quantitative information on remuneration per each business area, the number of individuals earning significantly high amounts,[102] etc. Finally, significant institutions must also disclose to the public the quantitative information related to the members of the management body.[103]

4.2 The Regulatory Regime for the Remuneration Structure

The most significant innovation of CRD IV in terms of remuneration policy is the set of rules on the structure of remuneration for "identified staff".[104] This represents the most contentious aspect of the regulatory regime and attracted harsh critiques in many academic studies.[105]

First, the Directive sets some general principles to set the variable part of remuneration. The evaluation of the performance must combine individual results and the results of the business unit. Moreover, the performance must be assessed with a multi-year horizon to capture the long-term component of the performance.

Besides, the Directive and the implementing Guidelines[106] extensively discipline all the aspects related to remuneration packages from their design to the pay-out phase. Figure 2 graphically shows the main building blocks of the "remuneration process", highlighting the main aspects of interest whose legal and economic rationale and implications will be detailed in the proceeding of this section.

The first phase consists of the design of the package. The cornerstone of this phase and the whole structural regulation is the cap on variable remuneration. The Directive makes a sharp distinction between fixed and

[102] On this see also Article 75 CRD IV on the cooperation between EBA and the Competent Authority.

[103] Article 450(2) CRR.

[104] In the context of remuneration policy, identified staff "means staff whose professional activities have a material impact on the institution's risk profile in accordance with the criteria set out in the Commission Delegated Regulation (EU) 604/2014 and where appropriate in addition based on institutions' criteria". See, Guidelines on sound remuneration policies, EBA/GL/2015/22 para 10.

[105] Among many other, see notably Ferrarini (n 75); Luca Enriques and Dirk Zetzsche, 'Quack Corporate Governance, Round III? Bank Board Regulation Under the New European Capital Requirement Directive' (2015) 16 Theoretical Inquiries in Law 211.

[106] Guidelines on sound remuneration policies, EBA/GL/2015/22.

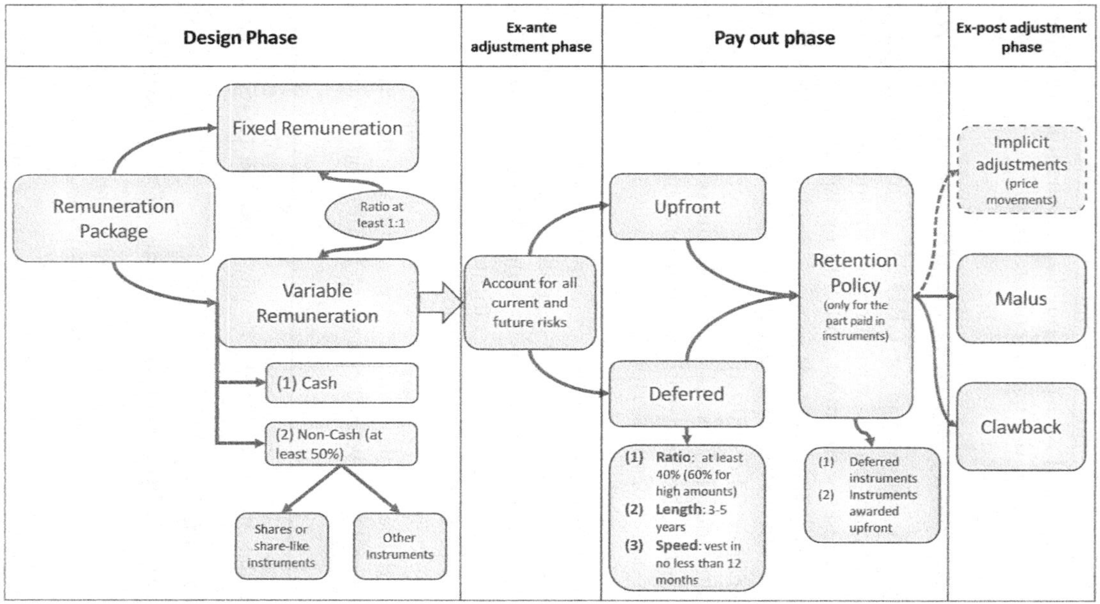

Fig. 2 Phases of the remuneration process

variable remuneration.[107] The former must reflect the professional experience and the organisational responsibility of the staff member, whereas the latter must reflect "sustainable and risk-adjusted" performance. The fixed and variable components of remuneration must be appropriately mixed.[108] In setting such an appropriate mix, the variable component of remuneration cannot exceed the fixed component.[109] Thus, the Directive limits the possibility to design the pay packages of managers and mandates that the ratio between fixed and variable remuneration is at least 1:1.

The Directive provides two possibilities to deviate from this principle, pointing at opposite directions. On the one hand, individual Member States can further limit the room for awarding variable remuneration to bank managers, imposing a lower maximum percentage.[110] On the other hand, shareholders can allow the institution to increase the maximum percentage up to 200%.

The following step consists of determining the composition of the variable elements needed. This aspect goes to the core of the matter of interest. For the time being, it suffices to say that the Directive[111] distinguishes between cash and non-cash bonuses and at least that 50% of the variable remuneration must consist of non-cash bonuses. Moreover, the Directive explicitly differentiates between shares and share-linked instruments[112] on the one hand, and "other instruments" on the other hand. Such differentiation and its implications are to be analysed in depth in Sect. 5. However, it is worth anticipating that both the letter of the law and even more its implementation lean towards a marked equity

[107] Article 92(2)(g) CRD IV.

[108] Article 94(1)(f) CRD IV.

[109] Article 94(1)(g)(ii) CRD IV.

[110] Belgium and the Netherlands took advantage of this possibility, setting the maximum percentage to 50% and 20% respectively.

[111] Article 94(1)(l).

[112] CRD V allows both listed and non-listed banks to use share-linked instruments whereas, under CRD IV listed banks were only allowed to pay with shares, which was deemed too costly and burdensome. See the new Article 94(1)(l)(i) that now states that the variable part of remuneration can be paid out in: "shares or, subject to the legal structure of the institution concerned, equivalent ownership interests; or share-linked instruments or, subject to the legal structure of the institution concerned, equivalent non-cash instruments".

bias, leaving the provision on "other instruments" as part of variable remuneration little more than dead letters.

As previously discussed, one of the key principles of variable remuneration is that it must reflect risk-adjusted performance, which represents the second phase of the process. Therefore, the Directive[113] requires that both the measurement of the performance and the allocation of variable remuneration should take into account all current and future risks and adjust accordingly.[114]

After the ex-ante risk adjustment, the pay-out phase begins. This phase consists of a complex set of tools and mainly focuses on deferral and retention policies. This provision wants to ensure the implementation of the long-term orientation principle for identified employees. The deferral and retention policies can shape the payment schedule so to reflect the long-term performance of employees. It is important to stress that the payment schedule has a twofold goal: on the one hand, it aims to influence risk incentives of employees and push them towards long-term orientation; on the other hand, it wants to make ex-post adjustment possible and effective.

Preliminarily, it might be worth defining the difference between deferral and retention policies within the meaning of the Directive and the Guidelines. Deferral means the period between the award of the variable remuneration and the moment when the employee legally becomes the owner of the remuneration awarded.[115] Retention means the period during which the employee cannot sell or access the variable remuneration; although, it has already been awarded and is already legally owned by the employee.[116] Hence, deferral policy applies both to cash and the non-cash component of variable remuneration, whereas retention policy can only apply to the part of variable remuneration paid in instruments. Moreover, the retention policy applies to both the deferred and the non-deferred part of variable remuneration.

[113] Article 94(1)(j) and (k).

[114] The procedures for performing such an adjustment are widely described and regulation in the Guidelines on sound remuneration policies (n 103) in para 217–232.

[115] See Guidelines, para 10.

[116] See Guidelines, para 10.

Deferral policies consist of three main characteristics: the ratio of deferred variable remuneration, the length of the deferral period, and the speed at which deferred remuneration vests.[117]

The variable component of remuneration packages comprises a part to be paid upfront and a substantial part to be deferred.[118] At least 40%[119] of the variable remuneration must be deferred for a period between 3 and 5 years[120] to align the risk incentives of the employee with their activities. However, the deferral period cannot be shorter than 5 years for the senior management and management bodies of significant institutions.[121] Finally, the deferred portion of remuneration can vest all at once, at the end of the deferral period, or through several payments throughout the deferral period. In this latter case, the first tranche cannot be paid out before 12 months from the award of the variable remuneration; moreover, vesting cannot take place more frequently than on a yearly basis.[122]

When it comes to the retention period, the Guidelines[123] specify that variable remuneration instruments are subject to an appropriately long retention period, so to align employee incentives with the longer-term interests of the institution. Retention periods play a different role when applied to deferred or non-deferred instruments. In the first case, on the one hand, a retention period exceeding the time of deferral allows

[117] In this context, vesting "means the effect by which the staff member becomes the legal owner of the variable remuneration awarded, independent of the instrument which is used for the payment or if the payment is subject to additional retention periods or clawback arrangements". See Guidelines, para 10. F.

[118] Article 94(1)(m) CRD IV.

[119] The minimum ratio increases to 60% for employees with particularly high variable remuneration. Institutions should define themselves what constitutes "particularly high amount" taking into account the available benchmarks issued by the EBA. See Guidelines, para 241 and 242.

[120] The CRD V prolong the deferral period to a minimum of 4 years (instead of 3) and, in the case of senior management, the minimum deferral is 5 years. See the new Article 94(1)(m) stating that: "a substantial portion [...] is deferred over a period which is not less than four to five years [...]. For members of the management body and senior management of institutions that are significant in terms of their size, internal organisation and the nature, scope and complexity of their activities, the deferral period should not be less than five years".

[121] Guidelines, para 240.

[122] Guidelines, para 245–248.

[123] Para 263.

for considering the underlying risks of special activities whose effects can materialise after the deferral period. On the other hand, applying a retention period to the instruments paid upfront by the institutions limits the incentives towards excessive short-term orientation. Besides, it grants the possibility to apply ex-post adjustments effectively. Indeed, the Guidelines[124] require awarded instruments to be subject to retention for at least one year, whereas a longer period is warranted if the ex-post risk adjustment relies on the change in the value of the awarded instruments.

Eventually, the remuneration process ends with the ex-post risk-adjustment phase. This consists of two main mechanisms: explicit and implicit risk adjustments. Malus and clawback arrangements are among the explicit risk-adjustment mechanisms. The Directive requires institutions to be able to apply such arrangements up to 100% of the variable remuneration.[125] Each institution, in specifying the criteria for the application of malus and clawback, should make sure that these cover the situations where the employee (i) participated in or was responsible for the conduct that resulted in significant losses to the institution; (ii) failed to meet appropriate standards of fitness and propriety.[126] Such arrangements, if efficiently designed, partially permit the institution to take a portfolio approach to remuneration, making the employee's performance impact on the total amount of remuneration received throughout years and not only on a yearly basis.

Finally, when staff is paid in instruments whose value is sensitive to the performance of the institutions (such as shares), the value of the variable remuneration after the deferred or retention period might vary (increase or decrease) according to the movement of the underlying price of the awarded instruments. This represents an implicit ex-post adjustment since the final monetary value of the instruments awarded depends on the overall performance of the institutions. However, the guidelines expressly state that implicit risk adjustments cannot be considered a substitute for malus and clawback arrangements.[127] Moreover, it is worth noting that explicit ex-post adjustments can only decrease the amount

[124] Para 267.

[125] In the aftermath of Brexit, in the UK the policymaker decided to erase this limitation. For an analysis, see Ricardo Cabral, 'The Banking Union's Resolution or Liquidation Approach' [2024] Journal of Banking Regulation.

[126] Article 94(1)(n) CRD IV.

[127] Para 277.

of variable remuneration initially awarded,[128] whereas, naturally, implicit adjustments can both increase and decrease such amount, according to the institution's performance and price movements.

4.3 Critical Assessment

"Poorly designed remuneration policies and incentive schemes are capable of increasing to an unacceptable extent the risks to which credit institutions [...] are exposed".[129] This is what the EU policymaker claimed as the rationale for the structural regulation of bankers pay and the specific powers granted to the competent authority on these issues.

It is now time to critically assess whether the new regulatory framework, as analysed in detail in the previous Sections, has increased the quality of the design of remuneration policies and incentive schemes. In so doing, the proceeding of this section will critically discuss the strengths and the weaknesses of the norms on structural regulation of managers' pay against the underlying economic arguments discussed in Sect. 2.1.

According to the theoretical framework proposed in Sect. 2.1, the main strength of the regulatory framework consists of its application not only to executives and senior management but also to the so-called "risk-takers".[130] Indeed, the aim to align the risk-taking incentives of a broader audience of high-profile employees represents a significant innovation as compared with the previous regime.[131]

When it comes to the criticism of the regulatory framework, for the sake of good order, the relevant arguments are split into two categories. First, I discuss the arguments related to the standard economic wisdom on remuneration, to the extent they apply in banking. Second, I address the specific issues pertaining to bank governance and discuss whether the current regulation efficiently and effectively addresses them.

[128] Para 275.

[129] Recital 68 CRDIV.

[130] Article 92(2). Those are defined as: "staff whose professional activities have a material impact on the institution's risk profile in accordance with the criteria set out in the Commission Delegated Regulation (EU) 604/20147 and where appropriate in addition based on institutions' criteria", see Guidelines para 10.

[131] With the same argument, see Armour and others (n 2) 386.

Pay Regulation and the Economics of Remuneration

The regulatory cap on variable remuneration has attracted the most criticism.[132] The European legislator was explicit in stating that such aims to avoid excessive risk-taking.[133] However, this provision cannot reach the desired goal and, besides, it brings about unintended and value-destructive consequences.[134] In the early phase of its implementation, the UK challenged the regulatory cap, as it was particularly hit by this reform. The Advocate General Jääskinen found the UK plea ungrounded, stating that EU legislation was fully proportionate and abode by the subsidiary principle.[135] In substantiating its opinion, the Advocate General stated.

To my mind this means that there was a danger of regulatory competition downwards and a risk that self-regulation by the financial institutions would not suffice to create the remuneration policies necessary for preventing excessive risk-taking. Moreover, it is evident that the goal of creating a uniform regulatory framework for risk management of relevant parts of remuneration policies of financial institutions could not have been better achieved by measures taken at the national level.[136]

Additionally, one might question even its effectiveness. The practice shows that in order to comply with the cap there is a tendency to increase the volume of fixed remuneration, so to keep variable remuneration high enough. Moreover, the cap is constantly circumvented by several banks via the so-called "role-based allowances" which are considered as

[132] Ferrarini (n 75); Kevin J Murphy, 'Regulating Banking Bonuses in the European Union: A Case Study in Unintended Consequences' (2013) 19 European Financial Management 631.

[133] Recital 65 CRD IV: "In any event, in order to avoid excessive risk-taking, a maximum ratio between the fixed and the variable component of the total remuneration should be set".

[134] Murphy (n 129) 648. Such consequences are even worse for investment bankers given the business model and the standard remuneration practice; i.e., below average fixed salary and above average performance-related bonuses.

[135] Opinion of Advocate General Jääskinen delivered on 20 November 2014, Case C-507/13 United Kingdom of Great Britain and Northern Ireland v. European Parliament and Council of the European Union.

[136] Ibid, para 102.

additional pay to the basic salary and therefore part of the fixed component of remuneration,[137] even though they work, de facto, as variable remuneration.[138]

Such a bias against variable remuneration springs from the pressure of political constituencies and media and not by efficiency and stability considerations.[139] The regulatory cap severs the link between pay and performance that is the very basic elements of good remuneration packages. As already mentioned, limiting variable remuneration incentivises banks to increase the fixed component of remuneration. This latter component cannot be tied to performance but "should primarily reflect relevant professional experience and organisational responsibility".[140] The EBA Guidelines further specify that a component of remuneration is fixed if it is based on predetermined criteria, reflects the level of professional experience, is permanent and non-revocable and, of utmost importance, does not depend on performance.[141]

Therefore, fixed components of remuneration must be paid upfront, cannot be deferred or retained, are not subject to *ex-post* adjustment. This means that none of the onerous and burdensome mechanism of control over the remuneration structure applies to fixed remuneration.

To provide anecdotal justification for such an argument, it is instructive to look at the remuneration policy of the UniCredit group.[142] Figure 3 shows data on the amount and structure of remuneration of identified staff for 2017. The compensation of the CEO, the other Directors, and the General Manager only or pre-eminently derive from fixed compensation. The remuneration packages of other executives have a higher

[137] See Opinion of the European Banking Authority on the application of Directive 2013/36/EU (Capital Requirements Directive) regarding the principles on remuneration policies of credit institutions and investment firms and the use of allowances, EBA/Op/2014/10, 15 October 2014, 2. See Also, EBA Guidelines, para 120 and followings.

[138] Andreas Kokkinis, 'Exploring the Effects of the 'Bonus Cap'Rule: The Impact of Remuneration Structure on Risk-Taking by Bank Managers' (2019) 19 Journal of Corporate Law Studies 167.

[139] The initial proposal of the Commission for the CRD IV did not comprise the cap on variable remuneration. The proposal was amended later by the European Parliament embedding the cap.

[140] Article 92(2)(g).

[141] EBA Guidelines, para 117.

[142] The remuneration policy of the group for 2018 is retrievable at https://compensationpolicy.unicredit.eu/assets/pdf/2018-group-compensation-policy.pdf.

variable component, slightly above 50% of fixed remuneration. The variable remuneration is paid mainly through deferred compensation, the upfront variable pay is mainly awarded in cash, whereas the deferred component is mainly awarded in shares. No other instruments are used for variable payments. Finally, the ratio of forward-looking[143] part of remuneration is between 46% (senior executive vice-presidents) and 26% (other identified staff).[144]

This brief yet informative overview of the remuneration policy of one of the biggest European banking group clearly shows that the link between pay and performance is particularly weak, especially at the apex of the group structure.

Another point attracting sharp criticism is the excessive complexity of the remuneration process and the burden for banks generated thereby. In particular, the problems related to overcomplexity are crucial when it comes to deferral and retention policies that represent one of the pillars of the whole framework in aligning risk-taking incentives to long-term horizon. Correctly setting those periods is one of the cornerstones of the current framework since it represents the channel to punish, implicitly and explicitly, bad performance and excessive risk-taking.

However, setting correctly the deferral and retention periods, i.e., setting them in such a way that makes it possible to correctly incentivise ex-ante and punish ex-post the performance of identified staff, is inherently problematic. To this end, Romano and Baghat[145] proposed to use only restricted stocks and restricted stock options in variable pay, restricted in the sense that the shares cannot be sold, or the option cannot be exercised for a period of at least two to four years after the executive's resignation or last day in office. The restriction to sell the shares or exercise the options lasts until 2–4 years after the last day in office of the employees. Such a proposal had two main goals: putting forward a

143 Forward looking remuneration indicate the variable part of remuneration that is not awarded upfront in cash. That part is prone to change its value overtime, depending on the future performance of the issuing bank.

144 Here, among the forward-looking components is comprised the award in shares and also the cash components not paid upfront. Indeed, these components are subject to malus arrangements and implicit ex-post adjustment. Hence, variable remuneration paid upfront in cash is not considered forward-looking as it reflects only past performance and has little potential to incentivise towards prudent risk-taking for the future.

145 Bhagat and Romano (n 74).

Population (as at Dec 31, 2017)	Num.	Fix[A]	Variable 2017			
			Upfront		Deferred	
			€	Shares	€	Shares[B]
CEO	1	1,200	0	0	0	0
Other executive Directors	0	0	0	0	0	0
Non executive Directors	17	3,606	0	0	0	0
General Manager	1	1,200	0	0	0	0
Deputy General Manager & SEVP	18	12,809	1,682	0	2,523	4,206
EVP	102	36,980	5,105	144	6,155	10,114
SVP	430	92,995	17,315	287	12,627	22,455
Other relevant staff	573	96,858	20,327	9	8,963	22,053

Data in k.

Fig. 3 UniCredit data on compensation structure for 2018[146]

146 See the Remuneration Policy report (n 140), 76.

simple and transparent regulation and fostering systemic stability incentivising high-profile employees to internalise all the risks of their activities, including tail risks. The idea is to prolong the time horizon of executives to a considerable extent. Those would internalise all the risks that may materialise throughout this very long timeframe.[147]

Even though the implementation of such a proposal would be particularly costly and burdensome for the banking industry, the difference with the existing regulation is clear. The current EU framework engineers a complex mechanism where deferral and retention period interplay, provides some fixed minimum deferral period, and asks banks to exactly determine it according to the specificity of their risk profiles, business models as well as the business cycle. On top of that, the competent authority has the power to supervise and to propose prompt corrective actions should the situation suddenly deteriorate.

The praiseworthy goals recommended by Romano and Bhagat are far from being reached. On the contrary, the risk is having a complex and somehow opaque system that is particularly difficult to supervise. Moreover, the current framework does not consider tail risk events in its incentive alignment process, as discussed in Sect. 4.2.

The current regulation loosens the link between pay and performance and creates an overly complex system, burdensome to build for the banks and difficult to supervise for the competent authority.

Pay Regulation and Bank Governance

The last step of this critical assessment is to understand whether the framework, despite its shortcomings, is able to tackle the specificities of bank governance. Again, the answer turns out to be negative, as the current framework still lacks a deep understanding of the specificities of bank governance. In particular, I will focus on three main elements: risk-shifting incentives, moral hazard and systemic externalities, and incentives for early recapitalisation.

Concerning risk-shifting incentives, the existing regulation does not improve the situation. Managers might pass on good risk-taking because of the cap,[148] since they are not able to enjoy the upside of their good

[147] Notably, the restriction could last decades. For instance, Richard Fuld, former CEO of Lehman Brothers, was in charge since 1993.

[148] Murphy (n 129) 647.

bets and have no incentives to do so. On the contrary, the regulation does not directly address risk-shifting incentives as the downside of bad bets is still massively externalised to creditors. As discussed above, it is extremely difficult to design malus and clawback arrangements and combine them with deferral and retention policies in such a way that employees are held fully accountable for the long-term consequences of their decisions,[149] including tail risk events.

The second point closely relates to the first one. The current pay regulation does not address the problem of ex-ante moral hazard either. Again, the combination of ex-post adjustment and deferral and retention policy is inherently unable to account for systemic externalities.

Finally, the existing regulation provides no incentives for prompt and early recapitalisation, which represents a crucial issue to timely address bank distress.

The outcome of this critical assessment is negative. The current regime does not efficiently address the general aspects related to the economics of remuneration, nor the specific aspects related to bank corporate governance. If any, both have been worsened. The fifth round of revision of the Capital Requirements Directive[150] maintains the very same regulatory approach to pay packages and mainly attempts to increase the proportionality of the framework. Hence, the overall negative evaluation of the efficiency of the existing pay regulation in EU persists.

5 Remuneration Through Bail-Inable Debt: A Proposal

Remuneration through bail-inable debt was already proposed at the highest policy levels in the so-called "Liikanen Report".[151] Nevertheless, the idea of remunerating managers also with bail-inable debt did not break into European best practices on remuneration.

[149] Ibid 652.

[150] DIRECTIVE (EU) 2019/878 OF THE EUROPEAN PARLIAMENT AND OF THE COUNCIL of 20 May 2019 amending Directive 2013/36/EU as regards exempted entities, financial holding companies, mixed financial holding companies, remuneration, supervisory measures and powers and capital conservation measures.

[151] Erkki Liikanen, 'High-Level Expert Group on Reforming the Structure of the EU Banking Sector' (2012) 2 Final Report, Brussels.

The group, chaired by the former governor of the Bank of Finland Erkki Liikanen, had the main mandate to explore the feasibility of a structural reform of the European banking market. Among the many recommendations of the group, the final report included the use of bail-inable securities for remunerating high-profile employees.

In particular, the final report states: "Bail-in instruments should also be used in remuneration schemes for top management so as best to align decision-making with longer-term performance in banks. The Group suggests that this issue should be studied further"[152]; and again "Building on existing requirements [...] a share of variable remuneration should be in the form of bail-in bonds".[153] Nonetheless, such recommendation experienced the same fate as the structural reform and was quickly put aside. The CRD IV took a different regulatory direction, and the idea of remuneration through bail-inable debt was not explored any further.

The legal analysis of the complex and rigid existing regulation provides some insights on the reason why it has not been the case, given the several foreclosures and mandatory requirements that are already required. However, it cannot fully explain this phenomenon worldwide, since, as discussed in Sect. 2.3, only UBS AG has implemented a similar policy. In this regard, it is worth remembering that the traditional approach generates negative externalities. Consequently, banks and especially bank managers would not enjoy all the benefits of opting out the traditional approach, and this very fact provides a powerful case for an ad hoc regulatory intervention.

The rest of the section discusses why and how remuneration through bail-inable debt can promote financial stability and enhance resolvability, making remuneration packages less complex and more aligned with the long-term viability of financial institutions. In so doing, the current situation of remuneration through debt needs to be analysed in detail, focusing on the regulatory elements that make it more difficult (Sect. 5.1). Subsequently, the proposal to remunerate bank managers (also) with bail-inable debt is discussed at length, focusing both on the general idea and the intertwining of the other elements of the pay regulation and the present

[152] Ibid 104.

[153] Ibid 106.

proposal (Sect. 5.2). Finally, the analysis outlines the strengths and weaknesses of remuneration through debt, focusing on whether it is able to address the shortcomings of the current regulatory framework (Sect. 5.3).

5.1 *Possibility to Remunerate Through Debt in the Current Framework*

As previously mentioned, the Capital Requirements Directive allows for the possibility to remunerate identified staff with instruments other than cash, shares, or share-like instruments.[154] The letter of the law provides that "where possible" variable remuneration can be composed of instruments that qualify as Additional Tier 1 or Tier 2 capital. Moreover, variable remuneration can also consist of other instruments that can be fully converted in common equity or written down. These instruments should "adequately reflect the credit quality of the institution as a going concern". This seems to hint to non-capital, bail-in eligible instruments but, as discussed later in this section, this is not the case.

Here, the caveat "where possible" represents the crucial element to start explaining why such provision remains little more than a dead letter. The EBA Guidelines on sound remuneration policies[155] and a Delegate Regulation[156] specify the requirement of the possibility of remuneration through "other instruments", de facto making it extremely expensive and unappealing.

The EBA Guidelines state that when such instruments are available, the variable remuneration should consist of a balance of different types of available instruments.[157] This means that such a requirement can be

[154] Article 94(2)(l)(ii) CRD IV.

[155] EBA Guidelines, para 249–259.

[156] COMMISSION DELEGATED REGULATION (EU) No 527/2014 of 12 March 2014 supplementing Directive (EU) No 2013/36/EU of the European Parliament and of the Council with regard to regulatory technical standards specifying the classes of instruments that adequately reflect the credit quality of an institution as a going-concern and are appropriate to be used for the purposes of variable remuneration.

[157] EBA Guidelines, para 250.

circumvented insofar as the instruments are not available.[158] The availability of "other instruments" depends on whether such instruments have been issued and on the sufficiency of such issuance.

In the case that all instruments are available, variable remuneration should consist of a balance of such instruments. The institution must be able to demonstrate that, in setting such balance, "that they have taken into account the interests of shareholders, creditors, bondholders and other stakeholders".[159] However, not all eligible instruments can be part of variable remuneration. Indeed, only the subset of eligible instruments that comply with the Commission Delegated Regulation can be used for such a purpose. This, de facto, kills both the market appetite and the competent authority attention towards such form of remuneration.

The Delegated Regulation provides a highly restrictive interpretation of the instruments that are appropriate for variable remuneration. AT1 and T2 instruments are allowed only if they match specific requirements[160] and "other instruments" are allowed only as long as they are linked to other appropriate AT1 or T2 instruments, i.e., options or futures of capital instruments. Therefore, non-capital bail-in eligible instruments cannot be awarded within the variable remuneration. This means that the power of the Resolution Authority to fully write down or convert into common equity such instruments is not deemed sufficient to adequately reflect the credit quality of the institution.

Furthermore, not all instruments that have a contractual trigger for write-down or conversion are appropriate either. The trigger event for write-down or conversion set at least to 7% of the ratio between CET1 and RWAs. Such a high threshold has a massive impact on both AT1 and T2 instruments. For the latter, it implies that—de facto—there is no appropriate Tier 2 instrument. The institution should issue non-perpetual high-trigger CoCos that qualify only as Tier 2 making them excessively expensive compared with the benefits they provide in terms of financial stability and regulatory compliance. When it comes to AT1 instruments, EU law qualifies as AT1 perpetual instruments that are written down or converted once the ratio between CET1 and RWAs

[158] CRD V provisions fix this allowing the use of share-linked instruments for listed stock corporations. See n 111.

[159] EBA Guidelines, para 255.

[160] Set down respectively in Article 2 and Article 3 of the Delegated Regulation.

falls below 5.125%. A higher trigger, such as 7%, still complies with the requirements for AT1 but make the instrument more expensive to issue. Therefore, it does not come as a surprise the fact that the trigger of the vast majority of Contingent Convertibles that qualify as AT1 instruments is set exactly to 5.125%.[161] Consequently, the sufficient availability of adequate instruments is by no means guaranteed.

In conclusion, the analysis of all the relevant legislation provides a picture where the possibility of remuneration through debt is much more foreclosed as compared with the idea one may have simply reading primary legislation. The Delegated Regulation is particularly attentive to guarantee the possibility of complete, certain, and non-discretionary write-down in case of distress, i.e., it wants to make sure that identified staff can be harshly punished ex-post, consistently with the approach that inspires the whole framework for regulating bankers pay. On the contrary, a more preventive approach, restraining excessive risk-taking in good times, is warranted and will be developed in the next section.

5.2 *Proposal for a New Regulatory Framework*

In this section, I propose a new framework to address the shortcomings of the current pay regulation. In structuring the variable part of remuneration, I propose to award bail-in eligible securities to bank's employees. This would tighten the link between pay and performance and, at the same time, directly tackle the specificities of bank governance. Moreover, remunerating managers through debt would have further positive spillovers, increasing the resolvability of financial institutions.

The main material consequence of this proposal is to magnify the importance of variable remuneration. Moreover, in structuring the variable component of remuneration, this proposal aims to strongly limit the use of cash bonuses and to resort mainly to shares (or share-linked instruments) and bail-inable instruments.

More specifically, as suggested by theory,[162] I will argue in favour of a balanced mix of instruments with a bias towards equity. Since the main goal of pay regulation should not be to dis-incentivise risk-taking as such.

[161] See descriptive statistics in Oliver Juhler Grinderslev and Kristian Loft Kristiansen, 'The Information Content in Contingent Convertible Bond Prices' (Danmarks Nationalbank Working Papers 2017).

[162] Edmans and Liu (n 46).

It is worth remembering that risk-taking is the core element of banking. On the contrary, the aim must be to dis-incentivise excessive risk-taking resulting in value destructing decisions. Thus, a balance of instruments with an equity bias represents the most proportionate way to proceed, closely mirroring the example provided by UBS Bonus Bonds.[163]

To this end, the proceeding of this section identifies the preferable type(s) of instrument(s) to form variable remuneration (5.2.1); the interaction of the proposed framework with the other elements of pay regulation, such as deferral and retention policies (5.2.2). Finally, this section discusses the relationship between paying bank managers with bail-inable debt and the resolution framework, especially in terms of compliance with MREL (Minimum Requirement for Eligible Liabilities and Own Fund) (5.2.3).

Remuneration Through Debt: Identifying the Instruments to Award

The first aspect to discuss is the type of instruments to be awarded as variable remuneration. So far only AT1 instruments have been tentatively awarded by UBS; yet the Swiss capital regulation sharply differs from the Capital Requirement Directive, and so it is the approach of the competent authority towards letting AT1 CoCos suffer losses. As it is neither possible nor proportionate to provide a one-size-fits-all answer, the flaws and virtues of AT1, T2, and non-capital bail-in eligible ("other") instruments are to be discussed.

On the one hand, AT1 contingent convertibles represent the natural candidate, since they count both as regulatory capital and, more specifically, as capital in calculating the plain leverage ratio requirement,[164] whereas Tier 2 instruments do not. As for the loss-bearing mechanism, "principal write-down" CoCos ought to be preferred to "conversion to equity" ones in order not to provide perverse incentives to managers once, if ever, the conversion happens.[165] Moreover, significant principal write-down CoCos in the portfolio of executives provide strong incentives towards early recapitalisation to avoid losses. However, in the European

[163] The variable remuneration at UBS consists for 20% of cash, for 30% of deferred contingent convertibles and for 50% of shares. See back Fig. 1.

[164] I.e., ratio between capital and total non-risk-weighted assets; whereas "typical" capital requirements comprise CET1, AT1, and T2 and risk-weighted assets are used as denominator.

[165] See, more at length on this topic, Chapter 5.

experience, both the supervisor and the regulator proved to be particularly reluctant to impose any loss on CoCos in going-concern, striving to avoid it even in the case in which the issuing bank has to skip a coupon.[166] Therefore, de facto, CoCos become little more than "common" bail-in instruments that are prone to suffer losses only at the point of non-viability, after a decision of the resolution authority.

On the other hand, there is no functional difference between Tier 2 and other eligible instruments since the most qualifying divergence between the two, i.e., maturity at issuance, can be efficiently dealt through deferral policy. Both Tier 2 and other instruments are prone to be fully written down or converted as a result of the decision of the resolution authority in case of distress. Again, writing down the principal amount of the awarded instruments must be strictly preferred to conversion for the same reasons discussed above.

For the equivalence between Tier 2 and other non-capital instruments to hold, ad hoc legislative provisions are warranted. Namely, a further element is necessary: in any case, the instruments awarded to banks' employees should be structurally subordinated. Awarded instruments can be more senior than capital instruments (CET1, AT1, and T2), but must be more junior than any other debt claim in order not to grant an unreasonable shield to managers in case of bank distress.

Finally, ad hoc issuances of instruments should be preferred over the use of available instruments already issued for other purposes. Ad hoc issuances allow tailoring the contractual arrangement to the specific case of variable remuneration in banking, such as the structural subordination mentioned above. Moreover, this also makes the task of the competent authority to effectively supervise the soundness of remuneration practices easier, since the competent authority can more easily oversee the contractual structure of the awarded instruments. Finally, ad hoc issuances allow for a real increase of bail-inable debt, enhancing the resolvability of the bank; whereas, awarding instruments that are already outstanding in the secondary market would merely re-allocate existing bail-inable debt.

As a result, I propose to grant the competent authority, in close cooperation with the resolution authority, a broad mandate to oversee the reasonableness of the instruments chosen for remuneration, considering

[166] Paul Glasserman and Enrico Perotti, 'The Unconvertible CoCo Bonds' in Douglas D Evanoff and others (eds), *Achieving Financial Stability: Challenges to Prudential Regulation*, vol 61 (World Scientific 2017).

the specific business and funding models of the bank.[167] The competent authority must also have sufficient power to impose corrective action in case the identified instruments and their balance are not in line with the long-term viability of the institution. In this respect, Article 104 of the Capital Requirement Directive listing the powers of the competent authority should be integrated accordingly.

Remuneration Through Debt in Context

On the one hand, remuneration through debt cannot be understood in an atomistic manner; instead, it should fit in the overall context of pay regulation: the regulatory design should magnify the complementary nature of this proposal with some aspects of pay regulation. On the other hand, it should acknowledge that this proposal can act as a (more efficient) substitute for other elements of the current regulation.[168]

On these grounds, I first propose to eliminate the cap on variable remuneration. Such a cap has been (mistakenly) introduced "in order to avoid excessive risk-taking".[169] This task, as widely argued above, can be taken over by structuring variable remuneration as balance of bail-inable instruments and share(-linked) instruments as well as a limited amount of upfront cash.

The fine-tuning of remuneration through debt with deferral and retention policies is more entangled, and no one-size-fits-all solution seems to be warranted. For instance, it does not seem plausible to impose the same deferral and retention policy to AT1 CoCos and bail-inable securities, given the sharp difference in their contractual design, liquidity in the secondary market, etc. Again, the competent authority should have a wide mandate to oversee the aptness of such policies to achieve optimal risk-taking incentives that foster the long-term viability of the institution.

However, it is possible to provide some guidelines to better integrate the remuneration through debt with the overall regulatory framework. The main aim is to guarantee that debt instruments granted as variable remuneration bear the losses, and that other outstanding liabilities do

[167] On the desirability of a supervisory approach, see Ferrarini and Ungureanu (n 81).

[168] On the possibility to relax some of the rigid incumbent regulation once a more balanced and tailored remuneration framework is in place see also Tung and Wang (n 32); Bebchuk and Spamann (n 22).

[169] Recital 65 CRD IV.

not shield managers from losses. This addresses large parts of the arguments against remuneration through debt proposed by Bebchuck and Jackson[170] and Alces and Galle.[171]

To this end, no instruments should vest faster than the minimum amount of time required for calling or redeeming instruments of the same seniority.[172] Moreover, as discussed in Sect. 5.2.1, the non-capital bail-in eligible instruments should be deferred for at least the same period of Tier 2 instruments.

Finally, no specific regulatory adjustment seems necessary for the ex-post adjustment phase. Malus and clawback arrangements, in their interaction with deferral and retention policies, have the potential to adequately work also with debt instruments. Moreover, it is worth noting that the mechanism of implicit ex-post adjustment, i.e., through price adjustment of the awarded instruments, would be enhanced. The balanced mix of instruments awarded as variable remuneration should reflect the long-term interests of shareholders in the stock component as well as the long-term viability of the institution as a whole in the "other component" part. Moreover, the latest revision of the resolution framework opened the door for an even more effective ex-post adjustment by the resolution authority in case of MREL breach. Section 5.2.3 better develops this argument.

Remuneration Through Debt and the Resolution Framework

One of the main strengths of remunerating bank managers through bail-in eligible instruments is that it creates a positive synergy between remuneration packages, the governance incentives stemming from them, and the resolution framework, yielding a more coherent regulatory environment.

The first, obvious, advantage is that awarding newly issued MREL-eligible instruments[173] eases the task of building enough MREL capacity and, consequently, makes the institution more resolvable. This aspect was

[170] Bebchuk and Jackson Jr (n 44).

[171] Alces and Galle (n 56).

[172] For AT1 instruments, see Article 53(1)(i) CRR that prevent issuing institutions to call or redeem such instrument before 5 year after the date of issuance. The same provision covers Tier 2 instruments as well, see Article 63(1)(j) CRR.

[173] On the specific requirement to be eligible for counting as MREL instruments, see Article 45 BRRD.

already stressed in the latest remuneration report by UBS, commenting on its Deferred Contingent Capital Plan (DCCP): "Therefore, DCCP awards not only support competitive pay, but also provide a loss absorption buffer that protects the firm's capital position".[174]

Moreover, the revised Bank Recovery and Resolution Directive grants the resolution authority with pervasive powers to address MREL breaches, tackling one of the more serious gaps of the original version of the BRRD. Specifically, in case of MREL breach,[175] the resolution authority can promptly intervene using the supervisory powers of Article 104 CRD and, more importantly for what is here of interest, can limit distributions on MREL instruments (i.e., coupon payments).

These new provisions enhance the enforceability and the preventive potential of the whole resolution framework. Furthermore, they can create positive synergies with the proposed remuneration through bail-inable instruments. In order to fully exploit the potential for such synergies, further reforms should allow for the possibility to cancel or diminish the distributions on MREL instruments awarded as part of variable remuneration. In particular, the resolution authority should have the power to restrict distribution on such instruments before MREL is breached so to incentivise the institution to build an adequate buffer. The resolution authority should also determine, on a case-by-case basis and in close cooperation with the competent authority, the required buffer on top of the minimum level of eligible instrument.

This has a twofold benefit: on the one hand, it helps to align managerial incentives with the long-term viability of the institution; on the other hand, it has a positive spillover on the political availability of using resolution tools so that it, de facto, increases bank resolvability. The overarching goal is to make this synergy one of the crucial elements to trigger a virtuous circle in which better bank governance enhances bank resolvability and vice versa.

5.3 Critical Assessment

This assessment explicitly mirrors the one on the current regulation on bankers' pay (Sect. 4.3) and, thus, its structure is similar. The impact

[174] See above n 68.

[175] See Article 45 k BRRD II in conjunction with Articles 16a, 17, and 18 BRRD II.

of the proposal is first discussed in the aspects related to the classical features of remuneration and its economic rationale (5.3.1). Thereafter, the focus shift into the capability of this proposal to tackle the specificities of bank governance (5.3.2). Finally, the discussion highlights the positive spillovers and synergies on the resolvability of banks (5.3.3). This latter element outlines how remunerating managers also with bail-inable debt, all else being equal, should be preferred since it generates positive spillovers and makes the overall regulatory framework more coherent.

Remuneration Through Debt and the Economics of Remuneration

The proposal tightens the link between pay and performance. The cap on variable remuneration is eliminated since, even taking for granted the official justification for it,[176] the purpose to limit (i.e., optimise) risk-taking incentives can be better achieved with remuneration through bail-inable debt.

Moreover, the proposal leans towards a supervisory approach,[177] consistently with the FSB approach.[178] This provides greater flexibility to individual banks, avoiding one-size-fits-all solutions as much as possible. Mandatory rules on structure, rather than standards, are limited to cases where the negative externality is clear, and so the market cannot achieve itself the optimal result.[179]

Admittedly, the complexity does not decrease sharply, and the analysis carried out so far showed that easy and straightforward remuneration packages for employees of complex banking institutions might simply be delusive: the remuneration process of complex institutions is inherently complex. However, providing flexibility allows for better tailoring the process to the specificities of each institution, especially in terms of size and systemic significance. In this perspective, the adjustments in terms of proportionality, as included in CRD V,[180] represent a significant step

[176] Recital 65 CRD IV: "In any event, in order to avoid excessive risk-taking, a maximum ratio between the fixed and the variable component of the total remuneration should be set".

[177] See also the proposal for implementation in Sect. 6.

[178] Strongly arguing in favour of a supervisory approach, as opposed to structural regulation, see Ferrarini (n 75).

[179] See also Sect. 6.

[180] Directive (EU) 2019/878 Of the European Parliament and Of the Council Of 20 May 2019 Amending Directive 2013/36/Eu As Regards Exempted Entities, Financial

forward. Overall, also the aspect of over complexity and calibration can be considered improved by this proposal, even though the improvement is not likely to be sizeable.

Remuneration Through Debt and Bank Governance

As widely discussed above, the main contribution of this proposal is to directly and explicitly address the specificities of bank governance. In this regard, remunerating bank managers with bail-inable debt can be considered a game-changer. Again, mirroring Sect. 4.3.2, three dimensions are to be discussed: bank leverage and risk-shifting incentives; ex-ante reduction of excessive risk-taking incentives; and incentives for early recapitalisation.

As for bank leverage and risk-shifting incentives, the benefit of this proposal is evident: once managers have (bail-inable) debt in their portfolio, shifting the risk to creditors implies that they shift the risk, to a certain extent, to themselves. More rigorously, bank employees would still enjoy the upside of their good risk-taking since a substantial part of their remuneration must still be awarded in shares. Bankers would also participate in the downside of the investment since they hold a substantial amount of debt. In this way, decisions that maximise the value of equity in expected terms but are detrimental to creditors are less likely to happen. In Sect. 2.4, I developed a simplified numerical example showing such mechanism: starting from a typical situation of risk-shifting,[181] the example shows that remunerating the decision-maker through a combination of equity and debt, she will pass on the negative net present value project, aligning managerial and societal incentives.

Closely related to risk-shifting, remuneration through debt would also indirectly address the problem of systemic negative externalities of banking activities. Once managers have both shares and bail-inable securities in their portfolio, they will strive to maximise the combined value of both parts of such a portfolio. Maximising the value of the bail-inable debt part implies to increase the institution's distance to default. In this regard, managers should be allowed to trade their securities in the secondary market before maturity. This latter feature ought to be

Holding Companies, Mixed Financial Holding Companies, Remuneration, Supervisory Measures and Powers and Capital Conservation Measures. OJ L 150, 7.6.2019.

181 For a simplified example on risk-shifting incentives see Becht, Bolton, and Röell (n 4).

balanced with appropriate deferral and retention policies. Moreover, even if the bank enters in distress, managers with a sizeable amount of bail-inable debt in their portfolio will be sensitive to the bank's liquidation value and, consequently, they will have limited incentives to gamble to resurrect.[182]

Finally, maximising the value of the debt part of a banker's portfolio provides incentives for early recapitalisation in times of turmoil. From the perspective of a banker that has both equity and bail-inable debt in her portfolio, early recapitalisation dilutes the equity part[183] but, on the other hand, shield the debt part from losses.

Remuneration Through Debt and Bank Resolvability

Creating positive synergies between different areas of banking regulation represents a crucial goal, especially given the extreme expansion of legislative bills of the last decade. Positive synergies create a more coherent regulatory framework and allow achieving the same effect with lower effort and regulatory burden. In this case, fine-tuning the resolution framework and the regulation of bankers pay has several advantages.

First, considering the ex-post nature of the resolution framework, i.e., once the bank is already in distress and the resolution procedure is triggered, remunerating managers with deeply subordinated bail-inable securities has positive spillovers in terms of the feasibility of resolution. The first anecdotal evidence showed high resistance to resolution, and especially to plain open-bank bail-in, from the media, public, and politicians. However, the fact that, following a decision of the resolution authority, bank managers are the first in line to bear serious losses makes a good political case for resolution. Section 6 details the possible implementation strategies to make bank managers the first in line in case losses are imposed through a decision of the resolution authority.

Second, looking more closely at the ex-ante potential of the resolution framework,[184] the synergies between pay regulation and the resolution framework again highlight the potential to trigger a virtuous circle. The combination of remuneration through debt and the new powers of the

[182] This follows the intuition by Listokin (n 47).

[183] Gordon (n 22).

[184] I.e., enhancing resolvability and, thence, fostering long-term viability of the business and funding model of the institution.

resolution authority appears as a promising avenue. Particularly so for the powers granted to the resolution authority to react to MREL breaches, through limitation on distributions to MREL instruments. This has the potential to enhance governance incentives as well as bank resolvability. In order to achieve such results, managers must be first in line to have their coupon cancelled or diminished and, consequently, minor legislative adjustments in this direction are warranted.

However, not all that glitters is gold: the positive yield of such synergies, especially when it comes to the enhancement of ex-ante resolvability, highly depends on the efficient and effective cooperation between the competent and the resolution authorities. This represents an issue that horizontally touches upon all the features related to the resolution framework[185] and, therefore, also the potential positive synergies between the resolution framework and pay regulation.

To sum up, the proposal of remunerating bank risk-takers through bail-inable securities, as compared with the current framework for pay regulation:

(1) improves the link between pay and performance;
(2) marginally improves the situation when it comes to complexity and calibration of remuneration packages;
(3) fine-tunes pay regulation with the specificities of bank governance, which represents the pivotal aspect of the whole proposal;
(4) generates further positive spillovers and virtuous synergies with banks' resolvability and the resolution framework.

6 Reforming Remuneration Regulation: Two Approaches

In the previous section, I described "the world as it should be". However, flipping the current regulatory framework upside down and remuneration practices is all but straightforward. Since it is known that the devil is in the details, in the proceeding of this section I propose two possible

[185] Most notably, the competent authority has the competence to declare an institution to be "failing or likely to fail" which is a prerequisite for entering in resolution. See Article 32 BRRD.

implementation strategies: the first focuses on opening up the possibility to use bail-inable debt for variable remuneration, removing the material impediments that currently exist. Such a strategy has the overarching goal of testing the market appetite towards such remuneration practice removing, or at least minimising, the biases in favour of the current practice (Sect. 6.1). The second proposed strategy is more radical and, to a certain extent, imposes the use of bail-inable debt in remuneration. Therefore, the attention focuses on correctly weighting the proposed implementation strategies so as to make it as flexible and proportionate as possible (Sect. 6.2). Both strategies increase the role of the competent authority in overseeing the soundness of remuneration practices and promptly correcting them if needed.

6.1 Unleashing the Possibility to Remunerate Through Debt

The first possible strategy can be labelled as "cautious", and its main aim is to deregulate the structure of variable remuneration and, at the same time, to remove any limitation on remuneration through debt instruments. This would allow eliciting market appetite in an unbiased manner.

In order to achieve this, modifications of both primary and secondary legislation, as well as guidelines, are warranted. Concerning primary legislation, Article 94(1)(l)(ii)[186] should be modified in two aspects. First, the incipit "where possible" must be erased. Indeed, up until now, such caveat made remuneration through debt a mere theoretical possibility and eliminating such exception represents the first unavoidable step for changing the current remuneration practices. Moreover, the appropriateness of the instruments indicated in the Article 94(1)(l)(ii) should not only require reflecting the credit quality of the bank but also to "foster the long-term

[186] Article 94(1)(l) CRD: a substantial portion, and in any event at least 50%, of any variable remuneration shall consist of a balance of the following:

(i) shares or equivalent ownership interests, subject to the legal structure of the institution concerned or share-linked instruments or equivalent non-cash instruments, in the case of a non-listed institution;

(ii) where possible, other instruments within the meaning of Article 52 or 63 of Regulation (EU) No 575/2013 or other instruments which can be fully converted to Common Equity Tier 1 instruments or written down, that in each case adequately reflect the credit quality of the institution as a going-concern and are appropriate to be used for the purposes of variable remuneration.

viability" of the institution. This further benchmark should, therefore, be included in the primary legislation. Those criteria apply to variable remuneration in its entirety and represent the benchmark to evaluate its adequateness.

On the other hand, the Delegated Regulation specifying the classes of instruments that can be part of the variable remuneration needs substantial modifications. The delegated regulation has to align the requirements for "adequate instruments" with the requirements for regulatory capital and open up to the use of bail-inable securities. To this end, AT1 instruments with a low trigger (5,125% CET1/RWA) should be included among the permitted instruments as long as the loss-absorbing mechanism of the instruments is the principal writ-down. On the contrary, instruments that convert to equity should have a higher trigger event to avoid the perverse incentives arising when the bank approaches the point of non-viability.[187] Such modification is crucial to open up the market of remuneration through debt. Even though it theoretically lowers the loss-absorbing quality of the instruments used for variable remuneration, this makes the possibility of remuneration through debt much more effective.

The second aspect needing severe revision is the category of "other instruments" that allows only for the use of instruments linked to (adequate) AT1 or T2 instruments. Indeed, the arguments put forward so far proved the necessity to include also deeply subordinated non-capital instruments among the ones that are "appropriate to use for variable remuneration". However, the delegated regulation should pinpoint that, to be considered "appropriate", such instruments must be senior to all capital instruments but junior to all other liabilities in the bankruptcy waterfall.

As for the guidelines on sound remuneration policies, no conceptual modification seems to be strictly necessary; yet the regulatory changes proposed above implies the need to update the Guidelines accordingly.[188]

Finally, the competent authority must play a quintessential role in this implementation strategy. The law should grant the supervisor with a wide

[187] On this point, see widely Chapter 5.

[188] So, for instance, some part would make no sense anymore and shall be cancelled. A good example can be found in the first part of paragraph 255: "Where both equity or equity-linked and other eligible instruments defined under Commission Delegated Regulation (EU) No 527/2014 are available, it is possible to pay variable remuneration as a balance of different instruments".

mandate in assessing the adequateness of the structure of variable remuneration. The evaluation criteria should be the modified criteria of the revised Article 94(1)(l), i.e., the mix of instruments awarded must reflect the credit quality of the institution and foster its long-term viability.

6.2 Mandating Remuneration Through Debt

If the first strategy has been labelled "cautious", as it is limited to open up a workable option for the use of debt in variable remuneration; the second strategy can be labelled "radical" as it aims at including debt via mandatory provisions. This strategy aims to impose, to some extent, the use of debt instruments in variable remuneration and, at the same time, not to make the regulatory framework excessively rigid and burdensome.

In so doing, again, both primary, secondary legislation and Guidelines ought to be modified. Specifically, the whole Article 94(1)(l) needs to be deeply revised. The reviewed version should establish that for the purpose of variable remuneration, the institution can award a balanced mix of cash, shares (or share-linked instruments) and other instruments. These instruments can be either Additional Tier 1, Tier 2, or non-capital bail-inable instruments as long as they reflect the credit quality of the institution and foster its long-term viability.

The specific criteria that those instruments need to comply with are set down by secondary legislation. Consequently, the delegated regulation ought to be modified accordingly, in line with the modifications proposed in the first strategy. Therefore, the requirement for Additional Tier 1 instruments ought to be harmonised with the requirements to count as regulatory capital if the loss-absorbing mechanism is principal write down. Moreover, bail-inable securities should be considered adequate insofar as they are subordinated to any other non-capital liability.

Again, consistent with the FSB standards, the role of the competent authority must be pivotal. The supervisor must have even wider powers than in the first implementation strategy. Hence, Article 94(1)(l) should not only be modified in its substance but also integrated so as to provide the competent authority with an explicit and pervasive mandate to oversee and promptly intervene if necessary. Specifically, the competent authority should ensure that, in structuring variable remuneration, the institution "[take] into account the interests of shareholders, creditors, bondholders and other stakeholders when setting the balance between different instruments".[189] If it is unlikely that the structure proposed fulfils the objectives discussed above, the competent authority should (have the power to) take adequate measures.

Finally, regulatory technical standards issued by the commission and drafted by the EBA,[190] should provide further explanation as for what can be considered a balanced structure of variable remuneration. Such standards should offer sufficient information to prevent uncertainty but, at the same time, should not be too rigid and static for allowing the banks to tailor the structure of variable remuneration to their own specificities.[191] Perhaps, the easiest way to do so is to set a quantitative benchmark. For instance, only for the purpose of the exposition, one might think of variable compensation packages composed by debt instruments for at least 33%, where no more than 15% can be paid upfront in cash. This proposal is in line with the example provided by UBS AG remuneration scheme, that proved to be successful over time. This approach is in line with the conclusion in Edmans and Liu,[192] where the authors argue for a balanced mix of equity and debt in remuneration packages, with an equity bias.

If the structure of the variable remuneration complies with such benchmarks, it can be presumed to be balanced. Otherwise, the institution must demonstrate that the structure of variable remuneration, given the specificities of its business and funding models, is still adequate to reach the objective.

7 Conclusion

This chapter shows the theoretical foundations of remuneration through debt and highlights how that has a beneficial effect in banking, given the specialty of Bank Governance. In particular, the core argument of the

[189] See EBA Guidelines, para 255, last part.

[190] The procedure is described in Article 10 of the REGULATION (EU) No 1093/2010 OF THE EUROPEAN PARLIAMENT AND OF THE COUNCIL of 24 November 2010 establishing a European Supervisory Authority (European Banking Authority).

[191] Ian Ayres and Joshua Mitts, 'Anti-Herding Regulation' (2015) 5 Harv. Bus. L. Rev. 1.

[192] Edmans and Liu (n 46).

study is that remunerating bankers through bail-inable debt would yield multiple positive outcomes.

Accordingly, this chapter proposes to sharply modify the EU regulation for bank managers' remuneration, embedding bail-inable instruments in the remuneration packages with the final aim to optimise the risk-taking incentives of high-profile bank employees.

This chapter discusses the optimal pool of instruments to form remuneration packages as well as the relationship between remuneration through debt and the other features of existing regulation. In this regard, the analysis reveals that remuneration through debt can act as a more efficient substitute for some of the existing rule (e.g., cap on variable remuneration), whereas it acts as a complement for other features (e.g., deferral and retention policies). In this latter case, the proposal for harmonising the regulation and optimise such complementarity are advanced.

Furthermore, this analysis also considers remuneration through debt in relation to the resolution framework, proposing specific marginal improvements to enhance the efficiency and the effectiveness of remuneration through debt on managerial incentives.

Finally, this chapter proposes two possible implementation strategies, one more cautious, based on standards, and the other more radical, based on rules. The analysis highlights the pros and cons of both the approaches in terms of political feasibility and regulatory efficacy. There is no clear-cut conclusion of which strategy is superior. However, a combination of the two strategies can turn to be the best solution, widely applying the proportionality principle so that the radical (rule-based) approach applies only for systemically relevant banks. In contrast a lighter (standard-based) approach should apply with less relevant ones.

Looking at the broader picture, the analysis shows that remuneration through bail-inable debt fine-tunes the specialty of bank governance with the resolution framework for ailing banks, using remuneration as a tool to connect the two spheres.[193] This line of reasoning hints at the fact that, from a positive perspective,[194] the impact of the resolution framework on

[193] For a general exposition of the relation between governance and regulation, see Chapter 2.

[194] See Chapters 4, 5, and 6 of the book.

bank governance is suboptimal and the potential synergies between these two dimensions can be exploited only carefully bridging their edges.

CHAPTER 8

Enabling Debt Governance: Bail-Inable Debt and Governance Rights

1 Introduction

Shareholders are the residual claimants on the assets of a corporation. Therefore, they are usually thought to have optimal incentives to maximise the value of the assets. Consequently, in virtually any jurisdiction, they are statutorily granted most of the legal rights to run the corporation. They are usually in charge of appointing the board of directors; moreover, they directly decide on a set of issues identified statutorily or through the corporate charter.[1]

On the one hand, creditors are fixed claimants, and their interest is merely for the borrowing corporation to remain solvent. Thus, a limited set of statutory and contractual provisions should protect them from possible abuses by the shareholders and management, decreasing the agency cost of debt.[2] However, corporate decisions should still be

[1] Frank H Easterbrook and Daniel R Fischel, *The Economic Structure of Corporate Law* (Harvard University Press 1996) 63.

[2] Jean Tirole, *The Theory of Corporate Finance* (Princeton University Press 2010) 389.

This chapter heavily draws from Edoardo Martino, 'Getting Bank Governance Right' (2022) 23 Journal of Banking Regulation 302.

E. D. Martino, *EU Bank Governance and Bail-In*, EBI Studies in Banking and Capital Markets Law,
https://doi.org/10.1007/978-3-032-20699-2_8

allocated to the management appointed, directly or indirectly, by the shareholders. On the other hand, creditors can only dictate some positive or negative behaviours to the management through contractual commitments. Any other possible externality or other market failure is better addressed through regulation than through the modification of governance arrangements.[3]

This represents a simplified explanation of the shareholder-centric model of corporate governance on which a fair degree of consensus has been reached over the last decades[4] and which has proved itself quite robust to the many critiques it attracted over the years.[5]

This chapter shows how profound adjustments to the standard model are warranted in banking because of the special nature of bank corporate governance and its relationship with incumbent financial regulation, with a particular reference to the resolution framework for ailing banks. The shareholder-centric model of governance for banks provides shareholders with incentives to excessively engage in risk-taking.[6] Moreover, shareholders lack the ability and the willingness to internalise the systemic externalities that banking activities generate.[7] However, the shareholders themselves are exposed to the market risk generated by such systemic externalities, as market risk is undiversifiable.

[3] Ian B Lee, 'The Role of the Public Interest in Corporate Law' in Claire A Hill and Brett H McDonnell (eds), *Research Handbook on the Economics of Corporate Law* (Edward Elgar Publishing 2012) 124.

[4] Henry Hansmann and Reinier Kraakman, 'The End of History for Corporate Law' (2000) 89 Geo. LJ 439.

[5] In this regard, the quintessential contribution is a brief article by Milton Friedman. See Milton Friedman, 'The Social Responsibility of Business Is to Increase Its Profits' *N.Y. Times* (13 September 1970). See also Steven M Bainsbridge, 'In Defence of the Shareholder Wealth Maximization Norm"' (1993) 50 Wash & Lee L Rev 1423. Hart and Zingales challenged this standard paradigm arguing that shareholders can have pro-social preferences that are not embedded in the share price. See Oliver Hart and Luigi Zingales, 'Companies Should Maximize Shareholder Welfare Not Market Value' (2017) 2 Journal of Law, Finance, and Accounting 247.

[6] Marco Becht, Patrick Bolton and Ailsa Röell, 'Why Bank Governance Is Different' (2011) 27 Oxford Review of Economic Policy 437.

[7] John Armour and Jeffrey N Gordon, 'Systemic Harms and Shareholder Value' (2014) 6 Journal of Legal Analysis 35.

Therefore, the arguments for opting out the shareholder-centric model of governance are particularly strong for banks as it would benefit shareholders' themselves. To date, only marginal adjustments to governance arrangements[8] have been deemed to be fit for purpose.[9]

In this landscape, the entry into force of the new EU resolution framework[10] for failing banks creates, as this chapter will show, the possibility to truly adjust banks governance arrangements. Such framework identifies a broad category of long-term non-runnable debt that is prone to suffer losses shareholder-like in case of financial distress.[11] These creditors, so the argument goes, should also monitor and discipline the bank ex-ante, to minimise the probability of experiencing losses.[12] Nonetheless, as the previous chapters[13] and a vast body of literature showed,[14] this mechanism functions better in theory than in practice. The proposed explanations are numerous, mainly focusing on the over-complication of the legal framework and the lack of credibility of resolution.

In the previous chapters, I also offered an additional argument, going beyond credibility and complexity, which is the discrepancies between

[8] Art 88 of the Capital Requirement Directive (CRD), Directive 2013/36/EU of the European Parliament and of the Council of 26 June 2013 on access to the activity of credit institutions and the prudential supervision of credit institutions and investment firms, amending Directive 2002/87/EC and repealing Directives 2006/48/EC and 2006/49/EC. OJ L 176, 27.6.2013.

[9] On the other hand, many academics found those marginal adjustments not to be fit for purpose. See, for instance, Luca Enriques and Dirk Zetzsche, 'Quack Corporate Governance, Round III? Bank Board Regulation Under the New European Capital Requirement Directive' (2015) 16 Theoretical Inquiries in Law 211; Christoph van der Elst, 'Corporate Governance and Banks: How Justified Is the Match?' (2015) 284/2015.

[10] Directive 2014/59/EU of the European Parliament and of the Council of 15 May 2014 establishing a framework for the recovery and resolution of credit institutions and investment firms. OJ L 173 12.6.2014.

[11] Christos Hadjiemmanuil, 'Bank Stakeholders' Mandatory Contribution to Resolution Financing: Principle and Ambiguities of Bail-In', *ECB Legal Conference 2015—From Monetary Union to Banking Union, on the way to Capital Markets Union* (2015).

[12] Jianping Zhou and others, 'From Bailout to Bail-in: Mandatory Debt Restructuring of Systemic Financial Institutions' [2012] Journal Issue 3.

[13] See Chapters 3 and 4.

[14] See, Tobias Tröger, 'Why MREL Won't Help Much' (2019) 20 Journal of Banking Regulation; Emilios Avgouleas and Charles Goodhart, 'Critical Reflections on Bank Bail-Ins' (2015) 1 Journal of Financial Regulation 3.

the regulatory framework and the specificities of bank governance.[15] Building upon this argument, this chapter proposes a reform of bank governance that aims to fine-tuning the resolution framework with the specific features of bank governance, focusing on the role of creditors.

With the law as it is, the BRRD creates more problems than it solves. So far, it has proved to be ineffective ex-post, in handling cases of resolution, and inefficient ex-ante in incentivising optimal risk-taking. Moreover, these components seem to reinforce one another and generate a vicious circle. However, the existence of a common resolution framework represents a significant achievement towards a genuine Economic and Monetary Union, at least within the Eurozone.[16] It has the potential to enhance the resilience of single institutions as well as of the system as a whole.

Therefore, this chapter proposes a deep statutory reform in the area of bank governance. The overarching aim of such a proposal is to fine-tune bank governance and incumbent substantive regulation and, subsequently, to truly enhance the quality of decision-making of banks in terms of risk-taking. At the same time, the proposed reform should increase the ex-ante credibility of resolution. In this vein, this chapter demonstrates how granting bail-inable creditors with ex-ante governance rights can represent a tool to correct for shareholders' perverse incentives and make debt governance work in banking.

This chapter proposes to make banks' decision-making process "sufficiently accountable" to the interests of MREL creditors. To this end, MREL creditors should have a limited set of appointment and decision rights. In particular, the right to appoint a common trustee as well as a qualified minority of strategic board committees, such as the audit committee, the remuneration committee, and the risk committee. Moreover, MREL creditors should have a say on remuneration and dividend policies with the aim of preventing disproportionate distributions in good times. The second part of this chapter will discuss the specific details of this proposal, how it fine-tunes bank governance and the resolution framework and the main implementation challenges.

[15] See, in general, Chapter 2. For an application to the remuneration structure of risk-takers, see Chapter 7.

[16] Herman Van Rompuy and others, 'Towards a Genuine Economic and Monetary Union', vol 5 (2012).

This chapter additionally argues that, on the one hand, rebalancing the relationship between shareholders and creditors in bank governance would achieve better alignment of private and social incentives since creditors cannot benefit from excessive risk-taking. This would act as a powerful complement to regulation and supervision, especially in good times when regulation is lax, and supervisors tend to delay actions.[17] On the other hand, a more central and better-defined role of creditors out of insolvency would increase the credibility of resolution. This, as opposed to the vicious circle described above, could trigger a virtuous circle where better-governed banks are more resolvable which, in turn, optimises market discipline (i.e., ameliorates corporate governance).

This chapter is structured as follows. Section 2 reviews and critically discusses the various strands of literature on "innovative" bank governance arrangements. Section 3 explores the theoretical arguments in favour of granting governance rights to creditors in financial institutions. Section 4 discusses the scope and borders of the policy proposal defining the creditors to which rights should be granted and the nature of such rights. Section 5 discusses the core issue of the proposal, i.e., the type of rights and governance status to be statutorily given to creditors, highlighting why and how those are functional to increase the resilience and resolvability of the single institutions. Section 6 concludes.

2 Governance Approaches to Account for Bank Specialties

In the aftermath of the global financial crisis, bank governance was heavily blamed as one of the drivers of the global burst.[18] An impressive amount of academic research, as well as policymakers' attention, stemmed from it. Policy reforms tackling bank governance mainly represented a political reaction against bankers and paid no attention to the distinctive features

[17] On the concept, cause and consequences of the so-called "regulatory pendulum", see Alessio M Pacces and Dirk Heremans, 'Regulation of Banking and Financial Markets', *Encyclopedia of Law and Economics - Volume 9* (Edward Elgar 2012) 593.

[18] See Jacques De Larosière and others, 'Report of the High-Level Group on Financial Supervision in the EU' [2009] European Commission. Brussels para 23. See also Grant Kirkpatrick, 'The Corporate Governance Lessons from the Financial Crisis' (2009) 2009 OECD Journal: Financial Market Trends 61. See also, Peter Laaper and Danny Busch, 'How to Behave Like a Good Banker?' (2022) 18 European Company and Financial Law Review 899.

of bank governance.[19] On the contrary, many academics pointed at the specialty of bank governance[20] and developed a proposal for reforming bank governance regulation accounting for such a specialty.

Therefore, before discussing the desirability of granting governance rights to creditors, it is worth briefly reviewing this strand of literature, which can be grouped into four main categories. First, studies looking at fiduciary duties of bank directors; second, studies looking at the role of the State in bank governance; third, studies focusing on modification of the liability regime of bank insiders; fourth, studies looking at the role of non-shareholders corporate constituencies.

All of these contributions aim at modifying governance incentives to induce optimal risk-taking and let bank decision-makers internalise the externalities they create. Before moving to the analysis of each of these categories, two preliminary caveats are in order. First, corporate governance research and policymaking in banking mainly dealt with directors' remuneration.[21] Although highly relevant, executive remuneration is not considered in this chapter, as the focus of this analysis is on governance rights and duties of corporate constituencies. However, it is crucial to highlight that remuneration practices represent a natural complement to governance rights,[22] and they need to co-exist to yield an efficient governance ecosystem. Second, most of the literature and proposals mainly deal with US banks; therefore, with US corporate law and financial regulation. Even though there is a certain convergence between US and EU regimes,[23] considerable differences persist. Thus, proposals that fit the US legal framework might not fit EU law and the national laws of the Member States.

[19] See Enriques and Zetzsche (n 10); van der Elst (n 10).

[20] See, in particular, Becht, Bolton and Röell (n 6); John Armour and others, 'Bank Governance' (2016) ECGI Law Working Paper 316/2016.Becht, Bolton and Röell (n 6); Armour and others.

[21] See, for instance, Lucian A Bebchuk and Holger Spamann, 'Regulating Bankers' Pay' (2009) 98 Geo. LJ 247; Kevin J Murphy, 'Regulating Banking Bonuses in the European Union: A Case Study in Unintended Consequences' (2013) 19 European Financial Management 631; Sanjai Bhagat and Roberta Romano, 'Reforming Executive Compensation: Focusing and Committing to the Long-Term' (2009) 26 Yale J. on Reg. 359.

[22] Se at length Chapter 4.

[23] Hansmann and Kraakman (n 4).

The first category of studies relates to proposals to alter the fiduciary duties owed by bank directors. In corporate law, directors and managers owe the corporation "fiduciary duties",[24] i.e., the duty to act with care and loyalty in its best interest[25] and, according to the vast majority of scholars, maximising shareholders value.[26] In banking, the claim for opting out, at least partially, of the shareholders' value maximisation paradigm is particularly robust. The peculiarities of bank activities give shareholders incentives to engage in socially inefficient risk-taking.[27] Therefore, some authors proposed to modify the fiduciary duties owed by the management, broadening their scope and opting out from the shareholders' centric paradigm.

In an influential study, Macey and O'Hara highlighted the vulnerabilities of bank governance well before the Global Financial Crisis.[28] According to the authors, the special corporate governance problems in banks weaken the case for fiduciary duties owed to shareholders only.[29] On the contrary, they argued that bank managers should owe fiduciary duties to equity as well as fixed claimants.[30] Such an argument is fascinating and theoretically grounded; yet, it remains unclear how the management would be supposed to discharge its fiduciary duties in times when the best interests of shareholders and fixed claimants might diverge.[31] Moreover, courts would be burdened with the impossible task

[24] The concept of fiduciary duties is proper of the US legal framework and scholarship. Yet, such paradigm can be used more in general to describe the functional feature of corporate law in different jurisdiction. Yet, the legal details and enforcement strategies may vary considerably cross-country, so that the general reference to "fiduciary duties" has to be understood as a simplified indication of the relation linking management and shareholders.

[25] Tamar Frankel, 'Fiduciary Duties', *The new Palgrave dictionary of economics and the law* (McMillan, London 1998) 127.

[26] Friedman (n 5). But see lately Hart and Zingales (n 5).

[27] Armour and Gordon (n 7) 58; De Larosière and others (n 19).

[28] Jonathan R Macey and Maureen O'Hara, 'The Corporate Governance of Banks' [2003] FRBNY Economic Policy Review 91. See also the post-crisis proposals, with similar outcome, by the same authors, Jonathan R Macey and Maureen O'Hara, 'Bank Corporate Governance: A Proposal for the Post-Crisis World' [2016] FRBNY Economic Policy Review 85.

[29] Macey and O'Hara, 'The Corporate Governance of Banks' (n 29) 97.

[30] Ibid 102.

[31] Bainsbridge (n 5) 1705.

of enforcing such duties and decide on directors' liability in case of conflicting legal obligations. In other words, multiple fiduciary duties are likely to work better in theory than in practice, since they would add little to managerial duties in good times and would create spectacular legal uncertainty in bad times.

There have also been other, more radical, proposals of shifting fiduciary duties. In particular, Schwartz argued in favour of a "public governance duty"[32] for directors of systemically important banks (SIFIs).[33] Such duty would entail "a duty not to engage in excessive risk-taking that could systemically harm the public".[34] Such a proposal could sound appealing at first; yet, at a closer scrutiny, it reveals to be even more problematic than the previous proposal. A duty to avoid the creation of systemic harms represents little more than a tautology,[35] and it is almost impossible to verify in courts. Thus, if extending fiduciary duties to fixed claimants would cause legal uncertainty, imposing a public fiduciary duty would generate a much more problematic legal vacuum.

The second category of bank governance reform proposals deals with the idea of granting the State pervasive powers to tackle excessive risk-taking incentives of the management. In particular, Omarova proposed a "golden share" approach[36] that would grant a state official a seat on the board with pervasive veto powers should the fear of systemic or idiosyncratic crises materialise.[37] This is based on the idea that the state is the real residual owner of the bank as it guarantees its solvency. Therefore, the State should act as a "manager of last resort".

This approach can be criticised both for its paternalism as well as for its inability to solve the underlying problems of bank governance. It is difficult to identify functional differences between the "manager of last resort" and the mandate of the supervisor. Additionally, there is no reason

[32] Steven L Schwarcz, 'Misalignment: Corporate Risk-Taking and Public Duty' (2016) 91 Notre Dame L. Rev. 1.

[33] For a relatively similar proposal see, also, Robert Hockett, 'Are Bank Fiduciaries Special' (2016) 68 Ala. L. Rev. 1071, 1071.

[34] Schwarcz (n 16) 28.

[35] David Min, 'Balancing the Governance of Financial Institutions' (2016) 40 Seattle UL Rev. 743, 763.

[36] Saule T Omarova, 'Bank Governance and Systemic Stability: The'Golden Share'Approach' (2017) 68 Ala. L. Rev. 1029.

[37] Ibid 1055.

why the classic supervisory problem of forbearance and delayed action should not apply in this case. Moreover, should a State official be sued for liability, as it is likely, given the times of turmoil during which he would need to act, a state liability for corporate wrongdoing would materialise, burdening taxpayers.

A third, more promising, stream of research on bank governance focused on modifying the standard liability regime. The rest of the section discusses both proposals to extend directors' and officers' liability[38] and proposals to extend shareholders' liability.

Armour and Gordon acknowledged that traditional private law tools, with special reference to tort law, are ineffective in the presence of systemic harms and that the shareholder' value maximisation paradigm incentivises excessive risk-taking.[39] Moreover, they observe that shareholder maximisation strategies carried out by individual banks can even turn out to be detrimental to diversified shareholders. If bank activities generate systemic harms, they increase overall market risk, which is undiversifiable.[40] Therefore, the authors argue against the application of the shareholder maximisation paradigm for systemically important financial institutions, to make risk-takers more risk-averse. In doing so, the authors propose to override the "business judgement" rule for bank directors and officers and impose a negligence-based liability regime. Such liability would be owed to the firm and should be triggered by shareholders through derivative actions in case of material losses. It is crucial to highlight how such tort liability suit should take place before insolvency to avoid the judgement proof problem.[41] This proposal attracted two main criticisms, pointing at the fact that quantifying "systemic harm" is likely to be an impossible task both for directors[42] and courts.[43] The

[38] Mostly based on Armour and Gordon (n 7).

[39] Armour and Gordon (n 8) 38 where the authors argue that "private law does not do an "imperfect job" of internalizing systemic harms; it does no job at all".

[40] Ibid 39.

[41] Ibid 77. Such liability regime should act as a complement to other regulatory and governance measures, such as regulation of executives' pay, ibid 61.

[42] Omarova (n 20) 1039, arguing that director might not be able to appreciate the systemic nature of bank risk-taking.

[43] Holger Spamann, 'Monetary Liability for Breach of the Duty of Care?' (2016) 8 Journal of Legal Analysis 337, 359.ibid. The author argues that courts might be unable

second criticism pertains specifically continental Europe, where the efficacy of such reform would be further undermined by the limited room for shareholders' derivative lawsuits.[44]

A second liability-based proposal is, somehow, to re-enact the extended liability of bank shareholders, partially overcoming the limited liability of the corporation.[45] This proposal builds on the old US regime of double shareholder's liability for banks. It served the purpose of "insuring" bank depositors in the absence of a public deposit insurer, minimising the risk of bank run.[46] The double liability regime ceased to exist after the creation of FDIC.[47] The double liability implied that shareholders' liability was not limited to the committed capital used to purchase the shares, but in bankruptcy was extended up to the par value (book value) of the shares each shareholder owned.

Relaxing the limited liability of shareholders, so the argument goes, would undermine the roots of excessive risk-taking incentives. Accordingly, it would induce equity holders to internalise the externalities generated by the shareholders' value maximisation paradigm. Lately, Macey and co-authors[48] reconsider the double liability rule, proposing an "extended" liability regime for SIFIs' shareholders. Under this proposal, the amount of the extension would crucially depend on the centrality of each institution in the financial network.[49] In other words, the more systemic externalities an institution is capable of creating because of its

to assess whether the risk undertook by director was "excessive", so that optimal liability could be close to zero.

[44] Martin Gelter, 'Why Do Shareholder Derivative Suits Remain Rare in Continental Europe' (2011) 37 Brook. J. Int'l L. 843.

[45] John Armour and others, *The Anatomy of Corporate Law: A Comparative and Functional Approach* (2017) ch 1; Giuseppe Dari-Mattiacci and others, 'The Emergence of the Corporate Form' (2017) 33 The Journal of Law, Economics, and Organization 193.

[46] See Macey and Miller (n 40) ch 31.; and Macey, J. R., & Miller, G. P. (1993). Double liability of bank shareholders: a look at the new data. Wake Forest L. Rev., 28, 933.

[47] Federal Deposit Insurance Corporation, that from 1933 act as the insurer of US deposits.

[48] Romano, Enriques and Macey (n 23).

[49] On financial regulation taking into consideration the specific topology of the financial system and building on network theory, Luca Enriques, Alessandro Romano and Thom Wetzer, 'Network-Sensitive Financial Regulation' [2019] The Journal of Corporation Law (forthcoming).see ibid.

size, interconnectedness, and complexity, the higher shareholders' liability should be.

Again, such a proposal sounds very appealing from a theoretical perspective. However, its implementation appears cumbersome: the enforcement of extended liability in court can be difficult and time-consuming, leaving aside the potential judgement-proof problem of shareholders. Moreover, such double or extended liability only works as a gone concern tool, so that its potential rest on the incentives provided to shareholders and ultimately on the credibility of the threat to impose such liability.

In contrast, Armour and Gordon's proposal is meant to work as a going-concern tool, as directors' and officers' liability is triggered by material losses while the bank is still solvent. Finally, this proposal attracted another, perhaps more fundamental, line of criticism, pinpointing the potential adverse spillovers of such regime in times of financial turmoil and liquidity scarcity. Such adverse spillovers can work in two directions. First, the liquidity of the stocks with enhanced liability would quickly dry out once the bank approaches insolvency, further decreasing the market value of equity. Consequently, this would endanger the resilience of the troubled bank at the worst possible time.[50] Second, issuing fresh equity would become extremely expensive, especially when it is most needed, i.e., when insolvency is approaching.

Finally, the last stream of literature considered here focuses on the role of bank creditors and debt governance.[51] Such literature largely consists of proposals for letting creditors' representatives seating on the board, building on the paradigm of German labour codetermination.

[50] On the disruptive effect of market and funding illiquidity, see Markus K Brunnermeier and Lasse Heje Pedersen, 'Market Liquidity and Funding Liquidity' (2009) 22 Review of Financial studies 2201. More in general on the role of liquidity in financial crises, see Markus K Brunnermeier, 'Deciphering the Liquidity and Credit Crunch 2007–2008' (2009) 23 Journal of Economic perspectives 77.

[51] Most of the literature related to creditors of banking institutions deal with their (in)ability of creditors to monitor and impose discipline on the borrowing bank. This topic has been largely dealt with also in the context of the newly established resolution framework. See Chapter 4. See also, Tobias H Tröger, 'Too Complex to Work: A Critical Assessment of the Bail-in Tool under the European Bank Recovery and Resolution Regime' (2018) 4 Journal of Financial Regulation 35.

Davies and Hopt critically reviewed such literature,[52] arguing that the scale of benefits of such proposals is likely to be rather limited, whereas the legal problems arising from such a governance adjustment would be considerable. The first of these problems is the compatibility of creditors' representation in the board and the codetermination system.[53]

This contribution adds to this last stream of research and focuses on the role of creditors. However, it departs from it quite considerably. Sections 3 and 4 discuss in detail the theoretical foundations of directly including bail-inable creditors in corporate governance. For the time being, it suffices to say that the distinctive aim of such proposal is to provide creditors with effective tools to police the building-up of excessive risk, replicating their role in non-financial institutions while accounting for the specificities of bank governance.

Finally, it is important to stress that various proposals put forward in the last decade are not necessarily mutually exclusive. In particular, a modified liability regime represents a good complement to this proposal, whereas the proposals pointing at including creditors in bank governance substitute proposals aiming at modifying fiduciary duties or granting governance rights to the State.

3 Good Governance and the Role of Creditors

Granting (some) governance rights to creditors in solvent banks represents an unusual proposal from a corporate finance and corporate law perspective. Voting rights are usually allocated to shareholders as residual claimants on corporate assets.[54]

Shareholders, so the traditional argument goes, have the incentive to maximise the overall value of the corporation since the value of their claim increases as the overall value of the corporation increases. Consequently, shareholders are better positioned to maximise social welfare. On the contrary, debtholders are fixed claimants whose claim is independent of the value of the corporation as long as it is solvent. Therefore, on the one hand, so long as the corporation is solvent, creditors protect their

[52] Paul Davies and Klaus J Hopt, 'Non-Shareholder Voice in Bank Governance: Board Composition, Performance and Liability' (2018) 413.

[53] Ibid.

[54] Easterbrook and Fischel (n 1).

fixed claim through monitoring and contractual arrangements.[55] On the other hand, in insolvency creditors have better incentives to maximise the liquidation value of the firm and, thus, increasing social welfare. Therefore, in insolvency, creditors become the "owners" of the corporation,[56] and most of the decision rights are allocated to them.[57]

From this brief and necessarily simplified overview, on the one hand, the clash between the conventional wisdom on corporate governance and the proposal of granting governance rights to creditors is clear. On the other hand, the fact that bank governance is special has already been highlighted.[58] Hence, this section discusses the distinctive features of bank governance in relation to creditors and highlights how such features build a strong case for regulatory intervention granting them governance rights. First, this section discusses the reasons leading to standard debt governance tools to be ineffective. Second, it proposes some on the welfare implications of effective debt governance in general and with specific reference to financial institutions. Finally, the discussion encompasses the potential positive spillovers in terms of legal certainty and credibility of the resolution framework.

Creditors usually protect their entitlements[59] from opportunistic behaviour of the management by imposing market discipline[60] through monitoring. Furthermore, debt contracts are used as a device to allocate control rights to creditors contingent on future and uncertain events.[61] However, previous chapters showed that in banking such channels are by and large foreclosed to creditors, making debt governance inefficient and

[55] For a broad overview, see Armour and others (n 47) ch 5.

[56] Jean Tirole, *The Theory of Corporate Finance* (Princeton University Press 2006) 389.

[57] In Coasian terms, in insolvency creditors are the ones that value control rights the most. Ronald H Coase, 'The Problem of Social Cost' (1960) 3 ournal of Law and Economics 1.

[58] Becht, Bolton and Röell (n 6).

[59] See the definition of Corporate Governance in Andrei Shleifer and Robert W Vishny, 'A Survey of Corporate Governance' (1997) 52 The journal of finance 737. The authors define corporate governance as "the ways in which suppliers of finance to corporations assure themselves of getting a return on their investment". ibid 737.

[60] Defined as "ability of financial markets to provide signals leading borrowers to engage in projects consistent with their solvency". See Timothy D Lane, 'Market Discipline' (1993) 40 IMF Staff Papers 53, ch 55.

[61] Philippe Aghion and Patrick Bolton, 'An Incomplete Contracts Approach to Financial Contracting' (1992) 59 The review of economic Studies 473.

ineffective.[62] Thus, one of the "special features" of bank governance is that debt governance simply cannot work as in non-financial corporations.

Most of the creditors of modern banks do not have proper incentives to discipline their borrowers towards long-term solvency. Junior unsecured creditors are the category that seems better positioned to exert efficient discipline. In contrast, previous research showed how market discipline through monitoring is impaired in banking because of the opacity of bank assets and the persistence of an implicit guarantee on bank solvency.[63] The possibility of the new resolution framework increasing market discipline has been heavily debated. It seems that the lack of credibility, the complexity,[64] and the legal design[65] of the resolution impair the possibility of bail-inable creditors to impose efficient ex-ante discipline.

A similar argument holds for contractual protection. Previous research has shown that the typical covenants attached to debt contracts to protect creditors' entitlements are not available, as they would disqualify junior instruments from capital and MREL eligibility.[66] There is, indeed, a trade-off between ex-ante discipline through contracts and financial stability. Breaching a covenant usually provides the right to speed up the repayment. In non-financial corporations, this provides incentives not to breach the covenant in the first place. However, should the bank enter into financial difficulties and breach a covenant, a contractual right to early repayment would cause a flow of funds that are, instead, supposed to be stable, such as senior unsecured debt or hybrid capital instruments.

Given the limited possibility to protect credit entitlements through usual mechanisms, the funding models of banks adjust accordingly, making long-term unsecured debt a less attractive and more costly way to fund bank activities. On the contrary, other sources of funding, such as short-term[67] and secured debt, arose as cheap and attractive channels.

[62] See Chapters 4–6.

[63] See Chapter 4. See also Mark J Flannery and Robert R Bliss, 'Market Discipline in Regulation: Pre-and Post-Crisis' in Allen N Berger, Philip Molyneux and John OS Wilson (eds), *Oxford Handbook of Banking* (3rd edn, Oxford Handbook of Banking (3rd edition), Oxford University Press, forthcoming 2018).

[64] Tröger (n 53).

[65] See, again, Chapter 4.

[66] See Chapter 5, Sect. 3.

[67] See Patrick Bolton, 'Corporate Finance, Incomplete Contracts, and Corporate Control' (2013) 30 The Journal of Law, Economics, & Organization i64, 75. Bolton

On the one hand, the excessive reliance on such source of funding made banks less stable and more vulnerable to liquidity shocks.[68] On the other hand, unsecured creditors pre-eminently relied on the implicit guarantee of the State on bank solvency as a way of protection. This kept the cost of capital low, giving banks an implicit funding subsidy over other corporations.[69] Such an implicit guarantee was, allegedly, eliminated with the post-crisis regulatory framework, so that the cost of long-term unsecured debt should rise considerably.[70]

Therefore, providing effective tools for protecting the entitlements of creditors would make long-term unsecured debt marginally cheaper as compared with current bail-inable securities. Moreover, it should make these securities comparatively more attractive as compared with other sources of funding that are less stable and more prone to liquidity shocks. This represents the first relevant theoretical advantage of granting governance rights to unsecured creditors. It is worth noting that if long-term creditors have tools to protect their entitlements the cost of capital will decrease.[71] However, lower cost of capital is ontologically different from the implicit subsidy provided by bailout expectations. It rests on a mechanism that is able to impose discipline on the activities of the borrower, whereas bailout expectations generate nothing but moral hazard.[72] Moreover, making long-term non-runnable debt marginally more attractive to issue and hold, as compared with short-term/secured debt would ease

argues that excessive reliance on short term funding for banks represent an inefficient equilibrium caused by limited commitment problems; namely, nonexclusivity. This view, based on the incomplete contract theory, is against the view according to which short term funding represent an optimal capital structure in banking to discipline management. On this, see Douglas W Diamond and Raghuram G Rajan, 'A Theory of Bank Capital' (2000) 55 The Journal of Finance 2431.

[68] Brunnermeier and Pedersen (n 52).

[69] João AC Santos, 'Evidence from the Bond Market on Banks''Too-Big-To-Fail'Subsidy' [2014] Economic Policy Review 29.

[70] As long as the elimination of the State guarantee is credible. For fist, partial, empirical evidence see Fabrizio Crespi, Emanuela Giacomini and Danilo V Mascia, 'Bail-in Rules and the Pricing of Italian Bank Bonds' (2018) 25 European Financial Management 1321.

[71] On the inverse relation between debt interest yield and the presence of covenants; see, Bradley, M., & Roberts, M. R. (2015). The structure and pricing of corporate debt covenants. The Quarterly Journal of Finance, 5(02), 1,550,001.

[72] Franklin Allen and others, 'Moral Hazard and Government Guarantees in the Banking Industry' (2015) 1 Journal of Financial Regulation 30.

the task of building sufficient MREL capacity.[73] Consequently, it would make the issuing bank more resolvable ex-ante.

Regarding the welfare implications of efficient and effective debt governance, there is now ample evidence that creditors are active players in corporate governance also outside of insolvency and that their influence generates value.[74]

In particular, Nini and co-authors[75] studied the impact of covenants violation on solvent non-financial firms. They demonstrated that the creditors played an active role both through the available legal mechanisms, explicitly forcing the renegotiation of the credit agreements and behind the scenes.[76] Such an engagement leads to two notable results. First, unsurprisingly, led the breaching borrower to more conservative investment and distribution policies, reducing risk-shifting and asset dilution, reducing the creditors' risk of bearing losses. Second, the engagement "produces" value for the corporation. Surprisingly, the corporations breaching covenants experienced positive abnormal stock returns in the quarters after the breach happened and stayed constant in the following quarters.[77] This shows that the ineffectiveness of debt governance in banking prevents from enjoying these welfare gains.[78]

Moreover, the ability of debt governance to reduce the agency costs of debt and, in particular, risk-shifting and optimal risk-taking incentives in banking has even more important welfare implications. As previously

[73] On the problem of building enough MREL capacity, especially linked to the holders of MREL Instruments, see Chapter 6, Sects. 2 and 3. See also Dominique Laboureix, speech at 6th Industry Dialogue: 2017 MREL Policy, accessible at https://srb.europa.eu/sites/srbsite/files/20171120_6th_industry_dialogue_item_2_mrel_dominique_laboureix. pdf. The estimation considers a sample of 76 banks, accounting for almost 80% of total assets of the banks subject to SRB authority.

[74] C Whitehead, 'Creditors and Debt Governance' (2012) 68 Research Handbook on the Economics of Corporate Law 75, 76.

[75] Greg Nini, David C Smith and Amir Sufi, 'Creditor Control Rights, Corporate Governance, and Firm Value' (2012) 25 The Review of Financial Studies 1713.

[76] For anecdotal evidence on behind the scene creditors engagement see Douglas G Baird and Robert K Rasmussen, 'Private Debt and the Missing Lever of Corporate Governance' [2006] University of Pennsylvania Law Review 1209.

[77] Nini, Smith and Sufi (n 77) 1747.

[78] According to the so-called "representation hypothesis", the supervisor should substitute debt governance, mimicking market forces. See Dewatripont Mathias and Jean Tirole, *The Prudential Regulation of Banks*, vol 1 (MIT Press 1994).

discussed, there is ample evidence that shareholder-centric governance paradigm incentivises excessive risk-taking, especially in good times, and that such excessive risk-taking contributes to build-up systemic risk. Effective debt governance would provide a "natural" solution for adjusting such shareholder-centric paradigm.

Thus, granting governance rights to creditors, hence making debt governance effective, has the potential to enable early policing of disproportionate risks in good times, complementing the role of the supervisor. For instance, a perpetual AT1 holder might not be willing to let the bank take such risks and might block it should they have the tools to do so.

Finally, granting governance rights to creditors might generate a positive by-product, increasing legal certainty in resolution. The protection of property entitlements of creditors subject to resolution has been one of the major criticisms raised in legal scholarship against bank resolution.[79] The use of the bail-in tool, so the argument goes, would violate the right to property of the creditors bearing losses. In the first cases disputed in front of the ECJ, the existence of the no-creditors-worse-off rules considered a decisive argument in favour of the constitutionality of bail-in.[80] Such rule implies that creditors cannot bear higher losses in resolution than the amount of losses they would have borne in the counterfactual liquidation scenario.[81] However, the practical judicial implementation of such safeguard is more complicated than it might seem at first glance, generating a great ex-ante uncertainty and negatively impacting the incentives of creditors to exert discipline.[82] In this regard, Chiu argued that: "the 'no creditor worse off' principle could also convince bail-inable debt holders that taking a back seat in monitoring would make no difference".[83]

[79] Karl-Philipp Wojcik, 'Bail-in in the Banking Union' (2016) 53 Common Market Law Review 91, 117.

[80] Judgment of the Court (Grand Chamber) of 19 July 2016. Tadej Kotnik and Others v Državni zbor Republike Slovenije. Case C-526/14.

[81] For more details on the no-creditors-worse-off rule see VPG de Serière, 'No Creditor Worse Off in Case of Bank Resolution. Food for Litigation' (2016) 31 Journal of International Banking Law and Regulation 376.

[82] For a detailed analysis of the impact of NCWO rule on incentives, see Chapter 4, Sect. 4.3.

[83] Iris HY Chiu, 'Corporate Governance: The Missing Paradigm in the Mandatory Bail-in Regime for Creditors of Banks and Financial Institutions' [2014] Journal of business law 611, 627.

Arguably, ex-ante governance rights provide better protection for property entitlements than an uncertain cap on losses that can be borne in resolution.[84] Therefore, providing ex-ante market-based safeguards could substitute the ex-post judicial (and uncertain) safeguard in terms of property right protections. This, in turn, would have two more general positive consequences. First, it would enhance the incentives of bail-inable creditors to impose market discipline on the borrowing banks. Second, it would make resolution more credible, eliminating one material impediment to resolution. Should the NCWO rule be breached, the creditors are entitled to ex-post compensation paid out by the Single Resolution Fund.[85]

Granting governance rights to junior unsecured (i.e., bail-inable) creditors in order to make debt governance work in banking firms also seems to be theoretically well-grounded. Nonetheless, finding suitable legal tools for efficiently implementing such a proposal is not straightforward. Many questions arise, none of which have an unchallenging answer. Which creditors should have governance rights? Should this right be contingent on financial deterioration? And, crucially, which kind of rights is proportionate to grant? Sections 4 and 5 attempt to solve these puzzling issues and develop a suitable legal framework interacting with various areas of law and regulation; namely, resolution regulation, supervision law and national corporate laws.

4 A New Governance Status for Creditors: The Boundaries

The remainder of this chapter develops the core of the policy proposal and highlights why and how it should achieve its overarching goal: fine-tuning bank governance and the resolution framework. Such overarching goals have a twofold nature: first, it aims at addressing the specificities of bank governance, with particular regard to debt governance. Second, it aims at enhancing the resolvability of financial institutions and, consequently, its credibility.

[84] For the proprietary foundation of property rights see John Armour and Michael J Whincop, 'The Proprietary Foundations of Corporate Law' (2007) 27 Oxford Journal of Legal Studies 429.

[85] Article 75 and 78 BRRD.

This chapter argues in favour of a "structured" legal approach in granting governance rights to bail-inable debtholders. Such a "structured" approach should primarily consist of a general principle of "sufficient accountability" towards bail-inable creditors in corporate governance. Building on this general principle, the reform should also provide a limited set of core rights at EU law level, to be implemented and detailed nationally according to national corporate laws.

Before discussing the advantages of such a "structured" approach, it is necessary to set the stage of the policy proposals, considering two crucial features and defining its boundaries. Namely, Sect. 4.1 deals with defining the pools of creditors to which the governance rights should be granted. Subsequently, Sect. 4.2 wonders whether such rights should be contingent on the deterioration of banks' solvency or should they be active at all times. Thence, once boundaries are defined, Sect. 5 digs into the contents of the proposal and discusses its advantages.

4.1 Creditors Holding the Governance Rights

The first step in building a coherent policy proposal is to identify the pool of creditors whose position and incentives align with limiting disproportionate risks. In doing so, this section proceeds by subtraction, skimming the unfit categories of creditors until only those that are fit for purpose remains.

First, it is easy to rule out all the creditors whose claim is not subject to bail-in.[86] Should the bank enter resolution, those are not going to bear losses shareholder-like as a consequence of an administrative decision of the Resolution Authority. Therefore, their incentives cannot be considered appropriately aligned with the willingness of limiting risk-taking ex-ante. As argued in the previous section, creditors seek protection through other mechanisms; for instance, security interests on some of the bank's assets. Moreover, there are examples of short-term creditors that are radically incompatible with holding governance rights. Think, for instance, of depositors or repo counterparties.

Second, not all bail-inable creditors are equal, at least from an ex-ante perspective. There are considerable discrepancies between the pool of creditors that can be subject to bail-in and a subset of those that are

[86] See Article 44 BRRD. For an in-depth discussion, see also Chapter 4.

eligible for MREL purposes.[87] Only committed, long-term non-runnable capital[88] can be counted for MREL purposes. Therefore, MREL functionally represents an additional capital requirement to be matched with own funds[89] and other eligible liabilities. Meeting such a requirement should ensure that the institution has a solid base of long-term funding in its balance sheet and consequently it is, at all times, resolvable.

Such functional goal cannot be ensured by any liability that, should the bank enter in resolution, is theoretically bail-inable. For instance, for the deposits exceeding the insured amount (i.e., 100.000 €), the uninsured amount is bail-inable[90]; yet it is not MREL eligible.[91] In the same way, a junior bond with a remaining maturity of 8 months is bail-inable in resolution[92] but does not count towards MREL.[93]

MREL-eligible creditors are better positioned to influence bank governance, and their incentives are more in line with socially desirable outcomes.

At this point, one might wonder whether the subtraction exercise is completed, and MREL-eligible creditors are the appropriate pool of creditors. MREL-eligible creditors represents an extremely heterogeneous class. The common characteristics of such broad class of creditors are that all MREL liabilities are long-term, with at least one year of residual maturity, and are not secured in any way by the issuing bank. Beyond such common denominators, AT1 perpetual CoCos are as MREL eligible as five years Senior Bonds are. Clearly, the risk of bearing losses in resolution

[87] Minimum Requirement for Own Funds and Eligible Liabilities, See Articles 45 and following BRRD.

[88] Capital is here used in its generic meaning of source of funding.

[89] I.e., capital in technical terms, as disciplined by the Capital Requirement.

[90] See the combined provision Article 44(2)(a) excluding covered deposits from bail-in and Article.

[91] Article 72a(2)(b) Capital Requirement Regulation, Regulation (EU) No 575/2013 of the European Parliament and of the Council of 26 June 2013 on prudential requirements for credit institutions and investment firms and amending Regulation (EU) No 648/2012. OJ L 176, 27.6.2013.

[92] Article 72(c)(1) CRR.

[93] Among the qualitative requirements to count as MREL instruments, the one of utmost importance is to have a residual maturity of at least 12 months. For more details on the legal framework pertain to MREL instruments see Chapter 4. For a critical assessment of such framework, see also Tröger (n 15).

sharply differs between the two types of MREL creditors[94] and, arguably, also monitoring and disciplining incentives differ accordingly. Therefore, one might wonder whether it is reasonable to grant the same governance rights to these different types of creditors. Or, in other words, should the subtraction exercise go any further?

Thus, there are arguments to further restricting the pools of "suitable" creditors, or at least to differentiate the rights to grant to different classes of equally MREL-eligible creditors. In contrast, two other elements are pushing to stop the subtraction exercise and grant the same governance rights to all MREL creditors.

The first argument relates to how MREL requirements are calibrated by the Resolution Authority.[95] The calibration of MREL considers the threshold of 8% of own funds and eligible liabilities[96] that needs to be bailed-in before accessing any resolution financing arrangement.[97] Therefore, at least in theory, if the bank enters in resolution, all MREL capital is going to be bailed-in before public funds are granted to the ailing bank. This harmonises, to some extent, the incentives of MREL creditors.

The second argument is more pragmatic and aims to avoid over-complications of an already complex proposal. MREL creditors share the core functional characteristics highlighted in Sect. 3 and, crucially, they are already identified for different regulatory purpose.

Therefore, MREL creditors should be considered as a class when granting governance rights. Moreover, alternative methods can better differentiate the position of different creditors. For instance, the voting rights of each creditor can be weighted based on a metric of the riskiness of different claims. It is not necessary to go deep into the details of how such mechanism should work. A simple example suffices to set the general idea: a creditor exposed for 1 million euro in T2 capital instruments should have more voting power than another creditor exposed for the same amount in senior unsecured debt.

As a further refinement, an ad hoc exclusion within MREL creditors is still warranted. For the purpose of this proposal, the so-called "internal

[94] Article 46 BRRD.

[95] On the differences between MREL and Total Loss Absorbency Capacity for Globally Systemic Banks, as designed by the Financial Stability Board, see Review of the Technical Implementation of the Total Loss Absorbing Capacity (TLAC) Standard, 2 July 2019.

[96] Article 45b (4) BRRD.

[97] Article 44(5) BRRD.

MREL" exposures should not be considered.[98] Internal MREL consists of eligible exposures of the holding company towards its subsidiaries to ensure that the group as a whole is resolvable under a Single Point of Entry Strategy (SPOE).[99] Thus, internal MREL has nothing to do with imposing discipline on the borrower, so that granting governance rights would make no sense as it would simply give rights to the holding that is already controlling the subsidiary.

Finally, it is now time for tackling the natural and foremost critique to this policy proposal: can it work? The concern is legitimate, as granting governance rights to creditors is rather unconventional. However, some elements suggest that creditors' rights could marginally improve bank resilience and resolvability. Chapter 6 documented the complex and mixed trends of the bail-inable creditors' composition. A clear path emerging from the evolution of such composition is the increasing share of professional investment in MREL-eligible securities. Moreover, bank crossholdings, although stable, are shifting towards more senior positions.[100] Therefore, it can be argued that MREL creditors are increasingly professional investors that are capable and willing to influence bank governance to ensure getting a return on their investment.[101]

Despite the above, in some countries, retail investment in junior bail-inable positions continues to be a burdensome legacy issue. For what is here of interests, granting governance rights to retailer investors represents a suboptimal outcome, as they are neither capable nor willing to efficiently exercise these rights because of insufficient sophistication and rational apathy. Moreover, retail holdings of bail-inable securities make

[98] The resolution of complex banking groups represents one of the major challenges for financial stability. On this intricate matter, see Jens-Hinrich Binder, 'Cross-Border Coordination of Bank Resolution in the EU: All Problems Resolved?', *Research Handbook on Cross-Border Bank Resolution* (Edward Elgar Publishing 2019). More specifically, on the governance of banking groups and on its impact on stability and resolvability, see Thom Wetzer, 'In Two Minds: The Governance of Ring-Fenced Banks' (2019) 19 Journal of Corporate Law Studies 197.

[99] On preferable resolution strategy, see Jeffrey N Gordon and Wolf-Georg Ringe, 'Bank Resolution in the European Banking Union: A Transatlantic Perspective on What It Would Take' (2015) 115 Colum. L. Rev. 1297. (arguing in favour of a Single Point of Entry Strategy).

[100] See ECB, 'Financial Stability Review - November 2016' (2016). In Box 7 there is the analysis: "The evolution of Sectoral holding of bail-inable debt".

[101] Shleifer and Vishny (n 61).

resolvability increasingly difficult and, ex-ante, not credible. For all these reasons, a final refinement to the subjective scope of this proposal is necessary. The governance rights embedded in the securities should remain inactive so long as the securities are held by non-professional investors.[102] This solution is milder than an outright ban on retail investors proposed by many scholars and policymakers.[103] Moreover, it is consistent with the approach taken by the EU legislation in the 2019 revision of the BRRD that aims to foreclose as much as possible the possibility of retailers to hold securities counting towards MREL.[104]

In terms of the legal design of the reform, on top of the other requirement to include liabilities in MREL, Article 45 of the BRRD should require MREL securities to include a contractual term granting the holders of such securities the rights conferred upon them, as specified in Sect. 5.

In the proceeding of the analysis, "MREL creditors" indicates the subset of bank creditors upon which governance rights should be conferred and has to be understood with this meaning unless it is explicitly stated otherwise. On the contrary, "bail-inable creditors" or simply "creditors" indicate the more general concepts discussed above in this section.

4.2 *The Nature of Governance Rights: Contingent v Absolute Rights*

The second step towards the definition of a new governance status for MREL creditors is to define the nature of their rights. In particular, defining whether such rights should be contingent on the deterioration of bank financial conditions.

In non-financial firms, debt governance mainly consists of control rights allocated through contracts and contingent on future events. For instance, a standard financial covenant can grant creditors a right

[102] On the definition of "professional investor", see the Annex 2 to the Markets in Financial instruments Directive (MiFid 2). Directive 2014/65/EU of The European Parliament and Of the Council of 15 May 2014 on markets in financial instruments and amending Directive 2002/92/EC and Directive 2011/61/EU. OJ L 173, 12.6.2014.

[103] Martin R Götz and Tobias Tröger, 'Should the Marketing of Subordinated Debt Be Restricted/Different in One Way or the Other? What to Do in the Case of Mis-Selling?' (2016).

[104] Article 44a BRRD.

to speed up the repayment of their exposure if the leverage of the borrower increases, breaching a contractually pre-specified threshold.[105] More generally, debt contracts can be seen as a tool to contingently allocate control[106] to creditors once the financial situation of the borrowing firm deteriorates to such a point that makes control rights more valuable to creditors than to shareholders.[107]

Contingently allocated control over corporate assets and decision-making to creditors decreases the agency costs of debt. Managers and shareholders are interested in retaining control so that they have appropriate incentives to avoid situations that are detrimental for the creditors and trigger the covenant. Additionally, should this situation materialise regardless, creditors are entitled with rights to minimise their risk of bearing losses. From an ex-ante perspective, this reduces the cost of debt capital, so that the borrowing firm is willing to restrict the set of available actions to be taken in the future to access cheaper funds.[108]

Therefore, if the governance status of MREL creditors is meant to merely mimic debt governance in non-financial firms, rights should be contingent. However, a clear parallel with the analysis by professors Armour and Gordon on directors' liability arises.[109] They persuasively argue that: "private law does not do an 'imperfect job' of internalising systemic harms; it does no job at all".[110] The same claim can be advanced for debt governance: debt governance does not work in banking,[111] but even if it worked as in non-financial firms, it would not be able to internalise any of the systemic risk generated via banking activities.

As previously discussed, the aim of granting MREL creditors a new governance status is not just to make debt governance more effective, but

[105] See, for instance, Adam B Badawi and Elisabeth de Fontenay, 'Contractual Complexity in Debt Agreements: The Case of EBITDA' (2019) Duke Law School DP 2019–67.

[106] Aghion and Bolton (n 63).

[107] Coase (n 59).

[108] There is an ample theoretical literature in corporate finance based on the limited possibility to credibly commit ex-ante. For an overview of this literature see Bolton (n 69) 71.

[109] Armour and Gordon (n 7).

[110] Ibid 38.

[111] For the reasons highlighted in Sect. 3.

to propose debt governance as a complement to regulation and supervision in enhancing the resilience of single institutions and the system as a whole.[112] Therefore, the governance status of bail-inable creditors must consist of absolute rights that can be exercised in any state of the world.

Moreover, it is worth noting that granting rights contingent on the financial deterioration of the bank would add little, if any, advantage and might generate serious negative consequences. Once the bank enters troubles, it gathers the attention of the supervisor and the market. At this point, both compliance duties and funding costs are likely to increase. In a moment of hardship, granting rights to MREL creditors would merely increase such hardship, with little room to impose higher or better discipline.[113] On the contrary, the governance status of bail-inable creditors intends to ease early policing of excessive risk-taking.

In conclusion, MREL securities should embed absolute, non-state contingent, governance rights. Such rights should act as a complement to supervision to prevent the accumulation of risk, especially in good times.

5 A New Governance Status for Creditors: The Contents

Having identified who should be granted governance rights and when such rights should be exercised, the next step is to define the content of the rights that are necessary and sufficient to achieve the goal of this proposal, i.e., complement financial regulation and supervision in minimising the creation of systemic externalities due to excessive risk-taking.

Defining the contents of the governance status of bail-inable creditors represents a tricky exercise as it faces two main perils: to "under-entitle" or to "over-entitle" bail-inable creditors. Under the first peril, bail-inable creditors have few and ineffective rights, and are unable to positively influence the decision-making of the borrowing bank. Conversely, if creditors are over-entitled with many and highly intrusive rights, the control powers of shareholders and the necessary discretion of the management over corporate decisions would be hindered.

[112] On the potential of governance arrangement to contribute in reaching macroprudential targets, see Enriques, Romano and Wetzer (n 51).

[113] On retrospective effectiveness of discipline see Constantinos Stephanou, 'Rethinking Market Discipline in Banking: Lessons from the Financial Crisis' (2010) 5227.

These scenarios are both value-decreasing. On the one hand, in case of under-entitlement little, if anything, would change in terms of preventing excessive risk-taking; whereas, non-trivial costs for setting up and running the new governance arrangements would be borne by the banks and probably by the creditors themselves, at least indirectly. On the other hand, in case of over-entitlement, the limitation of entrepreneurship would be excessive, with the risk of letting the bank passing on positive net present value projects for the mere reason that these entail some risk.

The exact calibration of the necessary and sufficient rights to grant bail-inable creditors is, therefore, at the same time, crucial and complex. Such complexity derives from two idiosyncrasies: the heterogeneity of banks' business and funding models (and the specific risks they entail) and the heterogeneity of national corporate laws.

That being the case, EU law should limit itself to identify a limited set of core rights and complement these with a general clause requiring both Member States and individual institutions to be sufficiently accountable towards bail-inable creditors in their decision-making processes and governance arrangements. What follows represents a first, tentative, attempt to operationalise this intuition: Sect. 5.1 discusses the desirability of a general clause including MREL creditors in the governance arrangements of banks; whereas, Sect. 5.2 proposes substantive rights to grant MREL creditors at EU level.

5.1 The General Principle

The general clause of "sufficient accountability" should be codified as one of the principles on governance arrangements itemised by Article 88 of the Capital Requirement Directive.[114] The principle should require the

[114] The other general principles listed in Article 88 CRD are:

(a) the management body must have the overall responsibility for the institution and approve and oversee the implementation of the institution's strategic objectives, risk strategy, and internal governance;

(b) the management body must ensure the integrity of the accounting and financial reporting systems, including financial and operational controls and compliance with the law and relevant standards;

(c) the management body must oversee the process of disclosure and communications;

(d) the management body must be responsible for providing effective oversight of senior management;

management body to set up governance mechanisms assuring sufficient accountability towards bail-inable creditors.

Sufficient accountability represents a vague and open-ended concept and voluntarily so. The goal of this principle is that banks, in their decision-making process, should take into account the interests of MREL creditors not to suffer losses and to receive the principal amount and interests when those come due. The generic formulation of the principle is important for two reasons. First, it allows individual banks to set up governance arrangements that are consistent with their business model and organizational structure and to experiment with different arrangements. Second, it gives the supervisor with some flexibility in determining the "sufficiency" of the governance arrangements of individual banks, allowing for a proportionate implementation of the principle.

This general principle should be further specified, expressly stating that these governance mechanisms should comply at least with the minimum set of rights provided by EU law, unless the law grants ad hoc exemptions for proportionality reasons.

Section 5.2 discusses the set of rights that should be granted to MREL creditors. Before moving to that part of the analysis, it is important to discuss the advantages of the "structured" legal design outlined so far. Two main advantages are worth mentioning.

First, including the "sufficient accountability" clause among the general principles of bank governance arrangements makes the implementation of such standard a matter that the competent authority must, by its own mandate, continuously supervise.[115] The review and evaluation of the bank's governance arrangements fall within the so-called "Supervisory Review and Evaluation Process" (SREP),[116] to be carried out by the competent authority at least annually. This would make the Competent Authority, hence the Single Supervisory Mechanism for the Euro Area, the gatekeeper of the governance status of the MREL creditors, overseeing its sufficiency at least on a yearly basis.

To assess the compliance with the "sufficient accountability" standard transparently and predictably, the European Banking Authority should

(e) the chairman of the management body in its supervisory function of an institution must not exercise simultaneously the functions of a chief executive officer within the same institution, unless justified by the institution and authorised by competent authorities.

[115] Article 98(7) CRD.

[116] Article 97 CRD.

issue appropriate guidelines. Such guidelines should allow for the widest diversification possible as for the specific governance arrangement to be considered "sufficient", to encourage experimentation and discourage herding behaviours.[117]

Second, this proposal allows for a proportionate and, potentially network sensitive, implementation of the "sufficient accountability" standard. Including the evaluation of the "sufficient accountability" within the SREP gives a gatekeeping responsibility to the competent authority which is legally mandated to apply it proportionally.[118] Clearly, what can be deemed sufficient for a medium-sized regional bank is likely not to be considered so for a Globally Systemically Important Bank (G-SIB). In this regard, requiring different governance arrangements to different banks can be considered a direct application of the proportionality principle. Looking at this from a substantive perspective, the differentiated application of the "sufficient accountability" principle can be implemented in a "network sensitive" manner,[119] accounting for the contribution of each institution to systemic risk.[120] In doing so, the competent authority should require higher standards for those banks generating higher systemic externalities because of their centrality and interconnectedness within the financial network.[121]

On top of the limited set of governance rights discussed below, institution-specific arrangements should guarantee sufficient accountability towards bail-inable creditors. To allow the management to

[117] Ian Ayres and Joshua Mitts, 'Anti-Herding Regulation' (2015) 5 Harv. Bus. L. Rev. 1.

[118] Proportionality can be considered a general principle of EU administrative law as an application of the principle of "open, efficient and independent European administration". See Article 298 TFEU.

[119] Enriques, Romano and Wetzer (n 51).

[120] For possible metrics measuring such contribution, see ibid 14.

[121] It is worth noticing that such account for systemic risk is necessarily qualitative and not strictly quantitative, contrarily to the examples provided by Enriques and co-authors. The governance rights and arrangements cannot be conceptualised as continuous variable assuming every possible value, but rather discrete and complex modules of rights and duties that can be target only by clustering covered institutions into various group with different coefficient of systemic relevance. An example of such an approach is the "bucket approach" employed by the Financial Stability Board. See BCBS, Global systemically important banks: updated assessment methodology and the higher loss absorbency requirement, July 2013.

discharge such duty effectively, EU law should mandate Member States to provide tools compatible with national corporate laws that banks can use to comply with the general principle of sufficient accountability.

Given the far-reaching nature of this proposal, digging into the details of possible creditor right regimes in various countries and types of institutions represents a far-reaching objective falling out of the scope of this research.[122] In evaluating these arrangements, the competent authority should consider two objectives: limiting switching costs to a minimum, adapting governance mechanisms that are already in place in a given jurisdiction, and incentivising anti-herding solutions.[123]

5.2 Governance Rights Granted at EU Law Level

General Features

This section discusses the minimum sets of rights allowing creditors to have a positive impact on bank governance, complementing regulation and supervision, and argues that a mix of targeted appointment and decision rights can be considered fit for purpose. An adequate "governance infrastructure" constitutes the prerequisite making the governance status of MREL effective. Therefore, it is necessary to preliminarily introduce the General Meeting of MREL creditors and their common trustee.

All the holders of MREL instruments should compose the General Meeting of MREL creditors. The voting rights at the meeting should be defined by the amount of exposure towards the bank and weighted according to the riskiness of the exposure. Riskier instruments grant higher voting rights. The General Meeting should vote on a limited and standardised number of items. Namely, the appointments discussed in Sect. 5.2.2 and the decisions to be taken according to Sect. 5.2.3, including the decision to start a liability suit if deemed appropriate.

The common trustee of MREL creditors should facilitate the coordination of the MREL creditors.[124] To this end, they should be responsible

[122] For an analysis of the complexities related to creditors' right in non-financial firms, see Rosemary Teele Langford and Ian Ramsay, 'The Contours and Content of the "Creditors" Interests Duty" (2021) 21 Journal of Corporate Law Studies 85.

[123] Ayres and Mitts (n 119).

[124] It is worth noticing that the type of trustee discussed here is different in means and scope from the traditional indenture trustee who has the power to enforce the indentures of a bond. As a means of comparison, the MREL trustee is closer to the figure depicted

for calling and organising the Annual General Meeting and representing MREL creditors in case of a liability lawsuit (see Sect. 5.2.3). They should possess all the required characteristics of independence required to independent directors.[125] In the same vein, the remuneration should be fixed and insensitive to the performance of the bank or other performance metrics.

As mentioned before, these two basic structural features are necessary for coordination purposes and enforcement. Sections 5.2.2 and 5.2.3 discuss, respectively, appointment and decision rights that should be granted to MREL creditors. Moreover, those explain the role of General Meeting of MREL creditors and the common MREL trustee in each specific instance.

Appointment Rights

According to the framework of the analysis, granting MREL creditors with some rights of appointment makes sense only if their appointees enhance the decision-making process of the bank, optimising its risk-taking appetite. Following this line of argumentation, MREL creditors should have the power to appoint qualified minorities of strategic committees[126]; namely, the risk committee, the audit committee, and the remuneration committee.

Such a choice needs a preliminary explanation and justification. The fact that the MREL creditors' representatives should count for a qualified minority of each committee aims to strike an appropriate balance between the risks of over- and under-entitlement previously discussed at

by Yakov Amihud, Kenneth Garbade and Marcel Kahan, 'A New Governance Structure for Corporate Bonds' [1999] Stanford Law Review 447.

[125] Note that the standard concept of "independence" in corporate governance, indicating individuals without significant personal and financial links with the company. Thus, the status of the trustee should be integrated by the requirement for independent directors set down in national corporate law or corporate governance code. This differs from the more substantive but vague concept of "independence of mind" introduced in the European Legislation as a feature with which each member of the management must discharge its duties. See Article 91(8) CRD: "Each member of the management body shall act with honesty, integrity and independence of mind to effectively assess and challenge the decisions of the senior management where necessary and to effectively oversee and monitor management decision-making".

[126] For instance, two fifth of the committee members should be MREL creditors representatives.

the beginning of Sect. 5. In the same vein, granting MREL creditors with the right to appoint members of the committee but not necessarily members of the board are meant to achieve the same balance. Moreover, such choice delivers two additional advantages. First, it allows for a certain degree of flexibility in the legal design of MREL representatives so that this can fit more easily in national corporate law and institution-specific arrangements.[127] Second, it allows for the design of a system in which the presence of MREL creditors' representatives can actually make a difference and where the representatives are incentivised to do so. The rest of this section better develops and explains this latter point, when it discussed the duties and responsibilities of the MREL representatives.

To ensure that the potential for a positive impact of bondholders' representatives in strategic committees is fully exploited, the rights and duties of the MREL creditors' representatives need to be further detailed. First of all, on the one hand, in terms of rights and duties vis-à-vis the management of the bank, the MREL creditors' representatives should be given access to all the relevant information as any other non-executive director. On the other hand, committee members should be held liable for unduly revealing confidential information or damaging the bank with intent or gross negligence.

The situation is more entangled and delicate when it comes to the relationship between committee members and MREL creditors. Evident agency problems might arise and the probability of committee members to be captured by bank management seems non-trivial. If this is the case, the presence of committee representatives would be irrelevant because their ability and willingness to voice the interests of MREL creditors in the committee would be impaired.

Standard governance strategies might help mitigate such agency costs. Committee representatives should possess all the characteristics of independence and integrity required to independent directors.[128] Moreover, committee representatives should owe fiduciary duties to MREL creditors. Thus, in discharging their duties, the representatives must act in

[127] The MREL creditors representatives might or might not have a seat in the board and if they are granted with a seat in the board they might or might not have a voting rights for all or some of the issues to be discussed. Yet, in compliance with the proposed general principle of Article 88 CRD, MREL creditors representatives should always have voting rights in the board committees.

[128] See note 125.

the best interests of the creditors. This duty is only mitigated by the duty not to intentionally or through gross negligently harm the bank, as discussed above. In this respect, having MREL creditors' representatives only seating in the committees and not on the board might alleviate possible legal problems arising from multiple fiduciaries owed both to MREL creditors and the corporation.

The liability regime of MREL creditors' representatives closely follows their fiduciary duties. Thus, committee members should be held liable vis-à-vis MREL creditors if they negligently avoid acting or to be appropriately informed on the matters to be discussed and decided within the committees and their inaction causes serious damage to bondholders.[129] The General Meeting of MREL creditors should decide on any liability lawsuits with a simple majority,[130] and the common MREL trustee should have standing. Moreover, a qualified minority of MREL creditors should be allowed to begin a derivative lawsuit.[131]

Finally, committee representatives should draft a comprehensive and detailed report on the activities of the committees and the impact of their decisions on the stability and resilience of the bank as well as the probability of MREL creditors to incur in losses. The report should be made available to MREL creditors before their Annual General Meeting. Particular attention should be devoted to the remuneration and dividend policies, as the report should represent the underlying material on which MREL creditors exercises the decision rights discussed in Sect. 5.2.3.

Decision Rights

The appointment of committee representatives might not be enough to efficiently impact on the decision-making of the bank management. As discussed in the previous section, the representatives of MREL creditors should count as a qualified minority of the committees, so that the rest of the members can overcome the reservations or proposals of the creditors'

[129] The standard of negligence mitigated by the duty not to harm the bank should be considered appropriate, further shielding committee representatives from liability, e.g., imposing gross-negligence standard, would not achieve the goal to minimise agency costs between MREL creditors and their representatives.

[130] See Sect. 5.2.3

[131] A derivative lawsuit is a legal action filed by an individual shareholder, in the name of the company, to redress wrongs or harms to the company that the Board of Directors or Officers will not address themselves.

representatives. Therefore, it seems also necessary to give the generality of creditors limited decision rights, complementing the role of creditors' representatives.

In particular, the right to vote on executive remuneration and dividends represents an effective set of core rights to be granted through EU law. Those would be relatively easy to implement in each jurisdiction and would complement the existing regulatory and supervisory framework. In this regard, the annual report of the MREL representatives discussed in the previous section represents an important background material. The report should provide a clear-cut and straightforward indication on the matters MREL creditors are asked to vote on, stating whether the remuneration and dividend policy takes in adequate consideration the interests of MREL creditors and, more generally, the solvency and stability of the bank.

Taking the law as it is, the competent authorities can limit both dividend and variable remuneration[132] only once the bank is in material breach of the so-called combined buffer requirement.[133] On the one hand, granting an unconditional right to creditors to block disproportionate distributions in good times would provide an important complement to the prudential tools currently in place. On the other hand, it does not seem proportionate to grant a generalised veto right on other types of distribution of corporate assets such as share repurchase or, more in general, capital instruments redemptions. The Competent Authority has already ample and non-contingent power to authorise such operations only if the bank satisfies stringent conditions.[134]

The most entangled aspect of the proposal consists of the legal effects of a bank's possible rejection of remuneration and/or dividend policies. Making the decisions of the MREL creditors binding might be considered an over-entitlement. In contrast, if these decisions are merely consultative, the opposite risk of under-entitlement arises. Moreover, in this matter is also important to provide some flexibility in the implementation, so to account for the heterogeneity of national corporate laws and bank's business models and strategic decisions.

[132] Article 141 CRD, setting the cases in which distributions can be restricted, the types of distribution that should be restricted and the maximum amount of distribution possible in case the combined buffer requirement is breached.

[133] Article 128 CRD.

[134] Articles 77 and 78 CRR.

There are three main dimensions to consider in designing the exact scope and effect of the voting rights granted to MREL creditors. First, the timing of the AGM of MREL creditors as compared to the AGM of shareholders. If MREL creditors vote on remuneration and dividend after the AGM of shareholders already deliberated on these issues, making the creditor's decision binding would be particularly difficult from a legal perspective and highly intrusive. On the contrary, if the opposition of creditors is on a managerial proposal, the law can oblige the management to revise its proposal accordingly. Second, the MREL creditors can be asked to vote on the policies on dividends and remuneration to be applied "pro futuro" and/or on the actual determination to distribute dividend or pay out remuneration. Third, hybrid forms in between consultative and binding decisions are possible and likely desirable.[135]

Finally, the MREL creditors during the Annual General Meeting can deliberate on the initiation of liability lawsuits. In particular, the common trustee should be allowed to act on MREL creditors' behalf against the committee representatives for breaching their fiduciary duties. Moreover, they should be allowed to initiate a derivative lawsuit against the directors and the management for damaging the corporation.

6 Conclusion

This chapter argues in favour of including (some) bank creditors in the decision-making process of their borrowers through statutory reforms. It shows how such a major adjustment to the standard governance arrangements is warranted.

In doing so, this chapter reviews several strands of literature proposing to sharply "alter" corporate governance arrangements of banks accounting for systemic externalities. Some of such proposals, such as the ones extending the responsibility of directors in the pre-insolvency phase, nicely complement the argument in favour of more robust debt governance. On the contrary, other proposals, especially those pointing at modifying the fiduciary duties of bank directors, are in a relation of mutual exclusiveness with granting governance rights to creditors.

[135] For an overview of the various policy options already implemented worldwide see Randall S Thomas and Christoph Van der Elst, 'Say on Pay around the World' (2014) 92 Wash. UL Rev. 653.

This chapter proposes two main theoretical justifications for statutorily including creditors in the decision-making process of their borrower. First, the specialties of bank governance make a particularly strong case for departing from a purely shareholder-oriented approach to governance. Second, analysing the problematic relation between governance incentives and financial regulation, this chapter argues that the room for debt governance in banks is particularly narrow. In contrast, functioning and efficient debt governance would be needed, especially in banks. Moreover, as an additional positive spillover, governance rights to creditors would increase the credibility of the resolution framework and, thus, the resolvability of the single institutions. This latter consideration highlights the potential for triggering a virtuous circle in which debt governance enhances the overall quality of bank corporate governance which, in turn, increases the credibility of the resolution framework. Being the resolution framework more credible, the disciplining pressure on banks risk-taking appetite increases, further enhancing the quality of the decision-making process, i.e., the quality of bank governance.

Finally, this chapter attempts to operationalise a framework for granting creditors some governance rights. It proposes to grant unconditional rights to creditors holding instruments that are eligible for MREL purposes. Moreover, it proposes to include among the principles on bank governance arrangements a general clause of "sufficient accountability" towards MREL creditors in decision-making. This approach has the advantage of including the quality of debt governance within the annual evaluation carried out by the supervisor. The adequacy of governance arrangements would become part of the annual SREP with the potential to put in motion a virtuous iterative procedure between the individual bank and the supervisor. This would help refining the governance role of the MREL creditors and fitting it to the specificities of each bank.

To complement such general principle and make it effective, a few specific appointment and decision rights should be granted to MREL creditors with the aim to balance the interests of both shareholders and creditors constituencies. Specifically, on the one hand, in terms of appointment rights, MREL creditors should be able to appoint a qualified minority of the members of some strategic committees, such as audit, risk, and compensation. On the other hand, MREL creditors should be asked to vote on the remuneration and dividend policy, complementing the role of committee representatives in restraining the possibility of the bank to engage in disproportionate risky projects in good times.

CHAPTER 9

The 2023 Banking Crisis: Lessons for Debt Governance

1 Introduction

The experience of the past years confirmed that banking crises are not a thing of the past. Despite the significant worldwide regulatory effort in the aftermath of the Global Financial Crisis, the events of March 2023 demonstrated once again how quickly confidence in large, complex financial institutions can vanish—and how ill-prepared existing institutional frameworks remain for managing adverse events. The failures of Silicon Valley Bank (SVB) and Credit Suisse occurred within advanced jurisdictions, subject to extensive prudential regulation and equipped with supposedly robust resolution regimes. Yet, when tested, these regimes failed to deliver. Instead, authorities relied on ad hoc interventions, discretionary actions, and improvised guarantees. These developments did not merely reflect isolated supervisory mistakes or idiosyncratic mismanagement. They revealed deeper and more structural weaknesses in the governance of contemporary banking systems.

The detailed analysis of the SVB and Credit Suisse cases is beyond the scope of this analysis.[1] Rather, this chapter analyses the 2023 turmoil as a

[1] For an internal encompassing report of the SVB and Credit Suisse Crisis, see respectively Michael Barr, "Review of the Federal Reserve's Supervision and Regulation of

E. D. Martino, *EU Bank Governance and Bail-In*, EBI Studies in Banking and Capital Markets Law,
https://doi.org/10.1007/978-3-032-20699-2_9

stress test of the theoretical claims developed in the previous chapters. The premise of the book is that bank governance remains structurally fragile because those to whom bank risk is allocated—especially creditors—face fundamental barriers to exercising effective oversight.[2] Previous chapters showed from different perspectives that the idea that debt governance can only function if supported by some institutional preconditions: predictable resolution frameworks, enforceable loss absorption, and credible supervisory activation. The fulfilment of these conditions can generate a virtuous circle, in which a strong resolution framework and effective debt governance reinforce one another. In contrast, the lack of these conditions generates a vicious circle, in which a weak resolution framework fuels ineffective debt governance which, in turn, weakens resolution even further.

This chapter shows that both in the SVB and Credit Suisse formal resolution frameworks proved ineffective at addressing the crisis and allocating losses in a transparent and predictable fashion. In the US, SVB's resolution was circumvented through the systemic risk exception, leading to a full bailout of uninsured depositors. In Switzerland, the Credit Suisse resolution was circumvented through a merger with UBS, creating a de facto monopoly in the Swiss banking market. This outcome was facilitated by the activation of discretionary regulatory powers to write down contingent convertible AT1 instruments cannot perform their intended function.

Based on this analysis this chapter moves forward and attempt to draw lessons for effective debt governance, looking both at what did not work and at what partially worked. Rather than discrediting the logic of debt governance, the 2023 crisis confirms its conditional validity. Conditional because to function properly, debt governance must be embedded in a framework that makes loss-bearing credible and timely.

Silicon Valley Bank" (2023) <https://www.federalreserve.gov/publications/review-of-the-federal-reserves-supervision-and-regulation-of-silicon-valley-bank.htm>. accessed October 29, 2025. For an independent overview of the crises also in a comparative perspective, see Ignazio Angeloni and others, "Much Money, Little Capital and Few Reforms. The 2023 Banking Turmoil" (2023) <https://cepr.org/publications/books-and-reports/geneva-27-much-money-little-capital-and-few-reforms-2023-banking> accessed October 29, 2025; FINMA, "FINMA Report -Lessons Learned from the CS Crisis" (2023) <https://www.finma.ch/en/news/2023/12/20231219-mm-cs-bericht/> accessed October 29, 2025.

[2] See Chapter 2, Section 5.1. For a broader theoretical framework on bank governance, see Marco Becht, Patrick Bolton and Ailsa Röell, "Why Bank Governance Is Different" (2011) 27 Oxford Review of Economic Policy 437.

This requires stronger supervisory mandates, earlier intervention powers, and greater legal and political clarity about resolution outcomes. As the earlier chapters have shown, debt governance is not a substitute for a strong supervisory and resolution framework—rather, it is their dependent variable.

This chapter proceeds as follows. Section 2 provides a concise narrative of the key events that led to the collapse of SVB and Credit Suisse. Section 3 offers a focused analysis of the governance failures exposed by the crisis, with particular attention to the functioning of loss-absorbing instruments and debt governance. Section 4 distils the key lessons for creditor-based bank governance and connects them back to the broader theoretical framework developed earlier in the book.

2 A Tale of Two Crises

2.1 Silicon Valley Bank

Silicon Valley Bank (SVB) collapsed on 10 March 2023. That was the second largest bank failure in United States history after Lehman Brothers and the largest since the global financial crisis.[3] The collapse unfolded over a matter of days if not hours, but its roots can be traced in underlying fragilities of the SVB business model, especially in structural imbalances and governance weaknesses.[4] SVB's failure triggered a wider loss of confidence in the banking sector, so much so that the federal authorities had to intervene with a de facto industry-wide bailout, launching the Bank Term Funding Program (BTFP), a discount window allowing all banks to post treasuries at the central bank receiving liquidity at par value.[5]

SVB experienced a steep growth in the years preceding its failure, especially at the beginning of the pandemic, fuelled by an influx of

[3] Andrew Metrick, "The Failure of Silicon Valley Bank and the Panic of 2023" (2024) 38 Journal of Economic Perspectives 133, 133.

[4] Ibid. 139.

[5] The programme was established by an administrative decision of the Federal Reserve Bank pursuing the Federal Reserve Bank Act 12 CFR 201.108(b). The programme required the approval of the Department of Treasury given its potential fiscal implications. See Federal Reserve, 'Bank Term Funding Program' (12 March 2023) <https://www.federalreserve.gov/financial-stability/bank-term-funding-program.htm> accessed October 29, 2025.

deposits from venture capital-backed technology firms.[6] By 2021, total assets had reached over $200 billion. However, unlike most banks of comparable size, SVB operated with an unusually low loan-to-deposit ratio and a deposit base that was weakly diversified. A substantial share of these deposits—over 90% by early 2023—were uninsured, and therefore exposed to loss in the event of failure.[7] Depositor concentration and limited retail funding rendered the bank acutely vulnerable to rapid outflows, especially in a digital environment with low transaction friction.

The bank's asset structure further exacerbated its vulnerability. Lacking a traditional bank business model, SVB invested a significant portion of its deposit inflows in US treasury bonds and mortgage-backed securities. As interest rates began to rise sharply in 2022, the market value of these assets declined, creating substantial unrealised losses. From an accounting perspective, these securities were considered in the "held-to-maturity" portfolio; however, the bank remained exposed to a severe duration risk.[8] At the same time, SVB's interest expense remained low, owing to its reliance on uninsured deposits. This extremely fragile construction was able to mask the bank's deterioration which did not appear in the standard regulatory metrics such as capital adequacy and liquidity coverage ratios but only materialised upon the run.[9]

Events escalated in early March 2023, as public information about SVB distress started to leak, fuelled by social media engagement.[10] So much so

[6] See Metrick (no 3) 134. For an analysis of the wider impact of the SVB collapse in the tech industry, especially in the crypto sphere, see Luca Galati and Francesco Capalbo, "Silicon Valley Bank Bankruptcy and Stablecoins Stability" (2024) 91 International Review of Financial Analysis 103,001; Gary B Gorton and Jeffery Y Zhang, "Bank Runs During Crypto Winter" (2024) 14 Harv. Bus. L. Rev. 297.

[7] See Metrick (no 3) 144.

[8] For a structural analysis of the massive exposure of the US banking system to duration risk, see Erica Xuewei Jiang and others, "Monetary Tightening and US Bank Fragility in 2023: Mark-to-Market Losses and Uninsured Depositor Runs?" (2024) 159 Journal of Financial Economics 103899

[9] Francisco Covas, "How Did Regulatory Tailoring Affect SVB's Capital Requirements?" (*Bank Policy Institute*, May 3, 2023) <https://bpi.com/how-did-regulatory-tailoring-affect-svbs-capital-requirements/> accessed October 29, 2025. On the accounting treatment of treasuries, see Joao Granja, "Bank Fragility and Reclassification of Securities into HTM" [2023] University of Chicago, Becker Friedman Institute for Economics Working Paper.

[10] Anthony Cookson and others, "Social Media as a Bank Run Catalyst" [2023] Université Paris-Dauphine Research Paper.

that the scale and speed of the run, concentrated among uninsured depositors with digital banking access and aligned liquidity needs, overwhelmed SVB's liquidity position.[11]

On 10 March, the bank was placed into receivership by the Federal Deposit Insurance Corporation (FDIC).[12] Under US law, if a failed bank is put in receivership depositors with an outstanding claim on the bank above 250.000 $—i.e., the uninsured—may suffer losses, depending on the severity of the distress and on the liability composition. Clearly, that would have been the case for SVB uninsured depositors. However, over the subsequent weekend, SVB depositors pushed for full bailout and, at the same time, the US banking system experienced worrying concerns about potential spillover effects on banks with a funding and asset structure similar to SVB.[13] This led US authorities to invoke the systemic risk exception under the Federal Deposit Insurance Act, allowing the FDIC to guarantee all uninsured deposits.[14] The approval of the Treasury and the Federal Reserve was necessary given the fiscal implications of the measure. When looking at the funding structure of SVB which disproportionately relied on uninsured deposits, this measured can be equated to an almost complete bailout, with extremely limited private sector involvement.

The decision to protect all depositors was framed as necessary to preserve financial stability. However, it also underscored the fragility of the post-crisis resolution framework in the face of concentrated, digitally enabled liquidity risk. The SVB intervention deviated materially from

[11] See Metrick (no 3) 144.

[12] On Friday, 10 March 2023, Silicon Valley Bank, Santa Clara, CA was closed by the California Department of Financial Protection & Innovation and the Federal Deposit Insurance Corporation (FDIC) was named Receiver. The FDIC transferred all the deposits and substantially all of the assets of Silicon Valley Bank to Silicon Valley Bridge Bank, National Association (N.A.), a full-service bank that was operated by the FDIC. See Federal Deposit Insurance Corporation (FDIC), 'Failed Bank Information for Silicon Valley Bank, Santa Clara, CA' (13 March 2023) <https://www.fdic.gov/resources/resolutions/bank-failures/failed-bank-list/silicon-valley.html> accessed October 29, 2025.

[13] See Marco Cipriani, Thomas M Eisenbach and Anna Kovner, "Tracing Bank Runs in Real Time" [2024] FRB of New York Staff Report 7. The authors report that twenty-two banks were effectively run between the announcement of the SVB collapse the introduction of the Bank Term Funding Programme.

[14] Marc Labonte, "Bank Failures: The FDIC's Systemic Risk Exception" (2023) <https://www.congress.gov/crs-product/IF12378> accessed October 29, 2025.

the commitment of private sector involvement in banks' failures, reintroducing a form of (almost) blanket guarantee last seen during the 2008 crisis.[15] This raised immediate questions about the credibility of existing resolution tools and the role of market discipline in a system where loss absorption by private creditors remains almost exclusively theoretical.

2.2 *Credit Suisse*

The collapse of Credit Suisse followed the turmoil generated by the SVB collapse and marked the end of a prolonged period of poor corporate governance, operational mismanagement, numerous scandals, and eroding corporate.[16] By the time market panic materialised, at the beginning of March 2023, the bank was already deeply vulnerable, both in terms of balance sheet structure and institutional credibility.[17]

Although formally well-capitalised, Credit Suisse had consistently failed to translate regulatory ratios into market confidence. Accordingly, FINMA's post-crisis report underscored that the bank's culture and governance had suffered from years of insufficient risk sensitivity, lack of board accountability, and a failure to act decisively on known weaknesses.[18]

After the SVB collapse, unsurprisingly, all the eyes were captured by Credit Suisse, whose share price plummeted. On March 14th, during an interview the chairman of the Saudi National Bank, a major Credit Suisse shareholder, ruled out the possibility of injecting fresh capital into the bank. This reinforced the concerns of investors surrounding the resilience

[15] Key Attributes FSB

[16] See, for instance, Kalyeena Makortoff and David Pegg, 'Crooks, Kleptocrats and Crises: A Timeline of Credit Suisse Scandals' (*The Guardian*, 21 February 2022) <https://www.theguardian.com/news/2022/feb/21/tax-timeline-credit-suisse-scandals> accessed October 29, 2025.

[17] Financial Stability Board, "Key Attributes of Effective Resolution Regimes for Financial Institutions" (2011).

[18] For a wide recollection of the mismanagement instances and scandals of Credit Suisse, see Duncan Mavin, *Meltdown: Greed, Scandal, and the Collapse of Credit Suisse* (Simon and Schuster 2025).

of Credit Suisse.[19] In the attempt to address these concerns, on March 15th the Swiss National Bank (SNB) and the Swiss Financial Market Supervisory Authority (FINMA) issued a joint statement declaring the bank solvent. In addition, the SNB pledged to provide liquidity assistance if necessary.[20] The day after, on March 16th the Swiss Bundesrat issued an emergency decree legitimising the SNB to provide liquidity assistance, as required by the Swiss law.[21] On March 19th, a few hours before the announcement of the merger deal, the Bundesrat amended the previous decree.[22]

As a result of the turmoil, on 19 March 2023, Credit Suisse was acquired by UBS for around 3bn CHF.[23] The deal was facilitated by FINMA, the Swiss supervisory authority for banks and financial markets. Within this construction, 17bn CHF of Contingent Convertible bonds (CoCos) were wiped out. The last-minute amendment previously mentioned legitimised FINMA to write down AT1 instruments in the context of a merger of systemically important banks assisted by a federal guarantee.

[19] Yousef Gamal El-Din and Marion Halftermeyer, 'Credit Suisse Reels After Top Shareholder Rules Out Raising Stake' (*Bloomberg*, 15 March 2023) <https://www.bloomberg.com/news/articles/2023-03-15/credit-suisse-top-shareholder-rules-out-more-assistance-to-bank-lf9gfhbr?in_source=embedded-checkout-banner#xj4y7vzkg> accessed October 29, 2025.

[20] FINMA and Swiss National Bank, 'FINMA and the SNB Issue Statement on Market Uncertainty' (15 March 2023) <https://www.finma.ch/en/news/2023/03/20230315-mm-statement/> accessed October 29, 2025.

[21] Bundesrat, Ordinance on additional liquidity assistance loans and the granting of federal default guarantees for liquidity assistance loans from the Swiss National Bank to systemically important banks, 16 March 2023 <https://www.newsd.admin.ch/newsd/message/attachments/76289.pdf>

[22] Bundesrat, Amendment to Ordinance on Additional Liquidity Assistance Loans and the Granting of Federal Default Guarantees for Liquidity Assistance Loans from the Swiss National Bank to Systemically Important Banks, 19 March 2023, <https://www.newsd.admin.ch/newsd/message/attachments/76290.pdf>

[23] For a discussion of the case, see Edoardo Martino and Tom Vos, 'The Bail-In of Credit Suisse CoCos: Why Principal Write-Down Made Sense' (*The CLS Blue Sky Blog*, 5 December 2023) <https://clsbluesky.law.columbia.edu/2023/05/12/the-bail-in-of-credit-suisse-cocos-why-principal-write-down-made-sense/> accessed October 29, 2025.

The decision raised numerous criticisms and a considerable level of confusion especially among legal scholars.[24]

To understand the relevance of this decision, it important to appreciate its wider context: supporting the merger between Credit Suisse and UBS is not merely a technical decision. Credit Suisse was the second largest Swiss bank and UBS the largest one. The result of the merger is that the Swiss banking market is fully concentrated in one financial conglomerate. This clearly raises concerns related to the competitiveness of the Swiss banking market and in relation to the too-important-to-fail nature of UBS, further reducing the credibility of resolution in case of a crisis.

Some elements that were discussed earlier in this book seem to have played a key role in reaching this decision. First, anecdotal evidence hint that the write-down decision mainly hit foreign sovereign wealth funds and hedge funds.[25] Second, a sizeable share of CoCo bonds were held by Credit Suisse's high-ranked employees, as the bank was paying part of their variable remuneration with AT1 instruments as an incentives compatible form of remuneration.[26]

[24] For an account of all these confusions and misunderstandings, see Javier Paz Valbuena and Horst Eidenmüller, 'Bailout Blues: The Write-Down of the AT1 Bonds in the Credit Suisse Bailout' (2023) 24 European Business Organization Law Review 409. For a deep criticism of this recollection, see Enrico C Perotti, 'The Swiss Authorities Enforced a Legitimate Going Concern Conversion' (*VoxEU*, 22 March 2023) <https://cepr.org/voxeu/columns/swiss-authorities-enforced-legitimate-going-concern-conversion> accessed October 29, 2025; Martino and Vos (n 23).

[25] Eleanor Pringle, 'One of America's Biggest Investment Managers Lost $340 Million in the Surprise Credit Suisse Bond Write-Off' (*Fortune*, 22 March 2023) <https://fortune.com/2023/03/22/pimco-america-investment-manager-lost-340-million-surprise-credit-suisse-bond-write-off/> accessed October 29, 2025. On the crucial role of bail-inable creditors counterparties, see Chapter 6.

[26] Robert Hart, 'Credit Suisse Workers Gear Up To Sue Swiss Regulator Over $400 Million In Lost Bonuses, Report Says' (*Forbes*, 22 May 2023) <https://www.forbes.com/sites/roberthart/2023/05/22/credit-suisse-workers-gear-up-to-sue-swiss-regulator-over-400-million-in-lost-bonuses-report-says/?sh=75d1a9a6e17c> accessed October 29, 2025. On the desirability of paying bank risk takers partly with CoCos, see Chapter 7.

3 Debt Governance in the 2023 Crises

3.1 Silicon Valley Bank

The proximate cause of the SVB collapse was a sudden depositor run; however, the underlying dynamics at play reflect structural weaknesses in the corporate culture, risk management and, ultimately, corporate governance of the bank as well as the ineffectiveness of the regulatory and supervisory architecture for non-globally significant banks in the US. Ultimately, the SVB failure illustrates the fragility of a governance model that relies on shareholders to discipline bank managers or on regulators and supervisory to substitute them, without meaningful involvement of loss-bearing creditors. Relatedly, the episode also raises important questions about the credibility of resolution tools and the continuing presence of implicit guarantees in the financial system, generating a vicious circle between bad governance ex-ante and bailout expectations ex-post. This section analyses the key features of the SVB collapse which related to debt governance.

Corporate Governance Failures

The collapse of SVB represents the archetype of corporate governance failures.[27] The internal governance structure failed to detect or respond to a highly concentrated risk profile, despite the fact that the bank's exposure to long-duration fixed-income securities was well documented in its public filings.[28] Yet the management and board of directors lacked the expertise or the willingness to act promptly.[29] This mismatch between board composition and risk profile translated into an inability to oversee basic asset-liability management functions. The interest rate sensitivity of the bank's portfolio, and the corresponding unrealised losses, were neither adequately hedged nor integrated into forward-looking capital planning.[30] These failures in strategic oversight were exacerbated by

[27] Michael Barr (no 1) 45.

[28] Greg Feldberg, "Lessons from Applying the Liquidity Coverage Ratio to Silicon Valley Bank" (2023) <https://som.yale.edu/story/2023/lessons-applying-liquidity-coverage-ratio-silicon-valley-bank> accessed October 29, 2025.

[29] Michael Barr (no 1) 47.

[30] Greg Feldberg, Carey K Mott and Jill Cetina, "How US Bank Regulation Failed SVB and Its Supervisors" (2025) 7 Journal of Financial Crises 313, 314.

managerial incentives focused on short-term growth, particularly during the low-rate expansion of 2020–2021.[31]

The idea that corporate governance mechanisms do not work properly in banking is not new and is one of the foundational elements of this book.[32] However, failures of this magnitude go beyond what one can reasonably expect and raise questions as to how this could be even possible for a bank with over 200 billion $ of asset under management. An encompassing analysis investigating the roots of such a radical corporate governance failure is beyond the scope of this chapter.[33] In contrast, this analysis focuses only on the lack of alternative discipline mechanisms, which is at the core of the argument of the book.

Creditor Composition—The Wrong Monitor

When contextualising the SVB failure within debt governance, the first aspect to consider is the bank's liability structure.[34] SVB was unusually reliant on large, uninsured corporate deposits, many of which came from venture capital-backed firms with concentrated exposures to the technology sector.[35]

Given such a liability structure, the uninsured depositors should have been the creditors class monitoring SVB risk profile.[36] In principle, these depositors had the necessary level of sophistication to discharge this role but had no incentives to do so. Unsurprisingly, uninsured depositors played no role in disciplining the bank ex-ante, but only "disciplined" the bank too late, when adverse news leaked and they coordinated their withdrawal making the collapse materialise.

[31] Metrick (no 3) 141.

[32] See Becht, Bolton and Röell (no 2) and Chapter 2, Section 2 of this book.

[33] For an analysis of how financial regulation failed to provide regulatory safeguards and governance incentives to prevent the collapse, see Sean Endres, "How Banking Regulation Failed to Stop the Collapse of Silicon Valley Bank" (2024) 50 J. Corp. L. 501.

[34] This line of arguments reflects the seminal contribution by Aghion and Bolton on debt contracts as a tool for contingently allocate control to creditors. See Philippe Aghion and Patrick Bolton, "An Incomplete Contracts Approach to Financial Contracting" (1992) 59 The Review of Economic Studies 473.

[35] Metrick (no 3) 134.

[36] See the analysis on creditors' monitoring and liability composition in Chapter 4, Section 5 of this Book. The analysis applies, mutatis mutandis, to the United States.

This confirms that even sophisticated depositors are poor monitors of bank risk because of the lack of incentives in good time, the coordination problems and herding behaviour in bad times and the expectations to be shielded from losses ex-post.[37] As analytically showed in Chapter 4, even assuming a smooth and credible resolution process, creditors will exert suboptimal effort in monitoring ex-ante. Mutatis mutandis, this applies also in the US context. *A fortiori*, this applies when the class which is supposed to monitor is that of depositors and not of long-term bail-inable creditors.

The SVB case confirms, once again, that placing residual risk in the hands of actors with no incentive to monitor and engage, not only has no positive effects on bank governance, but it even creates negative net effects as it allows shareholders to freely shift the risks of reckless bank activities onto society.

Supervisory Governance Failure

The SVB demise also exposed the limits of supervision as a credible substitute for debt governance. This is dense of relevant implications for the overall framework of this book. The standard argument is that corporate governance mechanisms do not work in banks, for the reasons discussed in Chapter 2. However, supervisors are there to mimic what the corporate governance mechanisms, internal and external, would have achieved if they had worked properly—the so-called "representation hypothesis".[38] This hypothesis is appealing and extremely useful to conceptualise the role of supervisors; however, it rests on unrealistic assumption—for instance, supervisors should be tasked with appropriate powers and should be willing and able to act promptly.[39] This was clearly not the case in the SVB case and, for that matter, in the Credit Suisse case.

According to the Federal Reserve's own review, supervisors had identified material weaknesses in SVB's risk management framework, interest

[37] This confirms the findings of Chapter 4 of this Book. For an early construction claiming that demandable debt could discipline bankers, see Charles W Calomiris and Charles M Kahn, 'The Role of Demandable Debt in Structuring Optimal Banking Arrangements' [1991] The American Economic Review 497.

[38] Dewatripont Mathias and Jean Tirole, *The Prudential Regulation of Banks*, vol 1 (MIT Press 1994).

[39] Edoardo D Martino and Enrico C Perotti, "Containing Runs on Solvent Banks: Prioritizing Recovery over Resolution" (2025) 7 Journal of Financial Crises 1.

rate exposure, and liquidity structure well before the bank's collapse. However, supervisors did not act upon these warnings, so that mismanagement and bad governance continued until it was too late to fix.[40] This inertia and forbearance is not solely the outcome of information gaps between the supervisee and the supervisor. The failure to escalate findings and the absence of timely corrective measures suggest that regulatory governance itself is subject to incentive problems—reluctance to intervene, coordination failures, or political economy constraints.[41]

As broadly discussed in the previous chapters, debt governance and supervision should complement each other and trigger a virtuous circle whereby, on the one hand, the existence of effective debt governance mechanisms eases up the task of the supervisor and, on the other hand, functioning and proactive supervisors makes debt governance engagement consequential. In contrast, the situation with SVB was that of a vicious circle, whereby supervisors were afraid to act fearing the run of uninformed and uninterested short-term creditors.

Predictability of the Resolution Outcomes

One of the central elements of this book is that effective debt governance requires resolution regimes to be predictable. The credibility of resolution and the predictability of its outcome remain the elephant in the room of the SVB collapse and, most likely, the most consequential element for the future of bank crisis management.

After the run, the bank entered receivership, under which uninsured depositors would face losses.[42] However, over the course of a single weekend, Congress voted to activate the systemic risk exception, enabling the FDIC to protect all deposits—insured and uninsured alike.[43] The bailout of all uninsured depositors at SVB effectively mimics a blanket guarantee for large corporate depositors. This outcome reaffirms the persistence of implicit guarantees in banking, notwithstanding more than

40 In its report, the Federal Reserve includes the need to 'change supervisor behavior' among the lessons learnt from the 2023 crises. See Michael Barr (no 1) 95.

41 Natalya Martynova, Enrico Perotti and Javier Suarez, "Capital Forbearance in the Bank Recovery and Resolution Game" (2022) 146 Journal of Financial Economics 884.

42 See Jeremy Kress, "'Least-Cost' Resolution" (2026) Yale Journal on Regulation (forthcoming).

43 Michael Ohlrogge, "Why Have Uninsured Depositors Become De facto Insured?" (2025) 100 NYU Law Review.

a decade of post-crisis reforms. Beyond lobbying efforts from uninsured depositors themselves, the rationale behind this operation was to avoid potential spillovers the U.S. banking system.[44] This is clearly sensible; however, it is also the outcome of extreme forbearance and delayed intervention. Moreover, this decision is likely to have longer-term implications, as large uninsured depositors and bank managers will update their preferences and beliefs based on the decreased likelihood of bearing losses in case of bank collapse.

This completes the vicious circle of bad bank management: (1) internal governance mechanisms do not work because of the possibility to externalise and socialise losses, expecting bailout support from the government; (2) debt governance mechanisms are impaired because creditors, either long-or short-term, expect to be shielded from losses; (3); supervisors do not effectively mimic internal and debt governance mechanisms because acting promptly may trigger adverse market selections, so that the bank deteriorates until the point of non-viability; (4) resolution procedures are not credible and their outcome not predictable because imposing losses on private parties may trigger adverse spillovers; (5) the government is forced to cover losses ex-post through bailouts, reinforcing the bad risk-taking incentives of bank shareholders and management. Therefore, it is fair to say that the post-crisis reforms were not able to break the vicious circle between bailout expectations and excessive risk-taking incentives of bank insiders. Debt governance had no space in these reforms, especially for banks not categorised as globally systemic important banks such as SVB.

3.2 Credit Suisse

The Credit Suisse crisis offers a distinct, but complementary, perspective to that of Silicon Valley Bank on the limitations of the current model of bank (debt) governance. In terms of debt governance, Credit Suisse holds more promises than SVB because of its better-balanced liability side of the balance sheet and the inclusion of high-trigger Additional Tier 1 (AT1) CoCo bonds. However, the way Credit Suisse demise unfolded reveals the fragility of expectations tied to contingent debt instruments because of flows in their legal and contractual design. On the other hand, the case

[44] The prospect was more than likely, given the evidence provided by Cipriani, Eisenbach and Kovner (no 13); Jiang and others (no 8).

exposes how remuneration structures and investor composition affect the disciplining potential of loss-bearing securities, especially when looking at the probability of actually bearing losses. Therefore, the write-down of AT1 CoCos may provide investors, banks and the supervisor the correct signals to trigger a virtuous circle between the credibility of the ex-post loss absorption and the ex-ante governance efforts.

Taken together, these dimensions reaffirm the broader theme of this book: debt governance mechanisms, unless institutionally anchored and predictably enforced, are insufficient to sustain market discipline or substitute for credible supervisory intervention.

The Role of CoCos

CoCos were introduced as part of the post-crisis regulatory reforms aimed at enhancing the loss-absorbing capacity by issuing hybrid instruments acting as pre-committed capital.[45] Their prudential appeal rests on a dual premise: first, markets could price contingent convertibility or write-down features; second, these instruments would absorb losses in going-concern and in a predictable manner. These conditions never properly materialise, and CoCos have not been activated in virtually any going-concern case before Credit Suisse.[46] Even in the Credit Suisse case there were severe enforcement problems that are currently being litigated. Accordingly, the market did not deem going-concern loss absorption as credible and, therefore, the prudential role of CoCos vanished.[47] At least until the Credit Suisse collapse, where CoCos actually absorbed losses in going-concern, albeit at a very late stage when the bank was already in the brink of default.

[45] Mark J Flannery, "Stabilizing Large Financial Institutions with Contingent Capital Certificates" (2016) 6 Quarterly Journal of Finance 1650006

[46] With the notable but also very peculiar exception of Piraeus Bank, whose CoCos were converted into equity in 2020. However, the holder of the converted instrument was part of the Hellenic Financial Stability Fund (HFSF). The fund held the CoCos as an outcome of a public recapitalisation operation carried out in 2015. Therefore, there was no private sector loss allocation in this case. For a detailed analysis, see Edoardo D Martino and Andrea Perini, "Rescued Banks Back to the Market?" (2025) 22 European Company and Financial Law Review 267, 283.

[47] Edoardo David Martino and Tom Vos, "Fixing CoCos in Bank Prudential Regulation-A Life-Cycle Approach" European Business Organization Law Review (forthcoming).

The analysis should therefore focus on the reasons of such a late write-down or, conversely, the reasons that prevented FINMA to act preventively. Two key complementary elements deserve particular attention: the supervisory incentives to forebear and the contractual design of the instruments.

Bank stability is by and large based on the trust that the public has on the bank itself. Signals revealing vulnerabilities may act as a self-fulfilling prophecy, generating runs and value destruction.[48] Supervisory actions imposing losses on a bank clearly provides a public adverse signal about the financial health of the bank. This puts the supervisor in a very uncomfortable and difficult position, as their activity to preserve bank stability may destabilise the bank, triggering a run. This generates incentives for the supervisor to delay action and forebear, to avoid providing adverse signals to the market.[49] Such forbearance is particularly apparent with CoCos and, more generally, early recovery actions.[50] Also in the Credit Suisse case, the decision to impose going-concern losses on AT1 instruments arrived very late, once the bank was extremely close to insolvency, so that the preventive potential of going-concern loss absorption was not exploited.

The incentives to forebear also generate incentives towards strategic contracting, i.e., creating a contractual design that makes it even more difficult for the supervisor to act preventively. In this setting, the issuing bank must include going-concern clauses for loss absorption, either in the form of write-down or conversion to equity, but it can make the enforcement by the supervisory authority particularly difficult.[51]

The AT1 instruments issued by Credit Suisse were structured to allow full and permanent write-down. The prospectuses included two alternative trigger events: first, an accounting trigger generally set at 7% of

[48] Following the famous model by Diamond and Dybvig. See Douglas W Diamond and Philip H Dybvig, "Bank Runs, Deposit Insurance, and Liquidity" (1983) 91 Journal of Political Economy 401.

[49] Martino and Perotti (no 39) 6

[50] For an overview of the problems linked to recovery measures and their triggers, see David Ramos-Muñoz, "'Twilight Troubles'. Early Intervention, Resolution Preparation and Triggers, and the Urgent Need to Reform Them" (2025) 26 European Business Organization Law Review 133

[51] Edoardo D Martino and Tom Vos, "CoCos in Europe: What Is Wrong–and How to Fix It?" (2024) EBI Working Paper Series no. 169, 15.

CET1/RWAs; second, a discretionary trigger—called "Viability Event". This second trigger was eventually activated by FINMA and covers the situation where the regulator deemed the write-down necessary to improve the capital adequacy of Credit Suisse in order to prevent its insolvency, or where extraordinary public support is granted to improve the capital adequacy of Credit Suisse in order to prevent its insolvency.[52] Such a discretionary trigger was part of the prospectus because of Swiss legal requirements for AT1, but it is formulated in an ambiguous and complex manner.[53] So much so, that the Bundesrat felt compelled to clarify the power of FINMA in relation to the write down of CoCos in an amendment in an emergency decree of 19 March 2023, just a few hours before the write down.[54] FINMA announced that its decision to write down the AT1 CoCos of Credit Suisse was based on the powers under the emergency decree.[55]

[52] See, for example: Credit Suisse, 'CHF 200,000,000 3.875 per cent perpetual tier 1 contingent write-down capital notes', <http://www.kcclle.net/document/887190023032 4000000000001> accessed October 29, 2025, p. 10–11. In full, the clause reads: '(a) the Regulator has notified CSG that it has determined that a write-down of the Notes, together with the conversion or write-down/off of holders' claims in respect of any and all other Going Concern Capital Instruments, Tier 1 Instruments and Tier 2 Instruments that, pursuant to their terms or by operation of law, are capable of being converted into equity or written down/off at that time is, because customary measures to improve CSG's capital adequacy are at the time inadequate or unfeasible, an essential requirement to prevent CSG from becoming insolvent, bankrupt, or unable to pay a material part of its debts as they fall due, or from ceasing to carry on its business; or (b) customary measures to improve CSG's capital adequacy being at the time inadequate or unfeasible, CSG has received an irrevocable commitment of extraordinary support from the Public Sector (beyond customary transactions and arrangements in the ordinary course) that has, or imminently will have, the effect of improving CSG's capital adequacy and without which, in the determination of the Regulator, CSG would have become insolvent, bankrupt, unable to pay a material part of its debts as they fall due or unable to carry on its business.'

[53] Martino and Vos (no 51), 20.

[54] Bundesrat, Amendment to Ordinance on Additional Liquidity Assistance Loans and the Granting of Federal Default Guarantees for Liquidity Assistance Loans from the Swiss National Bank to Systemically Important Banks, 19 March 2023, <https://www.newsd.admin.ch/newsd/message/attachments/76290.pdf> accessed October 29, 2025.

[55] FINMA, 'FINMA provides information about the basis for writing down AT1 capital instruments' (23 March 2023) <https://www.finma.ch/en/news/2023/03/20230323-mm-at1-kapitalinstrumente/> accessed October 29, 2025.

Who Holds Bail-Inable Securities

The political and distributional dimensions of the Credit Suisse resolution also deserve attention and are dense of lessons for debt governance in banks. The losses imposed through the AT1 write-down were concentrated among non-Swiss investors, including many based in far east Asia.[56] By contrast, the exposure of Swiss retail clients, depositors, and domestic counterparties was limited to non-existent. While this is perfectly legitimate as the composition of CoCo holders is determined by market forces, the effect was to shield politically salient stakeholders for Swiss authorities and allocate losses externally.

The governance implications of this feature are significant. As in the SVB case, the identity of the loss-bearers matters. In this instance however, what matter is not the sophistication and legal entitlement of the marginal monitor, but rather the political and societal position of creditors who should bear losses in case of a crisis. Not all creditors are created equal in practice, and resolution outcomes reflect institutional preferences.

Remuneration through (Hybrid) Debt

Another overlooked dimension of the Credit Suisse case is the fact that AT1 instruments were not held exclusively by external investors but there was also a significant portion of "inside debt", awarded to risk-taking employees as part of their compensation packages.[57] Therefore, CoCos were, at the same time, a loss-absorbing instrument and debt as a remuneration tool.[58] From a governance perspective, this design may appear

[56] Eleanor Pringle, 'One of America's Biggest Investment Managers Lost $340 Million in the Surprise Credit Suisse Bond Write-Off' (*Fortune*, 22 March 2023) <https://fortune.com/2023/03/22/pimco-america-investment-manager-lost-340-million-surprise-credit-suisse-bond-write-off/> accessed October 29, 2025. On the crucial role of bail-inable creditors counterparties, see Chapter 6 of this Book.

[57] The literature on the agency cost of debt and the role of remuneration through debt is long-lasting even if not widely developed. See Michael C Jensen and William H Meckling, "Theory of the Firm: Managerial Behavior, Agency Costs and Ownership Structure" (1976) 3 Journal of Financial Economics 305, 334; Alex Edmans and Qi Liu, "Inside Debt" (2011) 15 Review of Finance 75.

[58] Robert Hart, 'Credit Suisse Workers Gear Up To Sue Swiss Regulator Over $400 Million In Lost Bonuses, Report Says' (*Forbes*, 22 May 2023) <https://www.forbes.com/sites/roberthart/2023/05/22/credit-suisse-workers-gear-up-to-sue-swiss-regulator-over-400-million-in-lost-bonuses-report-says/?sh=75d1a9a6e17c> accessed October 29, 2025.On the desirability of paying bank risk takers partly with CoCos, see Edoardo D

aligned with the goal of internalising risk: employees who benefit from risk-taking are also exposed to its downside.

Once again, not all creditors are created equal even if they are formally entitled to the same legal treatment. The fact that the losses deriving from bank mismanagement could be partly allocated to the Credit Suisse risk-taker was another aspect making it politically viable to impose going-concern losses on contingent convertibles.

4 Concluding Remarks: Lessons for the Governance–Resolution Nexus

The 2023 failures of Silicon Valley Bank and Credit Suisse offered a unique opportunity to test the analytical framework developed in this book, starting from its very premise: the analytical framework proposed in Chapters 2 and 3. Debt governance in banking is the missing link but cannot work in a vacuum and, more importantly, it cannot be a substitute of public powers and public oversight. On the contrary, it rests on a set of institutional preconditions: the existence and credibility of an effective resolution framework, allocating losses to (long-term) creditors and avoiding bailouts. In turn, an effective resolution framework requires a strong and empowered supervisor who is willing to act preventively. This analysis carried out in this chapter and based on the collapse of SVB and Credit Suisse has shown that debt governance is neither inherently effective nor inherently futile; it is profoundly contingent on institutional design, political economy, and supervisory behaviour.

The SVB case stands as the perfect textbook example of the vicious circle between the resolution framework and (debt) governance, where each institutional weakness reinforced the next. First, the absence of a credible resolution framework—particularly for mid-sized banks under U.S. law—meant that uninsured depositors, rather than long-term debtholders, emerged as the marginal actors in the governance structure. Yet these depositors were poorly equipped to discipline the bank: they lacked both the incentives to monitor asset-liability mismatches or duration risk and the tools to impact bank decision-making. When panic did emerge, it quickly turned into a run dominated by large, uninsured

Martino, 'Fine-Tuning Bank Governance and Resolution: The Case for Remunerating Bankers through Bail-Inable Debt' (2020) 31 European Business Law Review.

accounts. In turn, the supervisory architecture also proved flawed: early warnings were ignored or downplayed, no credible recovery plan was activated, and intervention came only after insolvency was functionally inevitable. The invocation of the systemic risk exception, and the resulting blanket bailout of all depositors, completed the cycle. Far from reinforcing discipline, the episode signalled that political salience—not contractual position—ultimately determines loss absorption in practice.

The Credit Suisse episode offers a more nuanced but equally instructive example. Losses were imposed on holders of contingently convertible instruments which are designed to bear losses in going-concern. However, the activation of the loss absorption mechanism came extremely late, after prolonged value destruction and supervisory inaction. This delay was not merely tactical; it reflected years of supervisory forbearance, hesitation to impose recovery measures, and legal ambiguity surrounding the bank's viability status. As such, CoCos failed to serve their preventive (and governance function). The case also highlights that expectations matter at least as much as written laws. Since the resolution tools had never been tested in Switzerland and CoCos were perceived as quasi-equity instruments, neither market players nor internal stakeholders fully believed that losses would actually be imposed upon a crisis, especially on AT1 instruments. It is precisely this credibility gap—between legal form and external perception—that undermined the potential of debt governance.

Nevertheless, the Credit Suisse episode could also mark the beginning of a reversal in expectations. If AT1 losses are now politically and legally tenable, and if they are activated before the full erosion of value, they might yet form part of a more credible loss-bearing structure. Two contextual features made this outcome a more credible option. First, the geographical composition of bondholders—predominantly foreign institutional investors—muted the domestic political fallout. The absence of Swiss retail investors or pension funds among the losers reduced the pressure for compensation and made the hierarchy of claims more enforceable. Second, the use of debt instruments as remuneration mechanisms for senior staff changed the politics of bail-in. When risk-takers themselves are exposed to losses, the moral hazard critique of creditor bailouts loses force, and loss absorption becomes more defensible. These are not minor contextualities; they are structural enablers that shape the feasibility of debt governance in crisis. However, this expectation reversal was, in turn, reversed back by the recent decision of a Swiss tribunal of first instance that annulled the write-down declaring the emergency decree unlawful.[59]

Taken together, these two cases showcase a set of hard-earned lessons about what, when, and how creditor governance can and cannot deliver.

First, resolution frameworks must be usable and effective, not just available on paper. Legal hurdles and complexities, forbearance incentives, and bureaucratic complexity, or political pressure should not prevent authorities from activating recovery and resolution paths early when banks become distressed.

Second, contractual design making the enforcement of loss absorption events is key. Instruments like CoCos only work when triggers are timely, transparent, and embedded in a credible supervisory logic. Otherwise, they risk becoming deferred equity with no governance bite.

Third, and relatedly, supervisory powers on recovery must be strengthened. As emphasised in earlier chapters, recovery tools offer the best chance to realign managerial behaviour and creditor oversight before irreversible damage occurs and represents the crucial link between (debt) governance in good times and resolution. Yet both cases showed that supervisors either lacked the mandate or the will to act decisively in recovery. This is not a call for more intrusive state intervention per se, but for an institutional environment in which credible pre-resolution action supports the logic of financial stability and minimises the probability of ex-post state intervention ex-post through bailouts. Supervisory inaction erodes the very expectations on which debt governance relies.

Fourth, political economy matters. The identity of creditors—in terms of geography, sophistication, and institutional position—shapes the ability to monitor as well as the acceptability of loss absorption. If a virtuous circle is triggered, one reinforces the other. Where the creditor base is politically salient or deeply embedded in national financial systems, bailouts remain the most likely outcome. Where creditors are external, concentrated, or institutionally distanced from depositors and voters, loss absorption becomes more feasible.

Finally, the broader implication is clear: market discipline cannot be restored only leveraging on market forces. This must be embedded in a

[59] Dave Graham, John Revill and Oliver Hirt, "Swiss Court Rules $20 Billion Credit Suisse Bond Write-off Unlawful" (*Reuters*, October 14, 2025) <https://www.reuters.com/business/finance/swiss-authorities-analyse-court-decision-credit-suisse-bond-write-off-2025-10-14/> accessed October 29, 2025.

wider ecosystem of regulatory credibility, supervisory courage, and resolution realism. The promise of debt governance, as laid out in this book, depends on institutional trust: that losses will be allocated in line with formal rules, that early action will occur when needed, and that creditors will be allowed to perform their disciplining role. Where these conditions are absent, discipline turns to panic, and governance collapses into discretionary rescues.

This final analysis has therefore confirmed, rather than undermined, the theoretical claims advanced in the earlier part of the book. Debt governance is a key missing link towards a safer and more resilient banking system—but only if embedded in a coherent and effective institutional architecture. Creditor expectations must be shaped through repeated and credible signals as well as effective and enforceable contractual design, all paired with decisive supervisory actions and predictable resolution decisions. SVB and Credit Suisse showed what happens when (some of) these conditions fail. They also hinted, however imperfectly, at what might be salvaged. If these crises shift expectations—from guaranteed bailouts to contingent allocation of risk and losses—they may pave the way for a more durable model of bank debt governance.

References

1. Acharya V V, 'A Theory of Systemic Risk and Design of Prudential Bank Regulation' (2009) 5 Journal of financial stability 224
2. Acharya V V, 'Measuring Systemic Risk' (2017) 30 Review of Financial Studies 2
3. Adams RB, 'Governance and the Financial Crisis' (2012) 12 International Review of Finance 7
4. Adams RB and Mehran H, 'Is Corporate Governance Different for Bank Holding Companies?' (2003) 9 Economic Policy Review 123
5. Admati A and Hellwig M, The Bankers' New Clothes: What's Wrong with Banking and What to Do about It (Princeton University Press 2014)
6. Admati A and Hellwig M, The Bankers' New Clothes: What's Wrong with Banking and What to Do about It-New and Expanded Edition (Princeton University Press 2023)
7. Admati AR and others, 'Fallacies, Irrelevant Facts, and Myths in the Discussion of Capital Regulation: Why Bank Equity Is Not Socially Expensive' (2013) 23
8. Aghion P and Bolton P, 'An Incomplete Contracts Approach to Financial Contracting' (1992) 59 The review of economic Studies 473
9. Aikman D, Haldane AG and Nelson BD, 'Curbing the Credit Cycle' (2015) 125 The Economic Journal 1072
10. Alces KA and Galle BD, 'The False Promise of Risk-Reducing Incentive Pay: Evidence from Executive Pensions and Deferred Compensation' (2012) 38 J. Corp. L. 53

E. D. Martino, *EU Bank Governance and Bail-In*, EBI Studies in Banking and Capital Markets Law,
https://doi.org/10.1007/978-3-032-20699-2

11. Alexander K, 'Regulating Bank Governance and the EU Capital Requirements Directive' (2017) 28 European Business Law Review 809
12. Allen F and others, 'Moral Hazard and Government Guarantees in the Banking Industry' (2015) 1 Journal of Financial Regulation 30
13. Allen WA and Wood G, 'Defining and Achieving Financial Stability' (2006) 2 Journal of Financial Stability 152
14. Alvaro S and others, 'The Marketing of MREL Securities after BRRD Interactions between Prudential and Transparency Requirements and the Challenges Which Lie Ahead' (2017) 15 CONSOB Legal Research Papers (Quaderni Giuridici)
15. Angeloni I and others, "Much Money, Little Capital and Few Reforms. The 2023 Banking Turmoil" (2023) <https://cepr.org/publications/books-and-reports/geneva-27-much-money-little-capital-and-few-reforms-2023-banking> accessed October 29, 2025
16. Amihud Y, Garbade K and Kahan M, 'A New Governance Structure for Corporate Bonds' [1999] Stanford Law Review 447
17. Amorello L, 'Europe Goes "Countercyclical": A Legal Assessment of the New Countercyclical Dimension of the CRR/CRD IV Package' (2016) 17 European Business Organization Law Review 137
18. Anantharaman D, Fang VW and Gong G, 'Inside Debt and the Design of Corporate Debt Contracts' (2014) 60 Management Science 1260
19. Anginer D and others, 'Corporate Governance and Bank Insolvency Risk' (2014) 7017
20. Appel IR, Gormley TA and Keim DB, 'Passive Investors, Not Passive Owners' (2016) 121 Journal of Financial Economics 111
21. Armour J, 'The Law and Economics of Corporate Insolvency: A Review' (2001) wp197
22. Armour J, 'Making Bank Resolution Credible', The Oxford Handbook of Financial Regulation (Oxford University Press Oxford, UK 2015)
23. Armour J, 'Bank Governance' (2016) ECGI Law Working Paper 316/2016
24. Armour J, Principles of Financial Regulation (Oxford University Press 2016)
25. Armour J, The Anatomy of Corporate Law: A Comparative and Functional Approach (2017)
26. Armour J and Gordon JN, 'Systemic Harms and Shareholder Value' (2014) 6 Journal of Legal Analysis 35
27. Armour J and Whincop MJ, 'The Proprietary Foundations of Corporate Law' (2007) 27 Oxford Journal of Legal Studies 429
28. Asimakopoulos IG, 'The Veneto Banks Resolution: It Shall Be Called "Liquidation"' (2018) 15 European Company Law 156
29. Asimakopoulos IG and Tröger TH, 'Reform of the CMDI Framework—Driving Off With the Brakes On' (2025) 21 European Company and Financial Law Review 531

30. Avgouleas E and Cullen J, 'Market Discipline and EU Corporate Governance Reform in the Banking Sector: Merits, Fallacies, and Cognitive Boundaries' (2014) 41 Journal of Law and Society 28
31. Avgouleas E and Goodhart C, 'Critical Reflections on Bank Bail-Ins' (2015) 1 Journal of Financial Regulation 3
32. Avgouleas E, Goodhart C and Schoenmaker D, 'Bank Resolution Plans as a Catalyst for Global Financial Reform' (2013) 9 Journal of Financial Stability 210
33. Ayres I and Mitts J, 'Anti-Herding Regulation' (2015) 5 Harv. Bus. L. Rev. 1
34. Badawi AB and de Fontenay E, 'Contractual Complexity in Debt Agreements: The Case of EBITDA' (2019) Duke Law School DP 2019-67
35. Bainsbridge SM, 'In Defence of the Shareholder Wealth Maximization Norm"' (1993) 50 Wash & Lee L Rev 1423
36. Baird DG and Jackson TH, 'Corporate Reorganizations and the Treatment of Diverse Ownership Interests: A Comment on Adequate Protection of Secured Creditors in Bankruptcy' (1984) 51 The University of Chicago Law Review 97
37. Baird DG and Rasmussen RK, 'Private Debt and the Missing Lever of Corporate Governance' [2006] University of Pennsylvania Law Review 1209
38. Bank of Italy, 'Informazione Sui Detentori Di Obbligazioni Subordinate [Information about Subordinated Bond Holders]' (2015) <https://www.bancaditalia.it/media/approfondimenti/2016/obbligazioni-subordinate/index.html>
39. Bank of Italy, 'Financial Stability Report No. 1' (2016) <https://www.bancaditalia.it/media/notizia/financial-stability-report-no-1-2016/>
40. Barca F and Becht M, The Control of Corporate Europe (Oxford University Press 2001)
41. Barr M, "Review of the Federal Reserve's Supervision and Regulation of Silicon Valley Bank" (2023) <https://www.federalreserve.gov/publications/review-of-the-federal-reserves-supervision-and-regulation-of-silicon-valley-bank.htm> accessed October 29, 2025
42. Bates C and Gleeson S, 'Legal Aspects of Bank Bail-Ins' (2011) 5 Law and Financial Markets Review 264
43. Bauerschmidt J, 'Financial Stability as the Objective of the Banking Union' (2020) 17 European Company and Financial Law Review 155
44. Bauman Z and Bordoni C, State of Crisis (John Wiley & Sons 2014)
45. Bauman Z and Lawson N, A Chronicle of Crisis: 2011-2016 (Social Europe Edition 2017)
46. Bavoso V, 'Rethinking Banks and Banking Regulation in the Age of Financial Instability' (2023) 17 Law and Financial Markets Review 306
47. BCBS, 'A New Capital Adequacy Framework' (1999)

48. BCBS, 'Basel III: A Global Regulatory Framework for More Resilient Banks and Banking Systems' (2010)
49. BCBS, 'Principles for Enhancing Corporate Governance' [2010] Basel Committee
50. BCBS, 'Corporate Governance Principles for Banks-Guidelines' (2015)
51. BCBS, 'Standard. TLAC Holdings. Amendments to the Basel III Standard on the Definition Capital' (2016)
52. Bebchuk L and Fried J, Pay without Performance, vol 29 (Cambridge, MA: Harvard University Press 2004)
53. Bebchuk LA, Brav A and Jiang W, 'The Long-Term Effects of Hedge Funds Activism' (2015) 115 Colum. L. Rev. 1085
54. Bebchuk LA, Cohen A and Spamann H, 'The Wages of Failure: Executive Compensation at Bear Stearns and Lehman 2000-2008' (2010) 27 Yale J. on Reg. 257
55. Bebchuk LA, Fried JM and Walker DI, 'Managerial Power and Rent Extraction in the Design of Executive Compensation' (National bureau of economic research 2002)
56. Bebchuk LA and Jackson Jr RJ, 'Executive Pensions' (2005) 30 Journal of Corporation Law 823
57. Bebchuk LA and Spamann H, 'Regulating Bankers' Pay' (2009) 98 Geo. LJ 247
58. Becher DA and Frye MB, 'Does Regulation Substitute or Complement Governance?' (2011) 35 Journal of Banking & Finance 736
59. Becht M and others, 'Returns to Hedge Fund Activism: An International Study' (2017) 30 The Review of Financial Studies 2933
60. Becht M, Bolton P and Röell A, 'Corporate Law and Governance', Handbook of law and economics, vol 2 (Elsevier 2007)
61. Becht M, 'Why Bank Governance Is Different' (2011) 27 Oxford Review of Economic Policy 437
62. Beltratti A and Stulz RM, 'The Credit Crisis around the Globe: Why Did Some Banks Perform Better?' (2012) 105 Journal of Financial Economics 1
63. Bénassy-Quéré A and others, 'Reconciling Risk Sharing with Market Discipline: A Constructive Approach to Euro Area Reform' (2018) 91
64. Berg T and Kaserer C, 'Does Contingent Capital Induce Excessive Risk-Taking?' (2015) 24 Journal of Financial Intermediation 356
65. Berger AN, Imbierowicz B and Rauch C, 'The Roles of Corporate Governance in Bank Failures during the Recent Financial Crisis' (2016) 48 Journal of Money, Credit and Banking 729
66. Berle AA and Means GC, Modern Corporation and Private Property (Transaction Publishers 1932)

67. Bernard B, Capponi A and Stiglitz JE, 'Bail-Ins and Bailouts: Incentives, Connectivity, and Systemic Stability' (2022) 130 Journal of Political Economy 1805
68. Bhagat S and Romano R, 'Reforming Executive Compensation: Focusing and Committing to the Long-Term' (2009) 26 Yale J. on Reg. 359
69. Biljanovska B, 'Aligning Market Discipline and Financial Stability: A More Gradual Shift from Contingent Convertible Capital to Bail-in Measures' (2016) 17 European Business Organization Law Review 105
70. Binder J-H, 'Resolution Planning and Structural Bank Reform within the Banking Union' in Juan Castaneda and others (eds), European Banking Union. Prospects and challenges (Routledge 2015)
71. Binder J-H, 'The Banking Union and the Governance of Credit Institutions: A Legal Perspective' (2015) 16 European Business Organization Law Review 467
72. Binder J-H, 'The Position of Creditors Under the BRRD', Commemorative Volume in memory of Professor Dr. Leonidas Georgakopoulos (Bank of Greece's Center for Culture, Research and Documentation 2016)
73. Binder J-H, 'Cross-Border Coordination of Bank Resolution in the EU: All Problems Resolved?', Research Handbook on Cross-Border Bank Resolution (Edward Elgar Publishing 2019)
74. Binder J-H, 'Proportionality at the Resolution Stage: Calibration of Resolution Measures and the Public Interest Test' [2019] European Business Organization Law Review 1
75. Binder J-H, 'Bank Bail-in and Disputed Claims: Can It Cope? The Case for and against a Vis Attractiva Resolutionis' (2020) 21 Journal of Banking Regulation 54
76. Binder J-H, 'Towards Harmonised Frameworks for the Liquidation of Non-Systemically Relevant Credit Institutions in the EU?' (2021) 18 European Company and Financial Law Review 555
77. Binder J-H, 'Inter-Agency Cooperation Within the SRM: Legal and Operational Challenges for the Cooperation Between Banking Supervision and Resolution Authorities in the EU and With Third-Country Authorities' (2023) 19 European Company and Financial Law Review 900
78. Bliss RR, 'Market Discipline and Subordinated Debt: A Review of Some Salient Issues' (2001) 25 Economic Perspectives 24
79. Bodellini M, 'Greek and Italian "Lessons" on Bank Restructuring: Is Precautionary Recapitalisation the Way Forward?' (2017) 19 Cambridge Yearbook of European Legal Studies 144
80. Bodellini M, 'Corporate Governance of Banks and Financial Stability: Critical Issues and Challenges Ahead' (2018) 39 Business Law Review 160
81. Boermans MA and van Wijnbergen S, 'Contingent Convertible Bonds: Who Invests in European CoCos?' [2017] Applied Economics Letters 1

82. Bolton P, 'Corporate Finance, Incomplete Contracts, and Corporate Control' (2013) 30 The Journal of Law, Economics, & Organization i64
83. Bolton P and Jeanne O, 'Structuring and Restructuring Sovereign Debt: The Role of a Bankruptcy Regime' (2007) 115 Journal of Political Economy 901
84. Bolton P, Mehran H and Shapiro J, 'Executive Compensation and Risk-taking' (2015) 19 Review of Finance 2139
85. Bolton P and Samama F, 'Capital Access Bonds: Contingent Capital with an Option to Convert' (2012) 27 Economic Policy 275
86. Borio C, 'The Financial Cycle and Macroeconomics: What Have We Learnt?' (2014) 45 Journal of Banking & Finance 182
87. Bradley M and Roberts MR, 'The Structure and Pricing of Corporate Debt Covenants' (2015) 5 The Quarterly Journal of Finance 1550001
88. Brierley PG, 'Ending Too-Big-To-Fail: Progress Since the Crisis, the Importance of Loss-Absorbing Capacity and the UK Approach to Resolution' (2017) 18 European Business Organization Law Review 457
89. Brummer C, Soft Law and the Global Financial System: Rule Making in the 21st Century (Cambridge University Press 2015)
90. Brunnermeier MK, 'Deciphering the Liquidity and Credit Crunch 2007-2008' (2009) 23 Journal of Economic perspectives 77
91. Brunnermeier MK and others, The Fundamental Principles of Financial Regulation, vol 11 (ICMB, Internat Center for Monetary and Banking Studies 2009)
92. Brunnermeier MK and Pedersen LH, 'Market Liquidity and Funding Liquidity' (2009) 22 Review of Financial studies 2201
93. Busch D and Ferrarini G, The European Banking Union (Oxford: Oxford University Press 2020)
94. Cabral R, 'The Banking Union's Resolution or Liquidation Approach' [2024] Journal of Banking Regulation
95. Cadbury A, The Financial Aspects of Corporate Governance-Report with Code of Best [Cadbury Report] (Gee Publishing 1992)
96. Calabresi G and Melamed AD, 'Property Rules, Liability Rules, and Inalienability: One View of the Cathedral' [1972] Harvard law review 1089
97. Calello P and Ervin W, 'From Bailout to Bail-In' 30 The Economist (2010)
98. Calomiris CW, 'Blueprints for a New Global Financial Architecture' in Leonardo Auernheimer (ed), International Financial Markets: The Challenge of Globalization (The University of Chicago Press 1998)
99. Calomiris CW, 'Financial Innovation, Regulation, and Reform' in Michael Spence and Danny M Leipziger (eds), Globalization and Growth: Implications for a Post-Crisis World (World Bank Publications 2011)

100. Calomiris CW and Kahn CM, 'The Role of Demandable Debt in Structuring Optimal Banking Arrangements' [1991] The American Economic Review 497
101. Carmassi J and others, 'Completing the Banking Union with a European Deposit Insurance Scheme: Who Is Afraid of Cross-Subsidisation?' (2018) 208
102. Cartas J and He Q, 'Issuance and Holdings of Securities in a "From-Whom-to-Whom" Framework', Handbook on Securities Statistics (International Monetary Fund)
103. Chava S and Roberts MR, 'How Does Financing Impact Investment? The Role of Debt Covenants' (2008) 63 The Journal of Finance 2085
104. Chiu IHY, 'Corporate Governance: The Missing Paradigm in the Mandatory Bail-in Regime for Creditors of Banks and Financial Institutions' [2014] Journal of business law 611
105. Cihak M and Nier E, 'The Need for Special Resolution Regimes for Financial Institutions-The Case of the European Union' [2012] Harv. Bus. L. Rev 395
106. Cipriani M, Eisenbach TM and Kovner A, "Tracing Bank Runs in Real Time" [2024] FRB of New York Staff Report
107. Coase RH, 'The Problem of Social Cost' (1960) 3 ournal of Law and Economics 1
108. Coffee Jr JC, 'Systemic Risk after Dodd-Frank: Contingent Capital and the Need for Regulatory Strategies beyond Oversight' (2011) 111 Colum. L. Rev. 795
109. Coffee Jr JC and Palia D, 'The Wolf at the Door: The Impact of Hedge Fund Activism on Corporate Governance' (2016) 1 Annals of Corporate Governance 1
110. Commission E, 'Corporate Governance in Financial Institutions and Remuneration Policies'
111. Conlon T and Cotter J, 'Anatomy of a Bail-In' (2014) 15 Journal of Financial Stability 257
112. Cookson JA and others, "Social Media as a Bank Run Catalyst" [2023] Université Paris-Dauphine Research Paper
113. Cornelli F and Felli L, 'Ex-Ante Efficiency of Bankruptcy Procedures' (1997) 41 European Economic Review 475
114. Covas F, "How Did Regulatory Tailoring Affect SVB's Capital Requirements?" (*Bank Policy Institute*, May 3, 2023) <https://bpi.com/how-did-regulatory-tailoring-affect-svbs-capital-requirements/> accessed October 29, 2025
115. Crespi F, Giacomini E and Mascia D V, 'Bail-in Rules and the Pricing of Italian Bank Bonds' (2018) 25 European Financial Management 1321

116. Crockett A, 'Market Discipline and Financial Stability' (2002) 26 Journal of Banking & Finance 977
117. Cutura JA, 'Debt Holder Monitoring and Implicit Guarantees: Did the BRRD Improve Market Discipline?' (SAFE 2018) 232
118. Cutura J and Hesse H, 'Incentive Effects from Write-down CoCo Bonds: An Empirical Analysis' (2022) 8 Journal of Financial Regulation 162
119. D'Hulster K and Ötker-Robe I, 'Ring-Fencing Cross-Border Banks: An Effective Supervisory Response?' (2015) 16 Journal of Banking Regulation 169
120. Dari-Mattiacci G and others, 'The Emergence of the Corporate Form' (2017) 33 The Journal of Law, Economics, and Organization 193
121. Davies G and Dobler M, 'Bank Resolution and Safeguarding the Creditors Left Behind' (2011) 51 Bank of England. Quarterly Bulletin 213
122. Davies P and Hopt KJ, 'Non-Shareholder Voice in Bank Governance: Board Composition, Performance and Liability' (2018) 413
123. De Bandt O and Hartmann P, 'Systemic Risk: A Survey' (ECB working paper 2000) 35
124. De Bruyckere V and others, 'Bank/Sovereign Risk Spillovers in the European Debt Crisis' (2013) 37 Journal of Banking & Finance 4793
125. de Groen WP, 'Financing Bank Resolution: An Alternative Solution for Arranging the Liquidity Required' (2018) PE 624.423
126. De Larosière J and others, 'Report of the High-Level Group on Financial Supervision in the EU' [2009] European Commission. Brussels
127. de Serière VPG, 'No Creditor Worse Off in Case of Bank Resolution. Food for Litigation' (2016) 31 Journal of International Banking Law and Regulation 376
128. de Weijs R, 'Too Big to Fail as a Game of Chicken with the State: What Insolvency Law Theory Has to Say about TBTF and Vice Versa' (2013) 14 European Business Organization Law Review 201
129. Dell'Ariccia MG and others, Trade-Offs in Bank Resolution (International Monetary Fund 2018)
130. Demsetz H, 'Toward a Theory of Property Rights' (1974) 57 The American Economic Review 347
131. Devriese J and others, 'Corporate Governance, Regulation and Supervision of Banks' (2004) 2 Financial Stability Review 95
132. Dewatripont M, 'European Banking: Bailout, Bail-in and State Aid Control' (2014) 34 International journal of industrial organization 37
133. Dewatripont M and Tirole J, The Prudential Regulation of Banks, vol 1 (MIT Press 1994)
134. Diamond DW, 'Financial Intermediation and Delegated Monitoring' (1984) 51 The review of economic studies 393

135. Diamond DW and Dybvig PH, 'Bank Runs, Deposit Insurance, and Liquidity' (1983) 91 Journal of political economy 401
136. Diamond DW and Rajan RG, 'A Theory of Bank Capital' (2000) 55 The Journal of Finance 2431
137. Dias CS and Deslandes JJ, 'Recent Measures for Banca Carige from a BRRD and State Aid Perspective' (2019) PE 624.413
138. Duffie D and others, 'Financial Regulatory Reform after the Crisis: An Assessment' (2018) 64 Management Science 4835
139. Easterbrook FH, 'Derivative Securities and Corporate Governance' [2002] The University of Chicago Law Review 733
140. Easterbrook FH and Fischel DR, The Economic Structure of Corporate Law (Harvard University Press 1996)
141. EBA, 'Guidelines on the Interpretation of the Different Circumstances When an Institution Shall Be Considered as Failing or Likely to Fail under Article 32(6) of Directive 2014/59/EU. EBA/GL/2015/07' (2015)
142. ECB, 'Who Holds What? Nwe Information on Securities Holdings' [2015] ECB Economic Bullettin 72
143. ECB, 'Financial Stability Review-November 2016' (2016)
144. Edmans A and Liu Q, 'Inside Debt' (2011) 15 Review of finance 75
145. Eisenbach TM, 'Rollover Risk as Market Discipline: A Two-Sided Inefficiency' (2017) 126 Journal of Financial Economics 252
146. Ellingsæter SS, 'Could It Happen in the EU? An Analysis of Loss Distribution between Shareholders and AT1 Bondholders under EU Law' (2024) 10 Journal of Financial Regulation 194
147. Endres S, "How Banking Regulation Failed to Stop the Collapse of Silicon Valley Bank" (2024) 50 J. Corp. L. 501
148. Enoch C and others, From Fragmentation to Financial Integration in Europe (International Monetary Fund 2013)
149. Enriques L, Romano A and Wetzer T, 'Network-Sensitive Financial Regulation' [2019] The Journal of Corporation Law (forthcoming)
150. Enriques L and Zetzsche D, 'Quack Corporate Governance, Round III? Bank Board Regulation Under the New European Capital Requirement Directive' (2015) 16 Theoretical Inquiries in Law 211
151. Erkens DH, Hung M and Matos P, 'Corporate Governance in the 2007--2008 Financial Crisis: Evidence from Financial Institutions Worldwide' (2012) 18 Journal of Corporate Finance 389
152. European Banking Authority, 'Final Report on MREL-Report on the Implementation and Design of the MREL Framework-EBA-Op-2016-21' (2016)
153. Fahlenbrach R and Stulz RM, 'Bank CEO Incentives and the Credit Crisis' (2011) 99 Journal of Financial Economics 11

154. Fama EF, ‘Efficient Capital Markets: A Review of Theory and Empirical Work’ (1970) 25 The journal of Finance 383
155. Farhi E and Tirole J, ‘Collective Moral Hazard, Maturity Mismatch, and Systemic Bailouts’ (2012) 102 American Economic Review 60
156. Feldberg G, “Lessons from Applying the Liquidity Coverage Ratio to Silicon Valley Bank” (2023) <https://som.yale.edu/story/2023/lessons-applying-liquidity-coverage-ratio-silicon-valley-bank> accessed October 29, 2025
157. Feldberg G, Mott CK and Cetina J, “How US Bank Regulation Failed SVB and Its Supervisors” (2025) 7 Journal of Financial Crises 313
158. Fernández Acín I, ‘Caso Banco Popular (Banco Popular Case)’ (2018) <https://papers.ssrn.com/sol3/papers.cfm?abstract_id=3132293>
159. Ferran E, ‘New Regulation of Remuneration in the Financial Sector in the EU’ (2012) 9 European Company and Financial Law Review 1
160. Ferrarini G, ‘One Share–One Vote: A European Rule?’ (2006) 3 European Company and Financial Law Review 147
161. Ferrarini G, ‘CRD IV and the Mandatory Structure of Bankers’ Pay’ (2015) ECGI-Law Working Paper 289
162. Ferrarini G, ‘Single Supervision and the Governance of Banking Markets: Will the SSM Deliver the Expected Benefits?’ (2015) 16 European Business Organization Law Review 513
163. Ferrarini G, ‘Understanding the Role of Corporate Governance in Financial Institutions: A Research Agenda’ (2017) ECGI Law Working Paper Series 347/2017
164. Ferrarini G and Ungureanu MC, ‘Economics, Politics, and the International Principles for Sound Compensation Practices: An Analysis of Executive Pay at European Banks’ (2011) 64 Vand. L. Rev. 429
165. Ferrarini G, ‘Executive Remuneration. A Comparative Overview’ in Wolf-Georg Ringe and Jeffrey N Gordon (eds), Oxford Handbook of Corporate Law and Governance (Oxford University Press Oxford, UK 2018)
166. Financial Stability Board, ‘Principles for Sound Compensation Practices’ (2009)
167. Financial Stability Board, ‘Key Attributes of Effective Resolution Regimes for Financial Institutions’ (2011)
168. Financial Stability Board, ‘Principles on Loss-Absorbing and Recapitalisation Capacity of G-SIBs in Resolution - Total Loss Absorbency Capacity’ (2011)
169. FINMA, “FINMA Report - Lessons Learned from the CS Crisis” (2023) <https://www.finma.ch/en/news/2023/12/20231219-mm-cs-bericht/> accessed October 29, 2025
170. Fiordiponti F, ‘Le Aspettative Restitutorie Di Azionisti e Creditori Ai Tempi Del Bail-In’ (2016) 15 Analisi Giuridica dell’Economia 527

171. Flannery MJ, 'Debt Maturity and the Deadweight Cost of Leverage: Optimally Financing Banking Firms' (1994) 84 The American Economic Review 320
172. Flannery MJ, 'The Faces of "Market Discipline"' (2001) 20 Journal of Financial Services Research 107
173. Flannery MJ, 'No Pain, No Gain. Effecting Market Discipline via Reverse Convertible Debentures' [2005] Capital Adequacy Beyond Basel: Banking, Securities, and Insurance 171
174. Flannery MJ, 'Contingent Capital Instruments for Large Financial Institutions: A Review of the Literature' (2014) 6 Annu. Rev. Financ. Econ. 225
175. Flannery MJ, 'Stabilizing Large Financial Institutions with Contingent Capital Certificates' (2016) 6 Quarterly Journal of Finance 1650006
176. Flannery MJ and Bliss RR, 'Market Discipline in Regulation: Pre-and Post-Crisis' in Allen N Berger, Philip Molyneux and John OS Wilson (eds), Oxford Handbook of Banking (3rd edn, Oxford Handbook of Banking (3rd edition), Oxford University Press, forthcoming 2018)
177. Fleming MJ, Sarkar A and others, 'The Failure Resolution of Lehman Brothers' [2013] Economic Policy Review 175
178. Frankel T, 'Fiduciary Duties', The new Palgrave dictionary of economics and the law (McMillan, London 1998) 127
179. Freeman RE, 'A Stakeholder Theory of the Modern Corporation' (2001) 3 Perspectives in Business Ethics 144
180. Freixas X, Parigi BM and Rochet J-C, 'Systemic Risk, Interbank Relations, and Liquidity Provision by the Central Bank' [2000] Journal of money, credit and banking 611
181. Friedman M, 'The Social Responsibility of Business Is to Increase Its Profits' N.Y. Times (13 September 1970)
182. Galati L and Capalbo F, "Silicon Valley Bank Bankruptcy and Stablecoins Stability" (2024) 91 International Review of Financial Analysis 103001
183. Gardella A, 'Bail-in and the Financing of Resolution within the SRM Framework' in Guido Ferrarini and Danny Busch (eds), European Banking Union (Oxford University Press Oxford, UK 2015)
184. Gelter M, 'Why Do Shareholder Derivative Suits Remain Rare in Continental Europe' (2011) 37 Brook. J. Int'l L. 843
185. Gertner R and Scharfstein D, 'A Theory of Workouts and the Effects of Reorganization Law' (1991) 46 The Journal of Finance 1189
186. Gillan SL and Starks LT, 'The Evolution of Shareholder Activism in the United States' (2007) 19 Journal of Applied Corporate Finance 55
187. Glasserman P and Perotti E, 'The Unconvertible CoCo Bonds' in Douglas D Evanoff and others (eds), Achieving Financial Stability: Challenges to Prudential Regulation, vol 61 (World Scientific 2017)

188. Goodhart C and Avgouleas E, 'A Critical Evaluation of Bail-in as a Bank Recapitalisation Mechanism' in Franklin Allen, Elena Carletti and Joanna E Gray (eds), Bearing the Losses from Bank and Sovereign Default in the Eurozone (FIC Press 2014)
189. Gordon JN, 'Say on Pay: Cautionary Notes on the UK Experience and the Case for Shareholder Opt-In' (2009) 46 Harv. J. on Legis. 323
190. Gordon JN, 'Executive Compensation and Corporate Governance in Financial Firms: The Case for Convertible Equity-Based Pay' [2010] Columbia Law and Economics Working Paper
191. Gordon JN and Gandia CM, 'Money Market Funds Run Risk: Will Floating Net Asset Value Fix the Problem' [2014] Colum. Bus. L. Rev. 313
192. Gordon JN and Ringe W-G, 'Bank Resolution in Europe: The Unfinished Agenda of Structural Reform' in Guido Ferrarini and Danny Busch (eds), European Banking Union (Oxford University Press Oxford, UK 2015)
193. Gordon JN, 'Bank Resolution in the European Banking Union: A Transatlantic Perspective on What It Would Take' (2015) 115 Colum. L. Rev. 1297
194. Gormley TA, Johnson S and Rhee C, 'Ending "Too Big to Fail": Government Promises versus Investor Perceptions' (2014) 19 Review of Finance 491
195. Gorton G and Metrick A, 'Securitized Banking and the Run on Repo' (2012) 104 Journal of Financial economics 425
196. Gorton GB and Zhang JY, "Bank Runs During Crypto Winter" (2024) 14 Harv. Bus. L. Rev. 297
197. Gortsos C V, 'The Role of the European Banking Authority (EBA) after the Establishment of the Single Supervisory Mechanism (SSM)', Regulating and Supervising European Financial Markets (Springer 2016)
198. Gortsos C V, 'The European Deposit Insurance Scheme', Research Handbook on EU Economic Law (Edward Elgar Publishing 2019)
199. Gortsos C V, 'The Bank Recovery and Resolution Directive (BRRD): Evolution Within the System of EU Banking Law over the Period 2014-2024' (2025) 26 European Business Organization Law Review 5
200. Götz M, Krahnen JP and Tröger T, 'Taking Bail-in Seriously: The Looming Risks for Banking Policy in the Rescue of Monte Paschi Di Siena' (SAFE Policy Letter 2017)
201. Götz MR and Tröger T, 'Should the Marketing of Subordinated Debt Be Restricted/Different in One Way or the Other? What to Do in the Case of Mis-Selling?' (2016)
202. Graham D, Revill J and Hirt O, "Swiss Court Rules $20 Billion Credit Suisse Bond Write-off Unlawful" (*Reuters*, October 14, 2025) <https://www.reuters.com/business/finance/swiss-authorities-analyse-court-decision-credit-suisse-bond-write-off-2025-10-14/> accessed October 29, 2025

203. Granja J, "Bank Fragility and Reclassification of Securities into HTM" [2023] University of Chicago, Becker Friedman Institute for Economics Working Paper
204. Grinderslev OJ and Kristiansen KL, 'The Information Content in Contingent Convertible Bond Prices' (Danmarks Nationalbank Working Papers 2017)
205. Gropp R, Gruendl C and Guettler A, 'The Impact of Public Guarantees on Bank Risk-Taking: Evidence from a Natural Experiment' (2014) 18 Review of Finance 457
206. Gros D, 'Completing the Banking Union: Deposit Insurance' (2015) 335
207. Gros D and Schoenmaker D, 'European Deposit Insurance and Resolution in the Banking Union' (2014) 52 JCMS: Journal of Common Market Studies 529
208. Grossman S, 'On the Efficiency of Competitive Stock Markets Where Trades Have Diverse Information' (1976) 31 The Journal of finance 573
209. Grossman SJ and Hart OD, 'The Costs and Benefits of Ownership: A Theory of Vertical and Lateral Integration' (1986) 94 Journal of political economy 691
210. Grundmann S, 'The Banking Union Translated into (Private Law) Duties: Infrastructure and Rulebook' (2015) 16 European Business Organization Law Review 357
211. Hadjiemmanuil C, 'Bank Stakeholders' Mandatory Contribution to Resolution Financing: Principle and Ambiguities of Bail-In', ECB Legal Conference 2015–From Monetary Union to Banking Union, on the way to Capital Markets Union (2015)
212. Hadjiemmanuil C, 'The Banking Union and Its Implications for Private Law: A Comment' (2015) 16 European Business Organization Law Review 383
213. Hadjiemmanuil C, 'Limits on State-Funded Bailouts in the EU Bank Resolution Regime' [2016] European Economy 91
214. Hadjiemmanuil C, 'Monte Dei Paschi: A Test for the European Policy Against Bank Bailouts' (2017) Oxford Business Law Blog <https://www.law.ox.ac.uk/business-law-blog/blog/2017/05/monte-dei-paschi-test-european-policy-against-bank-bailouts>
215. Hadjiemmanuil C, 'Bail-in's Unfulfilled Promise' (2025) 26 European Business Organization Law Review 89
216. Hansmann H, 'Ownership of the Firm' (1988) 4 Journal of Law, Economics, & Organization 267
217. Hansmann H and Kraakman R, 'The End of History for Corporate Law' (2000) 89 Geo. LJ 439
218. Harner MM, 'The Corporate Governance and Public Policy Implications of Activist Distressed Debt Investing' (2008) 77 Fordham L. Rev. 703

219. Hart O and Zingales L, 'Companies Should Maximize Shareholder Welfare Not Market Value' (2017) 2 Journal of Law, Finance, and Accounting 247
220. Hau H, Radach T-O and Thum M, 'Insufficient Supervisory Board Competence as a Risk Factor for Banks' VoxEU Column (10 June 2024) <https://cepr.org/voxeu/columns/insufficient-supervisory-board-competence-risk-factor-banks> accessed 19 June 2025
221. Hellwig MF, 'On the Aggregation of Information in Competitive Markets' (1980) 22 Journal of economic theory 477
222. Hellwig MF, 'Valuation Reports in the Context of Banking Resolution: What Are the Challenges?' (2018) 2018/06
223. Heremans D and Bosquet K, 'The Future of Law and Finance after the Financial Crisis: New Perspectives on Regulation and Corporate Governance for Banks' [2011] U. Ill. L. Rev. 1551
224. Hill CA and Pacces AM, 'The Neglected Role of Justification under Uncertainty in Corporate Governance and Finance' (2018) 3 Annals of Corporate Governance 276
225. Hill J, 'Regulating Executive Remuneration after the Global Financial Crisis: Common Law Perspectives' [2012] Research Handbook on Executive Pay 219
226. Hirschman AO, Exit, Voice, and Loyalty: Responses to Decline in Firms, Organizations, and States, vol 25 (Harvard University Press 1970)
227. Ho JKS, 'Removing Bankers' Bonus Cap: Will This Enhance the Competitiveness of the UK Financial Market?' (2023) 18 Capital Markets Law Journal 556
228. Hockett R, 'Are Bank Fiduciaries Special' (2016) 68 Ala. L. Rev. 1071
229. Hofmann C, 'The Role of Deposit Insurance in Bank Resolution' (2020) 6 Journal of Financial Regulation 148
230. Holmstrom B, 'Understanding the Role of Debt in the Financial System' (2015) No. 479
231. Holmström B and Tirole J, 'Market Liquidity and Performance Monitoring' (1993) 101 Journal of Political Economy 678
232. Hopt KJ, 'Corporate Governance of Banks and Other Financial Institutions after the Financial Crisis' (2013) 13 Journal of Corporate Law Studies 219
233. Hopt KJ, 'Corporate Governance of Banks and Financial Institutions: Economic Theory, Supervisory Practice, Evidence and Policy' (2021) 22 European Business Organization Law Review 13
234. Huertas T, 'The Case for Bail-Ins' in Patrick S Kenadjian (ed), The Bank Recovery and Resolution Directive: Europe's Solution for" Too Big To Fail"?, vol 13 (Walter de Gruyter 2013)
235. Huertas T, 'European Bank Resolution: Making It Work!' (2016)

236. Huertas T and Nieto MJ, 'A Game Changer: The EU Banking Recovery and Resolution Directive', vol 19 (2013) <https://voxeu.org/article/banking-recovery-and-resolution-directive>
237. Hüpkes EHG, 'Insolvency-Why a Special Regime for Banks?', Current developments in monetary and financial law, Vol. 3 (International Monetary Fund 2002)
238. Hüser A-C, 'Too Interconnected to Fail: A Survey of the Interbank Networks Literature' (SAFE 2016) 91
239. Hüser A-C, 'The Systemic Implications of Bail-in: A Multi-Layered Network Approach' [2017] Journal of Financial Stability
240. Jackson P and others, 'Capital Requirements and Bank Behaviour: The Impact of the Basel Accord' (1999) 1
241. Jacobs G and Mitchell D, 'The No-Creditor-Worse-Off Principle from a Valuation Perspective: Standing in the Shoes of a Hypothetical Liquidator' (2014) 28 Journal of International Banking and Financial Law 233
242. Jansen D-J, Mosch RHJ and van der Cruijsen CAB, 'When Does the General Public Lose Trust in Banks?' (2015) 48 Journal of Financial Services Research 127
243. Janssen L, 'Bail-In from an Insolvency Law Perspective' (2017) 26 Norton Journal of Bankruptcy Law and Practice
244. Jensen MC and Meckling WH, 'Theory of the Firm: Managerial Behavior, Agency Costs and Ownership Structure' (1976) 3 Journal of financial economics 305
245. Jensen MC and Murphy KJ, 'Performance Pay and Top-Management Incentives' (1990) 98 Journal of political economy 225
246. Jensen MC, 'Remuneration: Where We've Been, How We Got to Here, What Are the Problems, and How to Fix Them' (2004) ECGI Finance Working Paper N°. 44/2004
247. Jiang EX and others, 'Monetary Tightening and U.S. Bank Fragility in 2023: Mark-to-Market Losses and Uninsured Depositor Runs?' (2024) 159 Journal of Financial Economics 103899
248. Joosen BPM, 'Bail in Mechanisms in the Bank Recovery and Resolution Directive', Annual Conference of the Netherlands Association for Comparative and International Law (2014)
249. Juks R, 'Asset Encumbrance and Its Relevance for Financial Stability' (2012) 3 Sveriges Riksbank Economic Review 67
250. Junge G and Kugler P, 'Quantifying the Impact of Higher Capital Requirements on the Swiss Economy' (2013) 149 Swiss Journal of Economics and Statistics 313
251. Kahn CM and Santos JAC, 'Allocating Bank Regulatory Powers: Lender of Last Resort, Deposit Insurance and Supervision' (2005) 49 European Economic Review 2107

252. Kashkari N, 'Lessons from the Crisis: Ending Too Big to Fail', vol 16 (2016)
253. Kirkpatrick G, 'The Corporate Governance Lessons from the Financial Crisis' (2009) 2009 OECD Journal: Financial Market Trends 61
254. Knight FH, Risk, Uncertainty and Profit (Harper & Row 1921)
255. Kokkinis A, 'Exploring the Effects of the 'Bonus Cap'Rule: The Impact of Remuneration Structure on Risk-Taking by Bank Managers' (2019) 19 Journal of Corporate Law Studies 167
256. Kokorin I, 'The Rise of "Group Solution" in Insolvency Law and Bank Resolution' (2021) 22 European Business Organization Law Review 781
257. Kornai J, 'Hardening the Budget Constraint: The Experience of the Post-Socialist Countries' (2001) 45 European Economic Review 1573
258. Krahnen JP and Moretti L, 'Bail-in Clauses' [2015] Financial Regulation. Cambridge University Press, Cambridge
259. Kress J, "'Least-Cost' Resolution" (2026) Forthcoming Yale Journal on Regulation
260. Kunde A, 'Legal Constraints on Resolution Measures and the Application of the Bail-in Tool under BRRD and SRMR', ECB Legal Conference 2015–From Monetary Union to Banking Union, on the way to Capital Markets Union (2015)
261. Kwast ML and others, 'Using Subordinated Debt as an Instrument of Market Discipline' (1999) 172 Report of a Study Group on Subordinated Notes and Debentures, M. Kwast, Chair. Board of Governors of the Federal Reserve System, Staff Study
262. La Porta R and others, 'Investor Protection and Corporate Governance' (2000) 58 Journal of financial economics 3
263. Laaper P and Busch D, 'How to Behave Like a Good Banker?' (2022) 18 European Company and Financial Law Review 899
264. Labonte M, "Bank Failures: The FDIC's Systemic Risk Exception" (2023) <https://www.congress.gov/crs-product/IF12378> accessed October 29, 2025
265. Laeven L and Levine R, 'Bank Governance, Regulation and Risk-taking' (2009) 93 Journal of Financial Economics 259
266. Laeven L, Ratnovski L and Tong H, 'Bank Size, Capital, and Systemic Risk: Some International Evidence' (2016) 69 Journal of Banking & Finance S25
267. Lamandini M and Ramos Muñoz D, 'Bank Resolution and Judicial Review: Lessons of the Banco Popular Litigation' (2025) 26 European Business Organization Law Review 47
268. Lane TD, 'Market Discipline' (1993) 40 IMF Staff Papers 53
269. Langford RT and Ramsay I, 'The Contours and Content of the "Creditors" Interests Duty" (2021) 21 Journal of Corporate Law Studies 85

270. Lannoo K, 'Uneven Progress in Implementing Cross-Border Bank Resolution in the EU' (2017) No 2017-26
271. Larcker DF, Ormazabal G and Taylor DJ, 'The Market Reaction to Corporate Governance Regulation' (2011) 101 Journal of Financial Economics 431
272. Lee A, 'TLAC Conundrums' (2015) 34 Int'l Fin. L. Rev. 17
273. Lee IB, 'The Role of the Public Interest in Corporate Law' in Claire A Hill and Brett H McDonnell (eds), Research Handbook on the Economics of Corporate Law (Edward Elgar Publishing 2012)
274. Lehmann M, 'Bail-in and Private International Law: How to Make Bank Resolution Measures Effective across Borders' (2017) 66 International & Comparative Law Quarterly 107
275. Lefeuvre E, 'The Strategic Importance of Public Recapitalisation in Banking Resolution, What Ireland Can Tell' (2024) 21 European Company and Financial Law Review 104
276. Lendermann UB, 'Automated Bail-in: Eliminating Regulatory Restraints' [2025] Journal of Banking Regulation
277. Lener R, 'Profili Problematici Delle Nuove Regole Europee Sulla Gestione Delle Crisi Bancarie' (2018) 37 Banca Impresa Società 13
278. Levratto N, 'From Failure to Corporate Bankruptcy: A Review' (2013) 2 Journal of Innovation and Entrepreneurship 20
279. Li DD and Li S, 'An Agency Theory of the Bankruptcy Law' (1999) 8 International Review of Economics & Finance 1
280. Liikanen E, 'High-Level Expert Group on Reforming the Structure of the EU Banking Sector' (2012) 2 Final Report, Brussels
281. Listokin Y, 'Paying for Performance in Bankruptcy: Why CEOs Should Be Compensated with Debt' [2007] University of Pennsylvania Law Review 777
282. Llewellyn DT, 'Inside the 'Black Box'of Market Discipline' (2005) 25 Economic Affairs 41
283. Lopez JA, 'Disclosure as a Supervisory Tool: Pillar 3 of Basel II' (Federal Reserve Bank of San Francisco 2003) 22
284. Lupo-Pasini F, 'The Credit Suisse Collapse and International Financial Law' (2023) 17 Law and Financial Markets Review 298
285. Lupo-Pasini F and Buckley RP, 'International Coordination in Cross-Border Bank Bail-Ins: Problems and Prospects' (2015) 16 European Business Organization Law Review 203
286. Macey JR and Miller GP, 'Double Liability of Bank Shareholders: History and Implications' (1992) 27 Wake Forest L. Rev. 31
287. Macey JR and O'Hara M, 'The Corporate Governance of Banks' [2003] FRBNY Economic Policy Review 91
288. Macey JR and O'Hara M, 'Bank Corporate Governance: A Proposal for the Post-Crisis World' [2016] FRBNY Economic Policy Review 85

289. Maggiolino M, 'The Tercas Case, State Aid, and Antitrust: Are There Holes in the Warp?' (2022) 8 Italian LJ 745
290. Main BGM and Johnston J, 'Remuneration Committees and Corporate Governance' (1993) 23 Accounting and Business Research 351
291. Maki U and Mäki U, The Methodology of Positive Economics: Reflections on the Milton Friedman Legacy (Cambridge University Press 2009)
292. Mann F and others, 'Market Discipline and UK Bank Bondholders' (2017) 57 Bank of England Quarterly Bulletin 26
293. Marinč M and Vlahu R, 'The Economic Perspective of Bank Bankruptcy Law' (Springer Science & Business Media 2011) 310
294. Marinč M and Vlahu R, The Economics of Bank Bankruptcy Law (Springer Science & Business Media 2011)
295. Martino E D, 'Subordinated Debt under Bail-in Threat' (2017) 2 University of Bologna Law Review 252
296. Martino E D, 'Bail-Inable Securities and Financial Contracting: Can Contracts Discipline Bankers?' (2019) 10 European Journal of Risk Regulation 164
297. Martino E D, 'The Bail-in beyond Unpredictability: Creditors' Incentives and Market Discipline' (2020) 21 European Business Organization Law Review 789
298. Martino E D, 'Fine-Tuning Bank Governance and Resolution: The Case for Remunerating Bankers through Bail-Inable Debt' (2020) 31 European Business Law Review 845
299. Martino E D, 'Towards an Optimal Composition of Bail-Inable Debtholders?' (2021) 21 Journal of Corporate Law Studies 321
300. Martino E D, 'Getting Bank Governance Right' (2022) 23 Journal of Banking Regulation 302
301. Martino E D and Parchimowicz KM, 'Go Preventive or Go Home–the Double Nature of MREL' (2021) 18 European Company and Financial Law Review 608
302. Martino E D and Perini A, 'Rescued Banks Back to the Market?' (2025) 22 European Company and Financial Law Review 267
303. Martino E D and Perotti EC, 'Containing Runs on Solvent Banks: Prioritizing Recovery over Resolution' (2025) 7 Journal of Financial Crises 1
304. Martino E D and Vos T, "CoCos in Europe: What Is Wrong—and How to Fix It?" (2024) EBI Working Paper Series n. 169
305. Martino E D and Vos T, 'Fixing CoCos in Bank Prudential Regulation-A Life-Cycle Approach' European Business Organization Law Review (forthcoming)
306. Martynova N and Perotti E, 'Convertible Bonds and Bank Risk-Taking' [2018] Journal of Financial Intermediation

307. Martynova N, Perotti E and Suarez J, "Capital Forbearance in the Bank Recovery and Resolution Game" (2022) 146 Journal of Financial Economics 884
308. Mavin D, *Meltdown: Greed, Scandal, and the Collapse of Credit Suisse* (Simon and Schuster 2025)
309. Matta R and Perotti EC, 'Insecure Debt' (Centre for Economic Policy Research 2015) No.1050
310. McCahery JA, Sautner Z and Starks LT, 'Behind the Scenes: The Corporate Governance Preferences of Institutional Investors' (2016) 71 The Journal of Finance 2905
311. Mecatti I, 'The Role of Deposit Guarantee Schemes in Preventing and Managing Banking Crises: Governance and Least Cost Principle' (2020) 17 European Company and Financial Law Review 657
312. Mesnard B and Magnus M, 'What to Do with Profits When Banks Are Undercapitalized: Maximum Distributable Amount, CoCo Bonds and Volatile Markets' [2016] European Parliament (Briefing, PE 574.399) 1
313. Metrick A, 'The Failure of Silicon Valley Bank and the Panic of 2023' (2024) 38 Journal of Economic Perspectives 133
314. Meyer LH, 'Market Discipline as a Complement to Bank Supervision and Regulation', Speech before the Conference on Reforming Bank Capital Standards, Council on Foreign Relations, New York, June (1999)
315. Mobius M, Mutual Funds: An Introduction to the Core Concepts (John Wiley & Sons 2007)
316. Modigliani F and Miller MH, 'The Cost of Capital, Corporation Finance and the Theory of Investment' (1958) 48 The American economic review 261
317. Mülbert PO and Citlau RD, 'The Uncertain Role of Banks? Corporate Governance in Systemic Risk Regulation' (2011) 179
318. Murphy KJ, 'Executive Compensation' (1999) 3 Handbook of labor economics 2485
319. Murphy KJ, 'Regulating Banking Bonuses in the European Union: A Case Study in Unintended Consequences' (2013) 19 European Financial Management 631
320. Myers SC, 'Determinants of Corporate Borrowing' (1977) 5 Journal of financial economics 147
321. Myers SC and Majluf NS, 'Corporate Financing and Investment Decisions When Firms Have Information That Investors Do Not Have' (1984) 13 Journal of financial economics 187
322. Nabilou H and Pacces AM, 'The Hedge Fund Regulation Dilemma: Direct vs. Indirect Regulation' (2015) 6 Wm. & Mary Bus. L. Rev. 183
323. Nabilou H and Pacces AM, 'The Law and Economics of Shadow Banking', Research Handbook on Shadow Banking (Edward Elgar Publishing 2018)

324. Nier E and Baumann U, 'Market Discipline, Disclosure and Moral Hazard in Banking' (2006) 15 Journal of Financial Intermediation 332
325. Nieto M, 'Bank Resolution and Mutualization in the Euro Area' (2016) 2 European Economy, Banks, Regulation, and the Real Sector
326. Nini G, Smith DC and Sufi A, 'Creditor Control Rights, Corporate Governance, and Firm Value' (2012) 25 The Review of Financial Studies 1713
327. Nölke A, 'Economic Causes of the Eurozone Crisis: The Analytical Contribution of Comparative Capitalism' (2016) 14 Socio-Economic Review 141
328. Occhino F, 'Debt-Overhang Banking Crises: Detecting and Preventing Systemic Risk' (2017) 30 Journal of Financial Stability 192
329. Ohlrogge M, "Why Have Uninsured Depositors Become de Facto Insured?" (2025) 100 NYU Law Review
330. Omarova ST, 'Bank Governance and Systemic Stability: The'Golden Share'Approach' (2017) 68 Ala. L. Rev. 1029
331. Oster P, 'Contingent Convertible Bond Literature Review: Making Everything and Nothing Possible?' (2020) 21 Journal of Banking Regulation 343
332. Pacces A, Rethinking Corporate Governance: The Law and Economics of Control Powers (Routledge 2013)
333. Pacces AM, 'Exit, Voice and Loyalty from the Perspective of Hedge Funds Activism in Corporate Governance' (2016) 9 Erasmus L. Rev. 199
334. Pacces AM and Heremans D, 'Regulation of Banking and Financial Markets', Encyclopedia of Law and Economics-Volume 9 (Edward Elgar 2012)
335. Parchimowicz K, 'Three Hidden Issues in the List of Global Systemically Important Banks' (2020) Oxford Business Law Blog <https://www.law.ox.ac.uk/business-law-blog/blog/2020/01/three-hidden-issues-list-global-systemically-important-banks>
336. Pardo JC and Santillana V, 'The European MREL: Main Characteristics and TLAC Similarities and Differences' [2014] European Regulation Watch
337. Paz Valbuena J and Eidenmüller H, 'Bailout Blues: The Write-Down of the AT1 Bonds in the Credit Suisse Bailout' (2023) 24 European Business Organization Law Review 409
338. Persaud AD, 'A Ticking Time Bomb: TLAC and Other Attempts to Privatise Bank Bailouts' [2016] Butterworths Journal of International Banking and Financial Law 160
339. Philippon T and Salord A, 'Bail-Ins and Bank Resolution in Europe: A Progress Report. Geneva Reports on the World Economy Special Report 4' [2017] International Center for Monetary and Banking Studies (ICMB), Geneva (Switzerland)

340. Pigrum C, Reininger T and Stern C, ‘Bail-in: Who Invests in Noncovered Debt Securities Issued by Euro Area Banks?’ (2016) 32 Financial Stability Report 101
341. Pisani-Ferry J and others, ‘What Kind of European Banking Union?’ [2012] Brugel Policy Contribution
342. Pistor K, ‘A Legal Theory of Finance’ (2013) 41 Journal of Comparative Economics 315
343. Ramos-Muñoz D, ‘“Twilight Troubles”. Early Intervention, Resolution Preparation and Triggers, and the Urgent Need to Reform Them’ (2025) 26 European Business Organization Law Review 133
344. Rasmussen RK, ‘The Ex Ante Effects of Bankruptcy Reform on Investment Incentives’ (1994) 72 Wash. ULQ 1159
345. Rau R, ‘Executive Compensation’ (2017) 10 Foundations and Trends® in Finance 181
346. Ringe W-G, ‘Bank Bail-In between Liquidity and Solvency’ (2016) 92 Am. Bankr. LJ 299
347. Ringe W-G, The Deconstruction of Equity: Activist Shareholders, Decoupled Risk, and Corporate Governance (Oxford University Press 2016)
348. Ringe W-G and Patel J, ‘The Dark Side of Bank Resolution: Counterparty Risk through Bail-In’ (2019) 31
349. Roberts DR, ‘A General Theory of Executive Compensation Based on Statistically Tested Propositions’ (1956) 70 The Quarterly Journal of Economics 270
350. Roberts R, Gambling with Other People’s Money: How Perverse Incentives Caused the Financial Crisis (Hoover Press 2019)
351. Roe MJ, ‘Corporate Short-Termism—in the Boardroom and in the Courtroom’ [2013] The Business Lawyer 977
352. Romano A, ‘Horizontal Shareholding: The End of Markets and the Rise of Networks’ (2018) Available at SSRN 3255948
353. Romano A, Enriques L and Macey JR, ‘Extended Shareholder Liability for Systematically Important Financial Institutions’ [2019] American University Law Review, Forthcoming
354. Sahut J-M and Boulerne S, ‘Flaws in Banking Governance’ (2010) 15 International Journal of business 319
355. Santos JAC, ‘Evidence from the Bond Market on Banks”Too-Big-To-Fail’Subsidy’ [2014] Economic Policy Review 29
356. Schildbach J, ‘Where Do European Banks Stand? 10 Years after the Start of the Financial Crisis. 10 Years after the Start of the Financial Crisis’ (2017) <https://www.dbresearch.com/PROD/RPS_EN-PROD/PROD0000000000450356/Where_do_European_banks_stand%3F_10_years_after_the_.PDF >

357. Schillig MA, 'CMDI Resolution Funding and State Aid Control' (2025) 26 European Business Organization Law Review 221
358. Schoenmaker D, Contagion Risk in Banking (LSE Financial Markets Group 1996)
359. Schoenmaker D and Oosterloo S, 'Financial Supervision in an Integrating Europe: Measuring Cross-Border Externalities' (2005) 8 International Finance 1
360. Schwarcz SL, 'Systemic Risk' (2008) 97 Geo. LJ 193
361. Schwarcz SL, 'Misalignment: Corporate Risk-Taking and Public Duty' (2016) 91 Notre Dame L. Rev. 1
362. Schwarcz SL, 'Rethinking Corporate Governance for a Bondholder Financed, Systemically Risky World' (2017) 58 Wm. & Mary L. Rev. 1335
363. Schwartz A, 'A Contract Theory Approach to Business Bankruptcy' (1998) 107 The Yale Law Journal 1807
364. Schwartz RE, 'The Clawback Provision of Sarbanes-Oxley: An Underutilized Incentive to Keep the Corporate House Clean' [2008] The Business Lawyer 1
365. Scott HS, 'Market Discipline for Financial Institutions and Sovereigns' in Claudio Borio (ed), Market Discipline across Countries and Industries (MIT Press 2004)
366. Seiler M and Fischer D, '"Bonus Bonds" for Bankers: A New Type of Debt-Based Remuneration in the Financial Industry' (2015) 425 ECFR 461
367. Sester P, 'Towards a Transnational Bank Restructuring Law-The Attempt of G20 to Initiative and Monitor Regulatory Responses to the Too Big To Fail Problem' (2010) 7 ECFR 512
368. Shin HS, 'Reflections on Northern Rock: The Bank Run That Heralded the Global Financial Crisis' (2009) 23 Journal of economic perspectives 101
369. Shin HS, Procyclicality and the Search for Early Warning Indicators (International Monetary Fund 2013)
370. Shleifer A and Vishny RW, 'A Survey of Corporate Governance' (1997) 52 The journal of finance 737
371. Singh D and LaBrosse JR, 'Northern Rock, Depositors and Deposit Insurance Coverage: Some Critical Reflections' (2010) 2010 Journal of Business Law 55
372. Sironi A, 'Testing for Market Discipline in the European Banking Industry: Evidence from Subordinated Debt Issues' (2003) 35 Journal of Money, Credit, and Banking 443
373. Skeel Jr DA, 'The Empty Idea of Equality of Creditors' (2017) 166 U. Pa. L. Rev. 699
374. Smith Jr CW and Warner JB, 'On Financial Contracting: An Analysis of Bond Covenants' (1979) 7 Journal of financial economics 117

375. Smits JM, 'Law and Interdisciplinarity: On the Inevitable Normativity of Legal Studies' (2014) 1 Critical Analysis of Law 75
376. Spamann H, 'Monetary Liability for Breach of the Duty of Care?' (2016) 8 Journal of Legal Analysis 337
377. Stanghellini L, 'The Implementation of the BRRD in Italy and Its First Test: Policy Implications' (2016) 2 Journal of Financial Regulation 154
378. Stark J, 'Clawback Provisions in Executive Compensation Contracts' (2021) 18 European Company and Financial Law Review 669
379. Stephanou C, 'Rethinking Market Discipline in Banking: Lessons from the Financial Crisis' (2010) 5227
380. Stulz RM, 'Credit Default Swaps and the Credit Crisis' (2010) 24 Journal of Economic Perspectives 73
381. Sum K, 'Bank Governance in the EU: A Substitute or Complement of Banking Regulation?', Post-Crisis Banking Regulation in the European Union (Springer 2016)
382. Sundaram RK and Yermack DL, 'Pay Me Later: Inside Debt and Its Role in Managerial Compensation' (2007) 62 The Journal of Finance 1551
383. Thomas RS and Van der Elst C, 'Say on Pay around the World' (2014) 92 Wash. UL Rev. 653
384. Tirole J, The Theory of Corporate Finance (Princeton University Press 2006)
385. Tirole J, The Theory of Corporate Finance (Princeton University Press 2010)
386. Tröger T, 'Why MREL Won't Help Much' (2019) 20 Journal of Banking Regulation
387. Tröger TH, 'Too Complex to Work: A Critical Assessment of the Bail-in Tool under the European Bank Recovery and Resolution Regime' (2018) 4 Journal of Financial Regulation 35
388. Tung F, 'Pay for Banker Performance: Structuring Executive Compensation for Risk Regulation' (2011) 105 Nw. UL Rev. 1205
389. Tung F and Wang X, 'Bank CEOs, inside Debt Compensation, and the Global Financial Crisis' [2012] Boston Univ. School of Law Working Paper
390. Tversky A and Simonson I, 'Context-Dependent Preferences' (1993) 39 Management science 1179
391. Ueda K and Di Mauro BW, 'Quantifying Structural Subsidy Values for Systemically Important Financial Institutions' (2013) 37 Journal of Banking & Finance 3830
392. Valiante D, 'Harmonising Insolvency Laws in the Euro Area' (2016) 153
393. van der Cruijsen C, de Haan J and Jansen D-J, 'Trust and Financial Crisis Experiences' (2016) 127 Social Indicators Research 577
394. van der Elst C, 'Corporate Governance and Banks: How Justified Is the Match?' (2015) ECGI-Law Working Paper 284/2015

395. Van Rompuy H and others, 'Towards a Genuine Economic and Monetary Union', vol 5 (2012)
396. Velliscig G and others, 'The Bail-in Credibility: Barking Dogs Seldom Bite' (2024) 25 Journal of Banking Regulation 1
397. Ventoruzzo M, 'The Disappearing Taboo of Multiple Voting Shares: Regulatory Responses to the Migration of Chrysler-Fiat' [2015] Bocconi Legal Studies Research Paper
398. Ventoruzzo M and Sandrelli G, 'O Tell Me the Truth About Bail-In: Theory and Practice' (2019) 13 The Journal of Business, Entrepreneurship & the Law 187
399. Véron N, 'Precautionary Recapitalisation: Time for a Review?' (Bruegel 2017) 21
400. Verrecchia RE, 'Information Acquisition in a Noisy Rational Expectations Economy' [1982] Econometrica: Journal of the Econometric Society 1415
401. Wagner W, 'Diversification at Financial Institutions and Systemic Crises' (2010) 19 Journal of Financial Intermediation 373
402. Walther A and White L, 'Rules versus Discretion in Bank Resolution' (2019) CERP Discussion Paper 14048
403. Wetzer T, 'In Two Minds: The Governance of Ring-Fenced Banks' (2019) 19 Journal of Corporate Law Studies 197
404. Whitehead C, 'Creditors and Debt Governance' (2012) 68 Research Handbook on the Economics of Corporate Law 75
405. Wiggins R, Tente N and Metrick A, 'European Banking Union D: Cross-Border Resolution—Dexia Group' [2014] Yale Program on Financial Stability Case Study
406. Williamson OE, 'Transaction-Cost Economics: The Governance of Contractual Relations' (1979) 22 The journal of Law and Economics 233
407. Wilson L, 'Debt Overhang and Bank Bailouts' (2012) 5 International Journal of Monetary Economics and Finance 395
408. Wojcik K-P, 'Bail-in in the Banking Union' (2016) 53 Common Market Law Review 91
409. World Bank, Understanding Bank Recovery and Resolution Directive in EU: A Guideline to the BRRD (Word Bank 2016)
410. Wu B (H. T), MacNeil I and Chalaczkiewicz-Ladna K, '"Say on Pay" Regulations and Director Remuneration: Evidence from the UK in the Past Two Decades' (2020) 20 Journal of Corporate Law Studies 541
411. Young T, 'Why TLAC and BRRD Discrepancies Will Fade' [2015] Int'l Fin. L. Rev.
412. Zalewska A, 'A New Look at Regulating Bankers' Remuneration' (2016) 24 Corporate Governance: An International Review 322

413. Zeissler AG, Piontek T and Metrick A, 'Ireland and Iceland in Crisis C: Iceland's Landsbanki Icesave' [2015] Yale Program on Financial Stability Case Study
414. Zhou J and others, 'From Bailout to Bail-in: Mandatory Debt Restructuring of Systemic Financial Institutions' [2012] Journal Issue 3
415. Zingales L, 'The Future of Securities Regulation' (2009) 47 Journal of Accounting Research 391

The manufacturer's authorised representative in the EU is Springer Nature Customer Service Centre GmbH, Europaplatz 3, 69115 Heidelberg, Germany. If you have any concerns regarding our products, please contact ProductSafety@springernature.com

Printed and bound by CPI Group (UK) Ltd, Croydon, CR0 4YY
22/09/2026
02220956-0001